CON
TEMPO
RARY
CARI
OCA

CONTEMPORARY
CARIOCA

CONTEMPORARY CARIOCA

TECHNOLOGIES OF MIXING IN A BRAZILIAN MUSIC SCENE

Frederick Moehn

Duke University Press

DURHAM AND LONDON

2012

© 2012 Duke University Press
All rights reserved.
Printed in the United States of America on acid-free paper ♾
Designed by Kristina Kachele
Typeset in Quadraat and Ostrich Sans by Tseng Information Systems, Inc.

Library of Congress Cataloging-in-Publication Data
appear on the last printed page of this book.

Duke University Press gratefully acknowledges the support of Stony Brook
University, which provided funds toward the publication of this book.

For Brazil's musical alchemists

CONTENTS

ILLUSTRATIONS

PREFACE

Globalization is not the weapon of a single country for dominating another. . . . It is sufficient that cultural institutions be attentive to the invasion of mannerisms and to the most alive expressions of the country's art, its music. Fortunately, samba is quite strong.
—José Celso de Macedo Soares of the National Commerce Confederation
  (*Jornal do Brasil*, 12 July 1999)

On 7 December 1998 the *Globo* newspaper sponsored a forum in Rio de Janeiro titled "MPB: Engajamento ou alienação?" (MPB: Engagement or alienation?). It brought together well-known musicians to debate whether Brazilian popular music (MPB) had lost the critical edge and national relevance it once had under the dictatorship, particularly from the mid-1960s to the mid-1970s, when politically engaged song was at its height (figure 1). The participants included Marcos Valle, a singer-songwriter who was at the center of what is often called the second wave of bossa nova, beginning in the mid-1960s, and whose grooves had recently been rediscovered by a younger cohort based in the United Kingdom; Fernanda Abreu, who first gained fame as a singer and dancer in the pop-rock band Blitz in the early 1980s and later pursued a solo career mixing disco, funk, and samba influences; Adriana Calcanhotto, a singer-songwriter from Porto Alegre, in the South of Brazil, who moved to Rio and made a name for herself there

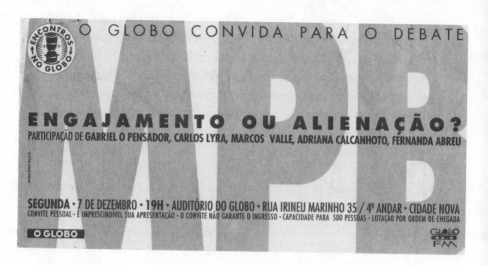

in the 1990s; and Gabriel O Pensador, a young rap artist who first gained recognition in 1992 for a song called "Tô feliz (matei o presidente)" (I'm happy [I killed the president]), a stark critique of then-president Fernando Collor de Mello, which Gabriel wrote while a journalism student at Pontifícia Universidade Católica do Rio de Janeiro (PUC-Rio).[1]

As the discussion began, Marcos Valle recalled that in the mid-1960s he was among the bossa nova artists who felt it was important to help "rouse the people from the stifling of the military government." The imperative to find ways to communicate past the censors through metaphors and double meanings in song lyrics, he recalled, provided "a very strong motivation for making real protest music." Even then, however, he sought to preserve his right to write songs that were not specifically political such as "Samba de verão" ("Summer Samba"), which was about "the sun, Rio de Janeiro, and sensuality." In the context of the dictatorship and the Marxist-oriented student protest movement of the mid-1960s, a culture had emerged in which one was either a politicized or alienated artist, Marcos observed. His musical circle felt a need to maintain an "openness with respect to expression" so as not to constrain creativity (his song "A resposta," composed with his brother Paulo Sérgio in 1965, was a "response" to this state of affairs, intended to assert that one could participate in musical protest "when one wanted to," he remembered). Now, in postdictatorship Brazil, there was no longer "that kind of . . . enemy," although there were of course still significant problems in the country, and reasons to speak out.

Adriana Calcanhotto similarly suggested that with democracy and free-

FIGURE 1. "MPB: Engajamento ou alienação?" debate invitation. Graphic design by Felipe Taborda. Used by permission.

dom of expression restored, there was no specific enemy to target. She did not feel motivated to write a protest song; she wondered who precisely she might target. For Gabriel O Pensador, one did not always explicitly need to say, "I'm against this, I'm against that." What was important was to question, "each one in his or her own style," and to get "into people's heads." Rather than asking whether contemporary Brazilian popular music was engaged or alienated, Fernanda Abreu thought, what was needed was a discussion of what it meant to be Brazilian at the end of the millennium, in an era of globalization, with information flowing ever more rapidly.

Was contemporary Brazil then no longer a good source for protest song?, the debate moderator, João Máximo (a *Globo* journalist), asked. Was there no necessity for political engagement in music because the country was doing fine? On the contrary, Brazil was a great source for protest song, Fernanda replied, but she rejected the moderator's either-or framing of the question. She didn't see herself "making a protest song in the sense of a militant, a partisan, taking a position A, B, or C of the left, arguing for A, B, or C proposal for a certain Brazil," because she was in fact optimistic about the country. She was cognizant of persistent social problems such as the high rate of poverty, but she had the sense that "in terms of humanity" things were gradually changing as Brazilians learned "to facilitate tolerance, generosity." It was not simply a question of alienation, because one's artistic production could be distinct from one's daily life as a citizen. What connected the two spheres of life was "opening up the mind" to an "understanding that the Other is different . . . but not worse."

"If you want to make a song about disco dancing, and someone else wants to make a song about misery in Brazil—this freedom of expression, and in particular *respect* for this freedom of expression, is what interests me," Fernanda said. In this newly open environment, people could finally "speak a little bit more about Brazil" and ask, "What country is this?" Citizens were moving away from the "accommodating attitude" that people manifested under the dictatorship, when no one "did anything because it didn't matter anyway." The political class, Fernanda said, "screwed up a lot of things," and it was now time for citizens to do something—"not necessarily to overthrow so-and-so—but to work on understanding the person at your side, to see if you have a prejudice, racial, or sexual . . . to have a relationship with the people around you," and this could come out in the music. A conversation was needed among music makers about, for example, what the pop rock of the 1980s represented. "What is happening differently now in the nineties, how are people producing music, what are they thinking, what do they think of the Brazil of today, since the *abertura*," that is, the political opening that led to redemocratization in the early 1980s? What was important, in other words, was contributing—as creative musicians—to a vibrant public sphere.

If the moderator of the debate viewed the songs of the late 1960s and 1970s that protested the military dictatorship and United States imperialism as the model for "engaged" music, he now saw a lowering of cultural standards on contemporary television (especially on the variety show *Ratinho*), and in the emphasis on sexualized dancing in the type of samba known as *pagode*. The commercialization of this latter genre and of *axé music* (a form of pop from Bahia, in the Northeast of Brazil) and *música sertaneja* (Brazilian country music) signaled for this apparently left-leaning intellectual the alienation of "the masses." What, he asked the panelists, did they sincerely think of the *música baiana* (a generic term for pop music from Bahia) and pagode trends? Were they "commercial, alienated, or what?" Media fabrications, Fernanda Abreu responded. What mattered was a *diversity* of cultural voices and options for cultural consumption. What was especially interesting about Brazil was its "musical richness." It was great that there was música sertaneja, pagode, axé music, MPB, rock, pop, dance, rap, and hip-hop, she said. The problem arose when these things became formulaic. Fernanda liked "the democracy of being allowed to choose."

Wasn't Fernanda "disappointed in the people for being alienated?," the moderator pressed. No, she replied, appearing to grow irritated with the framing of the questions. She did not want to think of "the people" as victims, she said, yet Brazil still suffered from misery, poverty, and a lack of education, of information. The political opening was relatively recent, she observed, and issues of inequality and development would not be "resolved in five or ten years." Nor were the media as such to blame, because there was actually "space for segmentation into every type of culture and art." The problem was that that the media often privilege cultural manifestations that do well in the IBOPE (Brazilian Institute of Public Opinion and Statistics) opinion polls, constraining the possibilities of expression. Marcos Valle similarly claimed not to be interested in "determining whether what the people like to hear is better or worse." Brazilians needed the opportunity "to hear every kind of music." If, when one turned on the television, one heard "one kind of music from beginning to end," then it was difficult to know about other options for listening. Once this was balanced out, he thought, "the people will be able to choose."

Notwithstanding reservations about mass media and markets, the musicians at this debate were by and large quite positive about Brazilian music at the end of the century, as the country was preparing to commemorate its quincentennial in extensive public celebrations. They were particularly excited about the freedom to mix influences, which they saw as a necessary condition for achieving universalism. Fernanda Abreu, for example, was happy that Brazilians could finally make music that expressed "the regional universal Brazilian." It was cool to see people from a new generation speaking of traditional Brazilian genres like *maracatu*, *côco*, *embolada*, samba, or *samba de roda*, she said, while mixing these with hip-hop, rap, and "scratch," using techniques such as sampling and digital audio media such as Pro Tools. To make "Brazilian" music, she enthused, it was no longer necessary to feature instruments such as the *pandeiro* (tambourine), *violão* (the classical-style guitar favored in samba and bossa nova, among other genres), or *tamborim* (a small frame drum used in samba). When the year 2000 arrived, Fernanda thought, Brazilians would manage to make a kind of music similar to what they had "always heard from abroad," that had a certain *liberty* that was "super interesting." Yet Brazilians would also succeed in making their own music. Brazilian music had the potential to be "a wonderful phenomenon in the world in the coming millennium." Fernanda was excited.

"After Blitz," Adriana Calcanhotto added, referring to the band in which Fernanda Abreu got started, "rock and pop in Brazil suffered a period of becoming old fashioned," while the media tended to saturate the market with anything that had already become a success, stifling other possibilities. Now, however, there was "a great effervescence," with artists like Chico Science mixing northeastern traditions with rock and hip-hop influences, or Gabriel O Pensador using rap. "It's completely cannibalistic," Adriana said. These musicians, Marcos Valle chimed in, were "doing something that is fantastic. . . . These connections between everything, this richness. . . . It is so many folks, everyone adding their contribution. I think Brazilian music is . . . the richest music in the whole world. Wherever we go, everyone notices, because there are many people doing good work." It was just necessary "to distribute this space a little better" so that "the people" could "choose what they want to hear."

Amid such optimism, however, Gabriel O Pensador—who, being the youngest artist on the panel, had experienced the dictatorship only as a small child—pointed to an adversary in an unexpected place: upper-middle-class Brazilian youths preoccupied more with international consumer culture than with local realities. "They don't want to participate," Gabriel lamented. "They're very egotistical. . . . They want to do well for themselves, and they don't believe very strongly in change." His social circle had money and studied in good schools in the South Zone of Rio de Janeiro, he noted. So when in 1993 he released his song "Retrato de um playboy (Juventude perdida)" (Portrait of a playboy [Lost youth]), in which he offered a scathing critique of the lifestyle of the privileged white middle-class Carioca male in his late teens or twenties, he sought to criticize his own generation, he said. The Little Playboy (playboyzinho) of the rap is a spoiled daddy's boy who, when not sleeping, lives a life of diversion, going to the beach, surfing, hanging out with his buddies drinking beer, practicing the martial art jiu-jitsu (but only for fun), and doing whatever all his friends are doing. He is a conformist who lacks personality and just fits into the system; he thinks that he is high class but actually "belongs to the worst race that exists." The Playboy treats with scorn and violence the humble maid who feeds him, washes his clothes, and cleans up after him; he enjoys ridiculing the poor beggar in the street. In the poor capitalist country that Brazil was, the playboys were "proliferating by the thousands," Gabriel warned. Neither patriots nor nationalists, they preferred the Stars and Stripes.

It is ironic, perhaps, that Gabriel, a young white musician of privilege, should choose rap as the musical medium for delivering a critique of his peers who looked to the United States in their lifestyle choices (see Bollig 2002). Such is the contradictory positioning of the middle-class subject in "emergent" economies. By the time of this debate, Gabriel had in fact grown disenchanted with rap music from the United States, he conceded, as the artists who inspired him when he began writing songs were recycling the same ideas about sex and drugs over and over again, having discovered that they sell albums. Protest and anger, then, could become little more than a false posture, Gabriel felt. What Marcos Valle had said about the freedom to choose what one sings about was therefore very important, he concluded, for market forces could constrain freedom of expression as much as a censoring dictatorship.

As Brazil re-democratized in the 1980s, it simultaneously entered a world in which market-oriented reforms were transforming the hemisphere and beyond. The so-called Washington Consensus promoted "free" markets rather than regulatory states as the engines of progress and development, and the "market-triumphalist" and United States–led character of capitalist expansion came to be called neoliberal globalization (Kingfisher and Maskovsky 2008, 116). Policies favoring privatization and the lowering of corporate income taxes, contraction of government and social welfare programs, the deregulation of industry and markets, respect for private property, the weakening of organized labor, capital mobility, and so on, seemingly spread from one country to another in recent decades, including Brazil. In fact, however, neoliberal projects have been messier than much of the literature suggests, and individual actors have promoted a variety of policy directions in hybrid, multiple, and contradictory contexts (Brenner and Theodore 2002, 351; Larner 2003, 509–10).

When I arrived in Brazil in August 1998 to begin field research for this book, President Fernando Henrique Cardoso, who first came to prominence as an influential dependency theorist but now was promoting market-oriented reforms, was in the middle of his reelection campaign. Contemporary reactions to his policies were sometimes strongly negative. For example, on 22 September 1998, when the Monica Lewinsky scandal was raging in the United States, the *Globo* columnist Arnaldo Jabor fumed that the "moralistic rigor" that "Old Testament Republicans" sought to impose on Bill Clinton was "equal to the rigor of the economic measures they prescribe to us." Not everyone was colonized by Puritans, he argued, into the Protestant work ethic. The United States wanted to foist "a tyrannical ideal of liberty" on the world, an ideal that was in reality characterized by open borders and markets in Latin America while the United States protected its own ones. "Reforms, yes, privatization, sure," Jabor quipped, but he counseled Brazilians to keep "one eye on the cat, the other on the fish that is frying" (making a reference to the samba musician Zeca Pagodinho's song "Velho ditado").

Brazilians voted to keep Cardoso in office in October 1998. Meanwhile, major financial crises in Asia and Russia had begun to affect Mexico and Chile. The International Monetary Fund viewed Brazil's stability as crucial to stopping the further spread of the crisis. Late in the year the IMF presented Brazil with a $41.5 billion loan package aimed at averting financial collapse; not surprisingly, it stipulated additional fiscal and administrative reforms to reduce government spending. In these first few months of my field research, anxiety was heightened as Brazil allowed its currency to float rather than continue artificially pegging it to the dollar. The fear of hyperinflation returned, but the loans stabilized Brazil's economy and inflation remained under control, allowing for modest economic growth as the decade came to a close. Cardoso's tenure, which ended 1 January 2003, marks a turning point in postdictatorship Brazil.

Brazil in the 1990s was thus consolidating into an "actually existing neoliberalism" (Gledhill 2004) that, rather than simply confirming the blunt transformational power of market-oriented policies, was "embedded" within a specific context that bore its own inherited political, institutional, economic, and cultural legacies (Brenner and Theodore 2002, 351). The "MPB: Engagement or alienation?" debate of late 1998 revealed different generations of artists thinking about making music under exciting new circumstances. Tropes of freedom, choice, and self-management could have a powerful effect among the consuming classes in a newly democratized nation. How did "the passions and the stakes of global connection" produce creative frictions (Tsing 2005, 269) and inspiration for Brazilian musicians in this period of national emergence? Could they finally be Brazilian and universal?

I surely heard songs written by Brazilian composers as a youth in New Jersey without necessarily taking note of it, if only because bossa nova and samba were incorporated into the jazz repertory that my parents enjoyed. Later, when I was a student at Berklee College of Music, I found the compositions of Luiz Bonfá and Tom Jobim in the *Real Book*, that is, the fakebook of lead sheets popular among students of jazz. Yet it wasn't until I began performing in New York City after college that I took a closer look at those bossa nova standards and grew increasingly interested in Brazilian music. At the time I was using the 1972 Fender Stratocaster electric guitar I had bought some years earlier when I played in rock bands — a prized instrument, but not well suited to the rhythmic subtleties characteristic of the bossa nova style, exemplified by João Gilberto's "stuttering guitar" patterns on the acoustic nylon-stringed classical instrument, the *violão*. As my knowledge of Brazilian music history deepened, I learned how electric guitars had in fact scandalized MPB musicians and audiences back in the late 1960s, when Caetano Veloso and the rock band Os Mutantes introduced them into the televised national song contests, and how they nevertheless quickly became an integral part of Brazilian popular music thereafter, while never really losing their association with foreign rock.

I first traveled to Brazil in January 1995 during graduate school at New York University. In Salvador da Bahia I heard samba, jazz, samba-reggae, *forró*, and *axé music*. In Recife I heard Chico Science; the *mangue beat* scene that he and his collaborator Fred Zero Quatro inaugurated in that city— a fusion of primarily rock, hip-hop, and traditional genres from the Brazilian Northeast—was in full bloom. My last stop was Rio de Janeiro, where I stayed in the home of two journalists who worked for the media conglomerate Globo Network, and who lived a block away from its headquarters on a quiet street bordering the steep, forested slope stretching up the mountain that supports the Christ Redeemer statue, directly beneath the so-called Armpit of Christ.

In Rio I saw Jorge Ben Jor perform on Ipanema Beach. In the 1960s Jorge (then known as just Jorge Ben) combined samba with rock, soul, jazz, and pop in hits like "Mas que nada" (roughly, No way; 1963), which Sergio Mendes would make popular in the United States in his 1966 version and then reinterpret forty years later with the Black Eyed Peas, and "País tropical" (Tropical country), which Marcos Suzano and Paulinho Moska would reinterpret on the latter's *Móbile* of 1999 (examined in chapter 5 of this book). This was my introduction to the South Zone of Rio de Janeiro. Among the most memorable experiences of this trip was my visit to the public rehearsal space (the *quadra*) of Brazil's oldest samba school, the legendary Mangueira (officially, GRES Estação Primeira da Mangueira), in the working-class North Zone of the city. Back in New York I had begun playing *caixa* (the samba snare drum) with Manhattan Samba, a percussion ensemble directed by Ivo Araújo, a Rio native. At Mangueira, during one of the hot weeks leading up to carnival, I first heard the swing of the massive drum corps inside that deafening, exhilarating, and intensely proud concrete enclosure decorated in the school's official colors of pink and green. Class was not the only thing that separated this part of Rio from the South Zone: while the residents of the Jardim Botânico neighborhood where I was staying are typically light-skinned, the inhabitants of the Morro da Mangueira—the hillside favela after which this samba school is named— tend to be of darker complexion.

That summer (winter in Brazil), I returned for an intensive Portuguese course at the University of São Paulo, and the following summer I visited again to begin formulating a dissertation topic. I first explored the music scene in Salvador, where I attended rehearsals and performances of groups such as Timbalada, Olodum, Ara Ketu, and Bragadá. I joined Margareth

Menezes's band atop a *trio elétrico*—an enormous moving truck with a stage on top and walls of speakers on the side. I had an interest in music production practices, which grew out of my undergraduate degree in that area, so I visited the studio of the axé music star Daniela Mercury while she was recording the album *Feijão com arroz* (Rice and beans). At the main recording facility in Bahia at the time, Estúdio WR, I observed a session of the group Gera Samba, who had popularized the 1996 song "É o Tchan" (It's the tchan), one of the biggest hits of the late 1990s in Brazil. This form of radio- and dance-oriented light samba, I later learned, inspired some anxiety among those who preferred a more rootsy, community-centered ideal of the genre, particularly middle-class listeners.

I again finished this trip in Rio de Janeiro, where the audio engineer Beto Santana took me to Companhia dos Técnicos, the country's principal samba studio and a place where many of the giants of MPB recorded. Later I would write about the recording of the annual carnival samba album at this facility, an intense experience that contrasted markedly with the setting I describe in this book (see Moehn 2005). I came to learn that Rio de Janeiro hosted several of Brazil's so-called international-level recording studios, and that the city, especially with the presence of the Globo Network, was still the media capital of the country. It boasted five major studios fully booked with banner clients and several medium-sized studios, as well as a growing number of computer-based recording facilities, and it remained a magnet for musicians. I decided I would conduct my field research in Rio.

Meanwhile, New York City hosted a five-day Brazilian Music Festival in 1997 with concerts at Central Park SummerStage, Avery Fisher Hall, and the Beacon Theater. (Lincoln Center also produced a series of Brazilian popular music concerts in July of that year.) "Brazilian music seems to hold endless bounties," the pop music critic Jon Pareles wrote of these concerts (1997). "Carnivals keep traditional songs, dances, and symbols alive, while local and regional pride hold homogenization at bay." There were "as many local rhythms" as there were "birds in the rain forest." The best Brazilian songwriters, Pareles proposed, "merge folklore and innovation, politics and entertainment, literary ambitions with graceful melody," and there was "a lot more talent awaiting export." Moreover, there were lessons to be learned about "the uses of folklore" in, for example, the way the singer-songwriter Lenine and the percussionist Marcos Suzano, who performed on SummerStage, together "conjured kinetic rhythms usually built by drum choirs" with only guitar and percussion.

Interestingly, not only do Pareles's comments demonstrate how Brazilian pop musicians were received abroad, his language mirrors the way the musicians themselves often talked about their work—as a kind of plentiful fount of brilliant eclecticism in a globalized world seemingly threatened by homogenization. Indeed, local versus global, traditional versus modern, diversity versus homogeneity—these were precisely the dynamics of "world music" that preoccupied many ethnomusicologists as the millennium came to a close. A tropical abundance, meanwhile, is a trope that dates back to the first Portuguese to land in Brazil, when the Crown's official scribe, Pero Vaz de Caminha, famously wrote of "an incalculably vast forest of rich foliage" in his letter to King Manuel I of Portugal in the year 1500 (1999, 53).

I returned to Brazil in 1998 and lived in Rio de Janeiro from August through July 1999, during which time I conducted many of the interviews and much of the participant observation for this book. I was skeptical of fears that global pop music was following a path of increasing homogenization as subjects struggled to maintain agency and difference in the face of the apparent cultural imperialism of, mainly, the United States. "To us," one Brazilian recording engineer told me in New York City in September 1997, "rock 'n' roll is world music" (Sólon do Valle, informal conversation). As I continued my research, however, I came to appreciate the music scene in Rio not simply as a case study useful for engaging in debates over, for example, national versus cosmopolitan sentiments, but rather as a vibrant setting contoured by local histories and discourses about global phenomena and problems, and suffused with the resilient sounds of genres such as samba and choro, as well as rock, funk, and hip-hop. Follow-up interviews after my initial fieldwork helped me to frame this book as a study of a specific period in Brazilian popular music.

ACKNOWLEDGMENTS

Writing, this book has taught me, can be a curiously solitary and yet also collaborative process. For all that one may strive to avoid distractions and even social contact in order to spend time alone in front of a computer, there are a remarkable number of individuals and institutions whose support and input are essential to any publication. I am forever grateful to the music makers I came to know in Brazil for their generosity of time and spirit. I extend special appreciation to each of the creative individuals I discuss herein for sharing some measure of their lives and work with me, especially Fernanda Abreu, Celso Alvim, Sacha Amback, Rodrigo Campello, Tom Capone, Walter Costa, Fausto Fawcett, C. A. Ferrari, Celso Fonseca, Lenine, Liminha, Pedro Luís, Ivo Meirelles, Suely Mesquita, Paulinho Moska, Mário Moura, Chico Neves, Maurício Pacheco, Lucas Santtana, Sidon Silva, and Marcos Suzano. There are, however, many others whom I do not specifically cite or mention in this book yet who did much to enhance my understanding of Brazil and its music; too numerous to name, I owe them all my gratitude.

New York University supported my graduate studies through a Henry Mitchell McCracken Fellowship and other awards and provided a challenging intellectual environment; my years there were wonderfully stimulating. The Foreign Language and Area Studies and IIE Fulbright programs of the United States government provided crucial funding to study Portuguese at the University of São Paulo and to conduct extended field research in Rio de Janeiro, respectively. I was able to complete follow-up research with help from the Faculty of the Arts, Humanities, and Social Sciences fund of Stony Brook University, which also provided a book subvention. For writing, I benefited from support from the Howard Foundation and from the Fundação para a Ciência e a Tecnologia of Portugal, the latter through the Instituto de Etnomusicologia–Centro de Estudo de Música e Dança (INET-MD) of the Faculdade de Ciências Sociais e Humanas at the Universidade Nova de Lisboa. Under the directorship of the indefatigable Salwa El-Shawan Castelo-Branco, INET-MD comprises a thriving community of engaged scholars and students who made me feel very much at home. The institute also supported my contracting of J. Naomi Linzer Indexing Services.

Generosity also characterizes those within academia who have guided me over the years, chief among them Gage Averill and Donna Buchanan, unfailing mentors to whom I am greatly indebted, as well as George Yúdice, the third member of my dissertation committee. Beginning with the Fourth Brazilian Studies Association Congress in Washington in 1997, Charles Perrone and Christopher Dunn have been particularly helpful instigators and collaborators. In Brazil, I had the pleasure of befriending Martha Ulhôa, and of benefiting from her expansive knowledge of Brazilian music and from her kindness. Through Martha I met Suzel Ana Reily, who has provided me with numerous insights in her own work, and through her readings of mine. At Stony Brook University I enjoyed the privilege of working with Jane Sugarman, whose scholarship and dedication to all facets of ethnomusicology are a continuing source of inspiration. Paul Gootenberg's moral support and professional stewardship were invaluable there too. Albert Fishlow has been a selfless mentor, first in his capacity as director of the Center for Brazilian Studies of Columbia University, where I taught seminars on Brazilian culture and society, and subsequently as a family friend always willing to provide advice or to prod.

Ken Wissoker at Duke University Press was an encouraging and thoughtful editorial director, and I could not have completed this work without the help of Jade Brooks, Beth Mauldin, Fred Kameny, Jennifer Hill, and Christine Dahlin. I am grateful to the anonymous readers of the manuscript for indicating ways to improve it. Other scholars who have inspired me along the way or provided helpful feedback include Barbara Browning, Larry Crook, Philip Galinsky, Paul Greene, Tomie Hahn, Cristina Magaldi, Bryan McCann, Louise Meintjes, Carol Muller, John Murphy, T. M. Scruggs, Thomas Porcello, Robert Stam, Thomas Turino, Michael Veal, and José Miguel Wisnik. Sandra Graham and Scott Currie have been steadfast pals since the days we performed together in the Near East Ensemble at NYU, with Donna Buchanan as our intrepid leader. Martin Kjendle spurred my first trip to Brazil in 1995. Kassandra Hartford, Darien Lamen, and Nicholas Tochka commented on early chapter drafts. A special thanks to Rodrigo Campello, Ana Fortes, Janaina Linhares, Jr Tostoi, Martha Ulhôa, and Liv Sovik for hosting me at various times in Rio, and to Claudio Gonçalvez Couto, Vanessa Elias de Oliveira, and Maurício and Sandra Faria da Silva in São Paulo for hosting me there. Some of these individuals have manifested admirable patience with me as I worked to complete this project. On this score, no one has been more giving than the members of my dear family, Teresa, Martín, Josefina, and Naomi. With such generous support, any shortcomings of this book can only be my own responsibility.

INTRODUCTION

In an article published in the Rio de Janeiro edition of *O Globo* in January 1998, the journalist Mário Marques identified a loosely collaborative group of musicians based primarily in what is known as the South Zone of the city who were making what he called *música popular carioca*, or MPC. The designation riffed on the older marketing label *música popular brasileira*—MPB—associated especially with major figures of urban Brazilian popular song from the mid-1960s through the 1970s. "Carioca" refers to someone or something from Rio de Janeiro and carries a host of established connotations. In coining the term, Marques thus indicated a connection with the mainstream history of urban popular song in Brazil while drawing attention to the importance of the local setting in the new trends he was describing. MPC musicians such as Pedro Luís, the group Farofa Carioca (whose lead singer, Seu Jorge, would go on to international stardom as a solo artist), and Celso Fonseca, Marques wrote, shared a desire to show that there was "intelligent musical life in the South Zone of the 1990s" (1998). They appreciated the poetic aesthetics of bossa nova and admired roots and classic samba, while they also mixed in rhythms and styles from the Northeast of Brazil, or rock, hip-hop, and funk from abroad.

Although not yet well known by the general public, Marques noted, some of the musicians making MPC were "beginning to arouse the curiosity of the record labels and to fill up nightclubs" as part of what he identified as a musical movement that was generating buzz in the media. Partying in the Ballroom nightclub of the Humaitá neighborhood, for example, and conversing in the bars of Santa Teresa and Baixo Gávea were among the favored activities of these individuals. "In the midst of the generalized mediocrity," the prominent bossa nova–era songwriter and guitarist Carlos Lyra commented for the article, "these young folk impress with this Carioca spirit." This was music "of the middle class," he said.[1] MPC artists were united, Marques asserted, in their aim to go beyond the celebration of Rio's attractions to offer constructive criticism of social life in the city. They sought to balance "the charms of the South Zone" with the "blemishes of the suburbs" in their lyrics, singing across the "divided city." In October a cover article published in the Rio edition of *Veja* magazine similarly spoke of a "Carioca way of making music," highlighting the samba-funk-pop singer-songwriter Fernanda Abreu and the bands Farofa Carioca and O Rappa (Tinoco and Weinberg 1998). Then in September of the following year another cover article published in *Veja Rio* represented Pedro Luís and Marcelo Yuka (the lead singer of the band O Rappa) as "voices of the street" who had different musical styles but nevertheless drank from the same fountain: "the Rio that pulsates outside the barred condominium windows" (Tinoco 1999).[2]

Carioca spirit. Middle-class music. Divided city. The language of journalism, perhaps, but Marques's characterization suggests a series of interesting questions. To begin, how did music makers in this setting weave themes and sounds recognized as Carioca into their work, and what role did the unique yet distressed social geography of the Cidade Maravilhosa, the Marvelous City, play in their lives? How, precisely, did they draw on established Brazilian genres and traditions while developing new musical vocabularies that spoke to contemporary local realities and also to global trends in popular music? Although they were hardly alone in reveling in the juxtaposition of elements from different styles, eras, and places, what drove *these* individuals to mix so intensely, and how did *their* mixtures engender distinct meanings in the local context? What production methods did participants use, and what forces shaped their musical tastes? What was the legacy of previous generations of MPB musicians for these music makers, and how did each of them pursue a distinct and original creative path? As the power of industry executives to push certain market sectors and of critics to shape tastes diminished in the first decade of the new millennium, how did these musicians increasingly come to self-manage their careers? Finally, what can their music making tell us about the middle-class experience in Brazil?

In 2007 I asked Pedro Luís to reflect back on the second half of the 1990s. "It was a moment," the songwriter, singer, and guitarist said, of "a certain effervescence" in the wake of the appearance of the musician Chico Science, the leading figure of Recife's then-burgeoning rock scene (called mangue beat), and of Pedro's own group, Pedro Luís e A Parede (Pedro Luís and The Wall), as well as bands like Boato and Farofa Carioca in Rio. "The industry took a breath," he said, "and grabbed onto the new things that were happening that the circles of opinion makers and the underground were unanimous in supporting." One of Pedro's band mates described how Brazilian pop musicians lost their "shame" in the 1990s, after a decade during which "the Brazilian music scene was really bad." The sound was awful in the 1980s, he thought. "When the music technologies began to arrive, people didn't know how to use them, and it was terrible." Fans of the Brazilian rock bands whose popularity exploded during that decade, he remembered, would always compare them to foreign groups. For the band Os Paralamas do Sucesso, it was the Police. For Legião Urbana, it was the Smiths. Each Brazilian group had a similar gringo counterpart. By contrast, two albums from the mid-1990s—*Olho de peixe* (Fisheye, 1993), by Lenine and Suzano, and the first album of Chico Science e Nação Zumbi (the full name of Chico's band), *Da lama ao caos* (From mud to chaos, 1994), "showed that you could make global pop music with a Brazilian aspect." After a decade that was more about imitation in Brazilian rock, he concluded, "things began to mix more" in the 1990s.

Marques's acronym MPC in fact gained little traction, and musicians such as Pedro Luís discounted the idea that there was a specific movement coalescing in the city at the time. But there was a *scene*, in the sense of there being a circle of local musicians (and their audiences, producers, audio technicians, publicity agents, etc.) who shared a sense of purpose and perhaps a kind of ethos about music making, and who were privy to deep-running histories that lent meaning to specific cultural mixtures (Straw 2006, 11, 13). The ways in which scenes can link tastes, affinities, and practices to the social experience of place, of the local, lend "depth to the theater of urban sociability" (16).[3] Scenes, however, also often involve affective links with other places, other scenes, other trends. They are loose, not rigid; they can be exciting arenas for participants to explore new identities (Shank 1994), yet they are, like other social spheres, partly shaped by power relations.

This book is concerned with how selected collaborators in this setting adapted their musical ways of living to new social, political, economic, and cultural realities beginning in the 1990s and continuing through the middle of the following decade. In a country that had emerged relatively recently from a military dictatorship and that was rapidly modernizing its economy, these individuals realized a collaborative celebration of Brazil's rich and varied musicality, finding in popular music an affirmation of their agency as creative subjects. Yet their music, lyrics, and talk are also characterized by the kinds of self-consciously ambivalent and contradictory sentiments that some scholars attribute to a specifically middle-class cultural space, particularly in nations where this group does not represent the majority (e.g., Liechty 2003). Although they might be regarded as comparatively privileged locally in social status, these music makers tended to think of themselves as somewhat disadvantaged in terms of access to equipment, specialized training (such as audio engineering programs), and career opportunities relative to their middle-class counterparts in the United States and Europe (this has changed in recent years). Meanwhile, they admired many forms of North American and European culture, even while they might simultaneously worry about imitating foreign models.

Consumption is a key dimension of middle-class life, yet these musicians usually professed distaste for *consumerism*. Similarly, they could appreciate the kinds of freedoms associated with liberal individualism yet be critical of market forces or of neoliberal globalization. Basically progressive in their politics, they also manifested mistrust of both populist tendencies and the political elite. They have celebrated roots cultural expression but have been wary of traditionalism; samba is a fundamental reference for these musicians, yet they resent stereotypes of Brazil as all samba, *mulata*, and carnival. They adore rock music but have sought to control its influence. Black diaspora musics have also been an important influence, but black identity politics less so. They could be pop, yes, but not too *popular* (meaning something like "of the people" in Portuguese), and especially not too commercial. Technology? Fabulous, but not if it erases sonic markers of Brazilianness. Their music should be Brazilian *and* universal. Their sonic practices have thus helped them navigate a socially constructed "space in-between" (Santiago 2001); in the process, they have continually, both individually and collectively, taken stock of themselves and their country in a figurative mirror.[4]

A "Promiscuous" Place

The South Zone of Rio de Janeiro is arguably well suited sociogeographically for incubating scenes, not least because it includes the Copacabana and Ipanema neighborhoods that cradle Rio's most famous beaches (see map). The culture of the beach is one of the defining aspects of Carioca life, even though many Rio de Janeiro residents live far from the shore or have little time to take advantage of it. The accessibility of sun and sand is commonly cited, for example, when locals contrast Rio with São Paulo (which is farther south and slightly inland). As one musician put it, "Sao Paulo is a city oriented toward more production, toward work, [while] Rio is oriented more toward—I don't want to say recreation, but the beaches make an enormous difference. The Carioca dresses differently [and] uses the body much more—there's that whole mystique of the Carioca woman, she shows more."[5] A little removed from the beaches are other comfortable residential neighborhoods such as Jardim Botânico (Botanical Garden, adjacent to the park of the same name), a neighborhood that hosts one of the higher concentrations of income in the city. Indeed, while the South Zone, like much of Rio, also includes some favelas (shantytowns) constructed on steep hillsides, it is most typically associated with comparatively privileged households, and its residents are predominantly of light phenotype.

The understated aesthetic of bossa nova took shape in this Rio de Janeiro of postcard beaches, the Sugarloaf (Pão de Açucar), and the Christ Redeemer statue (the Corcovado). The Brazilian rock that became so popular in the 1980s also blossomed in the South Zone. Poets, musicians, playwrights, actors, filmmakers, novelists, and the like, enjoy meeting for conversation, food, and drinks in the alimentary spaces of this area, such as the restaurants and bars of Baixo Gávea, which one writer has described as "frequented by the golden youth of the wealthiest classes, the jiu-jitsu

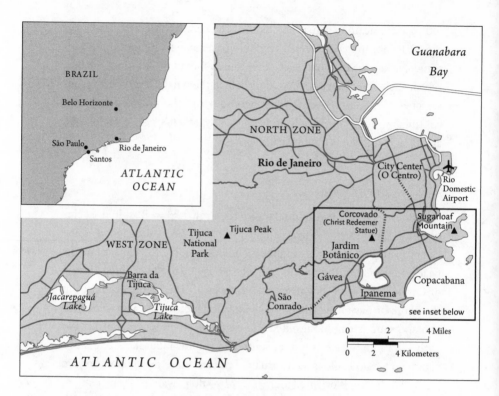

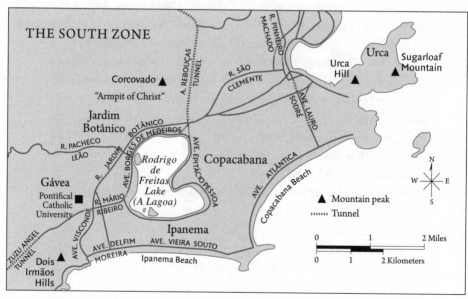

Map of Rio de Janeiro with inset of the South Zone

fighters, and the students of the best private schools of the city" (Gontijo 2002, 63).[6] There one could also find Tracks, a CD and vinyl shop for aficionados of international currents. Several of the recording studios that the musicians in this scene have utilized are in the South Zone.

This space of relative privilege has not been immune to Rio's daunting problems of violence. When I was staying with a friend in Jardim Botânico in 1998, the then-president of Sony Music Brazil was shot five times at a gas station nearby as thieves stole his Mercedes. (He survived.) The documentary film Bus 174 (2003) portrayed an armed bus hijacking that took place blocks away and resulted in two tragic fatalities. For Cariocas to live under such conditions, said one musician I interviewed in 1999, there had to be a certain tempering of hostilities that he believed was encouraged by social mixing. "You know, people mix daily . . . as if it didn't exist, this state of siege. . . . It's not like a place that's in conflict the whole time."[7] To be sure, the extent to which violence is a daily preoccupation in Rio depends largely on where one lives, with favela residents experiencing the bulk of it. (The "state of siege" has been somewhat exacerbated recently as federal police now battle drug gangs head on in an effort to ready the city for the next World Cup soccer championship in 2014 and for the summer Olympics in 2016.)

Social contrast in Rio is thus sometimes represented in terms of North Zone versus South Zone, or morro (poorer hillside communities) versus asfalto (paved spaces of condominiums). By the mid-1990s, the metaphor of the "divided city" had gained currency for Rio de Janeiro, particularly after the publication of Zuenir Ventura's book Cidade partida (1994), which described the "barbarity" of the "social apartheid" that he saw emerging from the rising violence in Rio de Janeiro. The shocking killings by police of street youths in front of the Candelária Cathedral in 1993, and of civilians in the Vigário Geral favela that same year, combined with middle-class anxiety over, for example, the arrastões (coordinated beach robberies in the South Zone), heightened this sense of social apartheid in the 1990s. But while Rio de Janeiro may in some way be divided, it is also, Beatriz Jaguaribe observes, "a tumultuous urban maze of inequality and social juxtaposition," as a close reading of Ventura's book suggests. "Between the favelas and the neighborhoods of the rich and the middle classes," Jaguaribe writes, "are numerous exchanges, and indeed it is the ambiguity of these contact zones that allows both violence and cultural socialization to simultaneously occur" (2007, 118).

Fausto Fawcett, a chronicler of Carioca life and, according to Mário Marques, one of the "icons of mixture" in this scene (he is a lyricist for Fernanda Abreu), described a "social promiscuity," a "very clear thing of mixture" in Rio. Whereas in São Paulo one encountered a radical distinction between the well-off professional classes living in the center of the city and the less privileged sectors spread throughout what is known as "the periphery," in Rio, and especially in the South Zone, Fausto asserted, there was a social intimacy (convivência) that was "very in-your-face." Middle-class neighborhoods in other areas of Rio were comparatively conservative and traditional socially: "A guy meets a girl, falls in love, gets a house, has children early, etc., you have a whole nucleus of family life," he said, conceding that he was oversimplifying to make a point. In the South Zone, however, there was a "promiscuity of poverty with wealth." Thus a local expression claims that the tunnels under the hills between the South Zone and other parts of the city mark passage to "a different world."[8]

Of course much that is pertinent to this music scene has occurred outside the confines of the South Zone, or between it and other places (or even in imagined transnational spaces). Moreover, Rio's capacity to host promiscuous, porous, or ambiguous contact zones has over time been mythologized, while the important question of who controls and benefits from specific forms of social and cultural proximity simmers beneath the surface of such observations. Despite this, discourses about mixture pullulate with ease in this city in part because they confirm the lived experiences of Cariocas.

The Most Brazilian Thing to Do

In fact, a series of circumstances and discursive confluences—some specific to Brazil, others not—accumulated to help elevate mixture as a cultural practice to a kind of creed in this music scene. For starters, there was the country's history of miscegenation dating to the earliest days of the colonial period. Rare is the Brazilian who does not cite the intimate contact between African, Amerindian, and European peoples as the foundational social dynamic of the nation.[9] While this history was a source of anxiety for the predominantly white elite in the first decades of the republic after its founding in 1889, by the late 1920s leading intellectuals of Brazilian modernism were seeing in miscegenation a defining national trait worth reexamining. It was above all Gilberto Freyre's classic book *Casa-grande e senzala* (1933, published in English as *The Masters and the Slaves*) — which famously elaborated theories about sexual license in the construction of a "Brazilian race" — that helped advance what effectively amounts to an official interpretation of Brazilian society: not only is it always already mixed, but Brazilians are by nature more adept at mixing than anyone else in the world.[10]

This much is still assumed and largely unquestioned in popular discourse to the present, despite public recognition that miscegenation has not led directly to racial democracy as such. Difference is thus structured into Brazilian discourses of mixture because they depend upon the idea that there exist original elements (e.g., African, Indian, and European). Likewise, a reflexive individual and group sense of becoming is always already inherent to Brazilian national identity: subjects who think of themselves as defined in good part by centuries of "racial" mixture are also, as Peter Wade argued for Colombia, in "a constant process of emergence, constituted by the genealogical intersections of their parental heritages and by living in mixed regional landscapes" (2004, 362).[11]

The formal end of the dictatorship in 1985 and the restoration of electoral democracy, along with the ratification of a new liberal constitution in 1988, gave musicians who grew up under the military government a renewed sense of liberty and hope for Brazil's future. (Some even expressed a degree of relief that they were no longer expected to protest the government.) However, the early years of the new democracy were also marked by political and economic instability as hyperinflation devalued currencies and prominent figures in the new government were found to be corrupt. Disgusted with their political leadership, some musicians coalesced around a project to *insert Brazil into pop*, in their words, that is, to find a musical language that would celebrate and reinvigorate traditions understood as distinctly Brazilian through adaptation to international forms and styles they regarded as universal. It was a project partly inspired by nationalist sentiment, to be sure, but it also explicitly rejected the national-popular paradigm associated with the university left in the 1960s, a paradigm these musicians viewed as overly xenophobic. Now musical mixture reemerged as *the most Brazilian thing to do* in these musicians' discourse.

The new currency program instituted by the finance minister Fernando Henrique Cardoso in 1994 (the Real Plan), coupled with broad structural reforms of the government beginning when Cardoso became president in 1995, paved the way for the establishment of a comparatively stable market economy that was briefly favorable to the music industry before the latter succumbed to piracy and the increasing popularity of the MP3 format at the end of the decade. This coincided with the growing popularity throughout the 1990s in the United States, Europe, and Japan, in particular, of so-called world music and of genres that emphasized rhythm and drumming. As a consequence, Brazilian popular music enjoyed increased recognition in the international sphere and there emerged greater opportunities for touring abroad.

In conjunction with this general development was the "rediscovery" of Brazil's Tropicália music movement and the rock band Os Mutantes from the 1960s, particularly in the United States and Europe. An impressive yield of international newspaper and magazine articles in the late 1990s fueled this revival, and it continued into the following decade with the reconstitution of Os Mutantes as a live band who toured the United Kingdom and the United States to critical acclaim (with Zélia Duncan as lead singer), and who recorded a new studio album in 2009, *Haih*. In 1990 David Byrne released a compilation of tracks from the oeuvre of Tom Zé, another participant in Tropicália, sparking a remarkable revitalization of his career. Caetano Veloso's autobiographical account of the movement was published in Brazil in 1997 and then in English translation (as *Tropical Truth*) in 2002. A museum retrospective of the broader artistic milieu associated with Tropicália opened at the Bronx Museum of Art in New York in late 2006, and in 2007 it was exhibited in Rio de Janeiro's Museum of Modern Art.[12]

These developments helped keep alive another discourse of mixture originating in Brazilian modernism: the cultural cannibalism famously proposed by Oswald de Andrade in 1928, and subsequently adopted by the Tropicalist musicians in the late 1960s to explain their fusion of Brazilian styles with electrified rock. Inspired by colonial-era tales in which the Tupinambá tribes of what would become Rio de Janeiro state were portrayed as cannibals who consumed their enemies in order to absorb their strengths (e.g., Jean de Léry's and Hans von Staden's accounts), Oswald wrote the provocative "Manifesto antropófago" ("The Cannibalist Manifesto"). "Cannibalism alone unites us. Socially. Economically. Philosophically," he proclaimed, referring to Europe and Brazil. "I am interested only in what is not mine. Law of Man. Law of the Cannibal" (O. Andrade 1999, 92). He called for the consumption of select elements of cultural models and advanced technologies from the more industrialized nations of the West in the creation of a "technified natural man" and an innovative mixed national culture that would be suitable for export (Berg 1999, 90). It was an aggressive "intellectual deglution" (B. Nunes 1990) that attributed agency to the formerly colonized.[13]

Pop musicians in Brazil delighted in the discourse of cannibalism in the late 1990s even more than the Tropicalists had, and they evoked it in a variety of playful ways in song lyrics. Several scholars, mostly in literature or cultural studies, have reexamined this discourse from a postcolonial or postmodern perspective (see, e.g., Rocha and Ruffinelli 1999).[14] For the musicians in this scene, its emphasis on incorporating foreign forms and technologies resonated with another development that quite literally aided practices of mixture: the transformation in music production, distribution, and consumption facilitated by computers and digital technologies. The late 1990s represented the effective end of recording to analog tape as standard practice. As music production increasingly came to depend upon computerized systems, it began to move out of large, expensive recording facilities and into small project studios that are often in people's homes. Mixing, in this instance referring specifically to the process of electronically combining and modifying musical tracks, gradually became accessible to nearly everyone, and the computer made it easy to sample, cut, paste, and loop sounds. Additionally, the Internet, cable television, the MP3 format, and other forms of communication made available—to those with access—massive amounts of information from all over the world.

Meanwhile, with the market for compact discs rapidly expanding as increasing numbers of Brazilians entered into circuits of consumption, the major recording labels pushed genres that many of the musicians I encountered regarded as overly commodified and largely homogeneous "product" of dubious artistic value. The bugbear of this dynamic was *pagode*, a form of light samba that exploded in popularity during this decade and earned significant profits for the recording labels, leading them to seek to capitalize on the trend as much as possible. A romantic variety (*pagode romântico*) was identified with São Paulo, while a more sexually suggestive type tended to be associated with groups from Salvador, Bahia, following on the phenomenal success of the Bahian group É o Tchan. The common practice of having young female dancers in tight mini-shorts or bikinis gyrate onstage for audiences and television camera close-ups did not help endear this music to the more intellectual members of the middle class.[15]

Some of those who viewed pagode with disfavor took to calling the genre "*bunda* music," employing a vulgar term for a person's rear. The blonde

Carla Perez, a dancer with É o Tchan, came to epitomize this aspect of the music. Where was Brazilian culture headed?, the keepers of *bom gosto*, or good taste, fretted in opinion editorials, music criticism, and other forums. On 6 March 1999 the *Globo* columnist Artur Dapieve published an editorial on the topic that deserves special mention for being indecorously scornful. In the previous week's column, Dapieve had characterized the pagode and música sertaneja (Brazilian country music) genres as "trash" (*lixo*), an assessment that generated "a record number" of e-mail responses—"38 approving and 3 disapproving." Among the latter was a message from the chief of MTV Brazil at the time, André Mantovani. In this fascinating communication, part of which Dapieve provocatively reproduced in his column, the executive, an economist by training, suggested that the market (that is, audiences, consumers) would sort out the good from the bad: "We are not just going to show Carla Perez's bunda; rather, we bring her to MTV to show . . . what she has besides bunda. It is up to the audience . . . to see if she has something or not. . . . MTV will be showing the entirety. . . . We believe that if we broaden the space for Brazilian music, more music videos will be produced and access to Brazilian music, of both high quality and no quality, will increase."

The music video channel, Dapieve worried, would "incorporate that which all the other networks are spouting to no end. . . . What is successful is what is already successful. Outside this model there is no salvation, not even on MTV anymore." Cardoso's Real Plan, he fretted, brought "something like 16 million people" who had previously been marginal to consumer society into the market. Since "no one gave the new consumer the conditions to appreciate" the traditional samba composer Walter Alfaiate or the modernist art music composer Heitor Villa-Lobos, Dapieve continued, "he can only continue to shake" to the pagode group Molejo. "Don't come at me with cultural relativist hypocrisy," he warned, for there was no way that Villa-Lobos's "Trenzinho do caipira" (Little country train, from the composer's *Bachianas brasileiras* no. 2, 1933) was equal to the song "Carrinho de mão" (Wheelbarrow) by the pagode group Terrasamba. "No!"

Dapieve's alarmist editorial exposes the anxiety that Brazil's changing social and musical landscape could cause for some of the country's more "disgusted" subjects at the time, to use Stephanie Lawler's term for middle-class individuals who worry that the "masses" represent a menace to good taste and culture, and who in the process reinforce their own sense of identity (2005).[16] Most of the musicians with whom I spoke, however, were not so baldly contemptuous of the tastes of the so-called popular classes. Rather, their concerns centered on massification, homogenization, and the problem of artistic freedom. For them, marketing labels were in themselves homogenizing. "We're terrible about fitting into a category," Pedro Luís told me of his band. The emphasis on musical mixture as part of a project to insert Brazil into pop music was thus also a moral-political move against the threats to creative liberty that once came from the dictatorship's censors and now seemed mostly to come from the multinational record companies.

Middle-class Becomings / Becoming Middle Class

How does class figure into this musical project to insert Brazil into pop? What is the relationship between the individual and the collective in this setting? Some scholars have described distinctive sentiments of "betweenness" among middle-class subjects, the result of a kind of assimilation of the conflict between elites "above" and workers "below" into an unstable social status and correspondingly anxious cultural practices (Liechty 2003, 18–19). These sentiments tend to be exacerbated in countries where the middle class is not the majority (or is newly emergent, as in the Nepal studied by Liechty), and where, as a result, middle-class subjects may feel pressure to mediate tradition and modernity, local and global, or to serve as the index of the nation's modernization and development. One historian described the Brazilian middle class as "stuck in the middle" during the 1930s through the 1960s, as subjects carried out their lives "in tangled relation to the middle class ideal" (Owensby 1994; 1999, 8). The anthropologist Maureen O'Dougherty similarly found a friction between ideals about being middle class and actual experiences in São Paulo during the 1980s and 1990s. The expansion of this social sector during the so-called Brazilian economic miracle of the early 1970s, she notes, gave rise to "collective aspirations and desires, with an idealized standard of how to be middle class" (2002, 8). The social category "middle class" is thus experienced in relation to ideals and in opposition to what is seen as threatening those ideals (9).[17]

The ambiguity, instability, and betweenness attributed to this experience remind us that class is not objectively "out there" as a given category into which subjects fit when, for example, they meet certain criteria of income, education, or habits. What we refer to as "capitalism," the anthropologist Sherry B. Ortner has observed, has a "massive" objective reality "as a set of discourses, practices, and institutions" (2006, 70). Its structural logic produces the economically stratified social positions that we denote as classes. There is, however, a subjective dimension to the ways in which class is experienced that is not so easily correlated to quantitative measures, and that is intertwined with other aspects of identity such as gender, race, and ethnicity (73). Class is, in this sense, also partly (re)produced by individual acting subjects, and like these other dimensions, it can be performed. Material conditions matter greatly, but class, and in some ways especially the status of middle class, may also be seen as a "cultural project" that is constantly in course, more of a social and cultural process than a product (Liechty 2003, 15–16, 37).

If the relationship of the individual to the collective is a fundamental question in the social sciences, it is so-called practice theorists grounded in sociology and anthropology who most rigorously sought to account for the dialectic, historical, and transformational dynamics that arise between the actions of individuals and the more or less structured social worlds in which they live. A key question for these scholars has been, How do historically constituted formations such as class (but also more broadly any reproducible abstract pattern of social relations, cultural forms, or established ways of doing things) constrain or enable the agency of individual actors, that is, their ability (or power) to choose courses of action that have the potential to transform the very patterns that, in part, realize them as subjects? From another angle, How do learned and deeply ingrained habits and ways of being-in-the-world predispose subjects to reproduce such patterns or structures in social life (Pierre Bourdieu's concept of *habitus*)? Music making, practice theory helped demonstrate, does not merely reflect apparently external social patterns, structures, and their associated meanings; it can also play a role in constituting or transforming them (Sugarman 1997, 27; Waterman 1993).[18]

In Brazil this observation could be said to hold true on a grand scale. As already noted, music is a vital component of Brazilians' collective view of the national character, and *making* music is therefore profoundly constitutive of social meaning(s) and even of social relations in this immense nation. The very notion that miscegenation defines Brazilian identity is daily reinscribed in musical sound and talk about music in an "intricate interplay between discourse and practice" (Sugarman 1997, 30). It follows that individual creative "agents" are integral participants in these processes. Ortner suggests that agency, in a practice theory sense, is best understood "as a disposition toward the enactment of projects" (2006, 152), or indeed the ability to protect the right to have projects (147). What she refers to as "agency-in-the-sense-of-power," defined largely in terms of relationships of domination and resistance (for which macro considerations such as class, gender, and race are particularly relevant), can analytically be separated from "agency-in-the-sense-of (the pursuit of) projects," in which the values and ideals of individual subjects come to the fore (145, 152).[19]

Gilberto Velho, who has studied middle-class and elite subjectivity in Brazil, argued that the notion of project is key to understanding the fragmented and heterogeneous nature of urban life, and that "humanistic-bourgeois-therapeutic discourse" serves to legitimate individual projects in such milieus (1992, 18). In the "intellectualized perspective of the middle class," he wrote, "the idea that each individual has a combination of unique potentialities which constitute an identifying mark" is naturalized, and each person's biography is central to the unfolding of projects, even while they are necessarily also socially negotiated (11).[20] Projects thus emerge from subjects' conscious reflection on their own conduct; they are predicated on the possibility that individuals can choose how to channel their energies, and that said projects can be communicated (14). For Liechty and O'Dougherty, a primary project of middle-class subjects is to participate in modernity, mainly through consumption (which they see as productive of class). By contrast, I am interested in individual and collective projects of musically being contemporary, and of being musical, while I also understand specific musical practices as productive of middle-class experience in this setting.

Insights from practice theory are helpful for situating acting subjects historically within the competitive "field of cultural production" (Bourdieu 1993), but the language of "structures" (or "structured" and "structuring" structures in Bourdieu's strained formulation), of "agents," "intentions," "dispositions," "schemas," and "motivated transactions" (Sewell 1992) — however analytically nuanced — can depict social life and the experiences of individual creative subjects through time as rather flat and calculated. Similarly, theories of subjectivity are often dehumanizing, the editors of a recent volume on the topic note, portraying people as "remote abstractions, discursive forms, or subject positions" (Biehl, Good, and Kleinman 2007, 13).[21]

Some anthropologists have taken inspiration from the writings of the philosopher Gilles Deleuze, and of Deleuze with Félix Guattari, for thinking about subjectivity and other social issues in a way that opens up to uncertainty or ambivalence, or to what Deleuze refers to as the "lines of flight" of individuals desiring and acting in social formations that "leak out on all sides" (2006, 127). This approach encourages greater recognition of the "unfinishedness" of individual and social projects, of becoming, while it recommends an embrace of the incompleteness of our theoretical reflections (Biehl and Locke 2010, 320).[22] The principal musician highlighted in chapter 5, Paulinho Moska, described in our first interview how he was influenced by Deleuze, but at the time I interpreted this as an aspect of his habitus that was consistent with the kind of education middle-class Brazilians tend to receive, which often privileges European thought. On one level this observation has validity, but was Paulinho's interest in Deleuze *merely* an indication of a specific habitus, a given location in a "field" of cultural production? I began to ask. Or could it be enrolled as an element of my own analysis of this setting? Could certain Deleuzian concepts complement practice theory's insights?[23]

Deleuze contrasts his "cartographic" approach to subject formation with the "archaeological" and arguably more top-down project of Foucault (Deleuze 2006, 126; Biehl and Locke 2010, 323), which focused on how subjects are constituted and constrained by regimes of power and expert discourses. In Deleuze's cartography, the analyst maps trajectories that desiring subjects navigate through *milieus*, "worlds at once social, symbolic, and material" (Biehl and Locke 2010, 323). Brian Massumi notes that in French "milieu" means "surroundings," "medium" (as in chemistry), and "middle," and that all three of these meanings are germane to the way Deleuze and Guattari use the word (Deleuze and Guattari 1987, xvii). I like this idea for the creative setting under consideration here, in which music is a medium for a Brazilian alchemy of becoming, and in which metaphors and sentiments of in-betweenness—a kind of middleness—are recurring. Deleuze saw social fields as "leaky"; he was concerned with "the in-between, plastic, and ever-unfinished nature of a life" (Biehl and Locke 2010, 323). A Deleuzian concept of becoming can evoke how people strive to free themselves, even in small ways, "from determinants and definitions," João Biehl and Peter Locke write, "to grow both young and old [in them] at once" (Deleuze 1995, 170), and to open up, existentially, to immanence, "to new relations—camaraderie—and trajectories" (Biehl and Locke 2010, 317).[24]

The singer-songwriter Lenine evoked the metaphor of a chameleon in a mirror to talk about Brazilian identity. It is a reference to a riddle that Stewart Brand included in his *Whole Earth Catalog* of 1974: "What color is a chameleon in front of a mirror?" When Brand posed this question to the anthropologist Gregory Bateson (at a moment when they were "lost in contemplation of the function—if any—of consciousness, of self-consciousness"), the latter proposed that the lizard would settle at a kind of middle color, while Brand imagined that the creature, "trying to disappear in a universe of itself," would "endlessly cycle through a number of its disguises" (1974, 453).[25] As with the chameleon's capacity to change its timbre, music making in the setting described here is a profoundly self-conscious and mutable endeavor that is continually adapting to social/environmental signals. The mirror trope, key to psychoanalytic theories of subject formation (e.g., Jacques Lacan's "mirror stage"), has also been used to refer to the way many Latin American intellectuals have felt compelled to compare local cultural manifestations, institutions, and identities with those of Europe or North America, particularly in relation to discourses of modernism, modernity, and processes of modernization (e.g., Morse 1988; see also Monteiro 2009). This mode of thinking has been prevalent in Brazilian music too, but the chameleon image also places emphasis on the becoming subject, at once attributing voluntarism to it, and—when coupled with the mirror—signaling the contingency of that voluntarism. Mine is a narrative of how an analogous reflexive tension has animated a particular music scene.

Inspirations

Rather than describing a specific musical style, the term *música popular brasileira* indexes a complex of genres, aesthetic preferences, ideological stances, and market interests in a field of cultural production that has consistently been debated (Napolitano 1998, 93; Stroud 2008). Nevertheless, some observers have pointed to the consolidation by the 1990s of a kind of "mythic narrative" about a relatively natural evolution of hybridizing genres with Rio de Janeiro as the primary incubator of "national" music and MPB, an acronym that came into use only in the mid-1960s, taken as the peak expression of Brazilian musical creativity (Lucas 2000, 42–43; see also Reily 2000). In this view, music critics and intellectuals in Rio and São Paulo, catering to the tastes of urban, educated middle-class audiences, have been guilty of giving excessive attention to bossa nova, Tropicália,

Jovem Guarda (Young Guard), and Brazilian rock while ignoring the varied forms of musical expression found in other parts of the country, identified as regional rather than national (Lucas 2000, 42).

For a variety of reasons, this tendency is not as pronounced today, and the scholarly literature has also diversified somewhat to include more musical manifestations missing from what Lucas refered to as the "official narratives propagated by MPB's middle class audiences" (2000, 43).[26] My research, however, took me to what might be thought of as a kind of epicenter of the discursive and sonic production of música popular brasileira, understood in a comparatively restricted sense as urban music made by individuals who have collectively shown a marked preoccupation with their own historical role in shaping narratives of Brazilian identity, who prioritize the *popular song* as a medium for communicating and revising that identity, and who actively dialogue with both established Brazilian genres (in this case, samba in particular) and international trends through continual, deliberate, and self-consciously savvy musical mixture.[27] To discount these preoccupations, genres, and processes as part of a hegemonic narrative and centralized culture industry, I hope to show, misses an opportunity to probe what is at stake in discourse about Brazilian popular music, and to account for changes in what sounds may edge into or out of the mix.

Rio de Janeiro *has* in fact historically been a vibrant center of cultural contrast and fusion, a hotbed of musical performance, creativity, and innovation. It is, of course, a port city and it was the nation's capital from 1763 to 1960. From 1808 to 1822, Rio hosted the Portuguese royal court in exile (a unique event in the history of colonialism), which boosted the city's status as a cosmopolitan center and enlivened its musical activity. European dances popular among the elite at the time such as the polka began to merge with Brazilian ones such as the *lundu* favored among the large African-descended population of the city. Mixtures like these gave rise to the *maxixe* salon dance and eventually to the *choro* that emerged in the late nineteenth century. As the plantation economy of the Northeast declined and coffee and industry boomed in the Southeast, Rio attracted a new population of African-descended laborers. Thus Rio's samba is thought to derive in part from the samba de roda (circle samba) and côco genres found throughout the Northeast. The Candomblé religion centered in Salvador but practiced in Rio by the celebrated "tias" (aunts) — knowledgeable women of the Afro-Brazilian community — most likely influenced early urban samba as well. As the music industry, radio, and eventually television established firm bases in the city, individual popular musicians made their way there too, especially from the Northeast, such as Dorival Caymmi, Luiz Gonzaga, and Jackson do Pandeiro, all of whom found tremendous success in Rio. Lenine, from Pernambuco in the Northeast yet an integral participant in the contemporary Rio music scene, has been living there since 1979. Numerous other musicians, such as the producers Chico Neves and Tom Capone, key figures in the chapters that follow, moved to Rio from other parts (Belo Horizonte and Brasília, in this case).

It is therefore hardly surprising that this city should have a dominant place in representations of Brazilian popular music. At the same time, the narratives produced about its music have not unfolded so naturally; instead, they been actively constructed and contested throughout their unfolding. Choro, for example, had largely faded from public attention until Almirante revived it and invented a choro tradition through his radio program in the 1940s (McCann 2004). In its early years, samba was hardly the favored music of the middle class, and the emergence of bossa nova in the late 1950s was partly a reaction against the dominance of heavily orchestrated samba-song on the radio. Yet bossa nova was controversial at first, as prominent critics such as José Ramos Tinhorão attacked what they perceived as a jazz influence in the music, or the "alienation" of the white middle-class musicians who played it (1997, 37; see also Naves 2000).[28]

Then, as the labor movement gained influence under President João Goulart in the early 1960s, college students began to advocate for a Gramscian, national-popular model of music centered on the singer-songwriter who treated themes of working-class life, giving rise to the "second wave" of bossa nova and other styles favoring acoustic instrumentation. Soon the media began promoting the term MPB (briefly preceded by MMPB, for moderna música popular brasileira; see Galvão 1976) as a label for the variety of styles performed at the famous televised national song contests of the mid-1960s. Around the same time, the Jovem Guarda musicians brought Anglo-American pop-rock sounds to Brazil, but their music was generally interpreted by critics favoring the national-popular paradigm as having no organic relation to the nation.

The Tropicália musicians—led by Caetano Veloso and Gilberto Gil, but also including Tom Zé, Gal Costa, and the band Os Mutantes, among others—challenged the national-popular paradigm in 1967 and briefly scandalized the song festivals by embracing the commercial aspects of pop culture, and by mixing electric guitars with Brazilian sounds and references. In 1968 the dictatorship turned hard line, again altering the course of the narrative. Through the 1970s a variety of urban styles grouped under MPB continued to flourish, occasionally drawing notice from government censors. This is the Brazilian music that until recently—and perhaps still today—has been most recognized abroad, and it encompasses several of the country's celebrated singer-songwriters (Chico Buarque, Caetano Veloso, Gilberto Gil, Milton Nascimento, Rita Lee, Martinho da Vila, etc.), and major interpreters such as Elis Regina, Gal Costa, Clara Nunes, and Maria Bethânia. Os Mutantes, however, delved into progressive rock, straying far from the MPB camp. Tom Zé, too, went "off-narrative" as he grew increasingly experimental. In the 1980s, Brazilian rock, initially antithetical to the MPB of the previous decade, grew enormously popular among middle-class youths. But in the 1990s urban middle-class musicians increasingly became interested in local genres again, as we shall see.

Even in this rough sketch of certain key moments in what might be a kind of mainstream narrative about urban Brazilian popular music history before the 1990s (ignoring various other tendencies), it is clear that its trajectory was socially constructed. Middle-class critics, academics, fans, media workers, and music makers perhaps would like to control the terms upon which the historical value of specific musical manifestations has been assessed, and perhaps some have during certain periods. In fact, however, the varied debates over música popular brasileira (whether labeled MPB or not) have just as much been driven by broader themes of development, nation building, modernization, and globalization. This book may be considered one chapter in one narrative (from among other parallel narratives) of a vibrant city's musical life. In the study of Brazilian music's invented traditions and forged identities, Marcos Napolitano writes, we can observe "the vibrancy of a society consciously taking stock of itself, its present, its past, and its future," and we can try to map Brazil's "most unfathomable contradictions" (1998, 104).

There is a growing literature on urban popular music in Brazil, including several monographs in English (Dunn 2001; Leu 2006; McCann 2004; Perrone 1989; Shaw 1999; Stroud 2008; Vianna 1999), as well as a variety of articles.[29] This book builds on such work as an examination of music makers of the generation sometimes referred to as the "children of the dictatorship," that is, individuals who were youths in the 1970s, then young adults in the 1980s, and who firmly established themselves in the music scene during the 1990s. While these musicians elaborated on creative tensions that have historically propelled música popular brasileira, particularly with respect to balancing national and international musical elements, as well as artistic and marketing priorities, they also introduced an intensified concern with their *sound*, conceptualized as a kind of interdependence between the new music technologies they began to integrate into their practice and the acoustic timbres predominant in genres traditionally represented as Brazilian. On this aspect, I take inspiration from ethnomusicologists who have been attentive to correlations between discourses of identity, production practices, uses of technology, and musical sound understood broadly (e.g., Meintjes 2003; Veal 2007; and the authors assembled in Greene and Porcello 2005; also Lysloff and Gay 2003). I augment the work of these scholars in drawing greater attention to the integration of technologies—and ideas about how to use them—into the career trajectories of individuals, into their becoming as creative subjects and agents, during a period of intense transition as digital production and distribution came to dominate music making.

Although various ethnomusicologists have integrated class relations into their analyses, the discipline cannot claim a sustained engagement with specifically middle-class pop music settings, especially in countries where that social sector is not as large as it is in the most industrialized nations.[30] A notable exception is Thomas Turino's meticulous examination of how discourses of identity and attitudes about music among middle-class Zimbabweans changed over a period of sixty years, with a particular focus on dynamics of colonialism/postcolonialism, nationalism, cosmopolitanism, and "modernist-capitalist" globalization. There are some broad parallels with the Brazilian context, but the two settings are probably more different than similar, if only because of the characteristic way race is experienced and talked about in Brazil. Additionally, my interest in detailing the practices of and discourses about musical mixture among selected collaborators in a rather unique urban milieu, and during a particular period of transition, makes this study different in scope and intent from Turino's.

Jocelyne Guilbault's *Governing Sound* (2007), a "critical genealogy" of the calypso genre in Trinidad, is sensitive to musical entrepreneurship and agency in an economy shaped by neoliberalism. Like Guilbault, I show how specific actors transitioned into more self-managed roles as the music industry transformed. Guilbault's attention to the "micropractices of power effected through music" and to how music can be a "field of social management," drawing on Foucault's concept of governmentality, offers a compelling prism through which to think about popular music and national identity in "developing" nations (4). Her focus on a single genre allows her to examine a broad range of competing projects of "governance" (including working-class, middle-class, and elite interests). The participants in the music scene under consideration here, by contrast, methodically destabilized genre definitions, and I seek to show how this effort was uniquely meaningful to a middle-class cohort.

In Rio during 1998–99, and in 2007 and 2009 for follow-up research, I spent many hours in recording studios. I took notes and interviewed musicians, producers, audio engineers, and industry personnel whenever and wherever possible. I attended rehearsals and concerts and took lessons from expert musicians.[31] The conversations I collected were fairly long and covered a broad range of intertwined topics; this interconnectivity of research themes came to serve as a central premise of my analysis. This is a setting in which social dynamics such as race, gender, class, place, national identity, and expressive practice are tremendously difficult to separate from each other, while these dimensions are further imbricated in local discourses about technology and the aesthetics of mixture. It is precisely these "audible entanglements," to use Guilbault's apt phrase (2005; 2007, 172) that are of interest, as these themes tend to converge around fundamental existential questions of the nation such as What is Brazil? Who are "the Brazilians"? What is the nature of Brazilian culture? and What future is there for Brazil? It is for this reason that narratives about music making often "allegorize" Brazilian national identity as a perennial "problem" that is rendered fabulous in the juxtaposition of seemingly incongruous tradition (or the "archaic," in Roberto Schwarz's formulation) and modernity— the dynamic captured in the popular metaphor of the "two Brazils."[32]

The place of individual musicians in the ethnomusicological literature is varied, ranging from musical biography to the recognition of the influence that especially creative people may have in local contexts, or of the fact that the researcher can only come to know a limited number of music makers (Stock 2001). The researcher may, however, be sympathetic to the uniqueness of particular musical individuals, or to the ways in which broad social changes have an impact on their creative lives, without claiming to document individuals as one's primary aim (13). I structured the chapters of this book around specific musicians or, in one case, a single band, not out of an interest in musical biography per se, but in order to allow various themes to weave through my examination of the talk and sounds of subjects whose careers and music making are closely intertwined yet also marked by sentiments of individual creative development.[33] Chapter 1 introduces percussionist Marcos Suzano, a central figure in this music scene. I examine his career trajectory over the course of several years, showing how, during the political opening of the 1980s, he began to turn away from the rock music he favored as a youth and to delve instead into two musical traditions closely associated with Rio de Janeiro and commonly considered "national" genres: choro and samba. I explore themes of masculinity, technology, and entrepreneurial self-management in his work, while I also devote attention to his percussion method, and to his interpretations of certain social changes.

Chapter 2 focuses on the singer-songwriter Lenine, who was Suzano's partner on the influential *Olho de peixe*, and who subsequently gained an international reputation with his solo albums. I pay special attention to the place of cultural forms and references from the *Nordeste*, the Brazilian Northeast, in the urban pop music of the 1990s, and to the ways Lenine has incorporated northeastern genres into his work. Chapter 3 is devoted to the band Pedro Luís e A Parede, whose most recent album Lenine produced. This group, which also goes by the acronym PLAP, explicitly sought to "dismantle" the rock drum kit and to revisit samba and other traditions steeped in percussion, while maintaining aspects of the rock influences so important to their early listening practices, such as the "heaviness" of groups like Deep Purple. As the turn of the millennium approached, the members of PLAP started a samba percussion workshop in the South Zone. It turned out to be much more successful than they imagined as it grew into a performing ensemble. It serves as an example of a kind of musical entrepreneurship that depends on a translation to the South Zone pop scene of musical practices originally associated with the working classes.

Chapter 4 focuses on Fernanda Abreu, who began her career as a singer in the new wave pop rock band Blitz in the 1980s and then enthusiastically adopted sequencers and other music technologies when she launched her solo career in the early 1990s. She embraced black dance musics from the United States, and then increasingly Rio funk and samba. Among the questions I ask here is what kind of vocabulary is necessary to discuss "whiteness" in this setting. Chapter 5 treats Paulinho Moska's album *Móbile*, produced jointly by Marcos Suzano and the singer-songwriter-guitarist Celso

Fonseca. It demonstrates how Suzano was able to bring his acoustic readings of techno and jungle influences into an MPB album. I also briefly follow Paulinho's subsequent career as he parted ways with his recording label and began to manage his own multimedia projects. Chapter 6 recapitulates certain key themes as a concluding discussion.[34] Appendix 1 provides information on the interviews I cite throughout the book. Appendix 2 offers supplementary information on Marcos Suzano's technique for playing pandeiro. It is now possible for the reader to hear most of the musical tracks and read their original lyrics at the websites of the artists examined herein.

MARCOS SUZANO

A CARIOCA BLADE RUNNER

Thanks to Ogum, I am a warrior. It is not my first instinct to hold my tongue in the face of untruth or justice, great or small. . . . I am a son of Ogum . . . He rules my head and molds my personality. He makes me strong like steel. Because of him, I am a pathbreaker, ever ready to invent or organize something new, to look at things in a new way.
—James Matory, *Black Atlantic Religion*, 246–47

I showed Marcos Suzano my new pandeiro today and he loved it. He knew immediately who had made it, and he marveled at the thick goatskin drumhead.
—Author's fieldnotes, 19 March 1999, AR Studios

The 1990s were interesting years for the percussionist Marcos Suzano and his colleagues in music, he recalls, precisely because they captured a specific phase of technological transformation. He recorded a lot analogically (i.e., on the tape medium), but also a lot digitally as new technologies emerged. In fact, he "dove headfirst into the digital thing," and by the time of our July 2007 interview, I could no longer discern what acoustic instruments Suzano used to generate the sonic raw material for the schizophonically corrupted grooves he delighted in playing back for me on his iPod nano.[1] Yet evidence of them was all around me in his cramped but sundrenched home studio. An Afro-Brazilian *berimbau* musical bow rested upright in one corner. Cuban congas filled another crook. I almost stumbled over a wooden *zabumba* bass drum from the Brazilian Northeast. Shiny metal *cuícas*, the unique-sounding friction drum of samba, were stacked atop one other. A handsome wooden *alfaia*, another bass drum from the Northeast, was perched against a *tarol* snare drum. Cymbals rested atop drumheads, and *cabasa* and *ganzá* shakers lay about. A Nigerian *dùndún* talking drum, Indian *tabla* drums, a wooden *reco reco* scraper, a *muringa* clay jug, an Afro-Peruvian *cajón*, various pandeiros, and sundry sticks, mallets, brushes, and instrument cases took up the remaining space to one side of the room.

The variety of wood, skin, and brass tones of these items contrasted with the grays, whites, and blacks of much of the electronic gear on the other side of the room, where Suzano had his Apple computer–based digital audio workstation (DAW) and electronic postproduction gear. Suzano might be merely an eclectic percussionist with virtuosic technique without his Pro Tools software and mixing console, Sherman V2 filter bank, Neve 1073DPD Class A transformer balanced two-channel microphone preamplifier, Rosendahl Nanosyncs DDS audio clock and sync reference generator, Universal Audio 2–610 Dual Channel Tube Preamplifier, Neumann TLM103 large-diaphragm cardioid condenser microphone, and Yamaha NS10 near-field monitors. To the left of the DAW a stand-alone ashtray held evidence of the percussionist's impulsive habits.

I first met Suzano at Estúdio AR, where he was co-producing Paulinho Moska's *Móbile* (see chapter 5). At the time, he was also working on his second solo CD, and on albums with Pedro Luís, Chico César, Zeca Balero, Lenine, Fernanda Abreu, Lucas Santtana, and Carlos Malta, among others, all released in 1999 and 2000.[2] He had recently recorded Otto's drum and bass–inspired *Samba pra burro* (roughly, Lots of samba), and performed on the soundtrack for the Oscar-nominated film *Central do Brasil* (*Central Station*, both 1998). He recorded with Marisa Monte on her *Rose and Charcoal* disc of 1994, and on Gilberto Gil's popular *Unplugged* CD and the corresponding concert tour that same year, as well as the Brazilian rock band Titãs's *Acústico* (1997). He also recorded on Gil's *Quanta* (1997) and the Grammy-winning live version, *Quanta ao vivo* (1998); on Sting's *All This Time* (2001); and on Gil's Grammy-nominated *Electroacústico* (2004).

In the early 1990s Suzano began to gain recognition in Japan, where he frequently travels to perform, record, and teach, and where he has recorded with the pop musician Kazufumi Miyazawa and with the drummer Takashi Numazawa.[3] His partnership with Lenine on the 1993 *Olho de peixe* CD is revered among many musicians and producers in Rio de Janeiro for reinvigorating the role of percussion in Brazilian pop. When the *New York Times* music critic Jon Pareles saw this duo perform on New York City's Central Park SummerStage in 1997, he wrote that Suzano "made a simple pandeiro (tambourine) into a polyrhythmic dynamo." The bassist Mário Moura of the band Pedro Luís e A Parede maintains that Suzano "turned everything upside down" by playing the pandeiro like a drum kit, and by bringing percussion to the foreground of pop music arrangements and productions. Indeed, while Suzano utilizes a great variety of percussive instruments in his music making, he is best known for his innovations on the pandeiro, the shallow, round, single-headed frame drum with metal cymbals that is probably descended from North African tambourines via the Iberian Peninsula.[4]

In sum, from the 1990s to the present, Marcos Suzano has remained a percussionist highly sought after for his musical skill and versatility, his recording and performing professionalism, his technological deftness, and his unique sounds. He claims to have played on over two hundred albums. It is fair to say that there exists a Suzano *brand*, and that he is a cultural entrepreneur who understands his sounds as capital to be managed within a market economy in a way similar to what Jocelyne Guilbault has observed among Trinidadian carnival musicians (2007, 265). As he has been a central figure in the South Zone pop music scene, an examination of his biography and musical practice is a good way to start looking more closely at the people active in this setting. What innovations made Suzano so in demand as a recording and performing artist? How did he adapt the traditional Brazilian pandeiro to changing music technologies and international musical trends? What can his musical practices tell us about race and gender in this setting, or about the image of Africa in musical constructions of Brazilian identity? In what ways do his career trajectory and musical becoming fit into the broader collective project of inserting Brazil into pop? First, some discussion of Suzano's musicianship, and a few observations about the context in which his musical activities have unfolded.

I begin by summarizing several interconnected innovations and practices for which Suzano is known among Brazilian musicians.[5]

He helped bring percussion to the foreground of Brazilian pop music. This may strike readers as an unusual claim, given the rich percussiveness of much Brazilian music. The argument, as I have heard it, is that in the 1980s when urban, predominantly white, middle-class Brazilian youths were increasingly identifying with international rock and pop music, percussion came to serve as a mere "complement" to an instrumentation structured around a drum kit.[6] With a commanding stage presence, virtuosic technique, and "contemporary" sounds, he was able to claim a new space in MPB for, in particular, the pandeiro.

He preferred thick, natural drumheads for his pandeiro, in order to achieve more low-frequency resonance. By contrast, many players were using comparatively thin skins or plastic heads in the early 1990s. Playing his somewhat heavier instrument requires physical stamina, and his favorite pandeiro, now three decades old, is bruised, beaten, and held together with duct tape (see figure 2).

He lowered the pitch of the pandeiro by loosening the drumhead. Traditionally, the instrument is tuned relatively tightly, giving it a medium-pitched and comparatively brief sonic envelope. Influenced by the drum and bass, jungle, and dub genres, Suzano was interested in generating a more sustained low bass.

He developed a playing technique that corresponds to these stylistic priorities, and that allows him to get at what he called the "Afro intention" of certain popular music grooves. In a typical samba technique for playing the pandeiro, open strokes with the thumb emphasize beat 2 in duple meter, analogous to the surdo bass drum. The surdo is said to have been added to samba by the drum corps director Bide (Alcebíades Barcelos) in the late 1920s as a way of keeping carnival marchers in rhythm as they parade. Suzano, however, keeps the thumb free to accentuate the offbeats, which he sees as closer to the role of the large rum (or ilú) lead drum in the traditional drumming of the African-Brazilian Candomblé religion (see, e.g., Béhague 1984, 232; Fryer 2000, 18). The smaller lé and rumpi drums in this tradition are typically responsible for steady patterns. Similarly, the cymbals on the pandeiro, in Suzano's method, generally maintain even sixteenth notes (that is, four subdivisions of the beat, without "swing") as they are shaken and clang against one another, providing the fastest pulse of a given rhythm and functioning as a kind of "density referent" (Koetting 1970). The middle range on the pandeiro includes various sounds such as a muted slap on the drumhead. I detail some of the basics of Suzano's playing technique in Appendix 2.

He captures and amplifies the sounds made on his pandeiro with a small condenser microphone that clips to the instrument's frame and is aimed at the rear of the drumhead, as seen in figure 2. He was thus able to collaborate with audio engineers to achieve an outsize sound

for the pandeiro both in live performance on the stage and in the
recording studio. This has also allowed him and his favored engineers
to control and electronically manipulate the sound of his instruments.

He, along with some of his colleagues, have utilized "mini-sets" (alt.
"mini-kits") of percussive instruments and odds and ends that allow
great varieties of timbres and are customizable to the particular musical context.

He adapted rhythms from a range of international influences such as rock,
techno, jungle, and drum and bass to the pandeiro and to his mini-kit.

He experimented with music technologies in his search for new timbres,
textures, and grooves. For example, he has used samplers and computers to record his acoustically performed beats and subsequently

FIGURE 2. Marcos Suzano's favorite pandeiro (underside) with
attached microphone and electronic foot pedal effects

to loop or modify them electronically. He also uses a variety of special effects in the form of foot pedals or rack-mounted outboard gear, especially filters. The pairing of the "natural" material to electronics is a central theme in his work, and he has taken it further than his predecessors in Brazil.[7]

In a conversation I had with Paulinho Moska he referred to Suzano as a "Carioca Blade Runner" who is "truly contemporary" and at the same time very rooted in Rio de Janeiro culture and life. Fusing the popular term for a native-born resident of Rio (Carioca) with the Hollywood reference, this characterization evokes the image of a savvy, somewhat aggressive, do-it-yourself solo male hero negotiating between nature and culture, emotions and programmed responses, humans and machines, corporate control and free will, like Harrison Ford's Detective Deckard, the Blade Runner. Deckard is charged with "retiring" rebellious "replicants," the bio-engineered slaves who are forced to live in a labor camp on another planet and who, after developing powerful emotions, seek to outlive their pre-programmed expiration date. In the end, Deckard chooses not to retire the last replicant, Rachel, with whom he falls in love and whom he invites into his home. He thus domesticates the threatening and alien technology much as Suzano has progressively domesticated imported music technologies and electronic sounds in his work and in his home DAW. Paul Théberge has observed that music technologies are often represented in advertising as women to impart a human "feel" to machines while simultaneously playing into male anxiety about the need for domination and control (1997, 124–25). This, he writes, is what is conveyed in Blade Runner's character Rachel.

Bearing these associations in mind, Paulinho's characterization of Suzano suggests some interesting ways to think about the latter's musical practices. If the Blade Runner aspect suggests a heroic domination of alien technologies, the "Carioca" modifier speaks to the percussionist's command of local and Brazilian musical styles (insofar as carioca samba is often understood—at least locally—as representative of "Brazilian" music). Did the sonic shift away from allowing percussion to serve as a mere "perfume" in the mix—as one musician described its place in Brazilian pop music "before Suzano"—toward a soloist man-and-his-tambourine sort of positioning index a broader shift in nationalist sentiment that at least partly played into existing sentiments about masculinity, control, power, individualism, and the "conduct of conduct"?[8] In fact, Suzano's desire to foreground percussion and to limit the role of the drum kit (understood as an import) complemented efforts by, for example, the members of the bands Pedro Luís e A Parede (PLAP) and Chico Science and Nação Zumbi (CSNZ), who similarly attributed to Brazilian percussion a reinvigorated role in the pop-rock ensemble.

Mário Moura explicitly expressed this kind of sentiment when he noted in one of our interviews that the band CSNZ emerged in Recife during a period of national anxiety following the impeachment of President Fernando Collor de Mello: "Brazilians got incensed with the lack of shame of this guy . . . He put his hand into everyone's bank account and . . . put [the money] in his pocket . . . And no one did anything beyond removing him from power. So that inflamed a nationalist movement of people, you know, 'I want a real Brazil, man!' And suddenly Chico Science and Nação Zumbi appeared with this totally different sound, mixing *tambor* [hand drum] with distorted guitar, hip-hop, rock 'n' roll, with agitated words, and it caught on. It was what the youth wanted to hear—strong, vigorous sounds, that seemed to say, 'Brazil is awesome [*do caralho*]!'"[9] The "strong" and "vigorous" sounds of CSNZ mobilized both new music technologies and the rather martial "no apology" (Crook 2005, 237) drumming of the Afro-Brazilian maracatu tradition along with other Afro-diasporic sounds to fortify beleaguered nationalist sentiments, and indeed to counterpoise the corrupted conduct of those in power (or removed from power because of their conduct). Suzano had already plugged into this sonic amendment through his collaboration with Lenine in 1993. (The title of Suzano's subsequent solo album, *Sambatown*, was in fact a play on the title of CSNZ's song "Manguetown.")

Some of Mário's language draws attention to the social construction of gender and sexuality. For example, one of the expressions Mário employed is associated with male sexuality: *do caralho*, which I have translated as "awesome," derives from a slang term for "penis" (*caralho*).[10] Similarly, Mário described Suzano as a *cara foda* (roughly, "formidable guy"), which derives from a vulgar slang term for sexual intercourse (*foder*). In our interviews, Suzano often used another popular Carioca word, *porra* (the double r sounding like an h), an interjection commonly used to express frustration, surprise, or anger or simply to stress a point. It is actually, however, slang for "semen." These terms, Richard Parker notes, "place emphasis on the potentially active quality of the phallus—on its aggressive quality, on its potency not merely as a sexual organ, but, in the language of metaphor, as a tool to be wielded, as a kind of weapon intimately linked to both violence and violation" (2009, 41). "In the play of words," he continues, "the phallus becomes, figuratively if not literally, an *arma*—a weapon, an instrument of metaphoric aggression, or in an extension of Pierre Bourdieu's expression, of symbolic violence" (42). The exclamatory interjection *porra*, "understood as both phallus and semen, as well as in its relation to anger and violence," Parker argues, "becomes a kind of essence of masculinity—a symbol of creative power, of *potência* (potency) and *vida* (life)" (42). These kinds of expressions, common in Carioca conversation and no less so in the male-dominated recording scene, are drawn from an extensive public repertoire of androcentric macho language in which the heterosexual male is represented as (sexually) active, in control, and producing (rather than reproducing), while women and gay men alike are passive, lacking control, receptive, or debased. Notwithstanding the ubiquity of such language, its use in this context adds to the sense that the modes of agency at stake in some of these musical developments have sexualized and gendered dimensions.

Suzano also calls on the Yoruba and Afro-Brazilian deity Ogum, a powerful, sometimes aggressive figure who presides over fire, iron, hunting, war, and, in some conceptualizations, politics (Ogun in Spanish-speaking Latin America, or Ogou in Haiti). Gage Averill and Yuen-Ming David Yih have noted that in Haiti the Nago dance for Ogou in the Vodou religion evokes military combativeness (2000, 276). As a blacksmith, Ogum is also understood in the Candomblé and the related Umbanda religions as the god of technology. He is often depicted brandishing a blade, and the *gonguê* iron bell of maracatu is sometimes associated with Ogum.[11] He can be a symbol of the struggle for justice (Shohat and Stam 1994, 45). In the minds of followers, Sandra T. Barnes writes, Ogum presents two images: "One is a terrifying specter: a violent warrior, fully armed and laden with frightening charms and medicines to kill his foes. The other is society's ideal male: a leader known for his sexual prowess, who nurtures, protects, and relentlessly pursues truth, equity, and justice. Clearly, this African figure fits the destroyer/creator archetype. But to assign him a neat label is itself an injustice, for behind the label is a complex and varied set of notions" (1997, 2).

As will become clear, Suzano identifies Ogum with what he understands as the diasporic power of low frequencies to lead or drive a given musical sound, while the associations Barnes describes resonate with the percussionist's broader projects to invert what he saw as certain incorrect hierarchies of music production, to subvert corrupt and centralized power, and to control the tools of his trade in his sonic smithing.

Suzano's evocation of Candomblé points to Bahia, the religion's ethnic and iconographic center, the most African of states in Brazil, the country's "Black Rome" (Dunn 2007; Sansone 1999, 20). At the same time, however, as José Jorge de Carvalho has argued, orthodox Afro-Brazilian religions such as Candomblé "suspend the question of who is black" because the deities worshiped "are universal and as such put themselves on top of whatever divisions are built on racial, social, political or sexual basis" (1994, 2). Instead of offering a black identity, he writes, these traditional religions "merely state ritually that anyone, black or white, can be an African." The "sound of Africa" (Meintjes 2003) can thus be called upon without necessarily engaging black identity politics.[12] Interestingly, in the Candomblé and Umbanda religions as practiced in Rio de Janeiro, Ogum is typically syncretized with Saint George, the chivalrous slayer of the dragon in popular iconography. It is not mere coincidence that in Mika Kaurismäki's documentary film *The Sound of Rio: Brasileirinho* (2007), Suzano can be seen performing onstage in a T-shirt with the figure of Saint George lancing a beast—an image, that is, of heroic manhood.[13]

The casual references to Harrison Ford's Detective Deckard and to Ogum in my interviews with musicians thus allude to a setting in which their efforts to bring percussion out of the background, central to the project of inserting Brazil into pop, can be seen as partly gendered and sexualized, while also drawing in complex ways on ideas about African sounds and Brazilian national identity. I bear these dimensions in mind when I contemplate the photograph I took of Suzano in his living room during one of our get-togethers (figure 3). The Carioca Blade Runner demonstrated how he runs his pandeiro through a series of electronic foot pedals—which I liken to Ogum's "frightening charms"—in the creation of compressed, filtered, sometimes distorted, often strange sounds generated through the percussionist's human, rhythmic mediation between the skin drumhead and the machines. The pandeiro itself might be thought of as Suzano's main weapon in his challenges to received sonic practices, akin to Ogum's sword or Saint George's lance.

Let me be clear that I am not saying these moves are only or even primarily an assertion of an essential(ized), heteronormative masculinity (possibly with racial and ethnic dimensions). Rather, I am seeking to

"embed" this musician's practices, his "desires and intentions," and his "plans and plots" into "motivated, organized, and socially complex ways of going about life in particular times and places," what Sherry B. Ortner calls "serious games" (1996, 12). Individuals play the "games of life . . . with intention, wit, knowledge, intelligence" (aspects of their "agency"),

FIGURE 3. Marcos Suzano demonstrating his pandeiro and electronic foot pedal effects setup

but these games are serious to the extent that "power and inequality pervade" them (12). Whether or not we adopt Ortner's metaphor, the point of it is to theorize "people-in-(power)-relationships-in-projects as the relatively irreducible unit of 'practice'" (13). Importantly, there is never just one game (13). So, for example, the project to "insert Brazil into pop" was a power move that reflected a specific shift in ideas about national identity and music making during the 1990s (particularly among middle-class subjects), but also historical anxieties over the "penetration" of foreign influences into Brazil (the drum kit displaces percussion, for example). It is worth remembering that the influences of jazz on bossa nova, and of the Beatles on the *iê iê iê* (yeah, yeah, yeah) pop music of the Jovem Guarda, were previously described in language that similarly evoked gendered power dynamics (*penetrar*, or even *violar* [rape]; see A. L. Barbosa, et al. 1966).

These same dynamics, however, can be read—and in fact were read locally—as related in not-always-obvious ways to questions of markets and, more precisely, in recent years, of neoliberal globalization, or even to problems of corruption in government, as the following passage from my 2007 interview with Suzano shows: "We have a serious problem that is reaching an unbearable level today, which is corruption. . . . It is endemic, it is one of our traits [*uma coisa nossa*]. The Brazilian is corrupt. It is depressing to admit it, but the Brazilian allows himself to be corrupted very easily. And we see this in music continuously—a corruption, for example, in the sense of accepting imported models, formulas for success, and people lower their heads and corrupt themselves to achieve success. How many great musicians, incredible people, caved to the requests of the record labels, the pressure? And the most basic example comes from our capital, Brasília. . . . Perhaps fewer than 10 percent of the deputies and senators have a clean police record. Either they . . . stole money, didn't pay their taxes, or were involved in some scandal, it's unbelievable!" Clearly what is at stake in these varied interpretations of foreign influence, market pressures, and individual creativity is power: (empowered) agency versus submission, an aversion to "lower[ing one's] head" and "accepting" (also a gendered/sexualized image consistent with tropes of the female being passive, receiving), or "caving" in.[14] With so many things having an impact on the games people play, a given influence or hybridizing practice can be good in some ways at some times to some individuals, and bad in other ways or at other times for other folks, or for the same ones. Thus we observe adjustments and readjustments over time of, for example, the role of the drum kit in Brazilian pop and rock (or of the electric guitar, the pandeiro, of samba, techno, "Afro" sensibility, and so on).

Yet there is something more to this story; there is also Suzano's emergence as a professional musician and experimenter with sounds and technologies. In this dimension, the percussionist's desires — realized not necessarily as clear intentions or as agency-in-a-project, but sometimes as a vague sense of frustration and search for a "line of flight" — are what make possible new musical and life experiences.[15] The following pages offer a more biographical narrative as I sketch out Suzano's career trajectory in relation to transformations in the political, economic, and technological spheres.

Formative Influences and Collaborations in Suzano's Early Career

Suzano was born in 1963 and grew up in Copacabana, a busy, eclectic, and intense neighborhood of condominiums, shops of all sorts, cafés, bars, restaurants, and nightclubs bordering the famous beach of the same name. In contrast to the previous generations of popular musicians that included many of Brazil's great singer-songwriters of the 1960s and 1970s, the influential Tropicália movement, and also the protest song associated with left-leaning student populations during those decades, Suzano reflected that his own youth was relatively removed from political concerns, and indeed from musical genres typically understood as Brazilian. He conceded that he didn't sense the dictatorship because his family "didn't suffer at all from any side — neither from the right nor from the left." He had no idea what was going on, he said, and only began to be exposed to the realities of the authoritarian regime once he began his college studies. He also made a point of observing that he only got to know the music of Os Mutantes, Caetano Veloso, Gilberto Gil, and Tropicália in the 1980s when he was older. Reacting against what he perceived to be an over-saturation of media attention to Tropicália at the time of our first interview early in 1999, he sought to distance himself from the movement. In doing so, Suzano affirmed how his own musical biography formed an independent narrative, rather than simply following a path broken by the Tropicalists. (And of all the people I interviewed for this project, Suzano was perhaps the least inclined to evoke the anthropophagy metaphor to explain his musical hybridizations.) As a youth playing around in Copacabana in the 1970s (between the ages of seven and seventeen), he remembered, he and his friends listened to rock groups from abroad such as Led Zeppelin and Black Sabbath; they were not paying attention to protest song.

In fact, in the early 1970s the Brazilian economic miracle of high growth helped keep many among the middle classes from agitating for democracy. By the late 1970s, however, economic expansion had ground to a halt while the new social movements coalesced around democratization during this period known as the *abertura* (opening). These transformations in the political sphere coincided with Suzano's increasing interest in two musical genres strongly identified with Rio de Janeiro and with Brazilian national identity: samba and choro. He was inspired to learn to play a variety of samba percussion instruments when he heard a carnival *bloco* in the early part of the decade. (A bloco is a musical association with percussion that parades relatively spontaneously through local neighborhood streets during the days of carnival, rather than in the media-ready sambadrome where the main competition between the big samba schools is held.) Traditionally, bloco repertoire focuses on samba or other favorite carnival genres like *marcha* (a fast march), with an emphasis on drumming and syncopated rhythms deriving in part from Afro-Brazilian influences, typically in duple meter.[16] It is easy to understand how hearing a street bloco could inspire a middle-class youth in Rio's South Zone to turn his attention from rock to samba during this period of political opening.

Choro, by contrast, is not associated with carnival or street processions. This primarily instrumental music emerged in mid- to late nineteenth-century Rio de Janeiro as Brazilians adapted European salon dances popular at the time such as the polka and the schottische to the syncopated inflections of genres like the *lundu*. By the 1940s a large body of repertoire had become standardized, and instrumental virtuosity had become a key feature of the genre, similar to jazz in the United States.[17] The pandeiro, used in many Brazilian genres, including samba, became an essential part of the contemporary choro ensemble as the main percussion instrument providing rhythmic accompaniment to the melody and harmony instruments. The popularity of choro suffered in the late 1950s and the 1960s with the explosive international success of the bossa nova genre. In the late 1960s, however, the mandolin virtuoso Jacob do Bandolim formed the Época de Ouro (Golden Age) ensemble in an effort to keep the genre alive. Among the original members of this group was Jorginho do Pandeiro (Jorge José da Silva), a master of the pandeiro. When Suzano heard

Jorginho play in the 1980s, he was inspired to concentrate more intensely on that instrument. In the 1970s a younger cohort of choro musicians in Rio furthered the revival of the repertoire and instrumentation; since then, a variety of groups and successive generations of musicians have maintained an active choro scene in Rio, São Paulo, Brasília, and other places in Brazil and even abroad (e.g., Choro Ensemble in New York City). It was in neotraditional choro and samba circles in the 1980s that Suzano first mastered the instrument with which he is most identified.

Not yet resolved to make music his career, Suzano attended the Universidade Federal do Rio de Janeiro (UFRJ) to study economics. Meanwhile, he also began learning Afro-Brazilian rhythms with the percussionist Carlos Negreiros, a specialist in Candomblé drumming, while performing with him in the group of the prominent choro and jazz clarinetist and saxophonist Paulo Moura. He eventually decided to abandon the idea of a career in economics (although he earned the degree). After college he participated in one of the new generation of choro ensembles, Nó em Pingo d'Agua (Knot in a Drop of Water), recording the critically acclaimed albums *Salvador* (1988) and *Receita de samba* (Recipe for samba, 1991) with that group. Founded in 1979, Nó em Pingo d'Agua has been one of the most active contemporary choro ensembles in Rio; they have incorporated jazz and funk influences, composed new repertoire, and collaborated with a broad range of talented musicians. Suzano left Nó em Pingo d'Agua after *Receita de Samba*. (Celsinho Silva, Jorginho do Pandeiro's son, replaced him.)[18]

In 1989 Suzano formed the Aquarela Carioca (Carioca Watercolor) jazz ensemble together with the saxophone and flute player Mário Sève (also a founding member of Nó em Pingo d'Agua). Aquarela Carioca performed at the 1989 Free Jazz Festival in Rio and São Paulo and released their debut album that year, winning the prestigious national Sharp Prize for instrumental music (analogous to the Grammy Award) the following year.[19] Their repertoire was eclectic; their second album, *Contos* (Stories, 1991), for example, featured original compositions alongside pieces by Villa-Lobos, Caetano Veloso, and Led Zeppelin. (Suzano even adapted some of John Bonham's distinctive rock drumming to pandeiro for their recording of Led Zeppelin's "Kashmir.") The group's third release, *As aparências enganam* (Appearances are deceiving, 1993), was a collaboration with the Brazilian pop singer Ney Matogrosso, and they released two more CDs after that (*Idioma* [Language], 1996, and *Volta ao Mundo* [Return to the world], 2002). It was with this group, Suzano noted, that he began "to develop [his] sounds" in collaboration with the recording engineer Denilson Campos, with whom he would work again on the Olho de peixe album and other projects.

While both Nó em Pingo d'Água and Aquarela Carioca had focused on choro and jazz instrumental arrangements, Suzano soon began to work with MPB artists. An early such collaboration was the singer Zizi Possi's Sobre todas as coisas (About everything) from 1991. Possi had ended her relationship with PolyGram, apparently because she wanted to perform and record a less commercial repertoire than the label preferred. Suzano suggested an acoustic instrumentation of percussion, cello, and piano (with Lui Coimbra, the cellist, doubling on other stringed instruments), moving away from the more typical MPB instrumentation based on a pop ensemble with drum kit. The CD, with some classic MPB repertoire, was recorded digitally in a small studio in Rio de Janeiro at a time when debates over the merits of digital versus analog media were not yet muted by the eventual triumph of digital culture. It was released on the independent São Paulo–based Eldorado label, yet it sold better than any of Zizi's previous recordings, and it won the national Sharp Prize for best singer and best MPB CD in 1991, an indication of the emergent trend toward digitally recorded independent projects. By this time Suzano had begun to develop his unique method for playing the pandeiro, allowing him greater rhythmic versatility beyond the traditional samba- and choro-style accompaniment. In terms of timbre, however, his overall sound remained quite traditional for the Possi recording.

In our 2007 interview, I asked Suzano to reflect back on the sociopolitical context of the early 1990s, a period when the process of democratization was still relatively recent, and the broad political and economic reforms that President Cardoso would later accelerate were still limited. Suzano recalled:

That was a very rough period because the musicians never received their pay right away, there was always a delay. With inflation of 1.2 percent per day, they would cheat us. . . . So we would do three shows per night—in the Cândido Mendes Theater with [my group] Aquarela Carioca at 7 PM, in the Ipanema Theater at 9 PM with [the MPB singer] Eduardo Dusek, and then around 11 PM at the Mistura Fina [nightclub]—to earn a buck a day, because there was no money around. You'd play the Canecão club with [the rock band] Paralamas for free. It was crazy. There was nothing we could do about it. At first people withdrew a bit, but at the same time, they began to get savvy about searching for options to continue working, for new ideas to attract the attention of the public. It's not for nothing that Zizi Possi appeared with her work during this period. . . . It was very important. It was exactly in 1990–91, and people heard that and said, "Wow, what is this, who is this singer?"—all the squares who were used to a different style. And that's when Marisa Monte came on the scene, and a little later came the reaction of the poorer population, favela funk, funk of Rio, man, you know, that was really serious.

Suzano was also a founding member in the early 1990s of a percussion-based ensemble called Baticum, which he formed with fellow percussionists Carlos Negreiros, Jovi Joviniano, and Beto Cazes. The group had several other percussionists as well (a total of twenty-four) and also featured Carlos Malta on winds and Rodrigo Campello on violão as an occasional guest. It was in this ensemble that the musicians experimented with the mini-kits mentioned previously, which consisted of an eclectic variety of instruments. Suzano's, for example, was structured around the cajón (a wooden box of Afro-Peruvian and Caribbean origin), in addition to, he said, "electronic things," while his colleagues Jovi Joviniano and Beto Cazes used samba instruments and miscellaneous small percussion. Carlos Negreiros's mini-kit featured *atabaques*, the tall single-headed drums used in Candomblé. The main idea with the mini-kits, Suzano observed, was the timbre, and the timbres of percussion in Brazil, he said, "changed *a lot* in the nineties."

Nashville, Jim Ball, and *Olho de peixe*

In 1992 the singer-songwriter Joan Baez invited Suzano to Nashville to record on her *Play Me Backwards* album. Working with Baez's audio engineer Jim Ball helped Suzano develop his sound as he became intensely interested in the technologies used to capture, mix, and produce his performances. In order to facilitate overdubbing several layers of pandeiro, he recorded for Baez with a click track (a kind of metronome, and a relatively unusual practice in Brazilian studios at the time). He recalled being amazed at the spatial organization of sounds between the left and right channels. Even with several overdubs, the tracks did not interfere with each other in the mix, a feat that requires technical skill with equalization, panning, volume levels, and the use of reverberation and other effects. "The pandeiro sounded so cool," Suzano related in one of our first interviews, and he was "shocked" by the breadth and detail of the stereo image. It was something he had never experienced "in the Brazilian style of recording," and it felt like he was "going ahead, going beyond."

After hearing the rich multitracked studio sound that Ball realized for his pandeiro, Suzano became increasingly convinced that the role of percussion in Brazilian pop music had become merely complementary, a kind of seasoning added almost as an afterthought. Major record label producers were relegating Afro-Brazilian-derived percussion sounds to the background of pop mixes, he reasoned, out of concern that such sounds were not appropriate for mainstream radio airplay. "By the force of the market," he recalled, "the drum kit took precedence in the 1980s and percussion became a complement. It became that kind of percussion of, you know, *clave*." It was "simplistic percussion."[20] Then in 1993 he teamed up with the singer-songwriter Lenine and the sound technician Denilson Campos (who had engineered the Aquarela Carioca albums and the live sound for the Baticum group) to record *Olho de peixe*. Mário Moura elaborated on the significance of this project. Samba and *batucada* (drumming, esp. Afro-Brazilian), Mário noted, had always existed, "but when someone went to make an album, the role of percussion was always reduced to an effect . . . [or used] to fill a space here or there." Suzano revolutionized percussion, Mário maintained somewhat hyperbolically, by bringing it to the forefront of a pop mix. "I couldn't believe it!" the bassist said of his reaction the first time he heard Suzano play. "The guy turned the pandeiro into a drum kit, man, it was no joke!" He made percussion into something fundamental to Brazilian pop music, Mário concluded, rather than a "perfume."

Suzano situated the album, which I discuss some more in the following chapter, within what he called an "explosion of ideas" in which the percussionist Carlinhos Brown in Salvador and the mangue beat groups of Recife played an important role. He was referring to the tendency among these musicians to move away from a standardized rock band instrumentation that had become well established in Brazil by the end of the 1980s. The "rhythmic options" that certain musicians in Recife, Salvador, and Rio presented, he noted, rejected traditionalist purism and gave local grooves a more contemporary treatment, most notably the combination of the backbeat of rock with the Afro-Brazilian drumming of maracatu that Chico Science and his band Nação Zumbi developed in Recife.

The explosion of ideas Suzano described required a parallel correction in the recording studio as producers had to learn to adapt to the new percussion sounds. There was a "bizarre" phase, Suzano reflected in 2007, of incomprehension on the part of pop music producers. The dependence on imported models became very clear to him, especially with respect to percussion. While he and his colleagues in the Baticum ensemble considered the arrangement of the low, middle, and high frequencies and sought to "fill in" all the sixteenth notes, as occurs among the three drums of Candomblé (lé, rumpi, and rum), the "hierarchy of music production," he remembered, meant that percussion was always the last thing to be recorded in the studio. When they tried to add their grooves, the producers would complain that they were "too busy" and "too full," according to Suzano, and they would ask if there was a way of playing the rhythm "with fewer notes." The "imported" hierarchy of pop music industry production models is precisely the inverse, in Suzano's interpretation, of the hierarchy of rhythms in the more traditional Afro-Brazilian Candomblé practice, in which not only is drumming predominant, but the low drum (rum) is the lead. He identified the place of the drummer in rock and pop as the main impediment to achieving his musical priorities in the recording studio: "There are many ideas that I use today that I already tried to use previously but the producers would cut them. . . . For example, you take a pandeiro and tune it low and play a groove like this [demonstrating a rhythm for me on his instrument] and the producers would ask, 'Man, what is that? There is already a drummer.' And I would say, 'All right, all right,' and think, 'Patience.' Then when I made [my solo album *Sambatown*] I began to use those grooves and people asked, 'Hey, what is that?!' It would be [the groove] I had tried to use four years before." The emphasis here on exercising self-control as Brazilian producers and listeners gradually caught up to Suzano is thus situated dialectically against the "explosion" and power of his ideas and methods.

To record *Sambatown*, an album structured around jazz-samba-choro instrumentation and arrangements, the percussionist was concerned to find "the ideal pandeiro sound." Ironically, given the problem of foreign models of music production, he sought the big stereo image that the recording engineer Jim Ball had created for him on *Play Me Backwards*. With Ball, he thought, he would make "a definitive pandeiro recording" with what he referred to as um puta som (which could be translated as "a bitchin' sound"). Ball gave him the "difference" that he sought through a wide stereo image that was not forced or exaggerated. The engineer, he held, "settled his style" and the direction of his sound. "It was, like, politically correct, but different," Suzano explained, by which he meant that the engineer did not use any electronic effects, distort the sound, or add anything to it. Rather, he "just recorded very well, checking which phase cancellation made the sound more interesting, with five tracks of pandeiro, and the stereo very wide." While multitracking five overdubs of this instrument was outside local production norms, Jim Ball's careful mixing tempered any sense of exaggeration, maintaining the album's jazz-like decorum, such that *Sambatown* represents a moment of transition between the unplugged aesthetic that is a prevailing tendency in much jazz (and MPB) and the percussionist's more radical dive into sonic manipulation as he began to take control of machines himself.[21]

Indeed, Suzano was animated when he detailed the hodgepodge of acoustic, analog, and digital instruments, technologies, spaces, and techniques they used: "I used my [AKG]98 microphone straight through an API preamplifier, and then I used two U67 [Neumann microphones configured] like this [and] a pandeiro here, with the phase reversed. Those two mics went through the Neve preamps, and there were two ambient mics that we put through the Demeter tube preamps. We cut straight to the tape, no console, and the tape machine was a very old MCI, sixteen tracks. . . . We only used near-field monitors . . . the NS10 [Yamaha speakers], with a Hafler amplifier, and on one tune, I think 'Airá,' we used some pitch-shift, like a fifth down. . . . [Jim Ball] spent some time just working on the phase problem of the pandeiro [between the various tracks and microphones]." The Carioca Blade Runner used this mix of prized retro and contemporary technologies, working with the North American audio engineer, to create the "politically correct" acoustic sound for this jazz-oriented recording.

Sambatown, which earned Suzano the Sharp Prize for new male talent ("Revelação Masculina"), opens with a two-part piece ("Pandemonium") featuring a four-minute pandeiro solo, the first two minutes of which are Suzano performing alone on pandeiro—and sounding almost like a drum orchestra, as music critic Jon Pareles put it (1997)—while for the second two minutes he is joined by an ensemble. Among the accompanying musicians is the wind multi-instrumentalist Carlos Malta, here playing baritone saxophone and ocarina. Suzano had already performed with Carlos in the latter's group Pife Muderno (Modern Fife), which drew heavily on the traditional fife-and-drum ensemble of the Brazilian Northeast. Pife Muderno adapted that rustic sound for Carioca audiences by mixing in some samba and jazz stylizations while maintaining an acoustic aesthetic and adding to the momentum of resurgent interest in northeastern music in the mid-1990s. Eduardo Neves, with whom Suzano had already performed in Nó em Pingo d'Água, added soprano and tenor saxophone to *Sambatown*, while the keyboardist Alex Meirelles contributed discreet synthesizer parts. The accompaniment is funky, bluesy, and jazzy; the remainder of the album follows this sound, with Lenine contributing a guest vocal on the song "Curupira pirou" (Curupira took off), which the two musicians composed jointly.[22]

For his second solo album, *Flash*, Suzano continued his research into timbres and unusual percussive sounds, this time processing and corrupting the acoustic timbres with electronic devices. He built further on the concept of arranging a jazz ensemble around the pandeiro with a quintet of trumpet/flugelhorn (Nílton Rodrigues), saxophone (Eduardo Neves), electric bass (André Carneiro), keyboards (Fernando Moura), and percussion. It was "very jazzy," he felt, but there was also the influence of techno and jungle (a fast-tempo dance genre characterized by frenetic snare drumming and dub reggae–influenced bass).[23] Now Suzano was using the Akai MPC 1000 sampler and discovering "a great richness in small variations" of timbres, as he explained to me in 2007.

> MS: With a small repertoire of instruments I managed to create many changes in the timbres through the alterations in the velocity of the sampler. So I began to discover, for example, that a pandeiro played at a certain velocity, sampled, and detuned creates a distortion that would be impossible to achieve playing more slowly and using a distortion pedal. So this began to make me think completely differently.

> FM: Always starting with the acoustic sound?

> MS: Exactly. The acoustic sound is always the starting point, and [then] I begin to alter it electronically. This period was very important because it also generated that idea of researching the material. I began to use wood, the cajón, and I built my mini-set, and so on.

The surdo, he said, is "good for playing more spaciously, at tempos of 90 to 120" beats per minute, or for a hip-hop-like bass drum sound, while for drum and bass Suzano prefers the "drier," less sustained sound of the wooden cajón.

Fellow percussionist Lucas Santtana described how Suzano's "rereadings" of, for example, jungle, ended up being something different from "a drum that you can program, *tss tss ftt ftt*," because of the physical aspect. With two hands, Lucas said, "it is unlimited what you can do." In one of our interviews Suzano detailed how he produces specific sounds through different uses of his right hand on the pandeiro. When he strikes the center of the drum head with the middle finger, for example, he tries to approximate something between the sound of the surdo bass drum from samba and the kick drum of a drum kit. On the other hand, when he has "the possibility of opening the thumb a bit more in a groove that's lighter," such as, for example, "things that are more ragga, you know, muffin, these things more reggaefied" (raggamuffin is a form of Jamaican-influenced dancehall), "then you can open up a bit, it sounds good." At the same time, Lucas Santtana noted, Suzano also "woke us up to this thing about amplification." Moreover, when Suzano added effects, he turned the pandeiro into "a powerful thing," a new instrument even—an *electronic* drum kit, "but with him playing."

The rich bottom end that Suzano sought for his pandeiro and other percussion sounds in his adaptations of techno and other Afro-diasporic beats at first inconvenienced producers, so here too an adjustment was required, as Suzano explained: "People would complain, 'You have too much bass.' . . . And I would say, 'Listen, haven't you ever gone to a samba school drum corps to hear some real low end?' . . . It's a radical beating [*pancada*]. Maracatu [drumming has this] too. This problem with the bass, in my opinion, comes from an ignorance about our origins, because . . . in Afro-Brazilian music the low end is the soloist. The low drum, man, the rum, *that* is where it's at. The bass from reggae, the [bass runs on] seven-string guitar [in Brazilian choro], the kick drum in funk, this is all rum, man, this is Ogum . . . because the African origin is the same. Listen to Fela Kuti in Nigeria, and you'll say that's the *ijexá* rhythm [from Candomblé], and of course it is." Although Suzano overgeneralizes the diasporic links here, it is noteworthy that he associates bass frequencies with the Yoruba deity Ogum, god of fire, iron, war, and technology. The term *pancada*, which Suzano uses to describe the sonic force of Afro-Brazilian drumming, means a powerful impact, a blow, or it can refer to a battle, a fight (recalling Averill and Yih's insights about militarism in Haitian music). Producers in the sphere of pop music, in this conception, lacked understanding of the power of the African roots (in this case West African) of Brazilian popular music. Meanwhile, Suzano made his own power play as he claimed space for bass in pop mixes, while he shrewdly narrated this move as a return to (national) origins.[24]

Interestingly, these *particular* genres from abroad, Suzano held, allowed musicians to foreground traditional Brazilian styles that emphasize busy and rapid percussion grooves, but that had been de-emphasized in the rock and pop of the 1980s. "The thing of jungle and drum and bass," he said, was "a relief" when it arrived in Brazil, because it demonstrated that percussionists could articulate all the sixteenth notes, with "everything full," like a *frevo*, referring to an up-tempo genre from the Northeast, or a fast samba, or even a *quadrilha*, a form of the eighteenth-century European contradance quadrille that is still popular in the June Festivals, or *festas juninas*, of the Northeast.

The New Samba

Meanwhile, the state of samba production after the emergence of the pagode subgenre incensed Suzano. In the 1960s to the 1970s, he reflected when we met in 2007, a number of distinctive samba singers were under contract with the major recording labels. Paulinho da Viola, Martinho da Vila, and the old guard of the traditional samba schools such as the singer-songwriter legends Cartola, Nelson Sargento, and Carlos Cachaça, Suzano felt, all had "their own sound," much as Suzano found his sound. The *sambistas* (samba musicians) of the era had "an incredible flavor." The problem, he maintained, was that after some samba musicians became commercially successful, a formula arose, and one producer emerged as the dominant force in the commercialization of pagode samba. This created a sort of sonic ghetto, Suzano felt, in which pagode albums and artists are entirely formulaic and interchangeable. "This is crap for samba!" he exclaimed. "Everything is the same," and it "doesn't reflect the reality of the way samba is played, because you have lots of people playing samba well, lots of different possibilities, great young rhythmicists, and they're not recorded—not by the major [labels]."

By contrast, an album of the samba musician Paulinho da Viola is "complete nobility." When you hear that, Suzano declared, you think, "Porra! It's just great," because it is at such a high level of musicianship. The samba musicians of whom Suzano speaks approvingly here tend to prioritize the richly polyrhythmic textures of acoustic roots samba, typically with memorable melodies and lyrics. We have already seen how, in contrast, some musicians and listeners have criticized the commercial pagode phenomenon as a comparatively homogenized form lacking roots in the communities that produced legendary singer-songwriters in samba such as Paulinho da Viola and Martinho da Vila. (Even some of the established samba musicians I interviewed voiced this criticism.)

At first glance, these viewpoints seem to reprise long-standing debates over what happens to music when it becomes commodified. Yet a simple correlation of the problem with the music industry is not precisely accurate, for, as Suzano noted, in the 1970s a diverse array of samba musicians possessing what he described as distinctive sounds and high levels of musicianship were contracted to the major labels. For Suzano, homogenization bore upon a larger question of *intensity* in samba, a characteristic of Brazilian music that represented a feeling for the groove that went "a little beyond" the more "cerebral" aspects of music making. Importantly, this meant that a musician could play the rhythm of samba but that didn't necessarily make it samba—at least not in Suzano's understanding of the music. There are lots of guys, he said, who invoke the characteristic samba rhythms on the pandeiro, yet the listener ends up thinking, "Porra, there's nothing there." By contrast, one might play an atypical rhythm that perhaps "allows for a situation that, porra, is more interesting harmonically, or whatever, but there's an element of intensity." (Suzano performed two contrasting rhythms on his instrument to demonstrate during this interview; see figures 4 and 5.) As a further example of this intensity of groove, Suzano described how the guitarist Gerson Silva had him on the edge of his seat at a dressing room rehearsal. It took one measure of 2/4, he remembered, and by the start of the second measure, he was entranced. "Porra! The guy was incredible," he exclaimed as he recalled this musician's remarkable swing.

It is the subtlety of execution that grabs Suzano's attention by the third beat; more generally, he values intensity, independence, and awareness of ensemble dynamics. Suzano described the third beat of Gerson's groove as the moment that "Dona [Lady] Judith" descended to inhabit the music, much like an *orixá* (deity). The spirit of Dona Judith, he informed me, "is an entity of the swing." When Dona Judith "arrives," he said, "the swing is there." Samba, in this conceptualization, is a "historically extended, socially embodied argument" about what goods "give point and purpose to that tradition" (MacIntyre 1984, 222; see also Guilbault 2007, 6). By contrast, recent trends in commercial samba recording, as well as the impris-

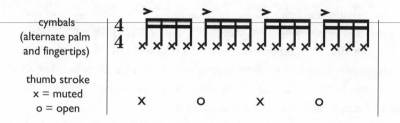

| cymbals (alternate palm and fingertips) | | |
| thumb stroke x = muted o = open | | |

onment of samba within set patterns of typical or generic rhythmic inflections, could lead to the "corruption" of musical ideals and constrain creative individuality in deference to market forces.

Nonlinear Recording, Filters, and Beatboxes

Working in his home recording environment with Pro Tools audio software and hardware, Suzano uses what he refers to as "nonlinear recording," a method that develops from the way in which the computer-based DAW represents audio tracks as compound waveforms on a computer screen. In this method Suzano records various "experiences," as he termed them, examines their visual representation, and then assembles "a mosaic of possibilities" from the parts that he likes. When I asked him in 2007 how the pandeiro fit into his recent work, he eagerly offered to demonstrate with audio examples. He opened a variety of digital files on his DAW and described how he used instruments such as his pandeiro, the cuíca friction drum and the surdo from samba, the cajón, and the Indian tabla, and how these instruments' acoustic timbres were all "corrupted" (*estragado*) beyond recognition by his Belgian-made two-channel Sherman filter bank.

To try to describe in words the "strange" sounds (Taylor 2001, 8–9) that Suzano played for me as he illustrated his new grooves at this meeting strains my ability to summon appropriate metaphors. Notating these grooves can only impart a minimal sense of some of the rhythmic organization, while one of the central functions of the filter is radically to alter the timbres of the acoustic instruments. (It can be understood as an example of what Cornelia Fales calls "timbral anomaly by extraction" [2005, 172].) One cyborgian groove, for example, derived from the sound of his pandeiro and cajón, based around a repeating 3 + 3 + 2 pattern of pulses (sixteenth notes in duple meter) heard in many Latin American genres (and elsewhere), but also featuring the oscillating sonic detritus of the fil-

FIGURE 4. A common basic samba pattern on pandeiro, as demonstrated by Marcos Suzano

cymbals (P & D)

slap (T)

mid slap (Ø or GØM)

open bass (G or GDM)

ter's corrupting authority. A high, ringing, space-age-sounding melodic part entered after a few measures. It turned out to be a filtered cuíca, the distinctive Brazilian friction drum from samba, but it bore not the slightest resemblance to the natural sound of this instrument.

Another groove featured Indian tabla and cajón, with the latter instrument improbably providing the *melody*. "Totally manipulated," Suzano said of it. If he were to remove the filter, he confided, the melody would "lose 80 percent of its attractiveness." As he played the excerpt for me, a driving bass line entered, also deriving from the cajón. So went this listening session as the afternoon wore on, with Suzano excitedly telling me what instruments produced the original sounds—an entirely unrecognizable pandeiro ("totally destroyed," in Suzano's words), a *moringa* (water jug) used to create a bizarre bass line, and so on. The appeal of the filter as a tool lies in the fact that it emphasizes the timbral aspect and allows the musician to create sounds that the unmodified instrument could not generate: one begins "to create syntheses through the filtering," Suzano said, and the Sherman was "heavy stuff [*barra pesada*]." One creates, in fact, by destroying through subtraction the timbral spectrum of the original sound (see figure 6).[25]

The machine's manufacturer describes the V2 filter bank as "a powerful analog filtering and distortion unit with a huge frequency range and a killing tube overdrive behavior," designed for "processing every sound source."[26] With "killing behavior," the device could be one of the creator-destroyer Ogum's "frightening charms." Suzano made a point of mentioning that the Icelandic musician Björk—whom Charity Marsh and Melissa West describe as a cyborg reworking the gendered distinctions between nature and culture, public and private (2003, 195–97)—also utilized the Sherman filter. Interestingly, Björk referred to her recording *Volta* (2007) as her "techno-voodoo" album (Pareles 2007), suggesting another associa-

FIGURE 5. One of Marcos Suzano's pandeiro patterns, as played during an interview with the author (see also Appendix 2)

tion between Afro-diasporic religion and machines for sonic manipulation ("Voodoo" is an alternative spelling for "Vodoun").[27] Suzano also singled out Björk's collaborator, the hip-hop producer Timbaland, as someone he especially admired. Timbaland is "a *genius* of the beat" for his conservative but effective use of multitracking and his ability to beatbox, that is, to produce electronic-sounding rhythms with his voice: "He does the basic grooves all with his voice, man! Porra! . . . For someone who works with rhythm, it's enough to make you stop playing! . . . And this is . . . a cool thing that the technology of the nineties facilitated. . . . That is to say, until the advent of the computer, recording and hard disk, nonlinear recording, it was practically impossible to hear [someone doing vocalized] beatbox. You could do it on tape, but . . . it was a headache. With a computer it is play, and the play became something serious." This serious play parallels Suzano's own adaptation of electronic beats on the pandeiro "always starting with the acoustic sound," while foregrounding human agency vis-à-vis

FIGURE 6. Marcos Suzano adjusting his Sherman v2 filter bank

machines. "Nature and culture are reworked" in such practices, while "the one can no longer be the resource for appropriation or incorporation by the other" (Haraway 1991, 151).

From Incomprehension to "Islands of Creation"

As recording technologies became increasingly accessible, "little islands of creation" emerged throughout the city at the expense of the major recording studios, and producers working with the major recording labels ended up having "to give space to new sounds." Today, Suzano enthused, "you have the advantage of this sort of do-it-yourself method, and you are not imprisoned." His collaborators send him recordings of sessions to which he adds tracks on his own DAW, and then he sends the accumulated tracks back. "I have everything here," he said, "and I make my sounds at home." Liberated from the imprisonment of a centralized music industry, at the time of this interview (July 2007), Suzano was working on his third solo album, *Atarashi* (meaning "new" or "fresh" in Japanese), which he described as heavily influenced by Jamaican dub, and which he recorded entirely in his home studio. "It's just percussion, completely processed," he explained. The word *processed* may evoke mass production (as in food), but here it describes Suzano's agency as a creative *processor* with command over the technologies he helped integrate into Brazilian pop. The electronic manipulation of acoustic percussion was part of Suzano's ongoing research into timbres, he affirmed.

The new project of which he was most proud at the time of our interview in 2007 was his collaboration with Vitor Ramil, a singer-songwriter from the southern state of Rio Grande do Sul. For Suzano, the double album they recorded, *Satolep Sambatown*,[28] was another example of how the established centers of musical sound are now "much looser" and more "spaced out" than the major recording studios were. Vitor's southern sensibility, or "aesthetics of the cold," he said, represents "a very different musical aesthetic," yet one that is equally "Brazilian." They recorded almost the entire album in Suzano's home DAW. With no rehearsal whatsoever, the percussionist somewhat immodestly noted, it turned out to be "an incredible album," his most mature duo collaboration in his estimation. "How I manipulated my sounds, man, I felt I found myself, and I think about how many percussionists could be doing work like this but who remain kind of trapped."

Some twenty years into his career as a percussionist, Suzano apparently encountered the creative self toward which he had been aspiring right in his very home, at his DAW, with unrehearsed spontaneous performances and a mastery of their subsequent processing with machines. Suzano's manipulation of the acoustic sounds contrasts with the "corruption" arising from the centralization of power in the major music labels, in the largest recording studios, in overly influential producers, and in homogenized aesthetics. Vitor Ramil and Suzano subsequently released the album on the independent MP,B label (MP,B plays on the established acronym MPB, adding a comma to *música popular brasileira*), retaining ownership of it for potential future releases. "It might work out well," he gambled, "or it might be bad." In the case of Suzano's solo album, *Atarashi*, there was to be "no label . . . nothing." Suzano would sell it at his shows and his percussion classes and take it to some stores himself. If somebody from abroad should want to buy it, he would "enter into business directly and export." He would retain complete control of the work and the stock and would thus earn more, he predicted.

Such retooling of music production and distribution to small-scale, artist-controlled, and often home-based configurations is complementary to certain realignments in cultural funding. Nongovernmental organizations and other nonprofit organizations and foundations have become increasingly important sources of support since democratization in 1985 and the institution of economic reforms in the 1990s. Suzano spoke approvingly of one government initiative at the state level: the corporate incentive laws that encourage private-sector support of cultural productions. These laws have roots in the 1940s, but the stabilization of the economy and economic growth in the past twenty years have turned such policies into something of a success story of private-sector arts funding, while musicians have become more savvy about utilizing them.[29] The incentive laws, Suzano explained, changed everything because "no one needs a record label." The once-influential figure of the recording label artists and repertoire director is today "completely unnecessary." He quipped: "These guys don't speak to anybody anymore, just to people who want easy success. They are irrelevant. You take a guy like Mr. ——, from [media giant] Globo TV. He puts down what you're doing and you think, 'What the hell is he talking about?' A little while ago you might have thought maybe he was right. Now you just laugh and say: 'Get serious.' They are a bunch of clowns."

Conclusions

Marcos Suzano was among Brazil's most-recorded percussionists in the 1990s and into the following decade in part because he is a skilled (and hard-working) pandeiro player who has managed to keep himself at the center of emergent trends in popular music and jazz. In his telling, part of his early success owed to the fact that he was a good sight-reader and was able to record quickly, playing "with swing, even when reading the music," as well as to the fact that he was "up to date" with the latest sounds. He learned to play his instrument in the traditions of two established genres strongly identified with Rio de Janeiro: choro and samba. By the mid-1990s, however, he had developed an idiomatic technique that allowed him to play more offbeat low pitches and, in general, a greater variety of rhythms. He saw this technique as more consistent with African-derived aspects of Brazilian musical culture (specifically, the drumming of the Candomblé).

The celebration of Afro-Brazilian culture has been a recurring theme in Brazilian social life for at least a century, but it has also met with resistance or ambivalence at times, and in certain contexts. In Brazilian popular music, the syncopated and polyrhythmic percussion characteristic of roots samba expression has often been relegated to the background. This was true of the bolero-influenced *samba-canção* (samba-song) of the radio singers of the 1950s, of bossa nova, and generally of MPB, which adopted a band format in which the drum kit tended to carry most of the rhythm. Beginning with the political opening of the late 1970s and early 1980s, Afro-Brazilian drumming came increasingly to be integrated into popular manifestations in the Brazilian Northeast, notably in the *blocos afro* of Salvador (Crook 1993), and subsequently with the resurgence of maracatu in Recife in the late 1980s and early 1990s. Suzano's efforts can be seen in part as responding to this tendency, and also as contributing, albeit in a limited and specific manner, to the growing revival of samba among the middle classes in Rio de Janeiro.

Suzano's early work with groups like Aquarela Carioca emphasized an acoustic sound with jazz influences, but he began to experiment with electronic effects and then samplers, filters, and of course digital home recording while incorporating new influences from international electronic dance genres such as jungle. He developed his mini-kit of cajón, tabla, and various other percussive instruments to augment the catalog of timbres upon which he could draw. Suzano, it could be said, invited a diasporic Ogum into his practice as the creator/destroyer in charge of policing technology and the public sphere, of sonically inverting incorrect hierarchies, and of "conjuring" the kinetic rhythms of drum choirs, as the *New York Times* journalist Jon Pareles described Suzano's performance at Central Park SummerStage (1997). At the same time, anxiety with respect to technology sometimes exists in a techno-voodoo dialectic with ambivalent and conflicting stances toward cultural practices that seem more traditional, and that are often racialized; the "question of who is black" may be "suspended" in such a move (Carvalho 1994, 2).

I suggested that the metaphor of a Carioca Blade Runner also pointed to a gendered, specifically masculine, dimension to the way this foregrounding of percussion was interpreted locally. I do not mean that Suzano illustrated some sort of essential masculinity defined by shades of aggressiveness, dynamics of control, and echoes of militarism. Musically constituted masculinity can assume different registers and Suzano is certainly a versatile instrumentalist.[30] Lorraine Leu has argued that in the late 1960s, the Brazilian pop musician Caetano Veloso used the visual vocabulary of style and performed femininity to "deregulate" the body in response to the ideologies of discipline, machismo, and the patriarchal family promulgated under the military dictatorship in its effort to control the national population (2006, 42–43). It is plausible that once disarticulated from authoritarian regulation of civil society and the body, those aspects of masculinity associated with power and control could take on new resonances. Suzano would be given a mandate to implement his musical priorities—a "line of flight" in a Deleuzian sense—when Paulinho Moska took him on as producer for his album *Móbile*.

LENINE

PERNAMBUCO SPEAKING TO THE WORLD

My best quality is being intuitive. I don't do music. Music is simply the conduit.
I deepen the human relationship. Actually, that is the only thing I do.
—Lenine

One of the characteristics of the pop music setting I examine in this book is the enduring legacy and influence of musicians who began their careers in the 1960s, especially individuals associated with the Tropicália movement. Caetano Veloso, in particular, has become somewhat of the gold standard for the figure of the Brazilian pop intellectual singer-songwriter; to receive his blessing is a powerful endorsement of one's work. In 1998 the French government invited him to perform for three nights at the Cité de la Musique in Paris as part of a Carte Blanche series in which the artist is given free rein to develop a show specifically for the venue. Caetano invited the influential concrete poet Augusto de Campos, from São Paulo, to join him for a multimedia presentation of Augusto's poetry and selected works by Mallarmé and Rimbaud, what he called an "anthropophagic musical manifesto." For the musical accompaniment, Caetano called on the singer-songwriter Lenine, originally from Recife, Pernambuco, whom he described as offering "the most comprehensive interpretation" of what was happening musically in that Northeastern state at the time, despite the fact that Lenine had lived in Rio de Janeiro for twenty years (D. Lopes 1999).[1]

Subsequently, Lenine became the next Brazilian to receive an invitation to perform at the Cité. The music critic Francis Dordor wrote the introductory program notes to the event. Titled "The Cannibal," this text (which presumably draws on Lenine's own discourse) reinforces narratives of Brazilian identity as rooted in mixture and appropriation, in this case also speaking to French readings of Brazilian culture, as Dordor refers to Lévi-Straussian dichotomies of civilization and barbarism (2004). "Long to take shape," the program notes state, Lenine's career "can be read as the patient resolution through music of this conflict that is as bitter as it is old." The "organ" he would develop to take in the eclectic influences of his youth, he writes, "was not the ear, but rather the stomach." Eating the music of others, he explains to the concert-going public, even more than listening to or producing it, constitutes "a fundamentally Brazilian act, a cultural cannibalism, the definitive form of the mixture." The luck or the misfortune of Lenine's generation, Dordor observes, is "to be the guest of honor at the greatest feast ever imagined: that of globalization." What renders Lenine "unusual and seductive" is his inclination to join his musical mixtures with the "at once urgent and melancholy dream of a less barbaric world." Noting that his namesake is Lenin (spelled "Lenine" in Portuguese), the critic concludes that "he is forcefully seeking to substitute utopia for the nightmare. Even if it means being a cannibal."

The cannibalist baton is thus passed, at least in this reading (which is, of course, designed to help promote the show), from Tropicalist to twenty-first-century humanist-socialist. Lenine describes his music as MPB, but he likes to think of the P as referring in his case to "planetary," rather than "popular," Brazilian music (Gilman 2006). Counting the planets outward from the sun, he told me, we are all "third world," and his lyrics sometimes refer to astronomical phenomena such as the big bang. He sees himself as a kind of troubadour, a "restless reporter" who is "plugged into the world, but who speaks of his tribe."[2] He is an energetic collaborator who has recorded with most of the central subjects of this book, in addition to many others. He likes "the plurality" that results from collaborating, and from the exercise, as he put it, of having "a small bunch of people around," especially in the recording studio. He is optimistic about the ability of the human spirit to triumph, through solidarity, over forces that potentially lead to social alienation. In this sense, Lenine may be said to have inherited some of the spirit of "revolutionary romanticism" that Marcelo Ridenti (2000) identified in the Brazilian left, and of the belief, prevalent among some musicians of the 1960s, that art can and should play a role in promoting the emergence of a more egalitarian social order in the country and the world.

In addition to his own endeavors, Lenine often works as a guest singer for live performances and as a guest recording artist, co-composer, and co-producer. His compositions have been recorded by a variety of musicians in Brazil, including a string quintet (Quinteto da Paraíba), and occasionally by artists abroad. He composed three carnival samba themes for the popular South Zone bloco Suvaco do Cristo. He has also had songs placed on Globo Network telenovelas (prime-time dramas), a coveted avenue for gaining publicity. Other activities include writing music for the São Paulo-based dance company Grupo Corpo for a 2007 work titled "A centelha" (The spark), which they performed in Brazil and abroad. He has won several Sharp Prizes, as well as five Latin Grammy Awards and three Grammy Awards.[3]

In this chapter I examine aspects of Lenine's career and several musical examples from his albums, exploring in particular how he incorporates into his work both thematic and sonic references to the Brazilian Northeast, a region known as much for its rich folklore as for its droughts and income inequality. Like Marcos Suzano, Lenine spent his teenage years listening to rock music, but in the 1990s he too trained his ear on Brazilian popular genres and sought ways to adapt the sounds and sentiments of rock and, subsequently, other international influences and technologies to the changing national context. As an artist who identifies strongly with the Northeast and yet is integral to the Rio-based music scene that is the focus of this book, Lenine bridges discursive formulations of cultural regionalism and Rio's "centripetal" claims to national representation—as well as its "centrifugal" claims to cosmopolitanism.

Writing about Dorival Caymmi, from Bahia, and Luiz Gonzaga, from Pernambuco—two influential musicians who established themselves in Rio de Janeiro in the 1940s—Bryan McCann has observed that northeastern cultural regionalism is generally not in opposition to constructs of national character but rather seeks a special place within that character (2004, 120). Caymmi's and Gonzaga's cultural projects, McCann argues, established a link between region and nation by rescuing "the vital folklore" of the Northeast "for the edification of the metropolitan center and, by extension, of the nation" (120). They thus communicated a fundamental part to the whole.

McCann's argument pertains to a distinct historical context, but the notion of the cultural "link" between a part and the whole is fundamental to Lenine's work as well. In this case, however, the nation is itself a part of the larger whole of humanity. Rather than salvaging folklore, Lenine's music takes the vitality of northeastern culture as axiomatic. His project is not merely sonically to reinscribe the importance of the Northeast to Brazilian national identity; rather, it seeks to universalize sonic representations of a local identity through their integration into the language of pop music. In this sense, it does not "folklorize underdevelopment," to borrow Caetano Veloso's words (1977, 21–24), but rather puts comparatively localized musical expressions on equal footing with international trends, conjoining them to Lenine's humanist vision of cosmopolitan solidarity. The Northeast is thus more than a fixed set of invented traditions; it is a kind of imagined and permeable community that is realized over time through the practices of individual subjects. For Lenine, the city of Recife, his hometown and the capital of Pernambuco, serves as his "lighthouse," as he put it, during his musical travels.

While Lenine has a very individualistic style of singing and playing guitar and a distinctly personal view of the world that manifests in his music, his career trajectory has also been shaped by his choice of musical partners. His fusion of northeastern traditional forms with electronic and sequenced musical sounds, for example, owes much to Chico Neves, who produced Lenine's first solo album. Chico related that when they were working on the album, he had a number of disagreements with Lenine because the latter was very ambivalent about "this world of machines." Lenine's work, like that of the other figures in this book, is thus the product of an emergent "art world" (Becker 1982), one that rather than being inevitable, took shape in part through negotiations over and experimentation with the way sound can be manipulated in the recording setting.

The Northeast: From Center to Region and Musical Heartbeat

The Northeast encompasses a massive territory consisting of nine states, including Pernambuco and Bahia, and containing about 30 percent of the country's population. The Portuguese captain Pedro Álvares Cabral landed on the coast of this region in 1500, and the city of Salvador, in Bahia, was the colony's first capital. Before attempting to enslave local Amerindian populations, the Portuguese traded with them for Brazil's first export product, *pau Brasil*, or brazilwood.[4] Later, male colonists procreated with indigenous women, and then with the African slaves who worked the massive sugarcane, cocoa, tobacco, and cotton estates (fazendas). For about a century and a half, the "Northeast" essentially was "Brazil" (Beserra 2004, 5). As a consequence, certain patterns of social interaction that have come to be seen as characteristic of Brazilian society are associated with the history of the Northeast—notably, paternalism, racial and cultural mixture, and also the vibrancy of traditional popular cultural expressions with roots in early modern and baroque Iberian forms, in popular Catholicism, in African cultures, and, to a lesser degree, in indigenous practices.

Two legendary rebellions took place in the Northeast. Palmares, a great *quilombo*, or community of runaway slaves, formed in the interior of the region in the seventeenth century and was structured as a neo-African state. Its population is believed to have reached 20,000, and it took years for the Portuguese to destroy it, which they did in 1694. The last leader of Palmares was Zumbi, who escaped during the final battle for Palmares only to be caught and beheaded in 1695. Zumbi has since become a symbol of Afro-Brazilian identity and struggle in Brazil. (Nação Zumbi, formerly Chico Science's band, takes its name from him.) The second rebellion took place at Canudos, a remote region in the west of Bahia, where thousands of peasant followers of the heretical religious leader Antônio Conselheiro (Antônio Vicente Mendes Maciel) assembled from 1893 to 1897 as a folk community independent of the recently proclaimed republic. They resisted centralized efforts to modernize and rationalize the administration of the nation-state. Surprisingly, three military expeditions failed to defeat the community, while the fourth, with 8,000 men and new cannons brought in from Europe, flattened Canudos, a decisive event in the consolidation of modern Brazil.[5]

The process by which this area came to be understood as a region rather than the center of modern Brazil really began in the early twentieth century and is directly tied to the southward shift of the economic and political center, and indeed to the nation-building project: as the state promoted industrialization in the Southeast, the Northeast, trapped in underdevelopment and "backwardness," was left to provide inexpensive labor. The idea that the Northeast was rooted in tradition and nostalgia for the past, one scholar has argued, was in fact fabricated by the local elites in response to their loss of economic and political space (Albuquerque 2004, 43). The Northeast is less a place than "a *topos*, a group of references, a collection of characteristics, an archive of images and texts . . . [and] a bundle of recurring memories." The establishment of a relationship of this "part" to the "whole," then, is infused with hierarchies of economic power and other forms of social stratification. Moreover, the identity categories of Nordestino (northeasterner), Paulista (native of São Paulo state), and Carioca, for example, speak to mutually constitutive national configurations of power (Beserra 2004, 7).

Larry Crook has argued that the Northeast provides the "musical heartbeat that has helped create and sustain the modern, ever-changing Brazilian nation" (2005, xxii). While Cariocas might wish to claim the same for samba, the folkloric traditions of the Northeast have a special purchase on popular images of "authentic" Brazil.[6] It will be helpful to describe briefly some of the genres from this region that Lenine incorporates into his pop music. Among them is the *côco*, which usually features a solo singer performing against a choral refrain in call-and-response, accompanied by percussion instruments such as the *ganzá* (shaker) or pandeiro. Singers often arrange themselves in a circle and clap, while a dancer may enter the ring until he or she chooses a replacement from among the other participants with a touch at the navel, a move known in Brazil as the *umbigada*. The côco is popularly believed to come from the Africans of Palmares, who are said to have created it as a work song to accompany the breaking of coconuts for food (M. Andrade 1999, 146). In Pernambuco the côco was often sung on sugar plantations. The rhythmic accompaniment typically places stresses on the first, fourth, and seventh sixteenth-note subdivisions of the beat (in 2/4), accenting the pattern of 3 + 3 + 2 that is found in much Brazilian popular music and indeed in much Latin American popular music. However, the overlaying of rhythmic variations can also create a subtle feeling of polyrhythm.

Embolada is similar to côco in its rhythmic structure and its use of call-and-response, but it tends to be more lyrically complex, while it often uses very simple melodies with limited, stepwise motion. Mário de Andrade held that embolada was not a genre at all but simply the "melodic-rhythmic process" utilized by northeastern singers called *repentistas* in the improvised construction of verses (1999, 199). It features virtuosic, alliterative, often tongue-twisting lyrics following standardized rhyme schemes (such as the *décima*) delivered in rapid-fire fashion, and wordplay such as the utilization of double entendres or the manipulation of similar-sounding terms that have different meanings. Embolada is typically sung without accompanying dance, and it may take the form of a vocal duel called *peleja* or *desafio*, in which the singers playfully (or not so playfully) insult each other. Lenine's "Jack soul brasileiro" is a good example of this kind of singing updated with funk and rock elements.[7] Embolada and desafio may also be accompanied by the steel-stringed double-course guitar of Portuguese origin called the viola, in which case it is also referred to as *cantoria* (or *cantoria de viola*) a broad category of rural styles with links to medieval Iberian traditions of improvised sung poetry. Singers of cantoria (*cantadores*) once traveled through the Northeast like bards, accompanying their song with a variety of instruments including the *rabeca* fiddle, the pandeiro, and the viola, or singing unaccompanied (called *aboio*).

With its doubled steel strings, some of which provide a drone, and simple harmonies centered on tonic and dominant chords, the viola, which is strummed as well as plucked, sounds quite different from the nylon-stringed violão, which, in the samba and bossa nova styles, is plucked in syncopated patterns that may feature comparatively complex harmonies. In cantoria, the viola provides a basic accompaniment; if it contributes melody, it is usually only in between song verses. Lenine's "O marco marciano" (The martian sign) is a beautiful ballad with viola accompaniment that utilizes the *abcbdb* rhyme scheme of the traditional *sextilha* of cantoria, while the melody uses a scale with raised fourth and lowered seventh degrees, customary alterations in the cantoria tradition (Crook 2005, 105). His song "Na pressão" (Under pressure) also begins with an ostinato figure on the *viola dinâmica*, a variety of the instrument featuring an aluminum resonator and an especially metallic timbre, while "Aboio avoado" (Senseless aboio) is a brief a cappella song modeled after the traditional cattle rancher's aboio.

Another important musical manifestation of the Northeast is the fife-and-drum ensemble (*banda de pífano*), which is popular in a variety of festivities in the interior regions. The pífano (alt. *pífaro*, or *pife*) is a side-blown cane flute generally played in pairs, with one flute usually taking the lead melodic part while the other plays a harmony. The ensemble includes a shallow two-headed bass drum called a zabumba and a shallow snare drum called a tarol (additional percussion such as a triangle may be added). In Rio de Janeiro, Carlos Malta's group Pife Muderno performs "rereadings," in Carlos's words, of the northeastern fife-and-drum repertoire, some of which is shared with the accordion-based forró bands. Lenine, who has also sung with Pife Muderno, utilizes a brief sampled recording of a pífano ensemble in the introduction to his song "Rua da passagem (Trânsito)" (Cross street [Traffic]), while the entire groove of the track is driven by the zabumba and tarol drums found in the banda de pífano country forró style.

The term *forró* came to be used to refer to a variety of dances associated with the festas juninas in celebration of Saints Anthony, John, and Peter. Again, a precise genre definition is elusive, and there are various subcategories, such as the *xote* and *xamego*.[8] However, its typical instrumentation of accordion, triangle, and zabumba bass drum; the often entertaining nature of the lyrics; and the genre's highly danceable swing make forró easily recognizable. The sixteenth–eighth–sixteenth-note rhythmic figure is also found in forró; tempos tend to be medium to fast. The genre *baião*, created by the Pernambucan accordionist Luiz Gonzaga in the 1940s, often uses the same instrumentation as forró, but it is usually performed at slightly slower tempos and emphasizes a driving dotted eighth–sixteenth-note rhythmic figure on beat 1 in 2/4.[9]

Perhaps the Pernambucan folk music that attracted the most attention through new pop fusions in the 1990s is the maracatu, of which there are two types. *Maracatu nação* (nation maracatu), also called *maracatu de baque virado* (maracatu of the turned-around beat), is the older type and is associated with a variety of Afro-Brazilian religions in Recife and surrounding areas. Singing is accompanied by a double-headed bass drum (alfaia, alt. bombo), snare drums (tarol and *caixa de guerra*, lit. "war box"), a gonguê, and shakers (usually the metal *mineiro*, but sometimes the *abê*, made from a gourd) performing a syncopated rhythm in a medium-slow tempo. Its origins are in the Afro-Brazilian tradition of crowning a king of the Congo or of Angola as an intermediary between the masters and slaves during the colonial era; it became a kind of demonstration of "acoustic power" (Crook 2005, 237). Against the steady groove of the ensemble, the bass drum plays "turned-around" syncopations, often utilizing the typical sixteenth–eighth–sixteenth figure of the côco.

Maracatu rural (rural maracatu), also known as *maracatu de baque solto* (maracatu of the loose beat), uses improvised vocal verses, brass accompaniment, and percussion such as the cuíca friction drum also found in samba (sometimes called *puíta* in the Northeast), and rapid snare drumming that some Brazilian pop musicians such as Marcos Suzano have hybridized with the jungle genre from the United Kingdom (which features the rapid electronic snare patterns). In the rural style, the energetic snare drumming and brass periodically stop to give way to the vocals. Both genres feature colorful costumes and pageantry and are performed on the street during carnival. Lenine's "Que baque é esse?" (What is this beat?) makes use of maracatu-like bass drum patterns.

Another lively carnival genre from Recife is the *frevo*, which took shape in the late nineteenth century and gained national recognition in the 1920s and 1930s. It has a percussive base of a fast march rhythm and characteristically syncopated brass and wind arrangements that derive from the European military and civic band tradition. The driving rhythm of frevo is a blazingly fast repeating eighth–sixteenth–sixteenth-note figure (in 2/4), often played on a pandeiro, while the brass and winds perform offbeat phrases in a kind of interlocking call-and-response.[10] Lenine favors côco/embolada and samba influences in his music, but his song "Leão do norte" (Lion of the north) from the *Olho do peixe* collaboration with Suzano features a frevo-inspired rhythm.

Lenine, *Cantautor*

Oswaldo Lenine Macedo Pimentel was born in Recife on 2 February 1959 (the day the Yoruba water goddess Iemanjá is celebrated, he pointed out in our interview). For his stage name, he uses only the name that his father, a member of the Brazilian Communist Party, gave him in tribute to the Russian revolutionary and statesman Vladimir Lenin. He likes to tell a formative story from his early childhood: His mother was a devout Catholic and insisted that he and his sister attend Mass on Sundays when they were young. His atheist father stipulated, however, that once Lenine reached the age of eight he would be allowed to choose between going to church and staying home with him to listen to music on the radio on Sundays. Lenine chose the latter, and this ritual of listening together, he explained, exposed him to an eclectic variety of music as a child. This musical diversity became a "hidden archive" when, as a teenager, he, like Suzano, began listening only to rock, especially Led Zeppelin and other "progressive" rock groups. While at the Pernambuco State Conservatory of Music in the late 1970s, he grew interested in MPB, particularly the Clube da Esquina (Corner Club) post–bossa nova group of musicians centered around the singer-songwriters Milton Nascimento and Lô Borges, who released the seminal *Clube da Esquina* in 1972, mixing elements of jazz and progressive rock into well-crafted songs with thoughtful, often moody, lyrics. This group of musicians impressed upon Lenine that it was possible, "technically speaking," to make a cosmopolitan album in Brazil. (Others made the same claim for bossa nova, or for Tropicália in earlier eras.) Equally important was his rediscovery of the more earthy Jackson do Pandeiro, a musician from Paraíba, just north of Pernambuco, whose musical career spanned the 1950s through the early 1980s; Jackson would become a fundamental reference in Lenine's music.

Lenine left the conservatory to move to Rio in December 1979 and his career began in 1981 when he performed his song "Prova de fogo" (Proof of fire, composed with Zé Rocha) on an MPB television show for the Globo channel (MPB-81).[11] In 1983 he released an LP with Lula Queiroga titled *Baque solto* (after the maracatu style). Despite the title of the album, there are few traces of maracatu in the sound, although there is some relatively subtle incorporation of rhythms such as the baião and frevo. The predominant aesthetic could be described as progressive rock-jazz fusion with local "seasoning." It hardly augured the sound Lenine would cultivate in the 1990s with Marcos Suzano's percussion and the manipulation of acoustic timbres through filters and other electronic means. After *Baque solto*, Lenine continued to work as a performer and co-composer, but ten years would pass before he released another album bearing his name: the *Olho de peixe* collaboration with Marcos Suzano. His first solo album would wait another four years.

Lenine's vocal timbre is both warm and edgy, alternatively slightly aggressive then gentle. He might sing a pensive ballad like "Paciência" or rap a tongue-twisting rock-embolada shout-out like the aforementioned "Jack soul brasileiro." In the studio, Lenine likes to "double" his vocal parts (that is, record the same part two or more times), combining them electronically for a full yet intimate vocal sound. He also uses his voice in the studio to produce a variety of percussive aspirations. His guitar-playing utilizes strong plucking and strumming in highly syncopated, funky, sometimes noisy riffs and grooves. He suggested that what he called his "virulent" style of playing guitar developed out of his urge to reproduce percussion and bass articulations on the instrument when accompanying his own compositions. He described exploiting the rhythmic incidentals that he is able to produce with this particular way of playing the instrument: "I discovered that when I would go to record, most people were looking for a certain perfection in the execution. [The guitar] would end up being cold

. . . and would lose some of the sonority. I was going to use the word *dirty* [to describe my playing], but in truth it's not dirty—it's with more frequencies complementing each other." His way of playing the violão, he elaborated, utilizes a lot of open strings and exploits "the noises of the strings."

It was a "summation of frequencies," he said, that you can only get on a "full" guitar, a guitar with "a body" (*encorporado*). Just as Suzano requires a special microphone to capture the full range of low frequencies on his pandeiro, Lenine places microphones at the bridge and the neck of the instrument to capture what he hears as he bends over while playing. "I experimented with various things," he said, "and through this process I was able more and more to exploit the *keh, kaw, shoo, fff*—the little syncopations, the dirty little sounds, that give it swing—the swing of the song." (These can be compared with the kinds of "participatory discrepancies" that the members of the band Pedro Luís e A Parede sought, described in chapter 3.) His choice of the word *virulent* to describe his sound suggests that his playing style, like Suzano's, is comparatively physical, even aggressive.

As a pop musician with an international presence, Lenine is clearly enmeshed in and conscious of markets and commercial trends. He professes to have a good relationship with BMG Brazil, his recording label for over a decade now, and to be an "anachronism" for working in the mass market "but in an artisanal manner" (in Pierre Bourdieu's terminology, something in between "restricted" and "mass" production, as I elaborate in the following pages).[12] Although he is savvy about managing his career, it is true that he has hardly prioritized marketability in his musical choices. He professes ambivalence about global capitalism, calling it "brutal." Those in the center, he complained (by which he seems to have meant primarily the United States), did not consider "the possibility that there might exist a mature poetry in Brazil, a mature literature. It's the third world. And, excuse me, culturally we have been first world for a long time. There is this freshness in all the arts," he said. And in fact, by the late 1990s, he observed, the world was discovering that Brazilian musicians were "doing it with refinement." If, before, Brazil was "just *exotique, très exotique*," to the first world, now there was more musical and cultural audaciousness, and a solidarity between a lot of people and various tendencies. "I know that what I do has refinement," Lenine asserted, adding that he was "speaking to the world," but it was because his music was a reflection of his country, his location, his universe.

Indeed, Lenine referred to his marketing strategy as "pulverizing," noting that by the late 1990s, there existed a significantly larger audience for world music than just five years before: "It is now possible to go and sell 4,000 albums in France, 12,000 in Germany, 5,000 in Japan, 600 in Belgium—you go adding this up. You pulverize it. . . . I saw one Japanese audience, man, [ages] nineteen to twenty-five, without speaking one word of Portuguese, singing along to my song 'Vai na ponte, Vai na ponte.'" It was, however, *Olho de peixe*, his album with Suzano, that "ignited this process" abroad, he recalled. For Lenine, the project grew out of his desire to "synthesize" his music into a stripped-down instrumentation. He had always performed with bands; now he wanted "a *diet* formulation" of his music. This formulation would be possible, he reasoned, because of the way he already "induced the harmony, the melody, the rhythm, all on the guitar." His style of playing filled in all the spaces and even provided bass lines.

Then he met Suzano, who showed up on the scene "with that face of a seminarian," Lenine recalled; loosened the skin of the pandeiro; and "made it like a drum." He "brought percussion to the front and got the spotlight on him," calling into question "the function of the drum kit." Suzano's pandeiro was "something else," Lenine reflected, and together the two effected "a marvelous synthesis." On the first track of *Olho de peixe*, "Acredite ou não" (Believe it or not), Lenine plays a groove utilizing only three tightly voiced triads (I, IV, and V), while Suzano complements Lenine's percussive and syncopated guitar playing with driving, steady sixteenth notes on the cymbals of the pandeiro. The predominant feel is a samba-derived duple meter, but Suzano also hints at a rock 4/4 rhythm by accenting a backbeat. The samba aspect is reinforced in the *agogô* (cowbell) pattern that Suzano adds beginning around two and a half minutes into the song. The percussionist's offbeat open strokes on the pandeiro head to produce bass tones similar to a kick drum in a rock kit, on the other hand, contribute additional syncopations from the lower-frequency range of the mix. The vocal part itself is highly syncopated, and during an interlude in the song, Lenine sings percussive vocables, further contributing to a richly polyrhythmic texture.

The idea for the song came from the *Ripley's Believe It or Not* television program (titled *Acredite se quiser* in Portuguese), which Lenine and the lyricist Braúlio Tavares liked to watch, and the refrain to the song adapts the opening line of the television show: "Strange! Bizarre! All of this happened, believe it or not." The lyrics describe a series of local events and practices that Braúlio sarcastically proposed were even more absurd than those on the television program (pers. comm., 30 August 2008), such as the seats of the sambadrome, where the carnival parades occur, being full of tourists paying ticket prices that average Brazilians can't afford. The song follows a verse-refrain pattern over the chord vamp, without any B (that is, musically contrasting) section. It develops through the increasing intensity of Lenine's vocal and Suzano's rhythmic performances. The latter's full and driving percussion, with each sixteenth-note subdivision of the pulse methodically articulated, remains perfectly steady, but he adds cymbal crashes, cowbell, woodblock, and increasingly insistent low-frequency strikes. Despite the restrained use of synthesizers and filters to add a hint of "strange" and "bizarre" sonic coloration, the aesthetic privileges acoustic timbres, and Jim Ball's mix keeps the various sources of sonic information discrete through careful microphone choice and placement, as well as studio equalization, panning, volume control, and use of reverb and echo.

The title song of the album was intended to reflect Lenine's "planetary vision" and humankind's connection with the cosmos, he said. The "fish eye" (*olho de peixe*) is a reference to the Great Red Spot on the planet Jupiter, photographed by *Voyager I* (the image found on the cover of the album; see figure 7). Lenine's lyrics express a vague statement about how the routine of the present can make one narrow minded. The mind is "a locker," and individuals decide what to put in it. The mind has a basement where "instinct and repression" reside, but what, Lenine asks, is in the mind's attic? The song "O último por do sol" (The last sunset) describes a supernova exploding, leaving Lenine alone on the earth, the last human on the day the sun died. The cosmic dimension of the album, however, was probably largely lost on local musicians. Rather, the predominant impressions they took from *Olho de peixe* were (according to conversations I have had with local music makers over the years) that (1) the rich texture was created with primarily acoustic guitar (violão) and percussion, especially the pandeiro (voice was a given); (2) the percussionist came to the forefront as a lead instrumentalist; and (3) the acoustic timbres were well recorded and tastefully mixed. (Figure 8 shows Lenine with the recording engineer for this album at Ministereo recording facility in the South Zone.)[13]

Artisanal Production and Real World

In 1997 Lenine released his first solo album, *O dia em que faremos contato* (The day we make contact, a title inspired by the 1984 science fiction film *2010: The Year We Make Contact*), again with Suzano contributing the percus-

sive backbone. Liminha (Arnolpho Lima Filho), a bassist who played with the band Os Mutantes early in his career (1970–74), and who is now one of Brazil's best-known producers of pop music, provided the main electric bass parts. Chico Neves produced the album and provided electronic programming of loops and effects, as well as additional electric bass parts. Lenine, Suzano, and Chico worked out the arrangements together. In his comments about this album shortly after its release, the ethnomusicologist and journalist Hermano Vianna interpreted it through the lens of the nation and cultural development. "Finally," he wrote, "Brazil has produced a record of this kind." It was a watershed mark in the history of MPB, with an "immediate liberating effect on the national musical life" (my emphasis). The first achievement of the album, he went on to explain, was that it

FIGURE 7. Album cover for Lenine and Marcos Suzano's *Olho de peixe*. Graphic design by Barrão (Jorge Velloso Borges Leão Teixeira).

updated MPB to the latest technologically savvy trends in music, a central trope of the modernist cultural cannibalism discourse. It was "post-hip-hop, post-techno, post-jungle, post-MIDI, post-sampler, post–personal computer," while it proposed a Brazilian use for these technologies. By contrast, most recent MPB music, Vianna noted, was "extremely restrained and well behaved in the use of new recording resources," and this owed perhaps to "shyness," or maybe to "narcissism," or even a fear of and prejudice against "the machine" that is characteristic of the "romantic and almost naturalistic songbook spirit" in MPB (referring to a series of published fakebooks covering the repertoire of canonical MPB songwriters).

It was Chico Neves's "impeccable production (even with all risks taken)" that was able to turn this "technological laziness" into "something of the past." Chico avoided "the great local studios in which the existence of the most modern equipment" is constrained by "bureaucratic and industrial working methods," choosing instead to use his personal studio. Lenine's

FIGURE 8. Lenine and the audio engineer Denilson Campos at the MiniStereo Studio, Rio de Janeiro

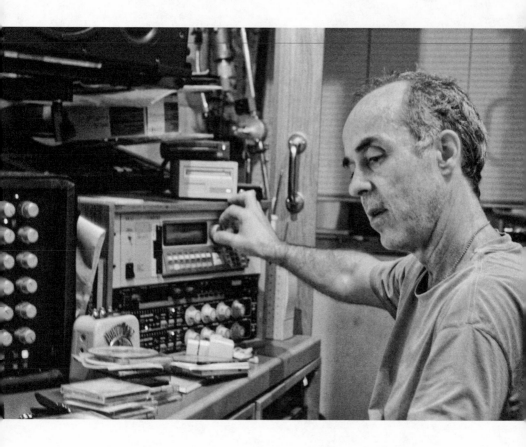

album, Vianna thought, was reintegrating other experiences "into MPB's well-known evolutionary line," but under a "Northeastern mentality." Brazil's chanters, its repentistas and *emboladores*, he suggested, had always had the habit of "sampling information of different origin" and tying it together into a single improvised line. Lenine was doing this "using the noise mode of our contemporaneous music," Vianna concluded (2000). We encounter in such comments the allegories of cannibalism, courage (risk taking versus behaving well), contemporaneity, rupture, modernization (versus laziness and backwardness), improvisatory evolution, and freedom (the liberation from industrial working methods).[14]

Chico Neves (figure 9) emerged as an important independent producer in Brazil in the 1990s, finding success with albums by the rock-pop band Os Paralamas do Sucesso (whose lead singer, Herbert Vianna, is Hermano's brother) and by Skank, as well as Gabriel O Pensador and Fernanda Abreu, among others. He views his way of working as a craft-oriented mode of

FIGURE 9. Chico Neves in Studio 304, Rio de Janeiro

production in direct opposition to what were, at the time of our first interview, the prevailing music industry models. As a producer who relatively early in the decade made the transition from working for a multinational label (Warner) to making records independently in his home studio, he anticipated the declining influence of the artists and repertoire director in this setting—and of the big recording studios—as occurred elsewhere. Even in 2009, the producer and guitarist Maurício Pacheco, of a younger generation than Lenine, related to me how important Chico's work on *O dia em que faremos contato* was in that it created a "magic carpet" on which Lenine—until then more of a songwriter than an artist with a distinctive sound—could fly. Before examining selected tracks from this album, I briefly profile Chico.

In my conversation with the producer, the central theme that emerged was the subordination of the industrial tools of music—technologies such as the Pro Tools digital recording and postproduction system—to his agency as a creative artist who carefully chooses which projects he will produce. In his view, the sampler and all technologies should be approached as the tools of a craftsman rather than as devices of mass production. Pierre Bourdieu would probably place him among the "dominated" fraction of the dominant class who, with relatively modest economic capital, seek to make up for this lack with cultural capital. In accordance with this fraction's efforts to accumulate cultural capital, those who are part of it tend to favor, in Bourdieu's framework, more "restricted" rather than mass production, and a comparatively high degree of autonomy from market forces (Hesmondhalgh 2006, 214; Bourdieu 1984).[15] This a compelling way to think about this producer's general outlook but it is not sufficient to explain his individual becoming, his minor history (or, for that matter, why some of his colleagues chose to continue in mass production), and it tells us nothing about the music he has made.

Chico moved to Rio at age seventeen and began working as a studio intern at the EMI/Odeon recording label, helping out on the productions of major MPB and samba artists. A year later, Liminha, then director of artists and repertoire at Warner Music, invited Chico to work as his assistant. From 1979 to 1986, he worked as a producer with Liminha and also began to work as an engineer at Liminha's and Gilberto Gil's recording facility, Nas Nuvens. By 1986, however, Chico had grown increasingly disillusioned with the music business. He quit his job at Warner and did not work for three years. He "was in a very bad state," he recalled, no longer able to identify with the people around him or with "the way that they worked with music," as he made an "interior journey" to find his own path.

In the process he came back to music after he bought a computer and a sampler and began to do things his own way, he said, "without trying to please anyone, without worrying about money." As with Suzano's career trajectory, we observe a process of individual becoming unfolding specifically in relation to emergent digital music technologies as Chico sought a "line of flight" out of an intolerable situation. With Fábio Fonseca, Chico developed much of the electronic programming and looping of the digital samples used on Fernanda Abreu's first two solo albums (see chapter 4). Then he did the same for selected tracks of Gabriel O Pensador's debut album. In 1994 he built a small recording studio in his apartment (Estúdio 302, which subsequently moved next door to apartment 304 and was renamed accordingly). Working independently, Chico claimed to have inconvenienced various people by not adhering to the rules of "the system," by which he meant not conforming to the profit logic and marketing plans he saw as driving the music industry. People who "sell themselves to the system," he said, are generally unhappy and not doing what they want. Sometimes, he conceded, he had money problems, but he found himself incapable of doing a project in which he lacked some sort of emotional involvement or interest. The recording process should be pleasurable rather than stressful, in his view, and this experience should be reflected in the music. "You need to find a way to make people happy in the studio and then you photograph that in sound." Chico noted that he spent two years recording Lenine's album (which is, of course, unusually long for a pop music recording). "I have no obligations to anyone," he said. He funds projects himself and follows his own schedule, so that he can "remain open to ideas coming when they will." This requires time, and projects mature and take form in their own way.

Not surprisingly, Chico contrasted his way of working in the studio (which Lenine called "artisanal") with the kinds of production models he thought tended to be utilized in the sphere of pagode music, singling out the group É o Tchan and "the things that are selling here." For him, these kinds of commercialized genres were "wrong," a word choice that reinforces how participants in this music scene have shared ethical views on correct practices. "I don't make music thinking about getting it on the radio," he asserted. It was regrettable that people saw albums and artists as "products," leading naturally to standardization; one recording label that Chico had approached about Lenine's album wanted to treat him as if he were a pagode artist. Not categorically against commercial music, Chico believed that within each recording system there had to be space for a variety of musical styles, echoing the position taken by the musicians at the MPB debate. "You can't pass everyone through the same prism, the same filter," he observed. Music makers do, of course, often attempt to position their work as art (or craft) rather than commodity for self-aggrandizement, but the case of Chico Neves's career is indicative of the wider shifts that occurred in the local music scene, as demonstrated by the fact that Chico became a much sought-after producer in the 1990s.

As was the case for many of the other music makers I interviewed, Chico's distaste for the more commercial aspects of the music business was matched by his optimism about the role of Brazilian music as globalization progressed. Brazilian music was quite rich, he felt, while "things abroad [were] very saturated." Foreign music makers saw "a cauldron of ideas" in Brazil, and he was confident that the country's music would become increasingly important in the world. His role in the recording studio was "to contribute to making this music more real." He correctly assessed that "the scheme of the recording label" as it existed in the mid-1990s was over.[16]

During pre-production discussions about *O dia em que faremos contato*, Chico and Lenine discovered that they shared a passion for the English musician Peter Gabriel and his former band Genesis. They decided that they wanted to mix the album at Real World Studios in England, owned by Gabriel and a key site for world music production during the early 1990s. Through Bruno Boulay, a producer and Brazilian music promoter based in France, Chico established contact with Real World, and they were able to do the mixing there. When he arrived at the facility, Chico said, he felt like he had "found his place, his way of working." It was "all about the music there, not about the money." One suspects that this was not entirely accurate, but this impression was important to Chico's narrative of his way of working, and it is noteworthy that as with Marcos Suzano's sonic epiphany of self-discovery while working with the North American engineer Jim Ball, it was abroad that Chico initially found the mixing space he was seeking.[17]

Making Contact and Speaking to the World

Lenine composed the opening track to *O dia em que faremos contato*, "A ponte," with his fellow Pernambucan Lula Queiroga (with whom Lenine had recorded *Baque solto* in 1983). The song was intended to express the possibility of communication across "islands" of difference, he explained. It takes inspiration from the geography of Recife, a city built around a network of canals and waterways, which Lenine imagines as a series of islands linked by bridges, and as representing a setting marked by a paradoxical state between isolation and connection. The geographical metaphor has its parallel in the Internet, an association made sonically explicit at the beginning of the song with a sample of the once-familiar digital noise produced by the initiation of a computer dial-up connection. The bridge, then, is also part of a "web of connecting—the possibility of going and coming." (The affinity that Lenine and Chico shared for the music of Peter Gabriel, which resulted in their mixing the album at Real World, exemplified the web.)

After eight seconds of the dial-up sound, the track makes a striking cut to a recording of the virtuosic embolada duo Caju e Castanha sampled from the soundtrack to the 1975 documentary *Nordeste: Cordel, repente, canção* (filmed when Caju and Castanha were twelve and seven years old, respectively). Their contribution to the documentary soundtrack (and to Lenine's album, via sampling) begins with Caju describing how they got started as musicians, singing in public squares before they were able to afford pandeiros. The sound of the dial-up connection spliced with Caju's narrative thus serves as a sonic metaphor symbolizing the linking of the traditional folklore and street performance of Pernambuco into new webs of communication.[18]

As Caju speaks during the introduction to the track, a heavily distorted guitar ostinato fades in, joined quickly by a synthesized non-musical sine wave moving through a harmonic series, and percussive bass and guitar ostinatos. Chico Neves programmed loops and the various "effects" that contribute to an urban sound removed from the conventional timbres of the traditional côco. A ganzá enters in the first verse, performing steady but swinging sixteenth notes in duple meter, with the accent on beat 2. An additional syncopated rhythmic pattern performed on knife and plate (used in traditional samba de roda) enters for a brief period. Then, beginning almost two minutes into the track, a sampled snare drum strike on beat 2 of every other measure suggests a rock 4/4 meter until, suddenly, the song breaks to samples of the young Caju and Castanha singing an embolada for a few seconds, and of the French duo Les Fabulous Trobadors, who similarly rap oral poetry, usually in Occitan.[19] The sampled and superimposed recordings of the two duos then cut out as Lenine's song reenters on the phrase "Nagô, Nagô, na Golden Gate," while heavily distorted rock

"power chords" (triads with roots and fifths doubled) on electric guitar follow the same rhythmic ostinato as the introductory portion. This change
toward a more forceful sound makes sense here, as Lenine is referencing
a popular song from the Recife maracatu Nação Porto Rico do Oriente:
"Nagô, Nagô! Our queen has been crowned!" the song goes, referring to a
West African Yoruba ethnicity (Crook 2005, 145).

Using wordplay, Lenine paints a loose association between the bridges
of Recife and San Francisco's Golden Gate Bridge. He takes advantage of
the fact that *Nagô* and *na Gol-* (from the line "na Golden Gate," meaning "on
the Golden Gate") sound the same in Brazilian pronunciation. "Accept my
hemispheric song," Lenine implores in the lyrics, "my voice on the Voice
of America," a reference to the transnational radio station of the United
States government. He also plays on the rhymes of *fonte* (fountain), *horizonte* (horizon), and *ponte* (bridge) in a call-and-response series of indirect
questions with chant-like responses, such as "This place is beautiful, but
how to get off the island? (On the bridge, on the bridge.)" The bridge, he
explains in the lyrics, is a metaphor for where his thoughts go, and it is
more important for the act of crossing it than it is for going somewhere in
particular. "A ponte" is thus a carefully constructed mixture of elements
taken from côco (e.g., call-and-response or question and answer between
verse and refrain, characteristic rhythms), from maracatu (Nagô), and the
specific references to the urban geography of Recife, as well as cosmopolitan references. It won the Sharp Prize for best song in 1998, while Lenine himself earned the Sharp Prize in the category of best new MPB artist
("MPB Revelação").

The song "Candeeiro encantado" (Enchanted lamp, composed with
Paulo César Pinheiro) was inspired by one of the classics of Brazilian
cinema, Glauber Rocha's 1964 Cinema Novo film, *Deus e o Diabo na terra
do sol* (titled *Black God, White Devil* in English). *Deus e o Diabo*, which takes
place during a severe drought in the *sertão* (arid backlands), allegorizes the
poverty, fanaticism, and injustice of life in the interior of the Northeast.
In the middle of Lenine's song, Chico inserted the audio from an excerpt
of the film when the character Corisco (Othon Bastos), the "blond devil,"
hears news of the capture and death of the notorious bandit of the sertão, Lampião (killed and beheaded by police in 1938), and incorporates
his spirit, promising to seek vengeance. The outlaw's name comes from
the word for the oil lamps that could be found in homes of the Northeast,
while a *candeeiro* is a gas lamp. Thus the refrain to the song is "É Lamp,

é Lamp, é Lamp, é Lampião / Meu candeeiro encantado" ("It's Lamp, it's Lamp, it's Lamp, it's Lampião / My enchanted lamp"), which also happens to play on the English word "lamp." With references to characters from the film; to the popular Catholicism of the Northeast; to the *mandacuru* cactus that grows—as northeastern legend has it—where blood has been shed; to Jackson do Pandeiro and Luiz Gonzaga; to the maracatu; to the traditional Afro-Brazilian dance *maculelê* (performed in a circle with *atabaque* drums and pairs of sticks that are struck against each other rhythmically); and to the *carimbó* (a musical genre traditionally performed on drums made of tree trunks), this song is an homage to the Northeast, an area, Lenine protests in the lyrics, that is still not given the respect accorded the more industrialized Southeast of Brazil.

In "Pernambuco falando pelo mundo" (Pernambuco speaking to the world), Lenine takes stock of the emergence of the mangue beat scene by singing a medley of Pernambucan songs. He wanted to express his solidarity with the younger generation, he explained, but also to cite other historical moments that he saw as ideologically similar "in terms of attitude and objective." The first song he cites in the medley is Luiz Bandeira's "Voltei, Recife" (I'm back, Recife), a beloved frevo from 1958 with a memorable melody. Lenine sings the first verse about returning to the city out of longing (*saudade*) and the desire to hear the classic carnival frevo "Vassoura" while parading with the crowds on the streets. He then segues into the song "Frevo ciranda" (1974) by the celebrated Pernambucan composer Capiba (Lourenço da Fonseca Barbosa), thereby referencing yet another traditional genre associated especially (but not only) with the Northeast, the *ciranda*, a circle dance and song primarily of Portuguese origin in which males and females (often children) separate into two circles. He continues with a citation of Alceu Valença's "Sol e chuva" (1976). Finally Lenine sings a few lines from the song "Rios, pontes, e overdrives" (1994) by Chico Science and Fred 04, leading figures in the mangue beat scene.

This composite medley, he said, was "a little congratulations" for his hometown at a moment when Recife was enjoying much media attention, but it was also a reminder to younger audiences that the city had a long tradition of great popular music. Recife has suffered from sentiments of self-deprecation, Lenine held, that alternatively cycle through moments in which people celebrate local culture. The main contribution of the mangue beat bands, in his view, was their ability to promote the development of self-esteem among an audience of students who listened almost exclusively to international rock, broadening the public for this music beyond "a ghetto of two hundred people" who previously constituted the audience for local progressive rock bands like Ave Sangria and Flaviola e o Bando do Sol. (Not surprisingly, he contrasted mangue beat with the pagode group É o Tchan, which dominated the airwaves at the time. "I'm speaking about a project that has a different kind of public as its object," Lenine said. The music has "a concept, a discourse.")

What Color Is the Groove?

The song "Que baque é esse?" (What is this beat?) also alludes to Recife's maracatu in a hard-driving, funky groove with a bluesy syncopated horn arrangement contributed by Carlos Malta (soprano, tenor, and baritone saxophone). Suzano plays a maracatu-like rhythm on the zabumba, a hip-hop-inspired rhythm on the pandeiro, and a shuffling backbeat on the snare drum. Lenine provides a harmonic base in characteristically funky acoustic guitar parts, but a distorted electric guitar adds bluesy rock power chords in parts of the track. A couple of minutes into the song, the guitars and voice drop out for a baritone saxophone solo over a hip-hop-samba-backbeat groove. Marcos Suzano plays snare drum with brushes, articulating figures that hint at the sixteenth–eighth–sixteenth note rhythm common in samba, côco, and other Brazilian genres. The sound of the drum is electronically panned from left to right channels and back in the stereo mix, in time with the beat. Another break later in the song features the syncopated, tightly arranged, and deeply funky horns with rock guitar in the background.

The lyrics describe a woman, probably African descended (nega), dancing at the front of a maracatu street procession on a hot, sunny day in early summer. The subject of the song, presumably a male (although not specified), is infatuated with her performance. The word baque refers to the thud or thump of things colliding or collapsing (and, as already described, is used to describe the heavy beat of the bass drums in maracatu). The verb form, baquear, means to fall noisily, or to ruin, to destroy. Lenine plays with these meanings as he sings "Ô Nega, que baque é esse? / Chegou pra me baquear," meaning, roughly, "Hey black woman, what is this beat? / You showed up to ruin me." Only one who follows behind the nega dancing to the pulsing of the bombo drum, Lenine sings, is capable of understanding all the "magic" of her dance, and of the crowd losing themselves in fantasy.

The word "nega," José Jorge de Carvalho observes, appears in countless songs. While its literal translation is "black woman," it is also a more generalized term of sexual intimacy that harkens back to the patriarchal setting of the colonial era, when relations between an upper-class white man and his wife remained very formal, while white men often had casual relations with black or mulatto mistresses (1994, 23). In this broader usage, *nega* need not indicate the skin color of a woman. "When a man calls a woman of fair skin nega," Carvalho writes, "this means she is able to preserve for him . . . something of the sexual mystery attached to the real other."[20] In "Que baque é esse?" the nega is similarly eroticized, although the lyrics represent the scene as natural to the context of the Afro-Brazilian maracatu. The reference to magic also suggests a kind of bewitching, enhancing a sense of otherness in the imagery. The rhythmic base and all the musical parts of the song were intended to "reinforce the question 'What is this beat?'" Lenine observed. Neither maracatu nor samba nor exactly hip-hop, the groove was "an innovative polyrhythm" of indeterminacy. Had the musicians played a more straightforward groove, Lenine felt, the song would have been banal. Instead, there was no *formula* to the song's "musical path." The indeterminacy of the rhythm in this song complements the sense of sexual mystery that Carvalho writes is associated with the word *nega*.

The song "Etnia caduca" (Expired ethnicity) treats the theme of racial mixture. "It's the chameleon in front of a rainbow / Smearing the eyes of the multitudes with colors," Lenine sings in the opening lines. A "cauldron mixing rites and races," the "Miscegenation Mass." Lenine uses the words *race* and *ethnicity* more or less interchangeably in the lyrics, drawing attention to several antiquated racial typologies and derogatory expressions (for example, um *mameluco maluco*, meaning a crazy *mameluco*, a term once used to refer to someone with Amerindian and white European parentage).[21] Why should miscegenation be the defining characteristic of Brazilian identity when other countries have also experienced racial and cultural mixture? I asked him when we discussed this song. "In any other place in the world," Lenine answered, miscegenation is less obvious. "Think about it," he continued. "We are completing five hundred years of what? Screwing [*fudelância*]! That's what colonization was like. They didn't *discover* anything. There were already thousands of races, hundreds of indigenous nations." Thus the mixture of peoples was "more explicit" in Brazil than elsewhere. It was in the libido, in the Brazilian character.

At the same time, with the expression *etnia caduca*, Lenine meant to say that the idea of ethnicity (actually meaning race here) has "expired" (*caduca* means "senile" or "failing"). Instead, the constantly changing color of the chameleon in front of the rainbow of global culture, he suggested, might be a more appropriate metaphor for Brazilian identity in the contemporary world. On the listening notes for the CD, he added a different question: "But what color is the chameleon when it is looking in a mirror?" In the context of this song, the metaphor of the chameleon seems to suggest that subjective aspects of self-identification, including how one's color contributes to one's racial identity, are in constant tension with externally imposed classifications. In front of a mirror, however, the chameleon is faced with the task of choosing its color based only on cues emanating from it. However we read Lenine's evocation of this riddle in this context, it certainly reinforces the sense that Brazilian identity is forever unfinished, that becoming is the permanent, quintessential state of being Brazilian (and that Brazilian identity is intensely racialized).

This short song begins with a looped and precisely even sixteenth-note rhythmic ostinato modified electronically with filters so that it is not clear what the sources were. Using different instantiations of this effect on a variety of percussive sounds contributes to the layered texture of the rhythm. In the introduction, the filter cycles through two beats, suggesting a duple meter typical to samba (and creating a sound somewhat like a strong wind whipping through a gully), while other unfiltered percussive elements such as the splash sound articulated every eight beats follow longer cycles or only articulate selected sixteenth notes rather than providing the consistent ostinato. Electric fretless bass and Lenine's customarily percussive and syncopated acoustic guitar accompaniment fill out the basic groove, while the mix is periodically adorned with odd electronically created or modified effects provided by Chico Neves. Beginning about fifteen seconds into the song, the percussion track fills up with Suzano playing various samba instruments: pandeiro, tamborim, surdo, caixa, and agogô. Later in the song, the guitar and bass drop out for an extended percussion break over which Lenine sings a rhythmic scat. The resulting rhythm is an intensely propulsive rethinking of samba that uses a relatively streamlined instrumentation. "What is the sound of samba in front of a mirror?" this song seems to be asking. It is a layered, electronically manipulated, and emergent samba integrated into these musicians' musical becomings.

For his album *Na pressão* (Under pressure), Lenine chose to work with the producer Tom Capone, then director of artists and repertoire at Warner Music. By 1999 Tom, who began his career as a rock musician (electric guitar and bass) in Brasília, had become an influential figure in Brazilian popular music production and an important presence in the South Zone scene. Occasionally, he recorded at his home, an impressive space located on a secluded, forested slope near the Barra da Tijuca area of the West Zone. In March 1999 I accompanied the wind instrumentalist Carlos Malta to a recording session there. Carlos had written an arrangement of Lenine and Braúlio Tavares's carnival theme "O suvaco é a maior diversão" (Suvaco is the most fun, referring to the Suvaco do Cristo South Zone carnival bloco), and it was to be incorporated into the album. My field materials document a discussion about carnival samba that Carlos had with a recording assistant (whom I knew only by his nickname, Tatú) before recording began. They were bemoaning what they perceived as a trend toward simplification of the melodies in *samba de enredo* (themed samba, the genre most commonly utilized in Carnival). "It's what's easiest to sing," Carlos complained of the newer sambas, as he began intoning, for contrast, the melody and lyrics to Edeor de Paula's "Os sertões" from 1976, based on Euclides da Cunha's classic account of the battle of Canudos. By the third word, Tatú was singing along. "Now that is so beautiful," they agreed. "It was from an era in which the melodic beauty of samba was also valued," Carlos asserted. Today, he said, the judges who choose the songs for a given carnival samba school reject melodies that they think will be "too difficult for the people [*povo*] to sing." How boring this was, Carlos lamented, because those sambas with beautiful melodies are "immortal."[22]

Tatú began singing, as an example of another unforgettable theme, "Kizomba, a festa da raça" (Kizomba, the festival of the race), which celebrates Zumbi, Palmares, and abolition. "Porra, man, this is beautiful," Carlos chimed in. Interestingly, these two sambas treat the two major rebellions described above, an indication of these events' importance in national culture. Carlos went on to mention some of the individuals he felt were great melodists of samba: Cartola, Nelson Cavaquinho, Paulinho da Viola. "All these guys," he said, "had a very healthy competition [to see] who could write melodies with staying power." This aspect, Carlos thought, was being "massacred by this thing of simplicity," whereby producers think the melody has to be "popular." These sambas *were* popular! he exclaimed, and everyone would sing along.

Carlos's march-like arrangement of "Suvaco é a maior diversão" for flute, piccolo, alto and tenor saxophone, trumpet, flugelhorn, trombone, bass trombone, euphonium, and tuba was utilized in the song "Rua da passagem (Trânsito)," on which it entered as a mere sixteen seconds of passing music. Co-composed with the São Paulo–based musician Arnaldo Antunes, the track establishes a distinct cinematic soundscape reflecting Arnaldo's lyrics about a busy intersection where impatient drivers honk at a motorist waiting for a dog to get out of the street. Slow down, the motorist-narrator requests; there's no need to run over the dog. Respect life. The song begins with the sound of a banda de pífanos, playing a duple-meter samba-like rhythm, which fades out after about half a minute. Simultaneously, there are sounds of traffic and cattle groaning. Rural and urban, rustic and modern, natural and manufactured collide in a kind of sonic metaphor for a rapidly developing late twentieth-century Brazil. At thirty-nine seconds, Carlos Malta's arrangement of "O suvaco é a maior diversão" fades into the mix for its quarter minute and then fades out. The calls of street vendors can be heard for a few seconds when, about a minute and a half into the song, an aggressive, driving groove is established on bombo and snare, suggesting a maracatu rural, and complemented by melodic riffs played by Siba, then of the Recife band Mestre Ambrósio, on the unmistakably northeastern rabeca fiddle. Tom Capone doubles Siba's melody on electric guitar before he leads into a distorted rock guitar solo late in the song. Electric bass propels the rhythm forward with a simple ostinato figure. Five minutes into the track, the music stops and the listener hears nothing but traffic (in stereo, with automobiles passing from one channel to another) for a long forty seconds. Then a programmed electronic beat with unidentifiable distorted sounds enters for the remaining twenty-five seconds of the song, concluding the brief film-like sonic story.

The first song on *Na pressão*, "Jack soul brasileiro," also begins with an aural reference to the Northeast, this time with DJ Marcelinho da Lua providing, on vinyl, a few seconds of the start of a maracatu rural with the alfaia drum, and a melodic ostinato plucked on the viola, the steel-string double-course guitar popular in the rural Northeast. The song is a tribute to master of the côco, embolada, and forró, Jackson do Pandeiro. It is a rousing rock-funk-forró-blues mixture in which Lenine incorporates verses and recorded samples from Jackson's songs "Cantiga do sapo" and

"Chiclete com banana" (1959) into his own verse. Charles Perrone and Christopher Dunn have described how the music and lyrics of "Chiclete com banana" demonstrated Jackson do Pandeiro's facility with the "interregional" mixing of forró with samba from Rio, as well as his use of international pop vocal stylings in the original recording, while subsequent recorded versions of the song inserted it into debates over popular music and globalization (2001, 4).[23] "The country of swing is the country of contradiction," Lenine sings in his lyrics, as he shouts out to the "king of the groove," following the percussive "rules of the embolada": "The dance, the *muganga*, the *dengo* / The swing of the *mamulengo* / The charm of this country." The word *soul*, as used here, is a reference both to the North American musical genre and to the "Brazilian soul." Not only does "Jack soul brasileiro" rhyme with "Jackson do Pandeiro"; it also sounds identical in Portuguese to the phrase "Já que sou brasileiro" (Being that I am Brazilian), another line from the lyrics. The words *muganga*, *dengo*, and *mamulengo*, with probable etymologies in African languages, are part of the lexicon of the Northeast. The mamulengo, for example, is a marionette play popular in Pernambuco.[24]

The poetic ring of the lines "a dança, a muganga, o dengo / a ginga do mamulengo" in their côco/embolada musical setting is tremendously musical, capturing the spirit of the northeastern oral poetry-song. There are also what might be called "Anglicisms"—words that have been appropriated into Brazilian Portuguese speech and orthography from English, such as *ringue* (ring), *suingue* (swing), and *charme* (charm). In the second verse, Lenine deepens the tongue twisting in rhymes, alliterations, and repetitions of one-syllable words. English words appropriated by Portuguese such as *funk* and *rock* are mixed with references to Afro-Brazilian culture such as samba and *batuque* (a generic term for Afro-Brazilian drumming and dance), and to Pernambuco (*repique* refers to a drum used in samba, but also to the traditional festive ringing of church bells in Pernambuco). The word *banguela* (meaning a toothless person) is probably another Africanism.[25] Much of the lyrical force of the words in this song thus derives simply from their sound. While the vocal to "Jack soul brasileiro" is grounded in the rhythms of the côco, programmed electronic drum parts suggest a 4/4 rock beat. Lenine adds a zabumba bass drum to his characteristically funky acoustic guitar groove, while Tom Capone plays electric bass.

Lenine takes his penchant for wordplay to an extreme on the song "Meu amanhã (Intuindootil)" (My tomorrow [Intuiting the tilde]), which begins as a love song but turns out to be a vehicle for the songwriter to juxtapose words that differ slightly in spelling (similar to "orthographic neighbors"), as well as words that sound similar but differ in meaning (paronomasia).[26] "Minha meta, minha metade" ("My goal [or limit], my half"), he sings, also using alliteration. Several of the pairings differ primarily in their diacritic markings: "Minha diva, meu divã / minha manha, meu amanhã" ("My diva, my divan / my whining, my tomorrow"), *fá* (as in the solfeggio for the fourth scale degree) and *fã* (fan), *massa* (pasta or paste) and *maçã* (apple), *lá* (the sixth scale degree in solfeggio, also "there") and *lã* (wool), *paga* (wages) and *pagã* (pagan), *sal* (salt) and *são* (health, soundness, also saint), and *Tao* (the Chinese word) and *tão* (meaning "as much as"). One of the most creative of these sets is the line "Nau de Nassau, minha nação," referring to the ship (*nau*) of John Maurice of Nassau, governor of Dutch Pernambuco from 1637 to 1644 (before Portugal reclaimed the area), and then "my nation," an ingenious reference to the importance of the contested Northeast in the formation of the Brazilian nation. Another clever phrase is "Amor em Roma, aroma de romã," or "Love in Rome, the aroma of pomegranate," and finally "O que é certo, o que é sertão," meaning "What is certain, what is sertão," yet another reference to the Northeast.

The song "Relampiano" (Lightning), co-composed with Paulinho Moska, describes the daily life of a poor family struggling to survive. It does so with a tone of resignation emphasized by the allusion to a well-known phrase attributed to Che Guevara: "One has to harden without ever losing tenderness" ("Hay que endurecerse, sin perder la ternura jamás"). In Lenine's song, the phrase is adapted as "One has to harden such a frail heart." (That it is a paraphrase of the popular saying is clear from the fact that the line is sung in Spanish and placed in quotation marks in the printed lyrics.) The possibility of revolution, however, seems distant, as the subjects of the song have become resigned to their lives: "It is lightning, where is the child?" asks the refrain. Selling candies at the traffic light is the answer. The lyrics describe daily toil as the child hits the streets to work and the mother washes clothes in the father's absence. A crying baby gets used to "the world outside the shack" and it is this child's frail heart that must be hardened, for its life "points down a one-way street." The second verse suggests that even with the passage of time, little has changed except that there is a new man in the household and the mother is pregnant. She is ironing the man's clothes. The baby soon to be born is "one more mouth in the shack." The music features the kinds of chord changes and temporary modulations one might hear in a moderate-tempo choro or a modinha (a sentimental song popular in the eighteenth and nineteenth centuries). Its winding melody, together with the accordion provided by the Pernambucan forró master Dominguinhos, gives the piece a melancholy serenade-like sound that serves to underscore the sense that the subjects' poverty has become normal for them, that they are resigned to a daily grind.

The text to this song was adopted for some academic tests in Brazil. For example, the 2005 entrance exam for one university asked test-takers to analyze the song lyrics. Multiple-choice answers suggested that the phrase attributed to Che Guevara might be a criticism of the "romantic" view that "proclaimed the innocence of poor families who freely bear children," or perhaps that in affirming that "the city grows together with the kid," the composer "recognizes that state strategies to restrict the movements of children through the streets are working," or that "the crisis of the family," poor schools, crime, and poverty are each "another kilogram of flour from the same sack" (a line from the song) of realities that characterize childhood in Brazil. A 2007 sample exam for a social services program at the Universidade Federal Fluminense similarly asked test-takers to contemplate specific lines of the song. "Lacking guarantees of its most basic rights," one of the possible answers proposes, "the child is obligated to mature and 'harden.'" The "kilo" in the lyrics, the test imaginatively suggests, "is an allusion to the low birth weight of the child, while 'flour from the same sack' compares the child . . . to all the children immersed in this universe of poverty, of abandonment, and of the absence of dignified conditions of living."[27]

Lenine has described the initial inspiration for the imagery of the song. He and his co-composer, Paulinho Moska, were stopped at a traffic light when a boy selling candies came up to their car. Just then, a bolt of lightning coursed through the sky, and the child said, "Tá relampiano" ("It's lightning"). The boy then noticed that there was an empty car seat in the rear of the automobile and said, "Where's the baby?" ("Cadê neném?"). In making a song out of the episode, Lenine and Paulinho turned the child's question into a social statement about the child himself, and about poverty in Brazil. The impoverished baby grows up fast. The answer to the question "Where's the baby?" is "Out in the street working."[28] What is striking about the lyrics to this song, their melancholy musical accompaniment, and the proposed readings in the university exams is the utter lack of agency attributed to the personages, especially the mother and child (perhaps the fathers mentioned in the song could be said to have some agency). There is an implied appeal to change those structures, but the individuals restricted by them are portrayed as basically resigned to their situations in life.

"Tubi Tupy" (To be Tupy) offers another allegory of the Brazilian nation in its narrative about the Tupinambá (alt. Tupi or Tupy) indigenous inhabitants as "liberated," "natural," "animal," and "digital" descendants of the big bang, while it makes a textual reference not only to Oswald de Andrade's modernist "Cannibalist Manifesto" (1928) but also to the band Pedro Luís e A Parede's 1997 album *Astronauta Tupy* (Tupy astronaut). The Tupy is a "tropical cannibal" reborn from the brazilwood after which the nation is named (possibly a reference to Oswald's earlier *Brazilwood Manifesto* of 1925), a liberated "Tupy astronaut" made out of the remains of exploding stars at the beginning of time. *Tubi*, a phonetic spelling of the English "to be," is a reference to Oswald's line in the manifesto, "Tupi, or not tupi that is the question" (as it appears in the original, a "cannibalization" of *Hamlet* [O. Andrade 1995, 142]).

Lenine sings the first verse over percussion only: a slow electronically programmed rock-like beat on bass drum and snare (provided by Plínio Profeta) establishing a rather bellicose atmosphere that is heightened by acoustic drums such as the caixa de guerra, referencing the storied aggressiveness of the Tupinambá. C. A. Ferrari, Sidon Silva, and Celso Alvim, percussionists in the band Pedro Luís e A Parede, add surdo, tarol, and hubcap (*calota*). The percussionist Marco Lobo plays the berimbau musical bow part during instrumental interludes. The berimbau, with a single steel string, a dried hollowed-out gourd resonator, and a very distinctive timbre, is believed to derive from African (Bantu) musical bows and has no links to traditionally Amerindian instruments. Nonetheless, it is often used in Brazilian popular music as a sonic symbol for purportedly "ethnic" or "tribe-like" dimensions of the country (see Galm 2010).

The refrain to the song is an aggressive-sounding chant. "My name is Tupy," Lenine sings, with his voice doubled several times as if a small tribe were chanting. This line is followed by the name of another indigenous people, the Gaikuru (or Gaykuru). "My name is Perí, of Ceci," it continues, in a reference to the mid-nineteenth-century nativist novel *O Guarani* by José de Alencar, a classic of Brazilian literature. In Alencar's novel, Perí is a "noble savage" figure and the chief of the Goitacá Amerindian tribe. He abandons his people, however, to serve a Portuguese woman and helps the Portuguese defeat the indigenous tribes of the area. Ceci is a chaste Native American woman who is often identified with the Virgin Mary. "I am the nephew of Caramuru," Lenine sings in a reference to Diogo Álvares Correia, a shipwrecked Portuguese man who lived among the native populations in the late fifteenth and early sixteenth centuries, and to whom the Tupinambá gave the name Caramuru. He is said to be the first European to live in Brazil, the mythical initiator of the process of miscegenation. He married the indigenous woman Paraguaçu and later helped found the city of Salvador and establish the first Portuguese government in Brazil.[29]

The last line of the refrain names "Galdino, Juruna, and Raoni." Galdino Jesus dos Santos was a Pataxó Indian whom five upper-middle-class youths burned alive while he was sleeping at a bus stop in Brasilia in 1997 (having traveled to the city to commemorate the Day of the Indian).[30] Juruna is an indigenous group in the state of Mato Grosso, in the northern part of the Parque Indígena Xingu. Raoni Metuktire is a well-known leader of the Kayapó tribe, an indigenous people also in Mato Grosso with a reputation as fierce fighters. Raoni became a public figure in the 1980s as he negotiated with the Brazilian government for the protection of indigenous lands and peoples. He also accompanied the British singer-songwriter Sting on a trip to Europe to campaign for indigenous rights. This song was adopted as the main theme for the film *Caramuru: A invenção do Brasil* (Caramaru: The invention of Brazil), a satirical take on the legend. The sweep and intertextuality of these lyrical and sonic references to historical and contemporary events, personages, and cultural practices is impressive.

Braúlio Tavares described the title track to the album ("Na pressão"), which he co-composed with Lenine, as a kind of a continuation of the song "Acredite ou não," as if they were "Part[s] I and II" of a portrait of contemporary Brazil. "In this case, however," he wrote me, "we spoke of the pressure of violence, of terrorism, of shootouts, of crime, etc." (pers. commun., 30 August 2008). The central image, he explained, is of a witch brooding over a cauldron, but instead of cooking up the typically Brazilian bean dish *feijoada*, she stirs in dynamite. The song begins with Lenine playing an ostinato on the ten-string *viola caipira*, using the same minor scale used for the cantoria tradition (and for Lenine and Braúlio's song "O marco Marciano"), with the raised fourth scale degree. The percussionist Naná Vasconcelos adds accents on the "Turkish drum" (a pitched bass drum), the West African talking drum, and the wicker *caxixi* shakers of Brazil. "Keep an eye on the pressure, it's boiling," the lyrics begin. "Oil on the pan / Dynamite is the bean cooking in her stew / The witch lit the fire and is stoking it, folks." The witch "is violence, war," Braúlio clarified. Into the broth the witch drips the saliva of a "ferocious devil-beast," stirring up violence throughout Brazil, but the lyrics make no references to specific incidents. Like "Relampiano," this song does not point toward an activist agenda, although it warns that society reaps what it sows.

Subsequent Work

Lenine released his third solo album, *Falange canibal* (Cannibal crowd), in 2002. His co-composers for the songs on this album were Paulo César Pinheiro, Lula Queiroga, Dudu Falcão, Bráulio Tavares, and Carlos Rennó, as well as the North American drummer Will Calhoun from the band Living Colour, who toured Brazil with Lenine that year. After several years spent establishing himself abroad, Lenine's collaborators for this recording comprised an especially cosmopolitan group. Among those from Brazil were the legendary bossa nova–era pianist Eumir Deodato; the literary scholar, composer, and pianist José Miguel Wisnik; the rock guitarist Roberto Frejat; Marcelo Lobato and Xandão from the rock group O Rappa; the electric guitarist Jr Tostoi and members of his group Vulgue Tostoi; Henrique Portugal and Haroldo Ferreti, of the pop-rock band Skank; and members of the old guard of Rio's legendary Mangueira samba school. Besides Will Calhoun, musicians from abroad included the singer Ani DiFranco; the jazz musician Steve Turre; the New York City–based "Afro-Cuban funk and hip-hop collective" Yerba Buena; the Russian musician Alexander Cheparukhin (formerly of the band Farlanders); Claude Sicre and Ange B. from Les Fabulous Trobadors; and the accordionist Regis Gizavo of Madagascar.

The album, which was nominated for a Latin Grammy in the category of contemporary Brazilian pop, is a tribute to a small bar from the late eighties in the Lapa district of Rio de Janeiro where, in Lenine's recollection, a variety of artists felt a great sense of liberty to make whatever kind of art they wanted (highlighting again the importance of the trope of creative freedom for the artists in this scene). For Lenine, the name *Falange canibal* also represented key aspects of his career: the cannibalist aesthetic, and the collaborative process (Carpegianni 2000). The opening track, "Ecos do ão" (Echoes of the ão) showcases Vulgue Tostoi's art-rock aesthetic. Jr's guitar on this track pays homage to Marc Ribot's guitar playing on Tom Waits's 1985 *Rain Dogs* album, and Lenine's voice is processed in a similar manner to Waits's on that album, giving it a kind of boxed-up shortwave radio–like sound. The lyrics to this song are again full of wordplay with nearly each line finishing with a word ending in *ão* (e.g., *são, ação, inauguração, civilização, nação*). The theme of the lyrics is a utopian vision for ending hunger and "slander" (*difamação*, an odd word in this context, clearly chosen for its *ão*) and inaugurating a civilization "as unique as our *ão*" that would realize "beautiful, free, and luminous" dreams for the nation.

The northeastern influences on *Falange canibal* are somewhat less obvious than on Lenine's first two albums, signaling in part the influence of various international personnel on the recording, but also the changed production context after the turn of the millennium, in which it seemed to be less urgent to manifest a resurgent sonic Brazilianness. The mixture is still there; it just doesn't draw as much attention to itself. In "Nem o sol, nem a lua, nem eu" (Neither the sun, nor the moon, nor I), for example, the electric guitarist Xandão utilizes rhythmic syncopations characteristic of bossa nova, while the text and melody are influenced by the ciranda song and dance. The most unusual sound in this restrained little song is the conch shell performance by Steve Turre. Lenine identifies the song as a "ciranda cyberpunk," noting that Turre's "divine conch shells" transport the song to "the sands of a remote beach . . . on Saturn!"[31]

The song "Caribantu" (from *Carib* [Amerindians] and *Bantu*, the African ethnicity) joins some thirty musicians from the musical cast of Chico Buarque's pop opera *Cambaio* and senior musicians of Rio's oldest samba school, Mangueira, into a mixture of samba de roda, Candomblé, and maracatu. "No pano da jangada" (On the sail of the raft) is a kind of côco referring to a simple fishing boat of the Northeast and the North, recorded with only Lenine's voice, along with percussion that he made with his mouth and also by sliding his feet around on sand that he had spread on the studio floor.

"Rosebud (O verbo e a verba)" (Rosebud [the verb and the money]), co-composed with Lenine's longtime collaborator and fellow Recife native Lula Queiroga, again emphasizes the lyrical possibilities of wordplay, such as in the opening chant of "Dolores, dolores, dolores. Dólares!" where *dolores* means "woes" in Spanish, while *dólares* is "dollars." The lyrics anthropomorphize "the verb" (*o verbo*) and "the money" (*a verba*), narrating a strange love story in which the talkative verb (gendered as a masculine character in the song) seeks the love of "cold and quiet" money (gendered female). With its trumpets and the *montuno* call-and-response and a refrain sung in Spanish near the end of the song by the members of the group Yerba Buena—"Ai que dolor, que dolor que me da los dólares" ("Oh what pain dollars cause me")—this song borrows from the *son* genre of Cuba while expressing a poetic pan–Latin American critique of the economic dominance of the United States.[32]

In 2004 Lenine released the DVD and CD of the Paris Cité de la Musique Carte Blanche concert, and then in 2006, the live *Acústico* MTV CD. The *In Cité* CD won a Latin Grammy Award for best Brazilian contemporary pop album in 2005, while *Acústico* MTV won the same award in 2007. In Brazil, Lenine won four Tim Prizes (formerly the Sharp Prize) in the categories of best song ("Todas elas juntas num só ser," co-composed with Carlos Rennó), best pop-rock singer, best pop-rock album (*In Cité*), and best singer by popular vote. A good portion, although not all, of the repertoire on these albums is taken from the earlier CDS. Lenine was now an acknowledged planetary minstrel, especially popular in France, and his sound on the live album is a polished, technically sophisticated jazzy global pop.[33]

Conclusions

At a time when the mangue beat bands drew media attention in Brazil and abroad to emergent youth cultures of Recife, Lenine found his voice in the Rio de Janeiro music scene with his mixture of northeastern musical genres, samba, rock, and newer electronic sounds. I have sought to provide details about the specific sounds for which he has become known, to examine several song lyrics from his early solo albums, and to show how his music fits into a longer history of popular musicians from the Northeast who have established links between region and nation, communicating a part to the whole, as described by Bryan McCann. If the Northeast is a topos more than just a geographical location, Lenine helped to augment its presence in international circuits of popular music.

During an interview I conducted in Rio in June 2009 with Maurício Pacheco pertaining to a separate research project, Lenine came up in our conversation. Maurício, who is of a younger generation of musicians to emerge from the South Zone, described how the Pernambucan was a trail-blazer in self-management, quickly accruing what Jocelyne Guilbault has referred to as an "assemblage of practices, knowledges, and technologies"

(2007, 265): "Lenine was the first younger guy, besides the great icons, who was able to enter into the European markets that were opening—the whole WOMAD thing, events where you mix business with shows and music and everything. . . . He went at the right moment and had the intelligence and the characteristics to take advantage of this development. . . . I remember in 1999 he made a tour here that was covered by Mondomix [based in Paris] . . . which was just a little website then, like a blog. These guys filmed his whole tour and Lenine would send [clips] to us. So a few people like me and some of our friends saw this and said, 'Oh . . . look what is going on. What an interesting site.' Two years later Mondomix already had an electronic magazine, and today it is . . . an important reference." It is important, Maurício added, to recognize "people who have not been there quite as long as Caetano [Veloso] and [Gilberto] Gil." Lenine was as much "a connecting thread" as they, he felt, the kind of person who "pulls the level of the music higher": "He is a guy who carries the boat. Paulinho Moska once told me, 'Every time I hear an album of Lenine's, I sit at home the whole day and think, Porra, how is it that I didn't have this idea?' . . . Besides the fact that we could spend hours talking about his compositions, I think he . . . is conscious that he's not making the music just for himself . . . [that] it reverberates among artists, among the public . . . And I think he knows that he doesn't always get it right. It took him a long time to find [his voice]. This makes him more human."

Jocelyne Guilbault's study of the Trinidadian carnival music scene since the 1990s shows how musical activities there came to be viewed as "cultural capital to be managed as part of a market economy" in contrast with the more nation-building emphasis of earlier times (2007, 264–65). Emergent forms of cultural entrepreneurship, she writes, demonstrate "a profound understanding of the processes, both discursive and material, at work under neoliberalism" (265). At the same time, however, Maurício pointed out that Lenine did not always "get it right," that his becoming took several years. Indeed, Lenine's emergence as a singer-songwriter speaking from Pernambuco to the world owes much to his collaborations with Suzano, Chico Neves, and Tom Capone, among others. He had his "ideas about things," Lenine said, but mostly what he did was "agglutinate," bring people together to do all his work jointly. "What people take from life is human relations," he reflected, sounding less like a rational "neoliberal subject" than like a humanist cultural cannibal. More than a set of market-oriented policies imposed from without, neoliberalism is a "set of cultural meanings and practices related to the constitution of proper personhood, markets and the state that are emergent in a contested cultural field" (Kingfisher and Maskovsky 2008, 120).

Is there a political project in Lenine's work? Probably not one that can forcefully agitate for a transformation of class relations, but in terms of transforming the space of music production, Lenine was central to this group project in Rio de Janeiro in the late 1990s. The enemy, for these musicians, was the stifling of creative freedom, whether by xenophobic nationalism or by homogenizing market forces associated with multinational corporations and neoliberal capitalism. Lenine came into Chico Neves's life precisely at the moment the latter launched his project of "resistance" against the conventional music industry as he knew it, his "line of flight." Chico, for his part, incorporated technology into Lenine's sound, giving him his "magic carpet," as Maurício Pacheco put it.

3 PEDRO LUÍS AND THE WALL

TUPY ASTRONAUTS

At the same time that one has to exchange information and to mix, one must not allow genuine manifestations to be diluted, because these differences make for a good mixture.
—Pedro Luís, 26 May 1999

During a research trip to Rio de Janeiro in 2007 I stayed in an apartment located in what one local audio engineer, in reference to the proximity of a number of music recording and rehearsal facilities in this area, called the "nexus" of the South Zone music production scene. Most of this apartment (save the small bedroom in which I slept, the kitchen, and the bathroom) had been converted into a recording and mixing space called the MiniStereo Studio. Jointly owned by the guitarists and producers Junior Tostói (Lenine's collaborator) and Rodrigo Campello, both members of Vulgue Tostoi, MiniStereo Studio features a view of the Rodrigo de Freitas lake and Ipanema from one side; in the other direction, up a steep slope, is the Corcovado, with its iconic Christ Redeemer statue. Discretion is the code in this exclusive neighborhood, where many houses are barely visible behind high walls or gates. I erred one day by leaving the street-side kitchen window at MiniStereo slightly ajar when I went out. (Although the window did not offer a view into the recording spaces, my gracious host later remarked upon my oversight.)

On a bright August day, I walked a couple of hundred yards from the studio to the condominium of the singer-songwriter Pedro Luís, also in this hilltop neighborhood. Pedro made tea for us and we entered his small home studio to talk. Suddenly our conversation was interrupted by a loud whistling sound from the street below. "With the guest participation of the knife sharpener," Pedro joked, by way of pointing out that the sound was captured on the digital recorder I had just turned on to document our talk. It was the ambulatory sharpener's distinct call alerting the neighborhood to his presence. I looked out the window and saw an older man standing next to the sharpening wheel that he evidently managed to get up the hill (for it was unlikely that the man lived in this neighborhood). "We really wanted to use it on our first album," Pedro said. "But he asked for too much. We were paying people three hundred *reais* for each guest participation; he wanted fifteen hundred. . . . The knife sharpener was too much of a 'pop star' for us," Pedro chuckled.

This chapter focuses on Pedro and his band, known collectively as Pedro Luís e A Parede (Pedro Luís and The Wall), or PLAP (see figure 10). In May–June 1999, they were recording their second album, *É tudo 1 real* (Everything's a dollar), at the nearby studio Nas Nuvens. The facility is nestled among tropical trees at a remove from the street and behind a wall with a steel door that a receptionist unlocks after verifying via intercom a visitor's identity and the reason for his or her visit. The street is blocked to unauthorized traffic by a guarded gate. During breaks in PLAP's recording sessions at Nas Nuvens I conducted interviews with the band members and Liminha, their producer for part of this album, and co-owner of the facility. I also attended live shows of the band that year. During my subsequent visit in 2007, I conducted follow-up interviews with Pedro and the PLAP percussionist Sidon Silva, and I attended rehearsals, workshops, and shows of their parallel musical project, Monobloco.

The singer, songwriter, and guitarist Pedro Luís was among the musicians whom journalist Mário Marques identified as making what he called *música popular carioca*, or MPC, in a 1998 article for the *Globo* (see introduction). These artists, Marques suggested, sought to balance "the charms of the South Zone" with the "blemishes of the suburbs" in their lyrics (as if Rio's charms and blemishes were so neatly divisible). Pedro was the first to emerge from this group, he wrote, with PLAP's *Astronauta Tupy* (Tupy astro-

naut) of 1997. Another journalist represented Pedro Luís as a "voice of the street" who is interested in "the Rio that pulsates outside of the barred condominium windows" (Tinoco 1999). How did Pedro find his voice and sound, and how did he come to lead PLAP? How do this group's music and the views of its members on the central themes of this book shed light on Carioca identity and social relations, particularly through the key metaphors of pressure, *suingue*, *batucada*, mixture, and the "Tupy astronaut"? What was the influence on this band of the mangue beat scene and the newfound vogue for folkloric musical traditions of the Northeast? What is the relationship between manifestations of live music making and this group's trajectory as a pop-rock band that also, of course, produces studio albums? How did the members of PLAP hone their management skills?

As the only band profiled in this book, PLAP offers the opportunity to consider ensemble dynamics. Specifically, I discuss how the group conceptualized their shift away from the rock drum kit toward the use of Brazilian percussion as a key aspect of their stage show. In association with this shift, I examine the group's engagement with samba, which culminated in the success of the Monobloco project, a hybrid of samba instructional workshop, carnival bloco, pop stage show, and recording ensemble that the members of PLAP founded and continue to run. PLAP's approach

FIGURE 10. Pedro Luís e A Parede. Photograph by
Guito Moreto, 2010. Used by permission.

to ensemble playing bears comparison with Charles Keil's preference for music that is full of "participatory discrepancies" (PDs), music that prioritizes process, groove, texture, and timbral heterogeneity over the "deferred gratification" of melodic-harmonic tensions (1987, 1995, 2002a, 2002b). For PLAP, the desire to "lay a groove in that eternal search for the perfect mantra," as the band's bassist, Mário Moura, put it during our interview, to perform with suingue (swing), to affirm "life-groove-play-party-pleasure-joy in the here and now" (Keil 2002b, 40), and to get their hands on as many acoustic instruments as they could took them deeper and deeper into discrepantly participatory forms of music making, and into samba especially. Their latest album, *Ponto enredo*, produced by Lenine, is in fact a pop tribute to the "sacredness" of samba and Afro-diasporic traditions.

Like Keil, the members of PLAP speak of the alienating and dehumanizing effects of market forces and globalization. They too have looked to musical forms that emerged in working-class communities for participatory inspiration. But there are also distinctly local dynamics of race, class, place, and nation that contour their musical practices. Mixture, as a method for increasing musical heterogeneity, can itself be thought of as a kind of discrepant way for PLAP—and other musicians in this scene—to participate in globalization, and they have a lot to say about it. Keil's dichotomous and intensely personal theorization of PDs through what he unabashedly refers to as a "Black vs. West" dialectic (2002a, 146; see Gaunt 2002 for a thoughtful critique) renders "groovology" an engaging but problematic framework for analysis, perhaps especially when taken out of the context of the United States, not to mention out of the "wild" (Keil 2002a, 142) and into the recording studio.

Also concerned with the distinctive dynamics of participatory music making, Thomas Turino (2008) proposes a framework of *fields* in which live performance practices are contrasted with recorded music making. He divides the former into the participatory field, in which all present take part in the performance or at least are free to do so if they wish (basically either in a musical role or as a dancer; Turino acknowledges inspiration from Keil for this one), and the "presentational," in which a clear distinction between musicians and the audience is drawn. The fields associated with recording practices are divided into those in which the role of technology is primarily oriented toward the capture of acoustically performed sounds—"high-fidelity" recording (more specifically, in which aesthetics of liveness influence the way sounds are recorded)—and those in which the relationship to live participatory music making is largely severed—"studio audio art." This typology can be helpful for sorting out some of the social values at stake in the developments examined in this chapter. In theory, each field of cultural production has value for those acting in it (although it is clear that Turino himself places highest value on participatory music making), and a given musical setting may draw from more than one field or may shift among them as values and goals change.

PLAP did not negate rock, pop, or technology in favor of live acoustic group music making, as Keil might prefer (nor have they ignored melodic-harmonic tension, especially on their most recent album). Rather, they found new ways to allow live and mediated (that is, recorded) fields of musicking to enrich each other. The "pressure" or "heaviness" of rock music in the 1970s was a strong attraction for these musicians during their youth, and as adults they called upon aspects of that sound in their project to invigorate Brazilian pop music. The samba schools also had that pressure, they felt, owing to the intense volume and full sound generated when so many drummers—sometimes over two hundred—perform together. "What is more rock and roll than a samba school?" PLAP drummer C. A. Ferrari asked me rhetorically. "What rocker," he said, "if you put him in the middle of a samba school, wouldn't be impressed with the sound?" The band describes their music as "batucada with rock 'n' roll pressure" (batucada typically refers to the percussion-driven grooves of Rio samba; it derives from batuque, an old generic term for Afro-Brazilian dance and drumming; see, e.g., Cascudo 1999, 58–59). This dual articulation also distinguishes their efforts from the middle-class phenomenon of revivalism that Tamara Livingston (1999) has described (such as the comparatively more tradition-oriented choro scene in Rio), or that Turino has found in old-time music and dance (2008, 155–88), even while the members of PLAP do value the preservation of musical traditions.

Turino's categories of musical practices thus usefully point to the specific goals that different spheres of music making may realize; however, his schematic (presented in a table as a continuum from participatory to studio audio art [2008, 90–91]) also seems to posit competing values as already constituted rather than emergent—as representing specific, primary, and theoretically incompatible ideals of which subjects are aware and to which they consciously aspire (even though Turino grants that these fields are not necessarily mutually exclusive). The examples of PLAP and the associated Monobloco project, I believe, reveal a richly complex web—a rhizome, perhaps—of sometimes competing, sometimes complementary, and often ambiguous values, goals, and contingencies that may or may not coalesce into "lines of flight" (and that sometimes generate failure) but that in any case present social "cartographies," to use Deleuze's term. In their clarity, Turino's terms serve as guideposts of specific musical-aesthetic mappings, but there is also more going on, or sometimes not going on, despite individuals' desires. And there is a messiness to things.

Pedro's Early Listening and Music Making

Pedro Luís Teixeira de Oliveira was born in Rio in 1960 to a Carioca father and a Portuguese mother who lived in a middle-class community in the Tijuca neighborhood. He grew up with eight siblings and described his childhood home as full of music, including regular singing and guitar playing, as well as listening to classical music, MPB, North American pop, and rock on radio stations such as Radio Tamoio AM, Radio Nacional FM, and Radio Eldorado FM. Radio Eldorado FM, he recalled, played progressive rock such as Yes and Led Zeppelin in the early 1970s. Pedro was attracted to the "big" sound of these bands, but especially "the sonority, the grooves, the instrumental pressure" of the English band Deep Purple: "It was heavy rock 'n' roll played really well, and well recorded. . . . Here in Brazil, good recording did not exist at the time . . . and this hormonal energy of the adolescent went very well with that heavy sound, a kind of masculine energy, you know. So it was the combination of these things— good execution, the heaviness, and good recording—that impressed us."[1] Live local music making, however, was equally important to Pedro's musical foundation. There were neighborhood guitar players and carnival blocos to be heard on his street, and his home was near the morro where one of Rio's major samba schools, Salgueiro, is located.

At school Pedro sang in choirs, including Cobra Coral (Choral Snake), which earned some notice after appearing on television and recording an independent album. With high school friends he formed his first group, Meio-Fio (Curb), in which he sang and played guitar. In the early 1980s, as the rock scene was taking shape among middle-class youths in Rio, Pedro formed a band called Urge, which mixed rock with samba rhythms and with the viola caipira steel-stringed guitar associated with rural musical traditions. He was also part of an ensemble called Paris 400, which provided the music for an experimental theater troupe called Asdrúbal Trouxe o Trombone (Asdrúbal Brought the Trombone). In the 1990s he began to take on the role of musical director of local groups, such as the wacky pop ensemble Boato (Rumor).[2] For a run of shows at a new restaurant in the South Zone, Pedro put together a cover band with Arícia Mess as lead singer, Mário Moura on bass, C. A. Ferrari on drums, and Sidon Silva on percussion (with repertoire from artists such as Sade, the Beatles, Aretha Franklin, and Etta James). The instrumentalists in this ensemble began developing a conceptualization of what they call batucada, giving new meaning to this general term for Afro-Brazilian drumming by applying it specifically to, as Mário put it, the practice of "using percussion not as an effect," but instead placing it "in the front line, driving the sound together with the guitar and bass."[3]

When Pedro was subsequently invited to perform at an experimental poetry event, he utilized this group (minus Arícia, for whom he substituted as lead singer). They continued experimenting with the sound of batucada, but their repertoire focused on Pedro's original compositions.[4] The drummer and percussionist Celso Alvim also joined them. As a teacher at a local school (ProArt), Celso had systematized into study guides rhythms from genres such as maracatu, samba, and maculelê (a Bahian dance). His expertise complemented the band's developing idea of "taking the drum kit apart and having three drummers performing the lows, mids, and highs," that is, distinct parts distributed into specific frequency ranges, analogous to Marcos Suzano's interest in adapting to his pop music performances the general contours of the arrangement of percussive sounds in the Afro-Brazilian Candomblé practice.

Batucada and The Wall

PLAP's instrumentation, C. A. Ferrari explained, was inspired by the forró trio of the zabumba bass drum, triangle, and accordion; by the marching of the samba percussion corps (*baterias*) in carnival; and finally by rock, in the sense that it was functionally related to the "power trio" of electric bass, drum kit, and guitar, but elaborated by five musicians instead. An additional motivation for breaking the rock drum kit apart and instead using three percussionists pertained to showmanship: they wanted the entire group to be able to move around the stage and dance, following the traditional practice of the bandas de pífano of the Northeast. When, at the rehearsal for the aforementioned poetry event, Pedro asked the band members to line up on the stage at the end of the show "like a wall," the band found its name. Celso Alvim and C. A. Ferrari elaborated on their approach to instrumentation and performance.

> CA: When you take the drum kit apart, if you are thinking in a Brazilian manner, the low frequencies will end up on . . . the zabumba or the surdo. So we began to work with these timbres, with these drums, and we began discovering the nuances within this arrangement. The zabumba has x possibility, the various sizes of surdo too have different timbres, different sounds. You cannot play phrases with a surdo [tuned] very low. It's more for making long notes, for example, for marking the first beat of a bar. For a surdo that cuts more [i.e., that can improvise rhythmic variations], you can tune it a bit higher . . . to have less resonance, and you discover that there are things that function well for getting a good sound out of that particular surdo, playing it lightly, [while for] other things, you need to bang it hard. And that's how it started and it became a characteristic of our sound.

> FM: [So] with the drum kit you have one person playing the various parts, but in this instance you have more bodies, more people, each one with a specific part.

> CA: Yeah, we even joke that there were three drummers but only one job opening, so we wrote a percussion arrangement to employ the three of us [laughs]. . . . But it is not just about reproducing the drum kit.

> CAF: No drummer has six arms.

> CA: Yeah . . . we create some grooves that go beyond this idea of just breaking down the drum kit. There is also the thing of sections, a section of surdos, which has a sound that a single surdo doesn't have, or even if you record in several separate channels one person playing the three surdo parts, it just won't have the same sound as recording five people together and on five different drums. So we use the idea of the section a lot.

> CAF: The proportional "out-of-tune-ness" of one drum to another creates a different kind of tuning that only that section playing together will have—the interferences of one instrument with another.

> FM: And this is something you look for?

CA: It is what already exists, for example, in a samba school, that effect of the collectivity—*massaroca*, we call it, not just in the samba school, in various other things. You can even see the way the people from samba record, everyone together in the room, and it has that massaroca, the sound of one invading the sound of another. So we incorporate this dirtiness, and it's a characteristic of our sound.

For music "to be personally involving and socially valuable," Keil wrote when he introduced his concept of PDs, it "must be 'out of time' and 'out of tune'" (1987, 275). Clearly, the percussionists were talking about the same phenomenon here.[5]

It is noteworthy, however, that the members of PLAP were seeking some of the "dirtiness" of samba percussion performance around the same time that in Brazil's premier samba recording studio (Companhia dos Técnicos), also in Rio de Janeiro, the producers of the annual carnival samba album sought precisely to edit out certain elements associated with the massaroca (a word that suggests the sound of "the masses," say, at a soccer game or at carnival) of the live event in their efforts to reach radio audiences for pagode samba and sell more albums. In the latter case, the producers were concerned that *too much* sonic "dirtiness" or "mess" would make the CD less marketable; PLAP, on the other hand, wanted some of what they regarded as the sonic grit of the collectivity who live, play music, and dance in greater proximity than what is typical of the comparatively privatized, gated spaces of the more privileged areas of the South Zone. In effect, this case approaches—from sort of the opposite direction—the same "schismogenetically mimetic" dynamic I analyzed in "The Disc Is Not the Avenue" (2005), wherein "the avenue" was the metaphor the samba producers used to index the participatory live carnival event, and the disc (that is, the CD) symbolized a commercial product for radio airplay (although there are some differences in the kinds of "dirtiness" and "messiness" that were at stake in the different settings).

Mário Moura elaborated further on the band's choice of instrumentation for the batucada. The kick drum in a rock kit is a dry sound, but the surdo, he said, pounding his fist on his breast, "beats much more here in the chest because of its resonance." C. A., he continued, plays the first and second surdo parts from samba, "boom, boom, boom, boom," in which the two drums, usually tuned an interval of a fifth apart and one generally larger than the other, alternate the two downbeats in duple meter. In some instances, depending on how a given instrument in the batucada is played, the band member may have a hand free to strike something else, multiplying the timbres and rhythmic accents. Sidon's "gigantic hi-hat" and snare drum, and Celso's various tin cans helped "fill in the spaces."

PLAP also integrate unconventional instruments (as well as traditional ones used in unconventional ways) into their concept of batucada. They like to use instruments, Pedro said, that can handle their way of playing loudly, with "limited technique," and with a "heavy hand." Inspired in part by the guru of Brazilian improvisatory music Hermeto Pascoal—who is known to play music on anything—the percussionists in PLAP utilize objects such as hoes, hubcaps, metal signs, a piece of the floor from a bus, and a beer keg that they brought back from Japan. They saw their project as partly building on the work of Marcos Suzano, Jovi Joviniano, and Carlos Negreiros in their percussion ensemble Baticum (see chapter 1), and of Chico Science and Nação Zumbi in Recife. Another aspect of their batucada pertains to the use of natural drumheads instead of the manufactured nylon ones that have become standard in samba drum corps. "The sound of the skin is *very* special," Mário reflected. "It sounds different, it sounds more alive, maybe it has more of the spirit of the animal that the skin comes from, I don't know, but something cool happens [*rola uma bossa*]. You play a pandeiro with nylon and then one with cowhide, you *feel* a difference there . . . and this is reflected in the sound."

The ensemble also often regards the batuque of what Pedro is playing on the violão as more important than the specific notes. It was as if Pedro were playing a pandeiro at times, Mário explained, rather than the guitar. This emphasis on batucada left the harmonic dimension of the music less fleshed out; Mário tries to bridge rhythm and harmony on the bass while finding a distinct sonic place for it relative to the surdo. This requires a different approach from playing with a drum kit, as it is more like "playing with three drummers." Moreover, since the surdo and the bass can sound very similar when played simultaneously, the group conceptualizes either the surdo in front of the arrangement with the bass responding to it or the inverse. The idea was sort of like "I am where you are not," Mário noted, echoing a practice typical of funk arrangements. Using a five-string instrument with an additional string below the customary four, Mário likes to keep his bass parts very low in the pitch range. "I like the fifth string too much," he admitted. "I'd even take the other four off." Not interested in soloing, Mário was into *groove*. It could be two notes, he said, "but you can play them for three days without stopping."

Suingue

Christiane Gerischer (2006) analyzed the "microrhythmic phrasing" of samba and Candomblé drumming that she recorded in Bahia, seeing these as a form of participatory discrepancy. Using computer software and Nazir Jairazbhoy's NUTS system of notating time durations (Jairazbhoy 1983), she demonstrated how percussionists do not articulate four even subdivisions ("pulses," typically sixteenth notes) of the steady downbeats but instead generally shorten the second pulse (or sixteenth note) and lengthen, especially, the fourth one that anticipates the next downbeat. This, combined with the fact that there are temporal micro-variations between the various percussion parts as well, creates the *suingue baiano*, the swing of Bahia. Over the years, I have heard musicians in Rio de Janeiro articulate a similar idea. One such discussion occurred when I interviewed the members of PLAP about their song "Caio no suingue" (I fall into the swing), to which I return in the following pages. The carioca rhythmic suingue is sometimes explained in terms of a kind of compromise (in a neutral sense) between quadruple and triple subdivisions of the beat.

According to Celso Alvim, this phenomenon occurred when the band recorded the song "Menina bonita" (Pretty girl), on PLAP's second album. They recorded an initial loop of caixa, surdo, and pandeiro, but when they tried to quantize it on the computer—that is, to lock the live tracks to an evenly subdivided digital pulse—they found that the groove did not correspond to a triplet or to a sixteenth-note pulse (assuming a quarter-note beat). "It's in between, in the middle," he observed, "but it is right there. That is what works in that moment." Thus, C. A. added, it is what happens in between two notes that is important for the swing. "In the space in between there is a variation that is neither this nor that [*ninguem de ninguem*]," he said. "It is the territory in between the two," Celso added. "It's not sixteenth–eighth–sixteenth, nor is it triplets. . . . You take a guy from samba who never studied music . . . someone of the people, that's what you get. That's the accent of the sixteenth note in Brazil." He had observed this phenomenon in the drumming at a Candomblé ritual he attended and in the tamborim (a small frame drum) patterns of the large samba school baterias.[6]

More metaphorically, C. A. described suingue as a "breath," and every place, every person, and every kind of music as having "its own breathing." Two people might play the same two notes in the same place, "but the distance between them will be interpreted differently. . . . Each person interprets silence differently." Sidon offered a different interpretation of suingue as a woman walking down the street *sambando* (i.e., moving in a samba rhythm). "That's where the suingue is," C. A. concurred, and indeed, if the "heavy" sound of rock and batucada tends to be associated with an aggressive masculinity, suingue may bear connotations of the female body and feminine sexuality in Rio. The bassist Mário Moura introduced yet another metaphor that he associated with suingue: "You have to have a certain *malandragem* to have suingue," he said, "and to be a *malandro*, you've got to have suingue," referring to the rogue-like archetype featured in many of the classic sambas of the 1930s and 1940s. It means being savvy. "It's . . . knowing how to arrive in any place, any kind of environment," Sidon added, while C. A. affirmed that malandragem is "knowing how to get along with various types of people, the idea of knowing how to deal with any kind of situation," because there is "always a big mixture of people."

If some of this seems vague, it is worth noting that Gerischer's interviewees in Bahia spoke in similar terms (for example, that what one does with one's body between articulations on an instrument is important, similar to C. A.'s idea of breath). As an ensemble, PLAP prizes this kind of suingue and the associated syncopations (on offbeat sixteenth notes, what Gerischer refers to as "double-time off beats"): it was precisely what had been *removed* from the commercial pagode popular at the time, Pedro thought. "Everything's on top of the beat, there's not a single syncopation," he exaggerated. "And that's it for the samba." Of course, some people might disagree with Pedro on this matter, including several of those interviewed by Gerischer, but the point here is that PLAP felt they were tapping into a kind of "authentic" Brazil they saw threatened by vulgar commodification symbolized by the massive sales that pagode was garnering. The concept of suingue, in sum, speaks to how syncopations are articulated and beats subdivided in music in ways that suggest physical movement, but also more metaphorically in the local context as a kind of ability to use to one's advantage the indeterminacy or ambiguity that may arise in social "mixing," or that inhabits the (musical) middle ground. As Prögler concluded about swing in jazz, it is about "participation and play, about 'touch' and feeling your way" (1995, 50).[7]

While suingue and the discrepant grooves of participatory music making can be talked about cross-culturally, the members of PLAP framed their broader musical methodology in relation to the established national discourses. Pedro called his music "absurdly mixed" and reprised the assertion that this is a cultural tradition that goes back to the arrival of the Europeans and the beginnings of Brazilian miscegenation. "What is most Brazilian is already mixed," he said, and he stated flatly that his is "the country of mixture." I wondered if the band members had familial connections with the Northeast, and our discussion about what parts of Brazil their parents were from demonstrates the tendency to talk at an "embodied level," as Peter Wade found in Colombia, of how individuals are constituted in terms of "blood" and heritage, and to conceptualize "personal traits and abilities" such as musicality in terms of a racialized (or ethnicized) view of history (2004, 362). After C. A. Ferrari noted that his family was from the Northeast, Sidon Silva joined in the conversation to say that his mother was from the state of Goiás, and his father from Alagoas ("the land of musician Hermeto Pascoal").

> CA: My grandmother was also from Alagoas, and the father of my mother from Bahia. The father of my father is from Minas Gerais. And my great-grandmother was [Amer-] Indian and married a Dutchman. My other great-grandmother . . . married an Italian immigrant. That is to say, it is mixture from way back.
>
> SS: Miscegenation. Brazil is all about this. It is all mixed race.
>
> CA: There does not exist a pure race in Brazil.
>
> SS: We are mongrels [vira-lata]. . . . And we are all Carioca, in this band.

Such talk may evoke well-trod narratives about Brazilian national culture (with Rio as a kind of epicenter of mixture, and with difference simultaneously preserved), but it also serves as a basic framework through which to rationalize the band's fusions not as radical breaks with the past but rather as perfectly consistent with what—in their view and in mainstream discourse—it means to be Brazilian. As such, it seems to have taken on heightened significance in the mid- to late 1990s as subjects found themselves increasingly anxious about the potential pitfalls of processes of globalization. That is to say, mixing elements of local or national cultural practices (such as timbral, textural, processual, and performative PDs from forró or samba) into the kinds of presentational pop-rock forms that Thomas Turino calls "cosmopolitan" (2000; 2008) provides a counterbalance to potentially alienating or homogenizing forces of (neoliberal) globalization. It remains important, Pedro said, "for you to have your national pride in order to preserve your characteristics and territory" from the economically powerful countries that have tended to exercise more control over cultural flows. There is so much information available through the communications media, and if you lack consciousness of where you live, of your culture, Celso added, "your identity may disappear." One might think of oneself "as a citizen of the world," he cautioned, but one can end up "not being from anywhere."

Since this act of preservation—resistance, if you will—was accomplished through purposeful mixture, it was possible "to preserve the particular stories of your life" without rancor or the kind of xenophobia that holds that if you use an electric guitar, it is no longer Brazilian music, Pedro said, referencing a debate going back to the Jovem Guarda and Tropicália movements of the 1960s. Had music from the United States "colonized" the world? I asked the percussionists. "Totally," Celso affirmed. "And I think it's a great thing," C. A. cheerfully added as he fell back—although with a degree of irony—on some stereotypes about cultural production in Brazil and the United States.

CAF: Americans have such discipline when it comes to music—not just in music but in everything. . . . But there is a bunch of good stuff here [too], which is our tribal music, without any discipline at all, extremely rustic, intuitive, [which we] ally with the discipline of American music, man. We ourselves make a music that is . . . completely filled with American music. . . . You mix good things from all over the place . . .

CA: This whole process also has to do with you knowing what it is you want. In our case, it is mixture; we are not interested in playing samba in a traditional way, or in playing funk completely American. It is precisely this mixture—

CAF: Because we play both things badly [laughter]. So we play somewhat bad samba, with somewhat bad rock, and it's already something else, understand?[8]

As noted previously, Chico Science and his band Nação Zumbi (CSNZ) were central to the process of reestablishing national pride among middle-class youths who, we might argue, had become alienated from Brazilian music during the 1980s, when rock predominated, and disillusioned with inept and corrupt politics in the early 1990s. PLAP certainly saw their project as building on the momentum sparked by CSNZ and the so-called mangue beat. (There is some similarity in the band names.) If CSNZ "discovered that hip-hop has everything to do with maracatu," C. A. pointed out, PLAP found that "rock 'n' roll has everything to do with samba schools." The point is that Chico Science "*researched this space in between* . . . [and] knew very well how to translate" (my emphasis). Specifically, they "opened the ears" of middle-class youths to folkloric genres like forró, baião, carimbó, *bumba-meu-boi* (a folk tale of the North and Northeast that is performed to music), ciranda, and maracatu—which they may previously have regarded as signs of underdevelopment—placed "in the middle of pop music."[9]

As part of their own research the percussionists recorded some of the rhythms from the music performed at an Umbanda ritual (similar to Candomblé, but more common in Rio de Janeiro and southern Brazil). They utilized part of this recording on the track "Cabôco," which ends their first album. ("Cabôco" refers to an Amerindian spirit in Umbanda, also written as *caboclo*.) For that track, the percussionists "sought to produce something closer to the authentic story," Celso explained. PLAP did things mixed, he said, but with a sense of the contexts in which specific musical genres emerged: "When I speak about what I know about Candomblé, I mean a specific person, Mestre Caboclinho, with whom I studied, who played Candomblé during a certain period in Rio de Janeiro. [If someone says], 'Ah, you know about maracatu,' [what I know is] Nacão Pernambuco, who are some guys from Recife who play maracatu today. . . . It's necessary for you to specify exactly what it is so that people begin to situate things. . . . If you have the notion of where each thing comes from in the history, you can situate what it is that you are hearing." Bearing in mind this understanding of a certain kind of authenticity as historically and socially contingent rather than fixed, C. A. affirmed of his band: "We don't play authentic samba, we don't play authentic forró, we don't play authentic rock." Yet there is an authenticity in their project of "being real," of saying, "I like this, this is my reality." For Sidon, "good music" is music "made from the heart," not, he implied, invented for the market.

This concept of authenticity is like the one developed by Turino in *Music* as *Social Life*, where he describes how "given practices that serve as signs of identity may be understood as authentic when they are the result of habits that are actually part of the person producing those signs," or, in the Peircean terminology that Turino uses, as "dicent articulations of the distinct cultural positions of participants" (2008, 161–62). Although Turino notes that this kind of argument can be used "to justify cultural appropriation, where members of dominant groups take up the traditions of less powerful groups and alternately claim them as their own," this risk is "partially alleviated . . . precisely by being clear about the nature of the tradition being performed" (162), as the members of PLAP were in our conversation.

The image of the Tupy astronaut, which would be the title of PLAP's first album (and the title of one of Pedro's songs, released on their second album), illustrates Pedro's approach to musical research and mixture. The Tupy were the indigenous group that populated the area that became Rio de Janeiro state, and that have been mythologized as quintessential cannibals of the Other. The idea was to pair the most advanced technologies of discovery with this kind of ur-anthropophagist to suggest "a being who is an explorer of a contemporary space," but who also looks to "foundations" for creative inspiration. The Tupy astronaut can thus be understood as an updated riff on Oswald de Andrade's modernist cannibal of the late 1920s, previously adapted by the Tropicália musicians in the late 1960s. Indeed, Pedro's song "Seres Tupy" (Tupy beings), from that first album, specifically evokes Andrade's line from his "Cannibalist Manifesto": "Tupy, or not tupy that is the question." (Pedro's version is equally existential, but it introduces the problem of poverty as a dehumanizing force: "Beings or not beings / That is the question / . . . / From Porto Alegre to Acre / Poverty just changes its accent.") Even in 2007 the image of the Tupy astronaut still framed Pedro's work: "It is my motivation. Whatever project I am involved with will have this as one of its bases. Such research is inspiring . . . in terms of what is traditional, as well as contemporary manifestations. . . . I have a messy, nonlinear background—I went to two universities and didn't finish either. I studied literature and music, both of them only halfway. So in reality my salvation is research, to search at the sources, and in goingson [*acontecimentos*]. And not necessarily in music—it can be in literature, in cinema. . . . But the research is fundamental, although it is not formal." Before discussing the Monobloco project, which was still more participatory, I turn to the recorded fields.

For their first album, *Astronauta Tupy* (Tupy astronaut), released in 1997 on the independent label Dubas Música, PLAP played all the basic tracks live as an ensemble in the recording studio, and then "built a structure on top of that" without knowing "where things would go," Mário Moura explained. "The idea was to capture that mess that we did in shows," he added, "capture it electronically, and transfer that to a CD." This description matches what Turino would label a high-fidelity recording, wherein "what is worked out for live performance influences what is recorded" (2008, 68). Stated in a more technical manner, in the field of high fidelity, recording practices are organized around an ideology that favors a representational relationship between live performance and the *signs of liveness* in the resulting studio sound (a relationship of *dicent* in Peircean terminology [Turino 2008, 67]).[10]

However, the transition to album was not merely one of capturing the band's live sound; there was also the building of the "structure on top of that." Their producer was Tom Capone, whom I introduced in the previous chapter; they recorded at AR Studios. Band members knew him before he became an executive at Warner Music because Mário Moura had played bass in his short-lived rock group Rotnitxe; they had become close friends. Tom was able to *seduce* "a structure like Warner," Pedro believed, because he could release more adventurous albums alongside comparatively mainstream recordings (such as Maria Rita's first CD, which received several Grammy nominations). Tom was "deft with the modern languages of recording and mixing"; in fact, he had a reputation in this scene for exploring "the extremes of each piece of equipment, of each technological resource," in Pedro's words. (Tom claimed that the first thing he would do with any device he bought was throw away the manual.) He would show up at recording sessions, "drop a grenade, and then leave," Pedro recalled, meaning that Tom would make comments that made the band members "look at things differently" and take the sound "in another direction" as they embraced the creative possibilities of studio work, in contrast to the presentational priorities of the live setting.[11]

Tom taught the musicians in PLAP how to translate their "presentational" performance with its aspects of "participatory" aesthetics into the pop-rock album format by settling them into a characteristic and more consistent sound *as a band* on the recorded medium, and by introducing them to the world of studio technology (without moving them into the field of "studio audio art," which, in Turino's conception, describes "recorded music that is patently a studio form with no suggestion or expectation that it should or even could be performed live in real time" [2008, 78]). Importantly, Tom did this without "exercising power" over the band but instead working with them on offbeat ideas. While most recording label executives are "very bureaucratic, or technicians, or economists," Pedro complained, Tom was a skilled musician and producer who also happened to understand "the commercial mechanism" very well. He represented for the members of PLAP a subject who could navigate the music industry and the market without surrendering his ability to act as a creative agent, and who had control over the technology that he manipulated. He alleviated potential anxieties about the commodification and commercialization of their project, recognizing band members' desires instead of crudely imposing industry priorities. This experience, however, altered the way PLAP approached live performance, reinforcing the interdependence between the two domains of music making.

The song "Caio no suingue" from this album is a fine example of the band's pop batucada. It begins with the driving rhythms of caixas with surdo punctuation in a samba-reggae hybrid groove (similar to the samba-reggae popular in Salvador, Bahia), and it does indeed have the "pressure" of rock to the extent that the sound of "the wall" is loud, "tight" (i.e., "compressed," in audio terminology, or electronically limited to a dynamic range that is kept at a high volume), and in the front plane of the mix. It is "in your face," if you will. There is also a "rocked-out" break in the middle that abandons the samba-reggae groove and adds distorted electric guitar. Lyrically, the song emphasizes the melodic refrain: "I fall into swing to console myself / You know this life is not easy/ I do this to hang on," while the verses are essentially rapped. Arícia Mess joins Pedro for an assertive rapping of the repeat of the verses, while a call-and-response section at the end of the song between Pedro's sung repetition of the refrain and a shouted counterpart from the band members adds to the sense of pressure. The lyrics describe the song as a funk "shot from a cannon," a "burst from a machine gun," to announce that Brazil is being "ambushed" by "the most unjust division." Although the song does not specify, it seems evident that Pedro means social divisions and inequality. His protest, Pedro sings, is in the form of a prayer: "Ave Mother, children, cousins / Spirits that inhabit the planet / Make your vote, write verses, get an attitude / To change things, because it's gotten really bad."

Suingue here indexes, first of all, the samba-reggae-like groove, full of the kinds of PDs Gerischer described for suingue baiano, but also the corporeal meanings associated with, as Mário Moura put it, "the swing of the swaying (*balanço*), the *suingue brasileira*." In fact, when it came time to film a video for the song, they exploited the sexual meaning of the term "swing." In the video the musicians appear nude (with their genitals covered by musical instruments, such as a hubcap for percussion), along with dozens of their friends, also naked. (The idea for this approach came from the video director.) They dance around, bump into each other, roll and writhe on the floor to suggest "swingers," but there is nothing overtly sexual about the imagery. Indeed, there are also naked children playing and a mother nursing a baby. It is the mother, the children, the cousins, and the spirits that inhabit the planet, exposed in their bodily diversity (although most of the bodies are rather light skinned). It was not, Mário specified, an erotic clip, "except for the eroticism that the body itself maintains." It was a "naturalist" video, in which the "nudity has an aesthetic function." [12] What was this function? Could it have been a kind of "falling" into Keil's "life-groove-play-party-pleasure-joy in the here and now" (2002b, 40), into humanistic participation as a form of consolation?

The track "Tudo vale a pena" (Everything is worth it), which Pedro co-composed with Fernanda Abreu, is a laid-back, shuffled, bluesy two-chord vamp, with Fernanda as a guest singer. The lyrics describe the happiness, musicality, and suingue that Pedro believed coexisted with poverty in Rio de Janeiro. Rio was experiencing a civil war, he lamented, "between the traffickers and the rest of the population." Yet even so, it was not Kosovo. It was not Yugoslavia in 1999, he said, when the war was raging there, where ethnic divisions were "so deeply rooted that sometimes the people don't even know why they're fighting." Rio is a city of "almost mythical" poverty, Pedro sings in the song, of heat and struggle that are partly offset by the festive nature of a people who love to fall into samba, to dance funk, who have suingue even in the way they look, and in the groove in their step. "Who thinks that there aren't treasures in the favela" or that "misery doesn't smile?" the lyrics ask rhetorically. "You see so much beauty too," Pedro said, "and sometimes the poverty seems lighter."

The refrain "Everything is worth it / your soul is not small" plays on the words of the celebrated Portuguese poet Fernando Pessoa (1888–1935). In Pessoa's "Mar português" ("Portuguese Sea"), the poet wrote, "Tudo vale a pena / se a alma não é pequena," that is, "Everything is worth it / if the soul is not small." The songwriters altered "*se a* alma" ("if the soul") to "*sua* alma" ("your soul"), which is phonetically similar but changes the meaning to an affirmation: "Your saints are strong / I love your smile / South Zone or North Zone / your rhythm is necessary / So everything is worth it, your soul is not small." These lyrics potentially expose Pedro to the criticism that he has an overly rosy view of working-class life in Brazil. However, such a reading seems facile; he is obviously aware that his experience of Rio is radically different from that of the city's poorest citizens, and that he cannot speak *for* the working classes. Without discounting Pedro's own class position, the lyrics can be read as affirming Rio's ability to swing during a period when the media dwelled on the rising violence, drug trafficking, and hardship of life in the favelas (and the threat that these posed to middle-class citizens).[13]

Another song, "Pena da vida" (Life sentence), is a criticism of the death penalty. It is an older song that Pedro performed with his band Urge and with Arícia Mess, and it became a kind of standard in the South Zone music scene as various other bands in Rio also performed it. (It even became a hit in Japan in 1998 after PLAP toured there.) In PLAP's version, this song is treated as a rowdy rock-funk with an almost shouted call-and-response between Pedro and the band members on the refrains, a "wah-wah" effect on the guitar, and the Hammond B3 organ (performed by the guest musician Maurício Barros) adding a gospel-like dimension to this mini-manifesto. "I am in favor of the life sentence," Pedro sings. A convicted criminal should "go to jail and pay dearly" but "pay alive." PLAP's music was not precisely activist (*engajada*), Celso noted in one of our interviews, but the group shared a general concern with improving conditions of living, working, and human relations.

Cleaning up the Pressure with Liminha

For their second album, *É tudo 1 real*, which is the one they were working on when I first interviewed members of the band, they recorded at Nas Nuvens with Liminha. By now, the band had "a more commercial objective," Mário observed at the time, and PLAP arrived in the studio with various ideas for the recording. How would this "more commercial" project be executed? With Liminha producing, the musicians discerned that their sound still had "a lot of pressure," Mário said, but it was "a clean pressure." With Tom, by contrast, "it was a dirty pressure, with more noise, more impurity." Neither was better, Mário diplomatically added; they were just different. So the new sound was less messy? I asked him. "A certain messiness is always present in our work," he reflected, but now it was "a very organized mess." It was clean, more commercial, "oriented to people who may not have understood the first album." It was aimed less at the Carioca public and sought instead "to take the things that are part of our local language and translate them for a larger audience."

The band was still in the process of making the album when this interview took place. Later it became clear that there were differences of opinion between PLAP and Liminha, who is known as a kind of "hit maker" of Brazilian pop, and Mário's responses to my questions about their new sound tiptoed around this issue. Liminha trained in the recording studios of Los Angeles, where he lived in the late 1980s. By the late 1990s, however, many of the younger bands in Brazil were looking for a different sound; they tended to disfavor the famously "clean" and well-behaved productions that had come to be associated with Los Angeles, with their reputation for technical perfection. Tom's work, by contrast, was inspired more by indie rock, grunge, and various "heavy" or "dirty" sounds. Liminha ended up leaving the project after producing eight of the twelve tracks, while Tom finished the remainder at his home studio. With Liminha, then, PLAP seemed to reach a kind of limit as to how far they were willing to "clean up" their sound for mainstream radio airplay.

In a press release, the guitarist Laura Campanér wrote of the album: "Sonic mass. Tons of bass. Hardness of the Walls. Batuque. Movement. Accelerated rhythm of the dance. Regurgitation of raw sentences." É tudo 1 real, she wrote, is rap, charme (a kind of Brazilian R&B), maracatu, axé, and hard funk (funk porrada). It is "rock with pinches of Olodum" (the Salvador-based samba-reggae band); it is "a refrain that sticks in your ear" and "social critique with an invitation to forget" (1999). That is to say, a radical aesthetic of mixture—even in some of the lyrics—with prominent doses of northeastern rhythms, rock, and the funk carioca grooves that would, in the following decade, circulate way beyond the local context. The title track opens the album with what seems to be a field recording of vendors at a street fair shouting about various goods for sale and chanting, "Um real! Um real!" ("One dollar!"). The song is a half-shouted funk-rap about a vendor of batteries, cassette tapes, crackers, peanut fudge, pumpkin sweets, coconut sweets, clock radios, and so forth, featuring a catchy choral chant at the end: "Water, limes, chocolate, one dollar, pah!" The second track, "Menina bonita" (Pretty girl, by Pedro Luís, Cabelo, and Alexandre Brasil), by contrast, begins with a mellow R&B groove (evoking the charme genre) with hints of forró in the triangle part and in some of the rhythmic accents, over which Pedro raps the lyrics. The band even recorded a version for the Japanese market with the refrain translated.

The track "Brasileiro em Tóquio" (Brazilian in Tokyo), a collaboration between Pedro and Miyazawa Kazufumi, draws on Recife's lively frevo carnival rhythm and Rio's similar carnival *marchinha* (fast march), mixed with a ska-like electric guitar part. It features the band Os Paralamas do Sucesso, who were known for their ska-rock in the 1980s. The lyrics are almost pure wordplay: "Eu ska-pei pro japão," Pedro sings, playing with the word *ska* (as in the musical genre) and the Portuguese word *escapei* to mean "I escaped to Japan." The song describes dropping a Portuguese dictionary on Japan from an airplane, resulting in a word "salad" that generated phrases like "Tóquio arigatô pau de arara" (a mixture of the word *Tokyo* with *arigato*, from the Japanese *domo arigato*, or "many thanks," and *pau de arara*, a term for a kind of flatbed truck with benches used in the Northeast to transport people). Another series of phrases mixes yet more references to the Brazilian indigenous Tupy peoples, the Afro-Brazilian deity Xangô, and Buddha without making much semantic sense. The meaning is in the mixture itself. Similarly, "Mergulho marítimo" (Ocean swim) is a hybrid of reggae with the somewhat similar northeastern xote rhythm and also features lyrics full of wordplay between Portuguese and English. "Eu disse xi! É ela / Ela disse ri! / É ele," Pedro sings, exploiting the *sh* sound of the Brazilian *x* and the *h* sound of the Brazilian *r* (when it is at the beginning of a word) to mean, "I said she [xi]! It's her. She said he [ri]! It's him." Pedro also plays with *xote* and the English words *short* (which in Brazilian pronunciation sounds almost identical to *xote*) and *shot*, displaying a penchant for wordplay comparable to Lenine's and to Tropicalists such as Caetano Veloso and Tom Zé (on Zé, see Dunn 2001, 196).

On the song "Aê meu primo" (Hey my cousin, by Pedro Luís and Pedro Rocha), the band inserts verses from two traditional songs in the public domain—the children's song "Ciranda cirandinha" and the march "Marcha soldado"—into a funk carioca groove over which Pedro and the band sing-shout the words in call-and-response, with funk bass and electric guitar added. Pedro spits out the lyrics on a single monotonous pitch, which serves to highlight the contrast between his somewhat vague rant about the state of the planet and the lighthearted, carefree children's dance, the ciranda, to which he refers. "Let's all dance the ciranda," he sings. The earth is "tired" and "the people are confused." It is not just Brazil, but rather a worldwide crisis. There is "a lack of structure" and "a lack of shame" and things will get worse "if we don't do anything." Rather than just waiting for a solution, Pedro implores, people must change things "in daily life." Change "the system" a little. Little changes in behavior, Pedro explained, could make the world more humane. That is to say, rather than following the revolutionary dialectic of the old left, change could be an incremental project (and so it has turned out to be under the Partido dos Trabalhadores, the Worker's Party, since 2003).

The album, which has a more dance-oriented pop sound and was released on the Warner Music Brazil label, earned PLAP a little more exposure outside Rio de Janeiro and on the radio. However, pop stardom was not in their future and band members would soon begin to devote more energy to a new project as the millennium came to an end and the music industry began to undergo radical transformation.

Monobloco: Pop Takes to the Streets

For one song on É tudo um real, "Cidade em movimento" (City in movement), the band decided they wanted to have "a dirtier sound." They came up with the idea of recording a small bloco (carnival street troupe), with each of the five band members playing a single percussion instrument but using only one (omnidirectional) microphone to capture the sound (as opposed to a stereo pair, or several microphones mixed down to stereo). As it was, in effect, a bloco in "monophony," the band thought of it as a "monobloco."[14] Subsequently, PLAP was contracted to perform for a week at the SESC Vila Mariana performance space in São Paulo. Aside from performing, they conducted workshops in which they taught some of their percussion arrangements, transcribed specifically for samba instruments. Based on their success with these workshops, they inaugurated similar weekly sessions in Rio as a way of earning some money and of creating a bloco with the students to parade during carnival.

This became the Monobloco project, and as its directors (from PLAP) grew progressively more entrepreneurial, they began to improve and professionalize their didactic methods. They were contracted to provide the bateria for regular dance parties at the Fundição Progresso space in the Lapa area of Rio on Fridays, using about 100–120 percussionists, the vast majority of them students of the workshops. They treated these shows as preparation for their bloco street procession, which, Sidon claimed, came to draw 100,000 people. (Photographs at their website seem to support this.) At first Monobloco's audience came primarily from the South Zone middle classes (it was *elitizada*, or elite-ified, Sidon conceded), but by around 2005, when the group began to perform in various cities in Rio de Janeiro state, and to reach other parts of the country, it had begun to have a broader appeal. "Because we use samba school instruments," Sidon observed, "it is something people identify with," even while the ensemble plays a variety of rhythms with those instruments.

By 2007 the group had split off a contingent of nine people led by Celso Alvim to go to the United Kingdom for a month to conduct workshops and perform shows under the Monobloco name there (they also have an online store for selling T-shirts and other merchandise in England). They capitalized on what Sidon referred to as a global "batucada movement," or the increasing popularity of samba drumming ensembles in cities throughout the world over the past two decades (perhaps especially among middle-class "cohorts" of what Turino refers to as a "cosmopolitan formation" [2000; 2008]).[15] Moreover, the development of this pop bloco coincided with a vibrant renaissance of the Lapa neighborhood in Rio de Janeiro as a center for live performances of samba, choro, and *gafieira* (a kind of ballroom samba dance generally accompanied with brass instrument arrangements) frequented by middle-class South Zone youths (see Herschmann 2007).

At the Monobloco workshop I observed in Copacabana (figure 11), the instructors used a whiteboard to write out rhythms and made sure students could clap or step certain patterns before playing them, making it similar to a classroom environment, in addition to using the more traditional watch-listen-and-repeat-after-me method for learning samba percussion. The group has a space on their website with didactic materials, including numerous short MP3s of various Brazilian rhythms, and the Monobloco grooves, as well as notated and other written materials for download. Ciranda, côco, congo, ijexá, maculelê, marcha, quadrilha, and xote are among the rhythms demonstrated there, as well as various examples of samba at different tempos. There is an online sound mixer on which the listener can raise or lower the playback volume of individual instruments in a given groove to hear how they fit together. Registrants of the workshops receive a password they can use to retrieve these materials. In short, the members of Monobloco developed a sophisticated, efficient, rational-

ized, and distinctly unmessy structure for teaching Brazilian rhythms, and thereby carved out a niche for themselves as musical entrepreneurs.

Meanwhile, one of the more significant changes in the music scene of Rio de Janeiro since the late 1990s was a revival of street manifestations during carnival (as opposed to the media spectacle in the sambadrome). "The city used to empty out during carnival," Sidon said. "Cariocas would leave. There was nothing to do. Today, there are various blocos filling up the streets, and the Carioca stays around." He elaborated his hypothesis that carnival, long interpreted as a period of suspension, inversion, or perversion of dominant social hierarchies, came to be viewed as a relief from the violence that plagued Rio de Janeiro.

> ss: No one is going to assault you [during carnival], so the Carioca takes advantage and hits the streets where the bandit and the prostitute mix—that mixture, everyone on the street. Carnival became more of a period of peace. . . . There are a lot of blocos, like in Olinda and Recife [in Pernambuco]. If you want to form a bloco, you begin by beating on a pail. The next year it already becomes a tradition. This kind of movement is going on here.

FIGURE 11. Monobloco workshop and rehearsal, Copacabana

FM: And this is more among the middle class, right? Because the working classes always stayed [in Rio for carnival], no?

SS: Yeah, I'm talking more about the South Zone, university students. The gang sticks around. What existed was [the bloco] Suvaco do Christo here in the South Zone. Monobloco took some of that same public but also opened up to another public.[16]

Recife's carnival has long been famous for still being a mass street phenomenon, while Rio's had, since the construction of the sambadrome in 1984, become a more controlled and mediated spectacle. Monobloco thus tapped into local desires to, as Sidon put it, "hit the streets."

However, Sidon sought to distinguish Monobloco from other street blocos in its more precise approach to musicianship. "We are musicians so we want to hear things played correctly," he said. "In these street blocos you've got thirty tamborins and each person playing their own way. It annoys me. If the person next to you is playing wrong, you're going to want to hear it played correctly." This kind of amateurish "messiness" was not at all the sound they wanted (and not what the best samba percussionists achieve). We may think of samba as a participatory form, but it is also presentational, and acceptance into Rio's most "authentic" baterias (that is, the older samba associations rooted in predominantly black working-class communities) requires extensive training. One popular bloco in the South Zone, Sidon claimed, "rents" drummers from the working-class neighborhood of Santa Marta morro, and then at carnival the *mauricinhos*, that is, the pampered middle-class youths who do not have such training, go out to play next to them. (Mauricinho is the diminutive of the name Maurício; it came to be associated with a stereotyped spoiled and privileged young male, similar to the figure lambasted in Gabriel O Pensador's "Playboy," described in the preface.)

In other respects, Monobloco sought to be *more* presentational than conventional blocos and samba schools through greater usage of microphones and the PA system. Their sound, Sidon observed, had "weight." "We like to have pressure," he said, with the surdos well tuned, and with "the punch of rock 'n' roll." Monobloco "put on *a real sound*," he said proudly. They took the instrumentation and the pressure inherent to the samba school format and gave it some of the amplified "punch" (they use the English word) associated with live rock and pop shows. (Recall that Paulinho Moska also used "punch" to describe Marcos Suzano's pandeiro sound.)[17] Interestingly, they do not have a proprietary "samba accent"—the nuanced differences in patterns of articulation, usually on caixas, surdos, or tamborins—that often form part of the distinctiveness of the biggest, oldest samba schools. Monobloco might play a groove utilizing, for example, the snare-drum pattern from the samba school Ilha do Governador, or a pattern associated with the Mangueira school. They also created signature grooves in, for example, their mixture of funk carioca with marchinha. (In fact, they discovered on YouTube a group in California playing one of their hybrid funk grooves.)

It is probably in their repertory, however, that Monobloco is most distinct from older street samba manifestations, as it consists of an eclectic mix of pop songs: Pedro's "Rap do real" and "Miséria S.A.," Tim Maia's "Imunização racional (Que beleza)" and "Do Leme ao Pontal," Raul Seixas's "Mosca na sopa," Rodrigo Maranhão's "Maracatu embolado," classic sambas like Silas de Oliveira's "Aquarela brasileira" and "É hoje" by Didi and Mestrinho (also in Fernanda Abreu's repertoire), as well as various recent compositions like Pedro's "Cirande em frente" from PLAP's repertory, and songs by the São Paulo rappers Rappin Hood and Xis. At the Monobloco stage show I attended at the Circo Voador in Lapa in 2007, the rather young crowd sang along with and danced to all the songs, including old sambas. Even on a rainy winter night, Monobloco filled the venue with fans, and I tried to imagine a scenario in which hundreds of dancing twenty-somethings would sing along to classic repertoire mixed with pop songs in the United States. Despite being a predominantly presentational setting, it was also what Turino would classify as a participatory event allowing for a sense of social cohesion.

Their samba repertory focused on compositions from before the mid-1980s. After that, Sidon claimed, there was no classic samba (samba antológica). Samba had become corrupted by money and standardization, he said, voicing a common complaint (which I heard even within the samba community). Recent sambas were "disposable." Samba had become primarily a way of making money, he lamented, as schools might, for example, make a samba celebrating a particular city in exchange for backing from that city's government (as a kind of tourism advertisement), or about, say, steel, to gain the financial support of a major mining interest. Another general complaint was that the numbers runners (bicheiros) and traffickers had too much invested in the schools and controlled which song would be chosen in the annual competition, among other matters. The culture of samba in the schools, in this interpretation, had been corrupted in a way similar to the corruption in the political sphere, and the music industry. Nevertheless, the big schools continued to serve as important sources of musical authenticity. Monobloco has, for example, often invited Mestre Odilon of the Grande Rio school to perform with them, and Sidon played for a year with Grande Rio, while C. A. Ferrari played in the bateria of the Mangueira school (and we have seen how the schools' proprietary rhythmic accents are valued). "Why did Monobloco become such a phenomenon even though it does not play on the radio or appear on television?" Sidon asked rhetorically in our 2007 interview. "Because it's bateria; the rhythm is contagious," he concluded as he produced a deft, swinging vocalization of an intense samba groove to emphasize his point.

For Pedro, what began as a modest project for the members of his band to earn some money on the side ended up becoming a phenomenon that was bigger in terms of popularity than PLAP, much to his surprise. More importantly, however, it provided the band with a forum in which to work out musical practices and administrative structures: "We became increasingly involved in creating our own structure of production, our own structure of thinking, our work philosophy. . . . Monobloco is founded and directed by we five but there are many collaborators who do this or that, from all sectors. Production, video, audio engineering—the technical team who together with us created the concept of how The Wall would sound live also helps us in Monobloco. So it is a very interesting concept of collectivity, without doubt—just as The Wall influenced Monobloco, after a while Monobloco ended up influencing PLAP too in terms of sound and structure." This collectivity that Monobloco evolved into may be emblematic of the new contours of the music industry, with more horizontal collaboration among relatively independent actors, rather than predominantly hierarchical models of corporate control.

These musicians' two parallel forums for creating and performing Brazilian popular music thus work in a complementary manner. If PLAP is primarily a pop band forum for Pedro's compositions, and for communicating about social concerns, Monobloco is aimed at the baile, the dance party, while it liaises more directly with the samba community, to some extent bridging South and North zones through musical practice. For example, at the Circo Voador show I attended, Arlindo Cruz, formerly of the roots samba group Fundo de Quintal, appeared with Monobloco as a guest singer.[18] Monobloco's function in Rio, Pedro summarized, was "to bring this tradition to pop, to bring pop to this tradition." Even the old guard from the schools came to the workshops and overcame "their traditional prejudice against contemporary manifestations," Pedro said, because when the group played samba, it really was samba.

Monobloco sought to translate their sound to the studio in 2002, when they released the album *Monobloco 2002*. They chose 25 percussionists out of the 150 or so who participated in the workshops and had a great number of guest participations (percussionists from the local groups Bangalafumenga, Boato, Rio Maracatu, Funk'n Lata, and Eletrosamba, for example; the local poet Cabelo; the singers Fábio Alman and Pedro Quental; certain individuals from the samba schools and the septuagenarian samba diva Elza Soares; and the rappers Rappin Hood and Xis). For Sidon, however, the end result was unsatisfying. "The group was very new then," he explained, "and we wanted the sound of everybody recording together, but it didn't work. We ended up losing ourselves in the middle of the process." Indeed, *Monobloco 2002* does seem to lack a clear conceptualization of the production sound; in this instance, the values and goals of participation did not translate into the high-fidelity field.

They returned to the workshops, the live shows, and the carnival bloco until 2006, when Monobloco released a DVD and CD of their live show in the Circo Voador. This recording was to be more like the baile, that is, more like the show. It has a better production sound than the first album and captures some of the excitement—although by no means all—of their live performances. It features guest vocals from Fernanda Abreu, Lenine, and the MCs Junior and Leonardo and mixes songs from MPB, samba, soul music, forró, and funk.

PLAP Continues

PLAP continued to tour as the new millennium began and, in between trips, assembled a third album, *Zona e progresso* (*Confusion and Progress*), at Tom Capone's Toca de Bandido studio (in a building on Tom's home property), released in 2001. They parted with Warner Music after the company asked Pedro to go solo and leave The Wall behind. "Being under contract with a major label with broad investments and various different artists to promote didn't work so well for us," Pedro told one journalist (M. A. Barbosa 2001). *Zona e progresso* was thus released on the local label MP,B (which also released the collaboration between Marcos Suzano and Victor Ramil

called *Satolep Sambatown*). The album title is a play on the motto of the Brazilian flag: "Order and Progress" (which comes from Auguste Comte),
where *zona* is the opposite of "order"—something like "mess" or "confusion." It was meant to indicate the global situation during an era of "incredible technological progress" that was paradoxically accompanied by
"an incredible mess in the mind of humanity [*na cabeça da humanidade*],"
Pedro said in an interview, as he also made reference to the "confusion
of terrorism and chemical warfare" that dominated the news in late 2001
(M. A. Barbosa 2001).

Pedro subsequently wrote the title song for the album in collaboration
with Suely Mesquita and Arícia Mess. "Dionysus is the god of confusion,"
he sings. "Bless this immortal confusion / That I bring to the surface."
(For Mário Moura, *zona e progresso* also characterized the very way the band
had evolved.) Lenine wrote an enthusiastic press release that evokes the
themes that dominated this music scene as the end of the millennium approached:

> The street raised to the fourth! The refinement of rusticity! Essence and
> excess! Maturity in the language! The radical-ness of the party! . . .
> The sound of Pedro Luís e A Parede is the face of Rio. It is the samba
> of the morro, the funk of the asphalt, and the peaceful coexistence of
> opposites. . . .
> The sound of Pedro and A Parede is the face of Brazil. It is the free
> transit of many tendencies, the agglutination of riffs and races, it is
> the chameleon in front of the mirror, it is the music of the future of the
> world, it is promiscuity and *mestiçagem* [racial mixing].
> Pedro's Brazil of Rio is universal and cosmopolitan, malandro and
> versatile, and it reflects the four corners of this continental country. The
> sound of these guys is without match!

Music making is again understood here as an allegory of the nation, where
the agglutination of musical riffs goes hand in hand with the promiscuous mixture of races. The "peaceful coexistence of opposites" turns into an
embrace of confusion in the name of a better future, in contradistinction
to the militaristic "Order and Progress," rendering music a kind of "audiotopia" (Kun 2005).

The lyrics of some of the songs continue Pedro's concern with social
questions, although they tend to remain very generalized. Northeast-

ern musical influences are again important. "Não ao desperdício" (Not to waste, by Cabelo and Gláucia Saad), for example, with a groove that draws on maracatu drumming, comments on consumer society: the pharmaceutical, automobile, and tobacco industries, the lyrics complain, turn harmful things into consumer goods. "Batalha naval" (Naval battle, by Pedro Luís and Bianca Ramoneda) addresses the anonymity of Brazilians engaged in a "social war": "In the land of happiness, country of carnival / In the marvelous city, things are going badly." Other songs are more lighthearted. "Ciranda do mundo" (Ciranda of the world, by Eduardo Krieger) again invokes the northeastern ciranda genre, while Pedro's "10 de queixo" (10 with slackjaws) mixes the cantoria ballad singing style and the distinctive viola steel-string guitar with a baião-like rhythm on the verses and maracatu-inspired drumming on the refrains in a song about ten males marveling at the young women dancing at a forró party. Pedro's "Parte coração" (Break heart) is a samba-canção (slow samba song) with choro accents and treats the old theme of the suffering heart. His "Mão e luva" (Hand and glove) is the least groove- and batucada-oriented track; it could be a Beatles song.[19]

Tragically, Tom Capone died in a motorcycle accident in Los Angeles shortly after the 2004 Latin Grammy Awards, where he received five nominations and two awards in the categories of best Brazilian rock album (with the band Skank) and best MPB album (with Maria Rita). PLAP deeply mourned the loss and would wait several years before releasing a new album, in part because they remained busy with Monobloco, but also because they did not know who could replace Tom.[20]

.enredo

Late in 2008 the group released Ponto enredo, produced by Lenine at AR Studios (of which Tom Capone had been a part owner), and at a smaller studio, Corredor 5. It is a richly layered samba-rock-pop album that seems free of the feelings of anxiety about commodification, the music industry, national identity, and globalization that characterized much of the hybrid Brazilian pop of the 1990s. Naturally, after over a decade working together, the musicians have a more seasoned sound. However, it also benefits from a more focused mixture of two principal musical ingredients: samba and rock. The result is a less "confused" musical concept than that of the earlier productions.

With Lenine, the band finally "succeeded in bringing Tom's energy back"; he understood PLAP's "musical language" (C. A. Ferrari, cited in Reis 2008). *Ponto enredo* is more melancholic than previous PLAP albums; it captures some of the quality of *saudade*—a sort of plaintiveness—that can be heard in some samba, while it still emphasizes danceable grooves. Pedro's compositions are much more melodic than the rapped or even shouted verses that characterized much of his early output. Samba is "worshipped" in these songs, as the title of the first track, "Santo Samba" (Sacred samba), by Pedro, suggests. Leave all problems, hurts, and useless things behind and call your friends together for a party, Pedro implores. "I will take care to samba," he sings. "I will sing for real / Samba is a sacred remedy / For whoever wants to live."

The song "Ela tem a beleza que nunca sonhei" (She has a beauty I never imagined) is a rock-samba piece utilizing the partido alto style, which emphasizes improvised lyrics and audience participation on the refrains, with guest vocals from a Carioca master of that subcategory of samba, Zeca Pagodinho (Jessé Gomes da Silva Filho), as well as Zeca's regular seven-string guitar player, Paulão 7 Cordas (Paulo Roberto Pereira de Araújo). The song begins with a distorted and filtered drone on the electric guitar with pandeiro and *repique-de-mão* (a medium-sized drum played with the hand) and a $3 + 3 + 2$ rhythm predominating. Soon the cavaquinho (a small, four-string, guitar-like instrument similar to the Hawaiian ukelele) joins in with strummed chords in common variations of syncopation (such as the sixteenth–eighth–sixteenth-note figure), and Zeca says, "What's up Pedro Luís, I was in the area. I'll strike up a partido with you," a characteristically informal way of beginning this kind of samba that has the effect of making it seem like a spontaneous meeting. As Pedro begins singing the first verse, the caixas join in, and soon Serginho Trombone adds short fills on his namesake instrument, which, together with trumpets, adds a gafieira flavor. Zeca sings the second verse, after which Pedro returns, and together the two sing the refrain as the samba concludes. The lyrics tell of Pedro's encounter with a kind of muse of the samba.

Pedro composed the title song of the album ("Ponto enredo") for a production of Shakespeare's *Midsummer Night's Dream* by the theater group Nós do Morro, made up of actors from the Vidigal favela in Rio. *Ponto enredo* hybridizes the word for an Afro-Brazilian Candomblé or Umbanda hymn (*ponto*) with the word for "plot" (*enredo*), as in *sambas de enredo*, the songs composed to a specific narrative theme for carnival each year. *Ponto* also means "dot" (or "period") and thus hints at the "dot-x" Internet address format, as if to suggest a web address that ends in ".enredo" (*ponto-enredo*). The song begins with the percussionist Léo Leobons playing a rhythm in 12/8 meter on conga drums, to which Mário soon adds a melodic fretless bass part. As the track progresses, it increasingly incorporates rock timbres as acoustic and electric guitars and drum kit enter, while it maintains the 12/8 feel on the congas, creating an appealing hybrid.

"Mandingo" (Witch doctor) is a collaboration between Pedro Luís and the samba de roda master Roque Ferreira, from the Recôncavo of Bahia. It opens with cavaquinho and electric guitar strumming chords, the latter with a "wah-wah" effect. Then it breaks to tamborim, conga, and hi-hat, as Pedro sings the first verse. The tamborim plays variations on a common samba ostinato (akin to the so-called timeline rhythmic figure of West African music, but not as consistent). On the second verse, the cavaquinho returns, and Mário Moura enters on bass, while Léo Saad plays a counterpoint to the melody on the viola ten-string guitar. The electric guitar returns on the repeat of the refrain. Its plaintive melody in G minor and the faint echo on Pedro's vocal give the song a melancholy, nostalgic tenor despite the rhythmic intensity it gains on the final repeats of the refrain as the drum kit becomes more predominant.

The lyrics tell of Afro-Brazilian sorcery: Be wary of the *nêgo mandingo*, for he "knows how to pick the leaf," how to say the prayer and work his magic. His drumming attracts the cabôco and orixá spirits; his dance calls all mediums to the floor. No one can undo the knots of love he secures. He controls time, the winds, the sea, the woods. This *nêgo male* (a West African Muslim in Bahia during the colonial era) had been a king in Senegal, and "his power comes from there." With a talisman in his pocket and a *tecebá* (a kind of rosary for Islamic prayer) on his belt, he cures with his medicine, while his poison kills. He bathed his necklace in the waters of Oxum (a Yoruba deity of rivers, love, beauty, wealth) but his Eledá (ancestral guardian) is Ogum Xoroquê. *Mandingo* is a term for an ethnic group in West Africa (of the Mande territory) who practice a form of Islam; in Brazil the term came to refer to Africans believed to have powers associated with Islamic amulets (called *mandingas*). Sylviane Anna Diouf describes how these amulets gave self-confidence to slaves, offering them "the sense of power over themselves, their family and their community that bondage denied them." The amulets were used like sorcery "in an attempt to control the slaveholders' behavior" (2003, 147). This image is mixed with Yoruba

Candomblé references in the song. The deity Ogum Xoroquê, for example, is said to be half Ogum and half Exu (two orixás who are already closely associated), taking the positive qualities of Exu, such as a resolute sense of purpose and principles, and the warrior quality of Ogum, resulting in a spirit of tremendous courage (Barcellos 1997, 16). Like Suzano, then, Pedro invokes the power of traditional Afro-Brazilian cultural practices in this song.

"4 horizontes" (4 horizons), by Pedro and Lenine, is another song that emulates the winding melodic contours of some classic sambas (weaving through II–V⁷–I chord patterns, or through modulations as alterations change a given chord from minor to dominant seventh, for example), against a common samba timeline-like rhythm figure (a 2 + 2 + 1 + 2 + 2 + 2 + 2 + 1 + 2 pattern of accents on cavaquinho and certain percussion). The counterpoint call-and-response between Pedro and Lenine on the repeat of the verse reminds the listener of the magnificent combination of melody and rhythm in the greatest of sambas. Lenine improvises a short vocal solo without words in a conversation with the distinctive cuíca friction drums of samba (an instrument that can sound a bit like a howling dog). For the final refrain, the driving, distorted rock guitar begins to take over, only to go silent, leaving a cuíca to have the last word (or wail, actually).

"Cantiga" (Ballad) is Pedro's musical rendition of a poem of the same name by the celebrated Brazilian poet Manuel Bandeira (1886–1968), performed as a kind of gafieira to a samba de roda 3 + 3 + 2 rhythm. "I want to be happy / In the waves of the ocean / I want to forget everything / I want to rest," Pedro sings in a call-and-response with the rest of the band. Bandeira's poem makes a reference to a traditional Candomblé hymn (ora) as the poet asks, "Who will come to kiss me / I want the Star of the Dawn [i.e., Venus] / the queen of the sea," to which PLAP adds a choral response near the end of the song on the name Iemanjá (alt. Yemanjá) in a reference to the Afro-Brazilian/Yoruba goddess of the sea. The music draws on the *ca-lango* dance popular in Minas Gerais, parts of Bahia, and rural areas of Rio de Janeiro.

"Repúdio" (Repudiation), by Pedro and the lyricist Carlos Rennó, is a bossa-rock hybrid that decries the notoriously appalling conditions in Brazil's jails, into which multitudinous prisoners are "squeezed" like "wild beasts." The prisoners could die of boredom, Pedro sings, until the moment when a prison revolt begins and amid the shooting there are "cries of murder and tears of blood" as "hate explodes." Such a scene was powerfully dramatized in the film *Carandiru* (2003, based on a book titled *Estação Carandiru* by Dráuzio Varella), about a prison riot in São Paulo in 1992 and its exceptionally violent suppression by the military police. "Luz da nobreza" (Light of nobility), by Pedro and Zé Renato, is a kind of *folia de reis* (traditional Three Kings Procession song performed between Christmas and Epiphany), with steel-stringed viola and a march-like rhythm on the snare drum, but in a 9/8 meter, rather unusual in Brazilian pop music.[21] Pedro Luís's wife, the singer Roberta Sá, joins him on vocal harmonies late in the song.

"Tem juízo mas não usa" (Possesses reason but doesn't use it), by Pedro and Lula Queiroga, is a samba-funk-rock mix with several layers of distorted and loud electric guitar (the beginning recalls Deep Purple), slap bass, and heavy batucada, especially on the catchy refrain. The use of electronic devices such as filters and an echo effect to process the sound in the recording studio is more evident on this track, recorded with Rodrigo Campello and Jr Tostoi (the MiniStereo production duo).[22] The remaining two tracks on this album are also collaborations. "Animal," which is about physical attraction, Pedro wrote with Suely Mesquita; it combines the 6/8 batucada that lends it an "Afro" feel with an increasingly heavy rock guitar sound as the song progresses. "Cabô" (It's over) is an older piece co-composed with Zé Renato; it is a lighthearted song about finding happiness through positive disposition. Interestingly, this track does not end when expected: after "Cabô" there is a brief period of silence before Léo Leobons leads a trio with Léo Saad and João Gabriel on the *batá* drums used to accompany Afro-Cuban Santería rituals (which bear similarities to those of Candomblé) in a chant to Yemanjá. It surprises the first-time listener, as it lacks its own track listing and is thus hidden, as if to recall the way African diaspora religious practices often had to be concealed from masters. The "sacred samba" that opens the album and the Afro-Cuban Lucumí (Yoruba) chant and drumming that close it thus frame the band's identification with—indeed, worship of—Afro-diasporic music.

Virtual PLAP

"Welcome to the PLAP BLOG! The blog of Pedro Luís e A Parede," read the announcement on the new PLAP website launched in September 2008. "This space is a virtual wall where you will be able to praise, suggest, criticize, and enter into contact with PLAP. We are expecting you. See ya, Mário Moura." With the release of *Ponto enredo*, PLAP inaugurated a new website.

As is typical, it offers a history of the group, brief individual biographies, the latest news, press releases and reviews, photographs and videos of the band, their performance schedule, a free MP3 promotional download, contact information, a blog, and a discography. The band's entire recorded repertoire is available in streaming (non-downloadable) audio under the discography section, along with song lyrics and basic album credits. This kind of virtual space is vital for bands working independently of major labels.

Despite the impersonal nature of cyberspace, the blog establishes an informal forum for communicating that works in conjunction with both the band's live shows and their recorded albums. A brief look at some of the posts demonstrates how the "virtual" and the "real" (the live shows, specific moments spent listening to the CD or attempting to learn the songs by ear, for example) are co-constitutive. As is to be expected, fan feedback is largely positive in such forums; I translate a few of the earliest entries to the PLAP blog, preserving some of the characteristic typography.

Eliana N. says: 1 de October de 2008 @ 22:28
I was in São Luiz do Paraitinga during the Week of Brazilian Song where I saw your show and Lenine's. MYGOD!!!!!!!!!! I returned to São Paulo with a Cleansed Soul. Do you have any idea of the importance of your magnificent work? The CD Ponto Enredo is the real Tribute to the forces of nature that live in us, subtly mystical without being sentimental. It touches the bottom of the soul and vibrates in every cell of the body. Thank God not all is lost. . . . CONGRATULATIONS!!!

Cristiane says: 23 November 2008 @ 14:10
. . . I went to the show yesterday, at the SESC Vila Mariana and I loved it!!! I had already heard talk about you but did not yet know [your music]. . . . Really good! I can only praise creative and competent people like you who make this delicious mixture of our music with the influence of rock! And that is not even speaking about the lyrics, which are formidable and intelligent! . . . We are happy to know that Brazilian music is not succumbing to Americanism and to globalization! In fact, long live the globalization that allows MPB to traverse frontiers!!! . . .

Marcelo W. says: 4 December 2008 @ 14:23
Hi PLAP! Each time I listen to Ponto I get more out of the CD. What a great partnership between PLAP + Lenine. You don't have any "making

of" videos to put on the site? . . . Any plans to post *cifras* [the chord changes to the songs]? Hearty embrace, Marcelo

Postings like these extend the impact of specific live shows by building anticipation or through post-show praise (which can create anticipation in others who await their turn to see the band). Moreover, in offering a place for fans to record their enthusiasm for Pedro Luís's rock-samba-Candomblé project, as well as recurring anxieties about Americanization and globalization, the virtual here offers another window into musically constituted senses of community "as real as any other human cultural production" (Cooley, Meizel, and Syed 2008, 92). PLAP has, in fact, recently added chord charts for the songs, as per Marcelo W.'s request. A major recording label would probably never have allowed that, at least not in the 1990s.

Conclusions

As youths in the 1970s and 1980s, the musicians in PLAP were, like Lenine and Suzano, attracted to the sound and instrumentation of rock bands. In the 1990s, however, inspired in part by Chico Science and Nação Zumbi, they began to rethink that instrumentation and to mix rock sounds with newly in-vogue northeastern folk genres such as maracatu and forró, for example, and especially with samba, the genre most associated with Rio de Janeiro. The band restructured to favor aesthetics that in many respects accord with the priorities Charles Keil emphasizes in his theory of participatory discrepancies. The group's engagement with samba eventually led them to form the Monobloco group, which both capitalized on and helped augment the renewed interest among the local middle classes in that genre and in carnival street manifestations as a whole. Throughout these developments, mixture remained a kind of creed, such that even Monobloco maintained a repertoire of pop songs alongside samba, with other influences such as rap. Thomas Turino's typology for different spheres of music making speaks to the different priorities these musicians juggled over the course of their careers and helps situate their work relative to broader currents that transcend this particular setting. But there are also other dynamics at play here that complicate, for example, the way participatory aesthetics are realized (e.g., Sidon's insistence on playing rhythms correctly in the street parade, and on using microphone technique to get a "real sound" on the street).

Turino's mapping of different values, while nuanced and taking their contingent nature into account, seems to fall largely along class lines within an anti-modernist teleology. Both Keil and Turino have isolated important issues of musical practice—Turino's model in particular encompasses an impressive range of possibilities and historical depth—but the explanatory power of PDS and of the four fields is tempered by assumptions that human society is increasingly becoming alienated through the machinations of capitalist formations. I do not doubt that this is one narrative of modernity, but subjects make and remake, or territorialize and deterritorialize, social relations (for example, late capitalism produces participatory revivalisms [e.g., Turino 2008, 155–88]). Class cannot be the irreducible social factor; it too is constituted by "people-in-(power)-relationships-in-projects" (Ortner 1996, 13), by people pursuing "lines of flight" through global assemblages, like a Tupy astronaut, for example.[23]

The trajectories of PLAP and the band's associated Monobloco project speak to the dissolution of the music industry model that prevailed through the late 1990s, and the gradual shift toward greater artist autonomy and entrepreneurship that has resulted from this development. The fact that the band settled on Lenine as producer for *Ponto enredo* further emphasizes how horizontal relationships with peers have come to characterize music recording more than the hierarchical structures of the older music industry models. "We had no idea back in 1999 when you were with us," Pedro told me in 2007, "that we were on the eve of the death" of the old ways of distributing music. "No idea." For about ten years, he reflected, music makers have been experiencing "an intermediate phase" in terms of the format, because it was still unclear whether musicians will release and distribute albums only virtually, and what this will mean for artists' livelihood. "I don't know either," he mused. "I know that I continue to make music, I continue to encounter other people who . . . are inspiring." Life, becoming, is unfinished, but new human relations continue to inspire music making.

FERNANDA ABREU

GAROTA CARIOCA

So face reality with the eye you have in front
And look at life in a different way
Because a decent woman can be much more attractive
Than a smiling *bunda*
So, *garota sangue bom*
If you take on the mission, if you take on this task
To be or not to be, that is the question.
—From the song "Nádegas a declarar," by Liminha, Fernanda Abreu, and Gabriel O Pensador

It is 9 August 2007. I am in Gávea, South Zone, visiting the singer, songwriter, dancer, producer, and official tourism ambassador of Rio de Janeiro Fernanda Abreu at her recording studio, Pancadão (meaning "A Hard Hit," or more figuratively, "A Heavy Beat"; see figure 12). We have been talking for forty minutes and as our conversation comes to a close, I ask Fernanda what she is listening to at the moment, motioning to some CDs I had noticed resting atop her mixing console. "I just bought these while on tour," she says. There is Prince's *Planet Earth* (2007), the French electro-tango group Gotan Project's *Lunático* (2006), and *Spok Frevo Orquestra* from Recife, who play blazingly fast swing band–like arrangements of Pernambucan frevo. In Portugal she picked up the Angolan-Portuguese *kuduro* group Buraka Som Sistema's *From Buraka to the World* (2006). Also from Portugal was the Portuguese/Cape Verdean Sara Tavares's *Balancé* (2006), which Fernanda found *super legal* (a positive slang term, like "awesome"). Friends such as Rio-based DJ Nuts and DJ and electronic musician Mar-

celinho da Lua, she tells me, also give her lots of recordings. "I listen to everything," she states. "I've paid a lot of attention to funk carioca." "And jazz?" I ask. "No, no, jazz I don't care much for," she concedes. Jazz seemed to her "like a closed club" in which it was "best not to get involved" if one did not know it well.

Perhaps more vocally than anyone in this book, Fernanda has celebrated mixture in her work, with a special interest in African American dance music and, as she noted, in the local funk carioca scene. In contrast to Marcos Suzano, she regards jazz as inhospitable terrain. Indeed, the driving dance beats, electronic and rock timbres, and pop choreography of her stage shows are far removed from the prevailing aesthetics of most jazz, especially post-swing jazz, in which the music's close associations with dance (and bodily expression) came increasingly to be subordinated to instrumental virtuosity and intellectualism.[1] After beginning her career

FIGURE 12. Fernanda Abreu in her recording studio, Pancadão

as a singer and dancer in the seminal pop-rock band Blitz in the 1980s, Fernanda emerged in the 1990s as a solo artist who would come to be known especially for blending funk, disco, and rap influences with samba. She embraced samplers and sequencers at a time when electronic dance beats were not typical for MPB (earlier than Suzano, and quite in contrast to Paulinho Moska, as the following chapter will show), and she has manifested a general fascination for studio technologies, a domain typically dominated by males.

A 1998 article referred to Fernanda as the "queen of samba funk rock" and included her in an emerging Latin American "rock sisterhood" with the Colombian singer Shakira and other artists (Padgett 1998). The article highlighted how these women were beginning to crack the "rock ceiling" and were "injecting a female perspective into a testosterone-fueled genre."[2] How have gender, class, and race inflected Fernanda's musical becoming, her desires, and her projects? What can Fernanda's career, music, and discourse contribute to discussions of anthropophagy (or cannibalism) and mixture in this setting? How might we understand the place of the body in her music and in discourses of mixture? What vocabulary is needed to begin discussing *whiteness* in a context of racially inflected musical mixture that involves various local and translocal border-crossings—between the South Zone and the western and northern suburbs of Rio, and between the United States and Brazil?

Rather than presume to be able to answer all these questions, I raise them in order to mark out the kind of problem space that some scholars, borrowing from Deleuze, designate as "assemblages." For Collier and Ong, for example, "global assemblages" are sites where "the forms and values of individual and collective existence are problematized or at stake, in the sense that they are subject to technological, political, and ethical reflection and intervention" (2005, 14). The anthropological application of Deleuze's assemblage concept is interesting because it "seems structural"; it has a kind of "materiality and stability of the classic metaphors of structure," but it tends to be evoked "precisely to undermine such ideas of structure," allowing for more open-ended understandings of the social (Marcus and Saka 2006, 102). Musical sound may itself be thought of as an assemblage, a momentary materialization of a problem space. Hence, as in previous chapters, one of my concerns here is also to describe the grooves, instruments, and other sounds mixed together on recordings, and to examine selected song lyrics.

Blitz and the Inauguration of the Decade of Brazilian Rock

In Brazilian rock, the singer-songwriter Rita Lee had in fact already cracked the proverbial ceiling in the 1970s. Rita began her career as singer for Os Mutantes, but when that band turned toward progressive rock "and left its more libertine side" (in Weinschelbaum 2006, 40), Rita decided to pursue a solo career, and today she is a kind of grande dame of a small Brazilian rock sisterhood. In an interview published in 2006, Rita singled out Fernanda Abreu, Marisa Monte, Adriana Calcanhotto, Zélia Duncan, and Cássia Eller as opposing the tendency in the mainstream media to represent women as "breasts, bunda [the commonly used slang term for the rear], silicone" (39). These artists are all *band leaders*, she emphasized, songwriters who do not need to display themselves physically in this manner. They are Rita's figurative nieces, grandchildren, and daughters, the rocker claimed.

Notwithstanding the groundbreaking Brazilian rock of Os Mutantes, Rita Lee, and other artists such as the Jovem Guarda musicians in the 1960s and 1970s, it was not until the 1980s that a full-blown rock *scene* would emerge—at first in Rio de Janeiro. Fernanda Sampaio de Lacerda Abreu, born in 1961 to a Carioca mother and a Portuguese father, would be at the center of that emergent scene as a young college student. She grew up in the relatively exclusive Jardim Botânico neighborhood of the South Zone (and had early exposure to dance as a student of ballet). At school she, like Pedro Luís, participated in choirs and music festivals, studied guitar and voice, and learned English. She then attended the prestigious Pontifícia Universidade Católica do Rio de Janeiro (PUC-Rio) in nearby Gávea, where she studied sociology and participated in campus theater and radio productions. She recalls, too, spending some of this time at the storied hangout of South Zone middle-class youths: Post 9 on Ipanema Beach.[3]

As Fernanda was about to begin her final year of studies in sociology at the university, she was invited to become a member of the band Blitz, a group whose success was so accelerated that she never completed her last year of college. The way the band came into being is quite typical of the South Zone arts scene, characterized by networks of personal connections linking one event to another. The actor Evandro Mesquita was part of an experimental and humorous theater group called Asdrúbal Trouxe o Trombone, which produced a show in 1980 at the Teatro Ipanema. (Pedro Luís performed with the troupe early in his career.) After the theatrical event, the singer Marina Lima performed and Evandro would sometimes stick around to sing with her band. When he was invited to perform at a new bar (Caribe) in early 1981, he invited Marina's musicians and created a show that combined music with humor and stage props. It was an immediate local hit and Evandro decided to put together a permanent band, Blitz, with the bassist Antônio Fortuna (who had played with Os Mutantes), the keyboardist William Forghieri, the drummer Lobão (João Luís Woerdembag Filho, from Marina Lima's band), the saxophonist Zé Luis (also from Marina's group), and the singer Ricardo Barreto. He then added Márcia Bulcão and her friend Fernanda Abreu as singer-actress-dancers to respond to his half-spoken/half-sung vocals.

In January 1982 the group won over crowds at the new Circo Voador stage constructed between Ipanema and Copacabana beaches, and their first single, the humorous "Você não soube me amar" (You didn't know how to love me, or How to make love to me; the meaning is ambiguous), quickly became a hit. The album that followed, As aventuras da Blitz (The adventures of Blitz), sold feverishly. By this time social movements advocating re-democratization had become increasingly vocal and the hardline military faction had yielded to the abertura process. Fernanda recalled the success of Blitz as partly related to the changing mood of the youths during this period. The humor and lightness of the band's pop-rock, she thought, tapped into a new generation that had never experienced a democratic Brazil but that was not part of the protest movements of the 1960s. In the 1970s "the truly politically correct thing to do was to try to liberate yourself from censorship and make interesting songs," she remembered during our interview. With censorship and the watchful eye of the dictatorship no longer a factor in the 1980s, sex, drugs, and politics could be themes for song lyrics, and rock seemed to offer a more direct language than the "refined lyricism" of MPB (Magaldi 1999, 320; also Walden 1996, 207–12). "After a country gets out of a dictatorship," Fernanda recounted, people want "novelty, and a lot of art comes from the subversion of things, of the transgressions that don't fit into a dictatorship." For many middle-class listeners at the time, popular music rooted in samba traditions was too closely associated with the Brazil of yesterday.

The group Os Paralamas do Sucesso, initiated by the Cariocas Herbert Vianna and Felipe "Bi" Ribeiro in the early 1980s, soon followed Blitz with a new-wave sound inspired by the ska-rock of the British band the Police. The bands Barão Vermelho, Legião Urbana, RPM, and Titãs, all formed by middle- and upper-middle-class (and predominantly white) youths, completed the explosion of what the journalist Artur Dapieve (1995) would call "Brock" (i.e., Brazilian rock).[4] After Blitz, the media began aggressively promoting Brazilian rock, and in 1985 the promoter Roberto Medina staged the seminal Rock in Rio festival to provide a performance venue for both major international bands that generally skipped Brazil in their tours (AC/DC, Rod Stewart, Queen, Iron Maiden, Whitesnake, and Ozzy Osbourne were among those who performed in 1985) and the Brock bands. Fernanda recalled criticisms during the era that the Paralamas, for example, were copying the Police, or that Legião Urbana was just a Brazilian version of another British band, the Smiths. But for her generation, she reflected in 2007, it was an important "evolution" (see also Madeira 1991; Perrone 1990; Ulhôa Carvalho 1995).

When I spoke about the 1980s with Fernanda's collaborator, the lyricist and author Fausto Fawcett, he pointed to an increased preoccupation in Brazil with "the sound" of pop music during the decade. "At least two generations of middle-class kids," he observed, listened to Deep Purple, the Rolling Stones, and above all Led Zeppelin. "It was a thing of well-educated kids who spoke English and had this connection." They "got used to that sound, to listening to good recordings, and there was this pressure in terms of . . . technological information, and [the desire to] express topics that were connected to an urban youth." The MPB songs one heard on the radio at the time, Fausto recalled, had "melodic and harmonic quality," but the production sound was weak. It was always the singer way in front of the mix, he complained, and the rest of the instruments in the back. There occurred "a generalized process of learning" about music production: "The producers learned together with the musicians, who were learning together with the audio engineers. So this decade was very important for these kids who were responsible for this turnaround in the thinking of musical production, of the technical formatting of musical product. . . . The slang expression . . . 'I want to tirar um som [get a sound]' seems . . . silly . . . but there is something important in it that ended up becoming serious." Blitz marked a division in 1982, Fausto argued, "not necessarily in the specific matter of techniques in the recording studio—but in terms of behavior." As wildly successful as the band was, however, Blitz dissolved shortly after Rock in Rio under the strain of touring and tensions between some members. (There were some later revival attempts.) By the end of the 1980s, the Brock scene had waned as recording labels shifted their priorities to new trends such as música sertaneja.

Around the time that rock was beginning to dominate the tastes of urban middle-class youths, in the lower-income suburban neighborhoods of Rio de Janeiro, where the population is more likely to be black or mixed-race, a different musical phenomenon was taking hold: funk carioca, which grew out of the dance parties of the 1970s. DJs would spin North American soul, rhythm and blues, and funk records that they acquired through circuits of couriers and other travelers. These *bailes da pesada* (heavy dance parties) attracted thousands of participants, at first at the Canecão nightclub but then, when the club decided to shift programming to MPB, in the working-class suburbs where the baile audiences lived. Huge sound systems were required for these events, and some producers built walls of speakers, which they would then give names. One of them, Soul Grand Prix, helped initiate a kind of "black is beautiful" trend in Rio beginning around 1975, which the press labeled "black Rio." The word *funk* came to refer to the set of varied black North American music styles to which participants danced at these events, while DJ Marlboro, who began to rap over his beats, emerged as the best-known disc jockey of the period.[5]

The foundational groove for what would subsequently emerge as funk carioca was Afrika Bambaataa's 1982 track "Planet Rock" (which sampled from Kraftwerk's "Trans Europe Express"). Bambaataa's track subsequently influenced Miami bass, a sound constructed around the use of the Roland TR-808 drum machine (808, for short), which in turn led to baile funk in Brazil. To this day, Paul Sneed observes, the vast majority of Brazilian funk songs "are based upon the electro funk style created by Bambaataa on his TR-808 programmable drum machine" (2007, 221). As the Rio funk scene evolved, local DJs and musicians began to produce original tracks strongly influenced by the Miami bass genre and using the Roland 808. Later, a gang-associated variety called *proibidão* emerged, with rough lyrics about violence and drug culture.

In 1990 the ethnomusicologist and journalist Hermano Vianna (brother of the rocker Herbert Vianna of the band Os Paralamas do Sucesso) described what he called a musical "apartheid" in Rio in the 1980s. Funk and hip-hop could not gain an audience among the middle-class youths of Rio's South Zone, he argued, precisely because it was popular among the lower classes in the North Zone suburbs (1990, 5). Moreover, many music critics contrasted funk unfavorably with samba as an inauthentic expres-

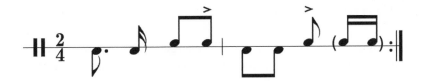

sion of the culture of the Carioca morros, that is, the hillside favelas (for being electronic and, initially, an import of North American grooves). At the same time, the genre was increasingly linked to violence and, in 1992, to a series of organized robberies that took place on South Zone beaches and alarmed residents of the nearby neighborhoods (Yúdice 2003). Sneed writes that Rio's funk music is often misunderstood by outside observers. "On the surface this somewhat deafeningly loud music . . . is deceptively childlike and simple," he concedes, with its "heavy Miami bass style sound, cheap keyboards, . . . rough and unpolished" vocal delivery, simple melodies, and "low-end drum machines" (2007, 221). Singers perform either alone or in duos, "sometimes yelling more than singing, in hoarse throaty voices, chanting out refrains reminiscent of the mass cheers at the soccer games in the Maracanã stadium on the north side of Rio." Its "violent reputation and overt sexuality have made Brazilian funk one of the most polemical musical practices in the world," but in Sneed's estimation, the genre has "evolved into a rich musical culture characterized by irony, complex maskings, and subversive messages and practices" (221).

Fernanda Abreu, already a fan of dance music from the United States, took a keen interest in the funk carioca scene as it developed, and she defended it as an important expression of favela life in addition to samba; when we met in 2007 she described it as "the cool groove" that still inspired her work. Besides the older style based on Miami bass, a newer funk carioca category is the *tamborzão*, for which the DJ and producer Sany Pitbull is known. (Figure 13 shows one typical funk carioca rhythm.) "Listen to this," Fernanda said to me in her studio as she called up from her iTunes library a recording which used this rhythm, a version of the so-called Duel between the Faithful Ones and the Lovers. The duel is not a song but rather a kind of live performance genre initiated by MC Kátia and MC Nem around 2006. It consists of a verbal battle between these two female MCs, one of whom represents the young women with steady boyfriends or husbands in the crowd, and the other rapping on behalf of those who want to be or already are the lovers of the boys or men who are taken. It begins

FIGURE 13. Example of a typical funk carioca rhythmic variation

without accompaniment as the two MCs taunt each other (although they point out in their introduction that they themselves are actually friends, and that they are "defending" the different camps). "Oh repressed faithful one," MC Nem (the "Lover") says. "While I kiss your husband / You end up there at the sink / Wash, iron, and cook / You do everything perfectly / Just to end up suspicious / I am kissing your husband."

"Stop getting excited, repressed girlfriend," MC Kátia (the "Faithful One") shoots back. "You think you are shaking things up / But you're being duped / If you want to keep going / This charade is worth it / I'm not worried / Because the husband is mine / If you don't like it, too bad [engole, also meaning "swallow it"]." And MC Nem sneers at her: "I'm screwing [comendo, lit. "eating"] your husband." Then the tamborzão beat enters, good and loud. "Imagine four thousand people moving [pulando] when this starts," Fernanda said to me as we listened through her prized Genelec monitors. "I have been to a baile funk there at Mineira with seven thousand people. It's incredible, in-cre-di-ble! Sensational! It's cra-zy! I love it," she enthused, adding emphasis in a characteristically Carioca manner by stressing each syllable, then changing her tone somewhat to note: "Now, it's very dangerous. I still go with DJ Marlboro. It's crazy. I think it's anthropological."[6] The bailes funk are massive participatory events (in terms of dance) and in this sense have something in common with the samba schools and the "massaroca" that attracted the percussionists of PLAP (but lacking the participatory discrepancies of the live samba instruments).[7]

Listening Racially

For the communications scholar Liv Sovik, Fernanda "assumes a discourse of one who sees funk carioca from outside the scene, as a white." She "advises the public to take an interest in the phenomenon. She supports the funkeiros ('funkers') and receives their support too, as she was the hit of the funk portion of the Rock in Rio festival in January 2001" (2004, 233). Fernanda's statement during our interview that the funk phenomenon is "anthropological" would seem to support Sovik's argument. In reviewing the emergent literature on whiteness in Brazil and elsewhere in the "white Atlantic," Sovik, following Ruth Frankenberg (1997), sees it as a context-bound "process" (rather than "a thing"), and "as a problem needing definition, a question to be asked, rather than a concept to be operated" (Sovik 2004, 316). Moreover, writes Sovik, when considered within international hierarchies of race, "there can be no universal definition of Brazilian whiteness. One can be white in Brazil but not in the United States, white in Bahia but not in Rio Grande do Sul" (323). It is a "comparative value . . . present even when race is not mentioned" (323), or, of course, often precisely as what is not mentioned, as the field of whiteness studies presumes. (The magazine article I cited earlier on the Latin American "rock sisterhood" breaking the glass ceiling, for example, made no mention of the fact that the women featured are all light skinned and from middle-class families.)

Consider the following passage in which Fernanda elaborates on her musical taste (having referred to the United States as "the king of black music"):

> I think that the United States is "the best" [in English] in terms of funk and soul, because it is a culture from there. It is the culture of the blacks that came from jazz . . . rhythm and blues . . . funk and soul, and then hip-hop, rap, *neguinho* will go on creating ever more things. . . . *Black music* [in English], in the world, had so much influence—in the United States . . . in Africa, in Brazil the samba. . . . Because I like to swing a lot, I like to dance. Music for me is very much a matter of taste. . . . I could even say, "Wow, Bob Dylan, you're amazing," and . . . I know how to value it, but it is not my taste. . . . Same thing with heavy metal. Sure, I like [the Brazilian thrash metal band] Sepultura. I find one thing or another interesting . . . but I'm not going to go out and buy a heavy metal album, or buy a new age album, a country music album. It's not my style. I like funk, I like samba, I like soul, I like—I like rhythm.

Dylan, metal, new age, and country music, offered as examples of genres that do not privilege dance rhythms, also seem, by implicit contrast, to index "white" music here, yet the word *branco* (white) is never used. Blackness, on the other hand, is specified, celebrated, and linked to dance. (In contrast to the males in this book, Fernanda did not show an interest in the heavy or progressive rock of the 1970s when she was growing up.)

At one point Fernanda utilized the term *neguinho* (the diminutive of *nego*, which derives from *negro*, meaning "black") as an indication of her affection for black culture. José Jorge de Carvalho notes that while "signifiers like *nega, nego, crioulo, preto, mulata, preta, pretinha, neguinho, neguinha, morena* [variants of "black" or "darker skinned"] . . . are found in hundreds (or even thousands) of commercial songs in Brazil, . . . signifiers like *branco, branca* (white man and white woman, respectively), *loura* (blonde), are almost non-existent" (1994, 3). For Carvalho, this multiplicity signals how complex "the universe of black identity" is in Brazil, but it likewise evidences how whiteness is not named.[8] In finding the white in such talk, we contextualize the complex discussion on race in Brazil within its immanently relational logic. However, even if we define whiteness as a discursively constructed index of privilege (consumption, education, mobility, freedom, safety, and so on) that transcends the individual, it seems necessary to consider the specificity of context-bound processes and practices. "Whiteness as a site of privilege," Ruth Frankenberg has observed, "is not absolute but rather crosscut by a range of other axes of relative advantage and subordination" (2001, 76).

Seeking to move whiteness studies into a more international and interdisciplinary framework than previous scholarship, France Winddance Twine and Charles Gallagher caution against descriptions of whiteness that work to essentialize it, preferring to theorize race in relation to other social dimensions. Whiteness, they argue, must be understood "as a multiplicity of identities that are historically grounded, class specific, politically manipulated, and gendered social locations that inhabit local custom and national sentiments within the context of the new 'global village'" (2008, 6; see also Bonnett 2002; Nayak 2007). One such local custom in Rio is the celebration of the female body.

The Garota Carioca: Engendered and Empowered

The sensual but independent *garota carioca* (Carioca girl) of the South Zone was famously portrayed in song in the 1962 bossa nova "Garota de Ipanema" (given English lyrics in "The Girl from Ipanema"). For the anthropologist Mirian Goldenberg, the actress Leila Diniz—who became a notorious icon of the 1960s and 1970s after she shocked society by appearing on Ipanema Beach in a bikini in late pregnancy (and unwed)—remains a symbol of the "Carioca woman," who embodies better than anyone the spirit of the city: "seminude body, beach, sun, carnival, party, youth, liberty, sexuality, happiness, irreverence, distraction, informality, creativity, hedonism" (2002, 7–8). Goldenberg points to the specifically classed dynamics of this body, describing a "culture of narcissism" among the middle classes of Rio de Janeiro. In this social sector, she argues, "the body and fashion are fundamental lifestyle elements, and the preoccupation with appearances is charged with personal investment" (8). The middle classes are "obsessed with physical perfection" and "crushed by the proliferation of images, by therapeutic ideologies, and by consumption." The body has become, she concludes, a key form of cultural capital in Brazil. Elaborating on the aspect of fashion specifically, Fabiano Gontijo argues that what is most important in the Rio style of dress "is to be different" (2002, 61). In contrast to São Paulo, he argues, where imported fashions from Europe and the United States are highly valued, "Rio de Janeiro seems to cultivate kitsch in the Ibero-Latin way of Pedro Almodóvar, the brega [tacky] and the démodé or, simply, what is different. To be in fashion in Rio de Janeiro means to be different, to create your own style" (61–62).

Fernanda has cultivated the image of the feminine Carioca body that Goldenberg describes, and she has shown an acute and original sensibility for fashion throughout her career, highlighted in her album art (overseen by her husband, Luiz Stein). The fragmented photomontage portraits of her on the Entidade urbana album, for example, play on the idea of an urban, cosmopolitan fashion diva, portraying Fernanda wearing various quasi-kitsch outfits, hairstyles, and accessories evidently culled from various world areas. The graphic design for her Da lata album, on the other hand, places her in a room full of shiny metal objects such as hubcaps, steel and aluminum pots and pans, and an oil drum, with shiny flooring. She appears in these photographs alternately draped in a robe of metallic miscellany, or with two frying pans hanging around her neck and over her otherwise bare chest as a kind of brassiere, or, as on the back cover to the CD, naked on a low barstool in the middle of the room. (A raised leg keeps the image discreet.) In this last photograph, the tones of the room are all silver-gray, accenting Fernanda's nakedness and indeed her gleaming skin (see figures 14, 15, and 16).

Fausto Fawcett, Fernanda's lyricist-collaborator, claimed that for her, music had "to touch a chord in the lascivious ancestral suingue, to refine the body in the twisting, to sharpen the sex in the swinging, igniting any event with her physical form." She always "commanded in a very carioca way," he declared, "this business about dance music exactly because Rio de Janeiro breathes, sweats, celebrates on every corner" (1995). The use of the word "command" here draws attention to Fernanda's agency; one (male) commentator playfully called her a "meddler," taking a term sometimes used pejoratively to describe women in positions of power and turning it into a positive attribute—into an allegory of the nation, in fact. She

was "plugged into the world," he noted, but not subordinated to anyone: "We all have to learn to be meddling like Fernanda, with a puffed up chest, a haughty look, and samba-funk in the feet, and to forget being the Brazilians of [writer] Nelson Rodrigues's chronicles, with our hands in our pockets, sucking on oranges, and reeking of the complex of third-world bums. God bless Fernanda's audaciousness. And her enchanting beauty of the cool, swinging Carioca girl" (Tas 1995). Fernanda's audaciousness has helped her negotiate between family and career. When I first interviewed her at her offices in Ipanema in 1999, I asked for her thoughts on being a woman in the music industry in Brazil. It was a very macho country, she responded, and women constantly had to fight and to learn to manage the competing demands of career, touring, and also being a mother and a

FIGURE 14. Album art for Fernanda Abreu's *Entidade urbana*. Graphic design by Luiz Stein.

housewife. "If you are an artist you have to travel all the time. . . . There are a lot of obligations, a lot of ambitions, objectives, conquests to realize in the professional sphere. . . . And here in Brazil there's the Catholic thing, lots of guilt for not being home with the children, not giving attention to your home, your family, your husband." Fernanda was pregnant with her second child at the time of this interview, and she was busy researching the themes, as she put it, for the album *Entidade urbana* (Urban entity). She had mixed her previous album in London, but now that she was expecting, she did not want to travel abroad. Instead, she would record at Nas Nuvens, the facility introduced in the previous chapter and which, Fernanda excitedly reported, had just acquired a "*mar-ve-lous*" new mixing board made by the coveted English brand Neve.

FIGURE 15. Album art for Fernanda Abreu's *Da lata* (pan brassiere).
Graphic design by Luiz Stein.

FIGURE 16. Album art for Fernanda Abreu's *Da lata* (back cover).
Graphic design by Luiz Stein.

Her plan was to record the basic tracks (e.g., some sequenced loops, keyboards) before giving birth and then spend a couple of months at home. "Then I will mix and do the voices," she elaborated, "and then a tour in the middle of the year. That's what I did with [my first born,] Sofia. It was a little hectic, but it worked out." In the autobiographical text she later posted on her website, Fernanda highlights the joys of becoming a mother as part of her professional life. (She deviated slightly from the plan for recording that she described in our interview.) "The most important thing I could add in terms of biography is the birth of my second daughter Alice on 7 December 1999 at 10:22 hours. I spent my pregnancy composing and working on the project for the album *Entidade urbana*. Two months after she was born I entered the studio to record. There were nine months between recording, mixing, mastering, album art . . . etc. And always nursing my little baby girl. . . . Now it's time to get the album on the streets, put together the show, and hit the road once again!" With this public narrative, Fernanda brings the female body out of the domestic sphere (without negating family life) and naturalizes it within the context of music production and recording, portraying a woman in control of her body, her career, her technology, and her family. Fernanda even claims that the album itself had a nine-month gestation, and she has featured her young daughters' voices on her recordings.

Fernanda's balance of her career ambitions—which include being viewed publicly as sexy, sensual, in charge—with motherhood within what she describes as a generally macho context seems sympathetic to third-wave feminism in its preservation of individual choice and agency. One of the things that characterizes the third wave is, in fact, ambiguity about what defines it, and the multiplicity of often apparently contradictory identities that are encompassed within it. Drawing on Foucault (1972), Valerie R. Renegar and Stacey K. Sowards have examined the potential of contradictions in feminine identities "to enhance agency by creating space for self-determination, transcending expected behavior and adherence to ideas, and exploring alternatives through counter-imaginations and creativity" (2009, 14). Society, they write, "is awash in artificial dichotomies, but contradiction challenges the either/or nature of forced choices and allows for complex combinations of options and new alternatives to emerge" (11).

Some third-wave feminists thus "embrace the messiness of lived experience" and engage "practical-evaluative agency to find new ways of thinking about seemingly black and white choices" (16). Contradictions can be part of "a deliberate strategy that includes interplays of oppositions. . . . Performative and participatory contradictions create possibilities for self-determination, transcendence, and counter-imaginations that foster and rely on a sense of agency" (6). Clearly, having both family and career is central to Fernanda's public identity. (Moreover, this kind of "and/and" strategy, as opposed to either/or, conforms well to the general discourse of Brazilian identity as located in "the middle ground" [DaMatta 1995], in between contradictions [see also Sansone 1996, 207].) A third-wave perspective is also more attentive to the ways in which class inflects gendered identities (and performances of identity); Fernanda's ability to engage what Renegar and Sowards refer to as "practical-evaluative agency" probably owes something to her class status. For example, as Judith Still has observed, "the relative freedom of middle-class Brazilian women, even those with small children," depends in good measure on low-wage domestic help (1999, 5). I do not presume to know the circumstances of Fernanda's domestic life, but it is likely she has some help that has facilitated her studio work and touring (and she has a supportive husband who collaborates on her projects).

However, while we can paint in broad strokes how privilege has historically tended to accrue to light-skinned middle- and upper-class Brazilians (glossing over gender issues), privilege and agency are not the same thing. Referring to the Duel between the Faithful Ones and the Lovers, Mirian Goldenberg (who wrote a book on the lovers of taken men, A outra) argues that the women of funk have succeeded in expressing a greater liberty than other women. "They are showing that they don't need to depend on the man, that they can also take advantage of being lovers simply because it is a personal choice of theirs" (cited in Lemos 2005). Thus the lovers' refrain goes: "I am a lover with pride, and I say this because I can." I am not sure if Goldenberg's claim would stand up to in-depth ethnography on the phenomenon of the Duel, but the discourse of the MCs, as reported by the journalist Nina Lemos (2005), supports the notion that they feel empowered.[9]

The funk movement has changed considerably since Fernanda began her solo career (MC Kátia and MC Nem are of a much younger generation), but it remains intensely sexualized, perhaps even more so as *popozuda* (slang for a woman with a large rear end) is so central to the visual staging of the baile, as exemplified in the rise to international stardom of funk dancer Andressa Soares, who goes by the name Mulher Melancia (Watermelon Woman). There remains a radical social gulf between Fernanda's daily life and that of the *funkeiras* (women of funk), and it goes without saying that it is important to expose social inequalities and work toward reducing them. But there is also a sense in which these women participate in the *same* assemblage, one in which race, class, gender, and musical sound are "constantly constructed, undone and redone by the desires and becomings of actual people—caught up in the messiness, the desperation and aspiration, of life in idiosyncratic milieus" (Biehl and Locke 2010, 337).[10] Let us look more closely at how some of these issues play out in Fernanda's musical recordings.

Embracing the Sampler

Fernanda's first solo album, SLA Radical Dance Disco Club, released in 1990, opens with a vignette of funk and soul samples such as the line "Shut up already, damn!" from Prince's "Housequake," excerpts from KC and the Sunshine Band's "That's the Way (I Like It)" and Sister Sledge's "We Are Family," and a James Brown scream. The album, produced by Herbert Vianna and Fabio Fonseca, and her subsequent SLA2—Be Sample of 1992, produced by Fabio Fonseca and Liminha, showcased the sampling and sequencer work of Chico Neves (whom I introduced in chapter 2). Fernanda sings in Portuguese, English, and French and quotes from songs like Cheryl Lynn's "Got to Be Real" (1979). SLA Radical Dance Disco Club was probably the first Brazilian pop album to make extensive use of samplers. (SLA derives from Sampaio de Lacerda Abreu, her full family name; the word radical in Portuguese can mean something like "extreme.") Although borrowing from abroad no longer sparked the kinds of debates that it did in the 1960s, we have seen how anxieties over the balance between "local" and "global" in pop music mixtures resurged in the 1990s. Hints of that anxiety are evident in the press release that Hermano Vianna (1992) wrote for SLA2—Be Sample. The music that is made in Brazil today, he wrote, "can sample any kind of other music and can also self-sample (the sampler is the perfect instrument for any kind of manifestation of anthropophagy). Caetano Veloso's voice, and Lemmy [Kilmister of Motörhead]'s voice, the cavaquinho of [the band] Novos Baianos, and the O'Jays' bass; everything has the same value in the digital blender of the sampler." For Vianna, the sampler in Fernanda's music "is in [the] service of dance music, and the dance music is in [the] service of Brazilian music." The (imported) machine simply enabled and accelerated the cultural cannibalism that was already natural to the Brazilian character ("making us conscious of what we had already done until that time," Vianna wrote), so there was no foreign colonization of Brazilian practice. Still, Vianna's defense of sampling here suggests that for local audiences some justification was expected.

One of the songs from SLA 2 — *Be Sample*, "Rio 40 Graus" (Rio 104 degrees [40 degrees Celsius is 104 degrees Fahrenheit]), co-composed by Fernanda with Fausto Fawcett and Laufer is a slow funk that anticipated the samba-funk swing Fernanda would refine on subsequent albums. Among the samples featured are the guitar riff that opens the O'Jays' "For the Love of Money" of 1973 (and the groove of "Rio 40 Graus" is similar to the groove of that song) and Gilberto Gil singing "O Rio de Janeiro" from his well-known song "Aquele Abraço" of 1969, digitally spliced with Caetano Veloso singing the words "Soy loco por ti" from his version of Gil's 1967 song "Soy loco por ti, America," so that the combination of Gil's and Veloso's sampled vocalizations generates the intertextual "O Rio de Janeiro, soy loco por ti," or "I am crazy about you, Rio de Janeiro." Liminha programmed electronic drum patterns and plays a funk bass line, while Fabio Fonseca takes up a Stevie Wonder–like keyboard accompaniment using a clavinet sound (as in Wonder's "Superstition").

Beginning at the lyric "Sou carioca, pô" ("I'm Carioca, man"), Marcos Suzano adds tamborim, the small frame drum associated with carnival samba, a relatively subtle sonic reference to local music. Then, with the line "batucada digital" ("digital drumming"), he adds the howl-like sound of the cuíca, which is readily identified with samba, signaling the acoustic batucada underneath the digital sequencing. The lyrics comment on the place of the drug trade and the associated violence that had come to dominate media representations of Rio de Janeiro by the early 1990s. The half-shouted refrain identifies Rio as the Marvelous City, but also as a "purgatory of beauty and chaos," and the "capital of hot blood," and of the best and worst of Brazil. The verses are rapped by Fernanda and Fausto Fawcett; they tell of the "commandos" into which the drug gangs are divided, of "sub-uzis" equipped with "musical cartridges" smuggled in by the military, and of the "informational machine gun."

One of Fausto's lines, "xinxa das esquinas de macumba / violenta escopeta de sainha plissada" evokes a series of images from street corner life in Rio. *Xinxa* is a vulgar slang term for the vagina (Berozu 1998), *escopeta* is a shotgun, and *sainha* is a miniskirt. "You could be passing a corner of Macumba, and there's a sexy girl [xinxa], and behind her there'll be a guy with a weapon," Fernanda elaborated when I asked her to explain these lines. "You're taking a walk, there's a pretty girl, she's the girlfriend of a [drug] trafficker, at the same time he's the friend of an arms trafficker, and she tries to involve you, a foreigner, in some business, perhaps to carry drugs somewhere. . . . There's a lot of this in Rio. Rio has a lot of sensuality, lots of bunda, lots of beach, lots of bikini, lots of *mulata*, lots of samba, lots of swinging of the hips [*rebolado*]. . . . It's not just in the samba schools, it's on the beach, all the time, [it's on] the bus . . . [But] it's all veiled . . . you don't really know exactly [what is going on]." Together, the lyrics and musical sound of "Rio 40 Graus" thus offer a poetic rendering of a street-level mixture of music, technology, sensuality, violence, informal economies, North American black music, hints of samba, the beach, traffickers, and the police — in short, Brazil's hot capital of beauty and chaos (perhaps specifically as seen by middle-class subjects).

In the song "Sigla latina do amor (SLA II)" (Latin sign of love, from SLA 2—Be Sample), with Fausto and Fernanda as co-lyricists, the SLA acronym is turned into a kind of word: "Sla on your body, Sla on your mind," Fernanda sings in English over a Prince-like groove. "It's an ancestral lascivious sentiment / a latent amorous sensation," she then sings in Portuguese, while throughout the track other sampled voices rap in Spanish. Marcos Suzano provides percussion, and DJ Marlboro, from the baile funk scene, adds scratches. "When I kiss, clandestine paradises mix, in heavens of an abstract sampler," Fernanda sings, linking the sampler with the sensual and sentient body.

Tin Cans, X-Rays, and Good Blood

After Fernanda's first two albums, which, as just described, emphasized the use of samplers and cannibalized black dance music from the United States, the album *Da lata* (Canned), which would earn the title of best Latin American album of 1995 from *Billboard* magazine, and the subsequent *Raio X* (X-ray) gave a more prominent place to samba, achieving an engaging samba-funk hybrid on several songs. The sound incorporates more acoustic instruments such as a drum kit and percussion, while sampled loops are part of the hybrid mix rather than the dominant musical material. Fernanda described the change in sound as a search for finding a "Brazilian" voice in her mixtures: "It was this very search, 'What does it mean to make dance music in Brazil?' Is it to copy Janet Jackson? [Is it] to copy Soul II Soul, and just add Portuguese lyrics? How am I going to make a consistent mixture of computer, Pro Tools, samples, with tamborim, violão, cavaquinho . . . and make it into something pop, danceable, with swing, funk, soul, made with this samba-funk mixture? It is a mixture I found interesting, because it takes instruments that are very much from samba, that were born in Rio de Janeiro, that were with me . . . with this city here. So, I think on *Da lata* and *Raio X* I was able to begin to translate much better what I really wanted with my music." Here Fernanda's musical becoming began to converge more clearly with the other projects going on in this scene contemporaneously as she searched for a more "Brazilian" way to incorporate (global) technologies while also bringing traditional acoustic samba instrumentation into the mix more directly. Meanwhile, the low-tech metaphor of the tin can (*lata*) evokes the sound of the batucada, that is, the beating of the drums in the morro. (Specifically, it was intended, Fernanda said, to reference how children in the favelas may begin their musical training beating on tin cans.)

There was, however, a double meaning to the album title, one that was very much an inside joke for the Carioca youth. In 1987, it is said, a Panamanian drug-smuggling vessel, upon being approached by the Brazilian military police off the coast of Rio de Janeiro state, unloaded its cargo of tin cans full of potent marijuana into the sea. For weeks, the story goes, Carioca youths snuck around the police to pluck the cans (the *veneno da lata*, "canned poison") off of the beaches at night. Subsequently, as the weed-smoking population deemed this herb to be of a very high quality, the expression *da lata* came to mean "good" in local slang. To say something *é da lata* ("is canned"), then, meant that it was of good quality. There are no specific references to the event in the lyrics; in her music video for this song, however, Fernanda wears a single white star on her shirt, an apparent reference to the Panamanian flag. (She sang about decriminalizing marijuana in the song "Bloco Rap Rio," borrowing a refrain from the local "rapcore" band Planet Hemp.)

Da lata, released in 1995, was produced by Liminha and Will Mowat, the British producer known for his work with the group Soul II Soul, although Chico Neves produced the title track. It was recorded at Nas Nuvens and Discover studios, both in the South Zone production nexus described in previous chapters, and mixed in Soul II Soul's London studio with the help of their regular engineer, Eugene Ellis. After coming across Fernanda's CDs in a shop in São Paulo during a visit to Brazil, Will Mowat contacted her about working together. Fernanda was thrilled. "I knew all their albums, completely, all the songs . . . and I always loved their sound," she said. In the United States the sound of dance recordings was sometimes "kind of heavy," but the albums of Soul II Soul (which, like Miami bass, utilized

the Roland 808 drum machine) were "softer," she thought. Da lata opens
with the song "Veneno da lata" (Canned poison) with a ganzá articulating steady but swung sixteenth notes (as from samba), a synthesizer pad
quietly establishing the bluesy two-chord vamp of the song (I^7–IV^7), and
Fernanda's three-year-old daughter Sofia reciting lyrics by the local poet
Chacal: "Rio de Janeiro, Marvelous City! The tin can. The tin can in the
middle of the night. In the dead silence of the night. Suddenly the groove
kicked in. The batucada began. Beat, beat, beat on the tin can! It's the tin
can of the bateria!"

Gradually, additional percussion instruments enter: pandeiro, drum kit,
cuíca, then electric bass and a restrained funk riff on the electric guitar.
Members of the venerable samba school Mangueira (officially, GRES Estação Primeira da Mangueira), the oldest such organization in Brazil, join
Fernanda on this opening samba-funk piece. However, their participation
is not merely captured in what Thomas Turino has referred to as the high-
fidelity mode of studio work (2008); it is, as Hermano Vianna commented
in his press release for the album, "reprocessed in Will Mowat's computer"
while "Marcos Suzano's pandeiro and Bodão's tamborim are digitized in Liminha's sampler" (1995). Technology, Vianna claimed, "is only accelerating
and facilitating the mixing acumen of Rio." For Vianna, the album signaled
that Rio de Janeiro was still a "marvelous" city even after several years of
negative press pertaining to the beach robberies, drug trafficking, and violence. Moreover, Fernanda's musical mixture, he proposed, extended the
kinds of cultural exchange between elites and "the people," between the
"asphalt" and the morro, between the South and North Zones that he had
researched with respect to the history of samba (Vianna 1999). When the
funkeiros were demonized in the media beginning in 1992, Vianna reflected,
he thought that Rio was heading for a radical apartheid following what he,
like most Brazilians, perceived to be the North American model wherein
"white is white, black is black, and the mulata (like samba and funk) is
nothing special [não é a tal]" (Vianna 1995, making a reference to Caetano
Veloso's song "Americanos"). Rio de Janeiro already provided "the ruler and
compass" with respect to mixture, Vianna wrote. Dance music could "teach
us the rest: namely, to use the computer to continue mixing everything." He
was referring not just to Fernanda's recording but to the funk carioca phenomenon as well: carioca dance music, he insisted in the enthusiastic prose
typical of album releases, was "the new malandragem, the new theory of cultural mestiçagem, the mulatto rhythm that is so great [é a tal]."

Alexandra Isfahani-Hammond has taken Vianna to task for this discourse about mestiçagem and the mulatto after Vianna evoked Veloso's song again in a newspaper editorial questioning the implications of affirmative action quotas in Brazilian universities (Vianna 2004). She characterizes it as consistent with an established rhetorical strategy that white writers in Brazil have used "to justify their incorporation of blackness" (Isfahani-Hammond 2008, 5). Such texts conflate "patriarchal white supremacism with resistance to US Empire," Isfahani-Hammond claims. Perhaps, however, both Vianna's and Isfahani-Hammond's interpretations of (white) Brazilians' views on race mixture oversimplify the matter some. Reflecting on a similar issue in the discourse of cannibalism, Zita Nunes describes the problem differently: "Although the philosophical trappings of anthropophagism would seem to imply a political vision of a democratic society, this is not the case. In fact, blacks have not been equal participants in a Brazilian 'mixture.' This is not the result of vulgar or individual prejudice; it lies at the heart of a notion of citizenship and is an enabling condition of a construction of a national identity. In the anthropophagist model, however, we discover that assimilation is unthinkable without the excretion. The law of assimilation is that there must always be a remainder, a residue—something (someone) that has resisted or escaped incorporation, even when the nation produces narratives of racial democracy to mask this tradition of resistance" (1994, 125).

Fernanda's cover of Caetano Veloso's "A tua presença morena" (Your presence morena) on this album is a slow, groovy, samba-reggae-dub-jungle hybrid. Her repetition of the words "your presence" (a tua presença) is double tracked (that is, recorded at least twice and layered in the mix) and split ("panned," in audio terminology) between left and right channels, giving the impression that multiple female voices are whispering the line into the listener's ears. The verses follow a cool, stepwise descending melody that almost suggests talking. The song tells of a human "presence" that enters through the eyes, the mouth, the nostrils, the ears ("the seven holes of my head") and "disintegrates and updates" the singer's presence, embracing the torso, the arms, and the legs, clearly suggesting intimacy between two people but also echoing tropes of cannibalism. Then, curiously, the presence is described in terms of colors, moving from white to green, then red, blue, and yellow, as if describing a rainbow. Finally, the lyrics settle on black, repeating it several times: "Your presence is black, black, black / Black, black, black, black, black, black."

This word cannot be heard as just another color in the list, especially given the morena (dark- or brown-skinned woman) of the song title. It is the remainder, that something that is always there to keep discourses of mixture meaningful. The progression of the lyrics in effect reverses the paradigm of Brazilian racial history expertly analyzed in Thomas Skidmore's classic study *Black into White* (1974), in which the historian described the whitening agenda of early twentieth-century Brazil. Here, in a transformation akin to Macunaíma's in Mário de Andrade's celebrated allegory of Brazilian identity—but inverting the change in color—white seems to become black (see Z. Nunes 1994 for more on race in Mário's *Macunaíma*). At the very end of the song, when a techno-samba jungle groove has taken over, Fernanda moves into a high register she rarely uses to sing, "It's black, it's black," as if to exalt blackness. Her rendition of the lyrics thus almost seem to describe how the embodied "presence and pleasure" often associated with black dance music (Danielsen 2006) have permeated Fernanda's body.

Fernanda's next release, *Raio X*, arose, she wrote in her accompanying press release, out of an urge to think about and confirm her musical identity, which "included the idea of location, origin, nationality, and experience." To do so she undertook a project of "remixes, rereadings, [and] re-recordings" and added a couple of unreleased tracks as a kind of "x-ray" of her career. A second motivation derived from her tour of Brazil with the *Da lata* show: "I saw a lot of corners of Brazil. . . . Lots of riches. Lots of misery. Lots of mixture. Lots of contrast. Lots of good people. . . . I left with Rio de Janeiro in my bags and returned with Brazil. . . . The look and swing of Chico Science's Pernambuco, of [Carlinhos] Brown's Bahia, of [André] Abujamra's São Paulo, of the Rio of Mangueira, for example, turned this project into a kind of . . . revised and amplified edition." Luiz Stein's album art suggests that Fernanda embodies the nation (via Rio de Janeiro): the front cover features a silvery-toned close-up of her face, evoking the visual language of the x-ray. She wears a pendant of Brazil on a necklace; inside the jewel box for the album, underneath the CD, is an x-ray of a torso, presumably her own. That the imagery and the music are intended as an x-ray of the nation *through* Fernanda is further suggested by the fact that she uses the title "Abreugrafia" for the autobiographical essay she posted on her website (*Abreu* + *biografia*, but also a reference to the Brazilian term for a radiography screen for tuberculosis invented by Manuel Dias de Abreu).

The opening "vignette" of the album ("Raio X [Vinheta de abertura]") is a brief, funky, confidently executed rap-manifesto of mixture, sampling, music technologies, and Brazil. It utilizes the kinds of language play I described for Lenine's and Pedro Luis's music, for example, using English words that can sound Portuguese, or playing with expressions such as *dizer na lata*, meaning speaking frankly and directly in someone's face (and referring back to the *Da lata* album as well). The text, penned by Chacal, describes a setting in which hip-hop, house, charme, samba, rock, funk, disco, and dub genres mix with pandeiros, samplers, and batuque on tin cans. "Presenting a different sound, creating a new style," she sings. "Inaugurating the sampler stressing what is needed." Her album SLA2—*Be Sample*, she chants, was just to confirm "that our traditions come from the verb to mix." Again the mediation between the working-class morro and the middle- and upper-middle-class "asphalt" is described as occurring "in a digital batuque."

Immediately following this manifesto-like introduction, Fernanda leads a joyous rendition of the uplifting 1964 carnival samba "Aquarela Brasileira" (by Silas de Oliveira; not to be confused with the earlier "Aquarela do Brasil," by Ary Barroso), which has a long, sinewy melody that draws the listener into its nationalistic celebration, with an uplifting modulation from minor to major and then back to minor again. This is a classic samba and Fernanda, again calling on members of the old guard of Rio's legendary Mangueira samba school for the percussion, along with Marcos Suzano, performs it entirely acoustically, following the tradition of gradually introducing more percussion instruments as the intensity of emotion increases. Beginning with pandeiro, ganzá, and voice, adding a tamborim ostinato, the distinctively grating sound of the knife and plate used in samba, then agogô, scraper, and caixa, then bass runs on the seven-string guitar, and—only when the modulation to major occurs, cavaquinho, surdo, cuíca, and the whistle used in samba schools to coordinate the sections, only to fade out on a triumphant choral chant of the syllables la, la ya la ya, back in minor. It is samba, she wrote in her listening notes, and "it remain[s] samba."

Fernanda's "Brasil é o país do suingue" (Brazil is the country of swing, co-composed with Felipe Abreu, Hermano Vianna, and Laufer), is a slow Prince-like funk-rap shout-out to Brazil inspired by "Aquarela Brasileira" (which describes traveling through Brazil and discovering the natural and cultural splendors of various locales). As explained in chapter 3, *suingue*, the Brazilianization of the English word "swing," refers not just to musical articulations but also to an embodied sense of rhythmic deportment, to the notion that the Carioca body—particularly the female body—has a musically sensual way of moving. "Come on fellows / everyone dancing," Fernanda calls out in the song, "dancing without stopping." The Brazilian, she sings, is of the baile and has carnival in the blood:

> I say, let that little ass [bundinha] hang out
> Let your hip loose and shout:
> "Brazil, Brazil, Brazil is the country of suingue!"

Fernanda calls all Brazilians to dance with her. To the north in Belém do Pará, she shouts out to the Tupinambá sound rig party, a massive mobile DJ equipment setup. She calls out to the reggae scene in Maranhão; the tambor da crioula (an informal Afro-Brazilian dance with religious elements), forró from Ceará; surf-reggae from Santa Catarina, a Japanese funk party in São Paulo, Candomblé and dancing in the streets with Timbalada and Ilê Aiyê in Bahia, the mangue beat in Recife, the rock-funk of Porto Alegre. "Come with me to Rio de Janeiro! The city of exceptional sensual swing!" Every corner, she delights, is samba-funk in the land of DJ Marlboro and his Big Mix bailes.

The sensual suingue described in this song is distinct, in Fernanda's estimation, from the phenomenon she referred to as bundalização (or "bundaization," a term at least one scholar has also used; see Lessa 2005). "Everyone wants to be beautiful and sexy," she told me. But this has to be put "in the proper perspective." The media "manufactures the woman as bunda," Fernanda complained. The head (cabeça, which can also mean "mind") of the woman is in fact the ass, she lamented. At the time of this interview, there was much discussion in the media about the model Tiazinha, who wore a thong negligee and gyrated in close-up camera shots on Luciano Huck's Programa H television show. "You look at Tiazinha," Fernanda said, "it's bunda." Look at pagode dancer Carla Perez from the group É o Tchan, "it's bunda." She recalled a popular joke from her childhood that plays on the slogan of the Brazilian flag: "Order and progress, bunda is success." Everything, she said, "is sort of about bunda."

For Fausto Fawcett, however, there is also "a more entertainingly serious aspect" to the term bunda when it is associated with "suingue, with sangue [blood], sensuality, rhythm," things that were "simply a part of our culture" and not "exaggeratedly commercial." He described the song "Garota Sangue Bom" (Cool girl), which he co-authored with Fernanda, as a kind of update to the bossa nova "Ela é carioca" ("She's a Carioca," 1963), by Vinicius de Moraes and Tom Jobim. *Sangue bom*, or "good blood," means someone who is "good people," who is "cool," who knows the codes of a given scene and is trustworthy. "Garota carioca, suingue, sangue bom!" ("Carioca girl, swing, good blood!") is the anthemic refrain to this romping mix of rhythm and blues, samba hip-hop, and rap full of attitude. The verses tell of "mocking hips" in the measured steps of the half-samba, half-funk "dancing scandal" of a woman; of the "Carioca feminine presence," suburban and South Zone, a "body that is a soul"; "sublime irresistible inspiration" from the Marvelous City; "a courtesan synthesized from the waves of a feminine body" with "an influence of a sensual caliber." "Check out her way of speaking," Fernanda sings, "of dancing . . . of looking . . . of walking . . . of flirting." Fausto's lyrics take the listener into "the suburban night" where there are girls of good blood, in the charme, of "inevitable desire," proffering invitations one cannot refuse, "the sugar of the Carioca feminine presence." It is a "hot paradise of excited spirit," of feelings "animated by the sun and the sea."

Clearly, all these images and metaphors speak to the male gaze, in this case, Fausto Fawcett's. How might this Carioca feminine presence be characterized? I asked the lyricist. "Suingue, rhythm. Explicit seduction," was his answer. "The Carioca woman has manners of seduction," he claimed. "She knows how to work with masculine fascination better. This is cool, and it's a tradition too, there is no denying this." But suingue, in Fausto's perception at least, also pertains more generally to social "contact," to "something even violent, of blood being synonymous with something vital to life, circulation." This was very pronounced in Rio de Janeiro, he felt, but especially in the suburbs, where suingue "*is the language*." Suingue is, he said, "the story" of the *comunidade* ("community," a term that refers specifically to the working-class population), and it is something that samba and funk share. Fernanda echoed Fausto's suggestive topography when she wrote in her press release for *Raio X* that "all that we want in Rio is to be able to listen to the sound that this new crowd from the morro is making, not just the sound of the asphalt, of the middle-class South Zone. After all, the morro is where the experts hang out."

One such expert is Ivo Meirelles, whom Fernanda invited—along with members of his samba-funk-pop group, Funk'n Lata—to record a rousing

remake of the classic samba "É hoje" (Today's the day), which she had already recorded in a more traditional style on *Da lata*.[11] Ivo grew up in the morro of Mangueira, and he has deep roots in that community's storied samba school, of which he has served as director (see figure 17). He started Funk'n Lata in July of 1995, he told me, as a project to turn the "rhythmicists" (*ritmistas*) of the samba school into "musicians of percussion" with the instruments of the samba school such as surdo, pandeiro, tamborim, caixa, and repique. "I wanted them to think musically like a pop-rock-funk band, not like a samba school," he said. That is, the percussionists had to move beyond thinking solely about their rhythmic role and consider the dynamics of a pop music ensemble that could record tracks for the radio. "I began to give them some patterns for how the surdo would perform the role of the kick drum, how the caixa would imitate the snare of a drum kit, how the tamborim and the repique would take the place of the missing tom-toms, and that's how Funk'n Lata began."

Like various other musicians discussed in this book, Ivo was interested in eliminating the drummer of the typical pop-rock band, but he was ap-

FIGURE 17. Ivo Meirelles, leading GRES Estação
Primeira da Mangueira in rehearsal

proaching the problem from precisely the opposite position of, for example, the members of PLAP. That is, *he was already in samba* and wanted to take the bateria associated with a classic samba school and combine it with electric bass and guitar, and with a horn section of trumpet, sax, and trombone. He sought to join batucada (unaccompanied samba drumming) to "black music," meaning funk, rap, hip-hop, and soul. (LL Cool J was among his influences.) The addition of the brass instruments to perform bright, syncopated fills gave Funk'n Lata a very danceable pop sound, and it is effective for Fernanda's recording of "É hoje." "Fernanda knows how to mix samba with funk and hip-hop," he said. "She does it well." The samba from São Paulo that was "in fashion," he complained, referring to the pagode phenomenon, lacked "a connotation of roots." When Fernanda makes a mixture, he said, "she knows the roots that carnival of Rio de Janeiro represents."

For Fernanda, beginning the album with people from the old guard of Mangueira and ending it with Funk'n Lata spoke to her concept for *Raio X*. Brazil was a "miscegenated and cannibalistic country" whose "cultural and racial tradition" came from the verb "to mix." *Raio X* mixed the various drums and drumming styles of tambor, maracatu, *timbau* from Bahia, electric *bumbo*, and the surdo from samba "in service of Brazilian dance music." Music technologies such as Pro Tools, samplers, and Macintoshes, on the other hand, were already part of "the universal pop language." The album, she felt, affirmed that Brazilian pop had begun to mix "Brazil" into its language more effectively. "To be Brazilian" is to be "of the world." Other tracks on the album include Fernanda's hip-hop-forró-samba-funk hybrid version of Lenine's "Jack soul brasileiro," with Lenine as guest singer, Liminha on bass, Suzano on pandeiro and ganzá, and Gilberto Gil on violão. The bossa nova–era legend João Donato added keyboards (clavinet and Fender Rhodes), while Rodrigo Campello and Berna Ceppas created loops from samples, in addition to Bodão's drum kit and tamborim and Fernando Vidal's electric guitar. It is quite a mixture of generations, influences, and instruments. Another song "Kátia Flávia, a Godiva de Irajá" (Kátia Flávia, the Godiva of Irajá), describes a sexually ambiguous character of Fausto Fawcett's invention from the underworld of Copacabana prostitution and crime, portrayed as a "hot blonde" (*louraça*) who is delicious and satanic and "only wears edible underwear."[12]

Urban Entities, Violence, and Consumerism

In preparing the album *Entidade urbana*, released in 2000, Fernanda researched "everything that has to do with humans in this space that is the city." The city is an "urban body," she told me, while Rio de Janeiro is "human, urban, and at the same time very difficult." She was preoccupied with "the violence, the tolerance, the generosity, also the nature" of cities like Rio, and she conceptualized a transhuman city as "a living organism" with "veins," "urban cloth," "vital city organs," "nodules," and "access highways." The sound of the album, which was produced by Liminha and Chico Neves at Nas Nuvens, Estudios Mega, and Chico's smaller Estúdio 304 (all blocks away from each other in the South Zone), continues Fernanda's interest in pop dance musics that originated principally in African American styles — mixed, of course, with samba or, in one case, with the maracatu rhythm.

The track "Roda que se mexe" (Circle that moves), for example, co-composed with Rodrigo Campello (of MiniStereo) describes the earth as a circle spinning, shuffling, and swinging, full of expanding and multiplying cities. The underlying rhythmic feel borrows from an American disco-funk sound of the late 1970s (it is similar to the groove in James Brown's hit "It's Too Funky in Here" of 1979), and the two-chord vamp (I^7–IV^7) in the verses give it a rhythm-and-blues flavor. At the same time, the musical accents performed on various instruments keep it rooted in a duple samba feel and mark it as a carioca groove. Percussion recorded live (e.g., Marcos Suzano on pandeiro and ganzá, and César Farias on tamborim), as well as subtle references in the instrumentation of Rodrigo Campello's and Berna Ceppas's programmed loops (the sounds of the cuíca, a knife and plate, and a box of matches played as a shaker) further highlight the samba influence on the track. Contributions from the MPB legends Gilberto Gil (violão, backing vocals) and João Donato (clavinet and Fender Rhodes piano), and from Jamil Joanes (slap funk bass), César Farias (drum kit), and Fernando Vidal and Davi Moraes (electric guitar), fill out the pop band instrumentation.

The word *roda* ("circle" or "wheel") is used in Brazil to refer to a circle of participants in a traditional musical or dance setting. In a samba de roda, for example, those present who are not dancing typically clap the rhythm (generally, a 3 + 3 + 2 pattern or similar), and sing a refrain in chorus — an eminently "participatory" formation. This pop roda, by contrast, is characterized not by the intensely localized and live manifestation of the circle dance but rather by a mixing, multiplying, cannibalizing, swinging, transhuman, transurban cosmopolitan loop. Everybody is moving at the same time, Fernanda sings. "The whole earth wants to swing." As the planet spins, cities are everywhere: the lyrics describe them climbing hills and descending valleys. They eat earth and drink ocean, creating new faces, new houses, and new corners for hanging out with friends, and for "making rhythm and rhyme." Cities are hotbeds of invention of new languages, dances, fashions.

The song "Meu CEP é seu" (My ZIP code is yours), also co-composed with Rodrigo Campello, is a mix of samba, acid jazz (club dance music influenced by jazz and funk), and jungle (a fast-tempo dance genre characterized by frenetic snare drumming and bass influenced by dub reggae). Rather than the city being like a body, the inverse is the case in this song: veins and arteries are compared to streets with traffic jams. "To navigate through your body," she sings, "is like walking through the city." She gets lost in the city-body, she changes her address to "inside your body." A deep, low electric bass line that follows fairly closely a characteristic samba syncopation (at a very slow tempo in 2/4 meter) is juxtaposed with an acid jazz–like drum part that feels more like 4/4 meter with even, slow, unaccented eighth notes played on a ride cymbal and snare-drum rim shots on beats 2 and 4. Filtered synthesizer pads (orchestral string backgrounding) add to the acid jazz ambience.

As Rodrigo Campello plays a chord vamp with syncopated samba accents on violão, Fernanda's voice enters, speaking the words rhythmically, then singing a hypnotic melody that mostly oscillates between the tonic and lowered seventh scale degree, but with accents that also emphasize the characteristic samba pattern. Her voice is modified by filters and electronically split into high and low octaves, lending it a machine-like, posthuman quality. On the refrain the groove switches to the rapid snare drumming common in the jungle genre. Also featured on the track is a flexatone, a spring steel instrument invented in 1924 to replace the musical saw and used in compositions by Arnold Schoenberg, Aram Khachaturian, and Alfred Schnittke, among others. Marcos Suzano performs on cajón and metal springs and platters, among the percussive odds and ends he includes in his kit.

From the same album, the song "Urbano canibal" (Urban cannibal), co-authored by Fernanda and Lenine, also features a jungle sound. City and body again blend into one another in the lyrics. Fernanda sings about being "an urban cannibal" made of flesh, steel, cement, "planted in the asphalt," "in the middle of everything," devouring, chewing "this city body of vacant identity" and "becoming what I am." The city body, as something to be consumed, is integral to this cannibal becoming. The rapid snare drumming of jungle percussion also reminds the listener of the maracatu rural of Lenine's home state, Pernambuco (see chapter 2). A violão adds a filtered harmonic vamp while distorted electric guitars scream and echo in the background, painting an aural picture of a tough, fast-paced, whirling urban environment that is half human, half street. In short, Entidade urbana expands the trope of the dancing, samba-ing body, of the incorporation of all things pertaining to one's identity, to include the urban landscape, evoking the kind of "cosmopolitan body" described by the geographer Nigel Clark: "It is not only human bodies that pass through a city composed of active matter," he reflects, "but matter which flows in and through bodies" (2000, 14).

The "city body" of Rio de Janeiro is also one threatened by violence, and Fernanda turned to this theme for the album Na paz (At peace), which she released in 2004. The striking album art, by Luiz Stein, features Fernanda in combat fatigue pants and a white T-shirt with a red heart on it, with small white flowers in her long brown hair. Her arms are outstretched in front of her, toward the viewer, and in each hand she holds a large caliber pistol, one black, the other silver, with sunflowers stuck in the barrels. The background is a blue sky with light cumulus clouds, and framing the white-lettered title of the album are two white pistols facing in opposite directions with flowers growing out of the barrels. One of the photographs inside the listening notes features a profile image of Fernanda holding an automatic weapon (also with flowers stuck in the end of the barrel), and Picasso's white dove of peace in the background. Similar photographs include a peace sign in the background.[13]

Fausto Fawcett describes the imagery as representing an "attitude of bellicose arrogance" (2004); perhaps it also reflects that "kitschy" impulse "to be different, to create your own style," that Fabiano Gontijo identified in the Carioca fashion sense (2002, 61–62). Given the context of the Rio de Janeiro of the past two decades, however, which includes the association in the media of funk with violence, as well as the more generalized problems that the various modes of violence (the war between traffickers and the police, the devastation of youth by drugs and the drug trade, armed robbery and assault, for example) pose for urban social life, Fernanda's incorporation of guns into her image for the album art is not mere aesthetization or trivialization. She wanted to take the images of weapons that saturated media coverage of the city, she said, and attach them to "a different message," that of peace.[14]

From this album, "Bidolibido" is a funk song (with the seven-string guitar of samba and choro) in which Fernanda aggressively raps accelerated lyrics by Fausto Fawcett about sexually charged encounters intertwined with sounds and images of violence. Fernanda's voice is modified electronically to sound like it is coming through a small speaker—a cellular phone? an answering machine? It is very *Sex and the City*, Fausto remarked in the press release. The jaunty, nervous verses, which are "treated like stray bullets . . . whirring by," Fausto writes (2004), give way to techno-samba groove accents on cuíca and tamborim on the refrains and again as the song ends. The violent city territorializes the sexualized body here, in the way Elizabeth Grosz described for "Bodies-Cities" (1998). Intertextual references such as a citation of Caetano Veloso's "De noite na cama" (At night in bed, 1974) and Gilberto Gil's "Aquele abraço," and the use of the English "I miss you" to rhyme with *edifício* (building) in a phrase describing sex in a hallway territorialize other assemblages. It reflects, partly, what Fernanda conceptualized as "your violent portion as a human being, . . . which generates other [forms of] violence, but which also generates energy [and] a number of things that are not all bad."

Another way in which Fernanda developed the themes for the album was in terms of the social violence of consumerism. In a city like Rio with its radical inequality, the dynamics of consumption were "cruel," she felt. Television made one feel that it was necessary "to buy Nike sneakers," and "that you have to be better than your friend, you have to be more beautiful than so-and-so," and this, she felt, generated a kind of violence. It was exacerbated by globalization and the policies of neoliberalism given free rein after the collapse of the Soviet Union, she said. Her generation, she reflected, read Marx and Engels and at least thought about socialism. "You had to think a little bit about fraternity, about inequality, generosity, the possibility of a life in solidarity, equality." Individualism was now liberated and the Other "can go to hell." The "yuppie" culture of Wall Street, in which "the idea was to get your first million dollars by age thirty," may have been "sweet [*bonitinho*] for the United States, where there is a certain standard of living," but in Brazil it was not a good fit. It was "savage" capitalism. Fernanda collaborated again with Ivo Meirelles for "Vida de rei" (King's life), a disco-funk-samba piece in which Ivo raps about being born in the favela, damned, and forced to "struggle with the devil" to gain respect and to stay out of gangs—a king without a kingdom. "You who doubt," Fernanda chimes in, "have everything in life" and do not want to recognize that the "maladies of the city are not in the shacks."

The dub- and rude boy–influenced "A onça" (The jaguar), co-composed with Rodrigo Campello and featuring the local hip-hop artist Black Alien, describes the kind of paranoia urban violence can generate. Fernanda sings of studying her surroundings while walking carefully through the city, alert to danger, steeled by hunger, asking Ogum to accompany her, with a cool mind and hot body, like a jaguar. She also sings a version of Jorge Ben Jor's "Eu vou torcer" (I will cheer), from the latter's A tábua de esmeralda (The Emerald Tablet), released in 1972 and regarded as a classic in Brazil. The song is about "cheering for peace," for "beautiful things" (spring, summer, winter, blue seas, dignity, lovers, happiness, understanding), and for "useful things you can buy for ten bucks," and it features Indian sitar (André Gomes) and tabla drum (Marcos Suzano), presumably to suggest a peaceful Buddhist or Ghandian spirituality. Ben Jor also joined Fernanda as a guest vocalist on the song "Zazuê," a melancholy tango-inflected track about a figure who wants to be a kind of Robin Hood of the morro.

She also includes on the album two irresistible sambas recorded largely acoustically. Fernanda shares the playful lyrics to the lighthearted "Sou brasileiro" (I'm Brazilian, co-composed with Fernanda's longtime percussionist Jovi Joviniano) with the samba artist Mart'nália. The final track on the album leaves no doubt of Fernanda's intense appreciation of samba as she covers the melancholic classic "Não deixe o samba morrer" (Don't let the samba die, 1976) by Edson Gomes da Conceição and Aloísio Silva and first made into a hit by the singer Alcione. The subject of the song— Fernanda, in this case—proclaims that when she can no longer parade down the avenue, when her legs can no longer carry her body along with the samba, she will hand off her place to someone else and watch her school from the sidelines, "winning or losing another carnival." And before kissing life good-bye, she will request that the youngest sambista never let the samba die: "The morro was made of samba, of samba for us to dance."

Conclusions

In the 1970s, soul and funk from the United States found enthusiastic audiences in Rio de Janeiro, particularly among the working classes. Disco music in Brazil had a precedent with the campy ensemble As Frenéticas, made up of six female singer-dancers (and band), at first as a novelty act at Nelson Motta's Dancing Days nightclub in the South Zone in the mid-1970s, but then, briefly, as a media phenomenon (Motta 2000, 290–303).[15] Fernanda Abreu began her career as a singer and dancer in the pop-rock group Blitz, which also became a media phenomenon in the early 1980s as Brazil re-democratized; when she wanted to launch a solo career, she was drawn especially to black dance music from the United States. However, together with her producers and arrangers, principally Chico Neves and Liminha, she also incorporated synthesizers and, more importantly, sequencers into her first two albums. In a country abundant in acoustic percussion traditions, in a city of samba, the practice of looping electronic beats on a sequencer could be interpreted locally as a dubious one—an "alienated" practice even, in the terms of the debate discussed in the preface. Fernanda did not use loops in moderation as a subtle update to the MPB aesthetic; she placed them at the center of her sound and her discourse about Brazilian music. Meanwhile, in the communities where samba was supposed to be rooted, funk carioca was emerging, also utilizing sequencers and beat boxes, and drawing on electronic dance rhythms. Fernanda Abreu was among the first from outside this scene—along with her friend Hermano Vianna—to recognize and embrace Rio funk as a legitimate expression of Carioca life.

After her first two albums, Fernanda began to include more samba in her mixtures, as she joined in the collective project to insert Brazil into pop. She also carefully balanced her career with motherhood in a context she identified as strongly macho. As Rita Lee pointed out, her career stands in opposition to mono-dimensional media representations of women as objects to be consumed—"eaten" in Brazilian slang for sexual intercourse. In "Nádegas a declarar," Fernanda's collaboration with Gabriel O Pensador, from which I quoted in the epigraph to this chapter, she addressed the issue of bunda in Brazilian culture. She is not interested in lecturing on morality, she rapped, because it is common knowledge that in a tropical country of soccer, carnival, and samba, "to shake a little ass" is "natural." Yet, while she did not claim to be a feminist, she recognized that bundalização was encouraged by a macho culture "full of chauvinist pigs." She wanted to rap about it not just for young girls but also to reach the males who "endlessly encourage" bundalização, especially on television. "This is for you!" she advised. The cover art for Gabriel's album Nadegas a declarar of 1999 (which features this collaboration) is framed as if it were a TV screen, with Gabriel tied up and muted with duct tape over his mouth, seated in a chair, looking upward toward the camera, his constricted hands opened upward in resignation, and surrounded by the bronzed backsides of some twenty or so young women wearing nothing but thong bikinis, lying in tight but more or less random proximity on the floor, none showing her face. Gabriel is suffocating in a sea of bunda in this image; the contrast with Fernanda's album art, which always features her face and front side, is striking (Fernanda's husband, Luiz Stein, oversaw the graphic design for Gabriel's disc, as he has for Fernanda).

"Historically," Heloisa Buarque de Hollanda writes, "Brazilian women have always found it uncomfortable to show public commitment to feminist struggles. As a result, it appears that the only reason for their present gains and outstanding leadership roles is their . . . administrative and financial talents and skills; skills that, not coincidentally, are today very appealing to neoliberal entrepreneurial management models" (2002, 322). Fernanda has shown these kinds of management skills and, like Suzano, adapted well to the new spaces opened up by transformations in the music industry. Na paz was the first album she recorded in her personal studio, Pancadão, and the first on her own label, Garota Sangue Bom. The studio is in a small house on a quiet street in the South Zone. She sought to make it into a comfortable space for working, a "home-like" environment, she said, with a kitchen and lounge as well as the studio itself. (It is not unusual for recording studios to have a small kitchen and lounge.)

She carefully chose the equipment, such as the Genelec control room monitors, which, she noted, had excellent bass, essential for mixing dance music. Most importantly for her, in keeping with broader trends as music production moved into smaller "project" studios, at Pancadão "you're not watching the clock." When you go to a commercial studio, you are paying by the hour, but "here a guy comes, turns on a pedal, turns on another, begins creating different things, because you have fewer limitations of time, money, schedule." The modernist thinker Oswald de Andrade's theory of anthropophagy, Sara Castro-Klarén has argued, attempted "to restore the figure of the woman-mother, in all her sexual stages, to the center of the anthropophagic scene, with a special consideration of the body as a place for Tupi thought" as part of his teleological vision for a final return to a Pindorama Matriarchy (2000, 305; Pindorama is purportedly an indigenous Tupi-Guaraní word for the land once inhabited by the Tupinambá, Brazil's quintessential "cannibals"). There may not be a radical project in

Fernanda's cannibalizations, but she has attributed a central role to the female Carioca body in this identity work.

Liv Sovik has discussed how the privileges that accrue to whiteness are masked in a context that celebrates miscegenation. Fernanda began an autobiographical essay for her website with the observation that she has in her blood the "mixture of the three races" that played a role in the formation of the Brazilian people (Europeans, Africans, Amerindians). Her sometime collaborator Ivo Meirelles—an Afro-Brazilian from the Mangueira community, also associated musical and cultural mixture in Brazil with miscegenation, but when I asked him if he thought racism exists in the country, he unhesitatingly affirmed, "Lots," and he added that it is perhaps worse than in the United States, where he thought it was more out in the open. In Brazil, by contrast, everyone is "fake" and there is "no confrontation." It is horrible because it is never clear who the "enemy" is, he said, echoing a theme from the "MPB: Engagement or alienation?" debate, in which participants noted that since the end of the military dictatorship, it had became harder to single out a target for protest.

Hollanda describes how Brazil's "'soft' ambivalence in gender and race discourses has begun to be understood . . . as a *process* of political articulations, which is proving more flexible and politically effective than the confrontational discourses of metropolitan feminism" (2002, 326). In contrast to Isfahani-Hammond, Hollanda feels that Brazilian gender and race studies are slowly moving beyond theories that interpret local discourses as primarily working to naturalize difference and inequality. By the late 1990s there was a growing sense, Hollanda writes, that Brazil's discursive "softness" was perhaps "an efficient survival strategy within the broader and violent scope of the relations between metropolitan and peripheral countries," *and* "a valuable way to negotiate the no less violent particularities of the logic of power relations in Brazil." Ambiguity may serve privilege more than the subaltern, and whether or not Hollanda's interpretation turns out to be valid in the long term remains to be seen. Nonetheless, Fernanda Abreu's career has shown a notable ability to navigate through music the divides of North Zone and South Zone, middle and working class, black and white, female and male, in the pursuit of new mixtures.

PAULINHO MOSKA

DIFFERENCE AND REPETITION

Music is a play of mirrors in which every activity is reflected, defined, recorded, and distorted. If we look at one mirror, we see only an image of another. But at times a complex mirror game yields a vision that is rich, because unexpected and prophetic. At times it yields nothing but the swirl of the void.
—Jacques Attali, *Noise: The Political Economy of Music*

Sensations are reborn from themselves without rest,
Oh mirrors! Oh Pyrenees! Oh Caiçaras! . . .
And the sighs that I make are distant violins;
I walk the land as one who sneakily discovers
On the corners, in the taxis, in the little dressing rooms, his own kisses!
I am 300 I am 350
But one day I will finally run into myself.
—Mário de Andrade, "Espelho, pirineus, caiçaras"

"That's my son at his seventh-birthday party playing capoeira and percussion," Paulinho Moska said as we looked at digital photographs on his laptop computer during my visit to Rio in August 2007. "He plays in Minibloco—the Monobloco for children," Paulinho explained, referring to the samba percussion workshops run by the members of the band Pedro Luís e A Parede (chapter 3). We happened upon the picture as Paulinho was showing me some of the strangely corrupted and distorted images he had amassed photographing Brazilian musicians through a marbled glass brick. Paulinho had been obsessed with photography since purchasing his first digital camera, a Canon G2, during a visit to New York City in 2001. At the time, he was experiencing a difficult period in his personal life; his malaise was heightened by the general gloom of the city following the attacks of 11 September that same year. Deeply contemplative, camera in hand, he was fascinated with the distortion of his image as reflected in the stainless steel faucets, showerheads, and other mirrored surfaces in the hotel rooms in which he stayed during tours. He began to generate hundreds of zany self-portraits by photographing these reflections. Some of the resulting images, he explained, inspired poems that subsequently inspired songs. These songs became his album *Tudo novo de novo* (Everything new again, 2003), and he displayed large mounted prints of the images at the corresponding live show, as well as in an exhibit in the Hélio Oiticica Arts Center in Rio de Janeiro. By 2007 Paulinho was even hosting a television program about Brazilian music that incorporated his digital photography.

When I met him at AR Studios in 1999, however, Paulinho had just begun making his fifth solo album, *Móbile* (Mobile), which would mark a turning point in his career. I observed several of the production sessions for the album, beginning with a recording at AR in Rio de Janeiro, and later mix sessions in New York City. Paulinho engaged Marcos Suzano as percussionist and producer for the album, with Celso Fonseca as a second producer. In this chapter I detail how the individuals involved in producing *Móbile* conceptualized the recording in relation to the main narrative threads of this book, particularly with respect to the reevaluation of the place of rock influences and instrumentation in their music. As I did for Pedro Luís e A Parede, I examine how participants in this project paid close attention to various aspects of sound, from prioritizing certain instruments in the arrangements to emphasizing specific aesthetic preferences in recording and mixing. Paulinho and Suzano intended *Móbile* to be different from — but also in some ways similar to — preceding trends in MPB, and different from Paulinho's own earlier albums. They also wanted it to be different from "Americanoid" rock and pop. These instantiations of difference were to be effected in broad strokes by eliminating drum kit and electric guitar from the instrumentation, and by adding what Paulinho conceptualized as deterritorialized "interferences" to the arrangements.

Other dimensions of difference, however, were less obviously instrumental, playing out in the ambiguous location of "Africa" in Brazilian cultural heritage, for example; in the presumed listening tastes of the "masses" versus comparatively restricted middle-class audiences; in perceived distinctions between mass-marketed versus specialist musical equipment, in comparatively subtle production and mixing preferences, or in a purportedly artisan-like search for aesthetic difference as such, in contradistinction to the tendencies toward homogenization inherent to industrial scales of production. While Paulinho was reconsidering the role of rock influences in his music, he simultaneously, under Suzano's tutelage, sought to incorporate into MPB certain sounds associated with electronica (an umbrella term for a variety of genres that privilege electronic instrumentation such as synthesizers, sequencers, and drum machines). I read *Móbile* as a recording that showcases Marcos Suzano's talent and influence as the end of the decade approached.

It is fair to say that Paulinho's creative work is driven in large part by the urge to explore his own emotions and processes of self-realization. As I describe in the following pages, he even recognizes a degree of narcissism in his motivations. His lyrics contrast with those of Lenine, Pedro Luís, and Fernanda Abreu and their collaborators in that they typically lack obvious references to characteristic markers of Brazilian social life, or to specific local cultural manifestations or dilemmas (although this is not necessarily the case when he records cover versions of others' songs). They seem strangely deterritorialized, in this sense. All the same, this musician's idiosyncratic artistic trajectory met with the broader debates about music making that unfolded in the Rio scene and beyond in the late 1990s. Paulinho spoke of an ethical connection (*ligação ética*) that he believed he shared with a variety of pop musicians of his generation, and that ran counter to a tendency in Brazil to interpret popular music "through movements with clearly defined aesthetics." In bossa nova, for example, "everyone had to sing the same way," Paulinho observed. If somebody tried to make a "heavier" sound, he said, it was unacceptable. Then came MPB, and the pop rock of the 1980s, he added, suggesting that these too had relatively constraining aesthetics.

In the 1990s, by contrast, Paulinho felt that something important happened: MPB artists had come to be "attracted to each other through difference." Paulinho enjoyed the music of Lenine, Chico César, Zeca Baleiro, Carlinhos Brown, Arnaldo Antunes, Cásia Eller, Zélia Duncan, Adriana Calcanhotto, Fernanda Abreu, and Marisa Monte, he said, precisely because they were different from him, and from each other. He appreciated "each in accordance with the aesthetic that they put into their work." There was no movement, "not even unconscious," because these artists, his friends, were all very different, and that was how they communicated. This development was a victory over the kinds of movement politics that often diminish "the freedom of the music itself." He seemed to be responding directly to the question posed in the "MPB: Engagement or alienation?" debate introduced in the preface: his contemporaries in Brazilian pop music had no banners to parade, he said, except for music that was "free." This was clear in their lyrics and in the way that they were "researching their sounds" so that they could be different, so they could "continue to be Brazilian but at the same time contemporary."

Difference and processes of differentiation as elaborated in music scholarship have generally been conceptualized in terms of race, gender, ethnicity, and geography, or along the divide between traditional and modern (or sometimes high and low art), and we have seen how these concerns inform music making in this setting.[1] In scholarship on so-called world music, the discussion has often positioned a presumed given "Western" subject against which "the Other" is articulated. This chapter, however, reveals these dimensions to be intertwined with Paulinho's intense desire to differentiate musical practices from both the established modes of production *within* MPB and from his own prior music making (which conformed to those more established modes). That is to say, making music different(ly) here is not only about dynamics of othering; it is also instrumental to individual and collective projects of becoming.

"Must the recognition of difference in music," Georgina Born and David Hesmondhalgh ask, "necessarily be fictive and devisive, ideological and hierarchical? Or can it be allied to a reflexive, analytical project?" (2000, 2). In Paulinho Moska's Deleuze-inspired understanding of his musical trajectory, repetition does not mean sameness; it means rather the possibility for newness. What is repeated is in fact difference—"everything new again," as in the title of one of his albums. This idea evokes Deleuze and Guattari's concept of a minor literature, described by Claire Colebrook as one that "repeats the past and present in order to create a future" (2002, 121). "Think of all the post-colonial texts that do not appeal to their own already given voice but repeat and transform texts of the past," Colebrook suggests. "The only thing that is repeated or returns is difference; no two moments of life can be the same. . . . The power of life is difference and repetition, or the eternal return of difference." For Deleuze, life is not "something that then changes and differs," Colebrook writes; life can be seen as "the power to differ" (2006, 1).[2]

The ways in which these concerns shaped the production of the *Móbile* recording form the focus of the first half of this chapter. In the second half, I examine how Paulinho gained independence from his recording label, EMI, and subsequently followed a distinct career path incorporating his digital photography and developing his television program *Zoombido*. Paulinho's multidisciplinarity, as he referred to it, serves as another example of emergent forms of self-management within transforming markets of cultural production (but for him, it was also a continuation of his Deleuzian project).

Early Career

Paulinho was born in 1967 to a Carioca father and a mother from Bahia. In the late 1970s his father managed the Dancing Days (later renamed Concha Verde) nightclub on the Urca Hill (the first stop on the famous cable car that ascends the Sugarloaf), where, as a child, Paulinho was able to watch performances by major figures in MPB.[3] He studied drama at a small local arts school (Casa das Artes de Laranjeiras) in the early 1980s and began to work in film, earning some minor roles. He was also a member of the choir Garganta Profunda, which performed an eclectic repertory including songs from the Beatles, nineteenth-century Brazilian *modinhas* (sentimental ballads), bossa nova, samba, and classical and early music.

In 1987 Paulinho formed a pop-rock group called Inimigos do Rei (Enemies of the King) with two other vocalists from Garganta Profunda (plus electric guitar, bass, and keyboard, as well as drum kit). Sérgio Dias, the guitarist for the Tropicália-era group Os Mutantes, heard the band one night and subsequently became Paulinho's musical mentor, producing the group's demo tape. Two years later their self-titled debut album generated two hit songs: "Uma barata chamada Kafka" (A cockroach named Kafka) and "Adelaide."[4] Paulinho began his solo career in the early 1990s during a period when he was influenced by rock acts such as Lenny Kravitz, Nirvana, and Pearl Jam. He described the urge to make music with more "attitude" than his previous vocal groups, and he saw rock as a "vehicle for a cry of liberation" from the lighter pop for which he had become known. He listened to rock "non-stop" and he bought a steel-stringed acoustic guitar of the type popular in the United States and Europe.

For his first album, *Vontade* (Wish, or Desire), from 1993, Paulinho sought what he referred to as a garage band sound. He had in mind the grunge bands associated with the Seattle rock scene at the time. He recorded on analog tape and as "live" as possible (that is, with limited overdubbing or postproduction treatment), consistent with the studio aesthetic priorities that Thomas Turino labels "high-fidelity" (2008). Although he recorded in Rio (at Nas Nuvens and Estudios Mega), he traveled to Los Angeles to mix and master the album because he thought it would be easier to achieve the grunge-like sound he desired there. In the album release, Sérgio Dias celebrated Paulinho's "courage" in leaving his previous pop successes behind to try a new sound, and he lauded Paulinho's good taste and compositional originality.[5]

Nevertheless, after the release of *Vontade*, Paulinho soon felt boxed in again when the press began to call him a rocker. "I love rock," he said, "but I immediately felt that I had escaped the label of 'the cute one' of Inimigos and had fallen into a different branch of the same tree of labels. I felt lost, questioning myself about why I was an artist," Paulinho wrote in an autobiographical essay (Moska 2004). Meanwhile, he had begun to participate in a philosophy study group organized by Professor Cláudio Piano, who hosted sessions in his home in the South Zone.[6] With Cláudio (who passed away in 1998), Paulinho read and discussed existential philosophy and Gilles Deleuze. The lyrics to his second album, *Pensar é fazer música* (To Think Is to Make Music), released in 1995, reflect the influence on his worldview of these readings. For Paulinho, the album, again recorded at Nas Nuvens, also represented a break with the idea that he needed to have a particular style. It is a mix of pop, rock, and blues with MPB influences such as a citation of Jackson do Pandeiro's "Cantiga do sapo" on the song "Careta," or the echo of a cuíca friction drum from samba on "Me deixe sozinho," from the same album. Gilberto Gil wrote an album release that praised Paulinho's "profound interest in incorporating the variety/complexity of being in the world."[7] From this recording, the song "O último dia" (The last day) was used as the opening music for the mini-novela (short-run telenovela) *O fim do mundo* (The End of the World), earning the track substantial airplay and giving Paulinho some national recognition. It remains one of his best-known songs.

The following album, *Contrasenso* (Nonsense), of 1997, continues this sound of rock-influenced MPB. The inspiration of the Beatles is audible in, for example, the George Harrison–like electric guitar of the opening track, "A seta e o alvo" (The arrow and the target), while other songs draw on more typically Brazilian styles, such as "Paixão e medo" (Passion and fear), which is in the melancholy style of a *seresta* (basically, a slowly sung choro) with a wistful accordion accompaniment.

Conceptualization and Planning of *Móbile*

I want to see a boogie-woogie with pandeiro and acoustic guitar.
—From the 1959 song "Chiclete com banana," by Gordurinha and Castilho

Although Paulinho enjoyed successes with memorable songs such as "O fim do mundo," "Relampiano" (the collaboration with Lenine, discussed in chapter 2, which the two also recorded on Paulinho's *Contrasenso*), and others from his first three solo albums, the predominantly rock-pop instrumentation and sound with some blues and R&B influences of those recordings, and of his fourth album, *Através do espelho: Ao vivo no Rival* (In the mirror: Live at Rival Theater), recorded in 1997, seems quite conventional in comparison to *Móbile*. The encounter that would eventually make the latter album possible was a show called "Cinco no palco" (Five on the stage), which headlined Paulinho and fellow singer-songwriters Lenine, Chico César, and Zeca Balero along with the percussionist Marcos Suzano, and which toured the various SESC theaters of São Paulo in 1998.[8] At this performance Paulinho observed Suzano "producing some sounds" with his mini-kit, and he was surprised at how the percussionist brought rhythm to the foreground in an MPB show rather than staying behind the band, "playing pique-poque, pique-poque" (i.e., a complementary or subordinate part). During subsequent performances together in Japan, Paulinho concluded that he wanted Suzano to produce his next album.

In December 1998, Paulinho began to visit Suzano at his home to introduce him to his new repertoire and to discuss the production of the album. Suzano, in turn, introduced Paulinho to Goldie, Roni Size, and a variety of other artists then associated with the cutting edge of techno, drum and bass, and related genres. Paulinho liked "the newness" and "the attitude" of the music, but not "the electronic thing," he recalled. "I hated techno," he told me (echoing Lenine's initial ambivalence vis-à-vis electronic music), and music that depended "on programmed patterns, on loops." Suzano, however, assured Paulinho that he could achieve those sounds with acoustic percussion and with his own samples. He insisted that he would be able to adapt the timbres of electronic-based grooves from drum and bass or jungle, for example, to a recording context that privileged acoustic percussion. Moreover, Suzano did not just show up at the recording studio with "a finished product," Paulinho emphasized, referring to the grooves the percussionist programs into his Akai MPC 1000 sampler and sequencer. "There really was an *encounter* of us playing together. I modified various rhythms on the violão; we adapted various arrangements, precisely because we were experimenting together. So we had moments in which the music happened in a very spiritual way. There were moments when we really caught on fire in that room." This was all the more startling to Paulinho because, as he put it, "what was there was an android, you know, the MPC 1000 was an android!"

Paulinho's astonishment and his use of the word *android* reveal how new Suzano's entire modus operandi was to a musician more accustomed to acoustic instrumentation (and it connects with Paulinho's portrayal of the percussionist as a Carioca Blade Runner).[9] At the same time, however, Paulinho's emphasis on their personal encounters and on their performative input and control meant that the musical outcome was more than an adoption of electronic sounds from abroad; rather, it was an intersubjective and localized process of aesthetic transformation that maintained a proprietary sense of human agency. It was the sort of selective appropriation and modification championed in discourses of cultural cannibalism (Brazil has, after all, always been "very anthropophagous," Paulinho reminded me)—not, crucially, merely in the sense of a hybrid of musical styles but also in terms of *process*: that is, it was important to Paulinho that the timbres and grooves of techno could be performed on acoustic instruments and worked out in an interpersonal setting.

Paulinho explained Suzano's vision of a new sound for the album, and how the latter suggested a change in the instrumentation:

I'll never forget, at [Suzano's] house, already working on the sequencing programs, when he said, "Man, we've got to give rock 'n' roll the boot, you know. To do something modern, we've got to go into the past, we have to go into jazz, and into what is most new, which is drum and bass, jungle, these more techno beats, and forget rock." So, to forget rock, the first thing that we did was get rid of the electric guitar, the symbol of rock. And the second was to take out the drum kit. Now, it's *rhythm*—it's no longer drum kit, it's *rhythm*. And with the electric guitar gone, I could experiment with sounds on my violão. So, many things that we recorded, you might think are made by keyboards but actually it's violão with a Mutator [frequency filtering processor], with the Sherman, which is another filter, or with the Mooger Fooger [also a filter]. So, I could consequently discover my own instrument, because I was being suffocated by a—quote-unquote—Americanoid structure of making an arrangement.

I saw a certain irony in this in 1999, for this interview with Paulinho took place in a New York City recording studio precisely as press coverage in the United States about the "rediscovery" of Os Mutantes, the band that introduced rock instrumentation into the televised MPB song festivals in 1967, was beginning to crest. (The interview with Paulinho took place on 22 April; Gerald Marzorati's *New York Times Magazine* feature article on the band and Tropicália appeared three days later.)

This seemed even more ironic given Paulinho's personal link with Sérgio Dias of Os Mutantes, his early mentor. Paulinho cautioned, however, that he did not "hate" the electric guitar, and that it was important that Brazilian music was "colonized" by Anglo-American popular music so that it could have these sounds (and technologies) as additional options for the great mix. (Cultural imperialism can be read as an enabling force.) It was a matter of historical context: in the time of Tropicália, "there was no worldwide promotion. People didn't have access to this." Bossa nova may have been wildly successful internationally in the 1960s, but few abroad would have thought to listen to Brazilian rock in 1968 when it had to compete with, for example, Jimi Hendrix, the Beatles, and Eric Clapton. (Only thirty years later did David Byrne and others "discover" Os Mutantes in their own globalized search for difference.)

At a holiday gathering late in 1998 in the hills a few hours outside the city of Rio, Paulinho, Suzano, and the singer-songwriter-producer Celso Fonseca further conceptualized the *Móbile* project.[10] Celso introduced Paulinho to a variety of "new artists with new sounds" (such as Portishead), insisting that Paulinho could still foreground his violão. With Suzano and Celso, Paulinho thus developed a plan to move away from the drum kit and the electric guitar, and to prioritize instead the *couro* (hide or skin) of the pandeiro, the "natural" materials of other percussion instruments, and the *cordas* (strings) of the violão as sonic markers of Brazilian musicality. The sound of popular music in Brazil, Paulinho said, "had become unbearable," following a "structure of drum kit, keyboards, [electric] guitar and bass." In the Deleuzian vocabulary, Paulinho sought a "line of flight" out of an intolerable situation. But it was also a difference in repetition. "Brazil was always acoustic," he noted. "As a poorer country, its great music was born in the morro, in the skin of the percussion and on the strings of the violão. This is perhaps what differentiates us most clearly from other cultures—principally American culture."[11]

Móbile was obviously not a traditionalist effort to return to the music of the morro, so to speak, or even to "classic" MPB. Suzano, Paulinho related, elevated Miles Davis as an example of someone who changed the history of music several times, and he urged Paulinho to take risks in the production. It was "not a negation of rock"; it was "to search for an attitude of the contemporary" in jazz and other African diaspora musics. It was not about being "modern," for trying to be modern was "very damaging to the one who is creating." Instead, as a *contemporary* album, *Móbile* would "be attentive to the new things that are going on in the world" such as "loops, spatial sounds, noise, the inclusion of interferences," and what these could "bring in terms of musicality." In this manner they would be able once again to make an album structured around rhythm and violão, like classic samba, choro, and bossa nova. "We are once again Brazilians," he concluded, "but we have succeeded yet again in being different just when we were no longer believed that this combination would continue to produce something different." Jorge Mautner, who wrote a press release for *Móbile*, and who collaborated on one of the tracks, said of the recording that it represented a "marriage" of the familiar and the strange, "like a dream that we have already had several times, but with the presence of a frightful and scandalous newness" (1999).

Interferences, Electronica, and Difference

There was another key participant on the album who would help in achieving the desired "contemporary" aesthetic: the keyboardist and electronic music programmer Sacha Amback, whom Paulinho had met years earlier in his philosophy study group. Professor Cláudio Piano, perhaps thinking of Deleuze and Guattari's writings about the synthesizer, had in fact urged Paulinho to work with Sacha.[12] Only now, however, when pushed by Marcos Suzano to consider electronic sounds, did Paulinho think of Sacha for making a connection with European art music and electroacoustic sounds. Sacha was a devotee of European composers such as György Ligeti and Luciano Berio; even after working in pop music for many years, he told me, these were the two composers who most "moved" him in music.

In 1985 he began playing with the pop musician Ritchie (born in England but living in Brazil), and from 1987 to 1998 he worked with Lulu Santos, another major figure in Brazilian pop. He also worked with the singer-songwriter Adriana Calcanhotto (one of the participants in the "MPB: Engagement or alienation?" debate). Sacha's familiarity with both pop and contemporary art music would be ideal for the *Móbile* project, Paulinho decided.

For Paulinho, Sacha was to be distinguished from the typical keyboardist in a pop-rock band because he would never just play a standard piano or organ accompaniment through an entire song. Rather, Sacha played *interferences*. He "samples everything," Paulinho explained, and "constructs with a mosaic of references"; his work was "fractal." Paulinho wanted the keyboardist to incorporate "apparently non-musical sounds" into the music, to "insert noises in the service of the song." Not "noise for the sake of noise," but an "interference" that could "be a part of the music, the naturalness of the music, of the musical chaos." Paulinho envisioned a "pseudo-place," a "non-physical place where all the noises, silences, pauses, and rhythms" already existed; to compose a song was "to dive into that place and take out a few things" to combine.

Gilles Deleuze utilizes the French word *brouillage*, which translators have glossed as "interference" or "noise"; his usage seems to derive from the work of fellow Frenchman Michel Serres, whom Deleuze frequently cites (Brown 2002, 1). Serres recognized interference and noise as essential to the process of communication. The reasoning behind his argument derives from information theory, in which there is a distinction between a sender and a receiver and there is a signal that passes from one to the other. Noise or interference is external to the classical model of communication; it *interferes* with ideal transmission. Serres proposed, by contrast, that noise is "the necessary ground against which the signal stands out as something different," making it recognizable as communication: "In order for there to be any kind of relationship between sender and receiver, some form of noise or interference, that is, an injection of difference, is required. This comes about by the very opening up of a passage, which inevitably exposes the signal to noise, and thus also to potential transformation. Serres then arrives at the interesting paradox that successful communication necessarily involves the risk of failure. Communication may be thwarted or 'betrayed' by the medium through which it passes. But if we take the position 'downstream,' at the point of destination rather than departure of the message, we may see this failure, this betrayal, as also the process of invention" (Brown 2002, 7). Paulinho conceptualized noise "downstream" on *Móbile*, that is, as part of the process of invention and communication, while the "pseudo-place" he described resembles Serres's concept of the "chaos-cloud," the founding noise from which differentiation potentially emerges (Brown 2002, 14).

It was important, Paulinho stressed, that Sacha's interferences were to be in the service of the music. "The *interference itself has a human interference on top of it*, placing it into a context within the song in which the noise becomes beauty" (my emphasis). For Paulinho, then, Sacha's "studio audio art," to use Thomas Turino's term for recording practices that privilege electronic or computer-generated or mediated sound removed from the context of live performance (2008), in fact had to be connected to a subject-centered ideal of aesthetic value (the beauty of a song). "I am a composer of songs," Paulinho asserted. "I'm not a musician who wants to make a twenty-minute-long techno track without words. I want to say something with my words." Even so, within that context the noise itself was detached from specifically located subjects. Asked if there existed a "Brazilian" noise, or a Brazilian preference for a certain type of noise, Paulinho responded: "I'd like to have noise in the territory of non-nationality. Maybe this is a virtue of noise, that it doesn't have style. . . . Maybe in a hundred years people will succeed in nationalizing noise, but . . . it still has this function for us of liberation, of denationalization, of deterritorialization." Noise, in this conceptualization, can help free a song from being merely "national." And yet Paulinho was sure that "that the majority of the population" in Brazil would understand the noises on *Móbile* as foreign, as representing an influence from abroad. If noises are supposed to be deterritorialized, existing in a pseudo-place, listeners nevertheless inhabit specific national spaces; Paulinho feared that his new sound would seem very strange, un-Brazilian, to many.

Suzano's idea was that Sacha would also contribute interferences along the lines of what the British electronic musician William Orbit had done for Madonna's *Ray of Light* album (1998). As an admirer of Orbit's work, Sacha was pleased with Suzano's suggestion. Orbit exemplified Sacha's broader aesthetic preferences for "the sound from England, and from Germany," he told me. Specifically, he felt that "in English music there is a sonority of German electronic equipment" that he found more appealing than the sonority of American popular music. Even English pop, he thought, is "much more infused with alternative influences" than American pop. Sacha appreciated synthesizers such as the German-made Waldorf (e.g., the Attack percussion synthesizer, the Microwave XT, or the Q virtual analog synthesizer), and the German-made Quasimidi Polymorph analog emulation synthesizer popular in techno music. He also preferred English and German microphones, pre-amplifiers, equalizers, and compressors. Sacha elaborated:

> The way they use filters, which today is very much in fashion, they were always doing it. The English filters, the Belgian-made Sherman, the German ones, and others that I may not even know. They always used these things, and I always liked them. I'm attracted to this even more than the synthesizers from Korg, Roland, Yamaha in general, which I love, but the kind of sonority that they look for there [in England] is something that I think is more serious. It's not about making a synthesizer that plays drum kit, piano, that does everything. . . . People think that they buy one of these and they have an orchestra. The equipment [that I like] is for another kind of music. It's a sound with some personality, something that only *that* synthesizer can do well. . . . It's an instrument that does a special kind of thing that may not be so palatable to everyone's taste, but which has a very strong personality.

Sacha's preferences recall Chico Neves's discourse about artisan music making; the synthesizers Sacha disfavors are mass produced in much greater economies of scale than the more specialized (and more expensive) gear he prizes. (In fact, Sacha saw in Chico a fellow "instigator" who did not fit in well with the music industry.)

Sacha also held up Walter Costa, the audio engineer for *Móbile*, as a technician who was willing to experiment, someone to whom one could say, "Walter, I have a new piece of equipment, I brought this new spice," and he would respond, "Mmm, what can this new spice do for our sound?" Sure, Sacha wanted technical excellence in a mix, he said, but he was much more content "to discover *one* thing different and unusual" than he was with technical perfection. Celso, too, had advocated Walter for the project as "a kind of scientist" who would truly "mess" with Paulinho's sound and "ruin everything" but "in a good sense," Paulinho recalled. A spirit of experimentalism simply did not exist in the music industry, Sacha lamented, at least not as he had experienced it in Brazil. Industry personnel were interested in "filling up [retailers'] shelves" with CDs, and with "making music to play on the radio, for the market."

Recording and Difference

Shortly before beginning the project with Paulinho, Walter Costa recorded an album of one of Brazil's leading MPB singers with Celso as producer. They traveled to New York to mix it. He thus had a freshly comparative perspective and was able to elaborate some differences in production preferences that he had observed abroad. The singer in question had "an American vision" in mind for her album, said Walter. She wanted it "to sound different" from a Brazilian recording, and the production team was at first onboard with this plan. Walter, however, had a feeling that such an approach would not work out for the mix sessions in New York. There existed a concept of what one could call a Brazilian sound, he said, which was difficult for Americans to understand. Specifically, Americans tended not to understand the place of the percussion: "If you have an album constructed completely around percussion and you put it in the hands of somebody who puts the percussion in the background, I think the album is lost. If you give it to someone who thinks of the skeleton of the album—around which the whole album is constructed—as secondary, the rest doesn't have support."[13]

According to Walter, a similar dynamic occurred when a prominent British producer-engineer came to mix a project by another MPB singer: "He used sounds in a very touristic way. He liked those things that were *very* characteristic, and he liked them simply as mentions. He used the minimum possible for something to characterize a Brazilian rhythm. As soon as he reached the point where he thought the Brazilian characteristic was established—*for an English person*—the rest was unnecessary, as if the rest was an overdose of the same idea, but it wasn't. When it is an overdose, that's where the idea is." Despite the local production team telling this visitor what their priorities were, the latter "didn't do the necessary homework," Walter said, and instead thought it was "too much" percussion. As Louise Meintjes has observed, "mediation embeds layers and layers of experience in the expressive commodity form" and "opens up multiple possibilities for interpretation of those embedded experiences" (2003, 261). The British listener of that mix (now fixed onto the CD) may find it satisfying, while the Brazilian listener may sense something off about it. Brazilian music makers, meanwhile, may take lessons from such cross-cultural collaborations and seek to assert their priorities in subsequent work, as they did for *Móbile*.

Celso Fonseca (*Móbile*'s co-producer, with Suzano) had also observed differences precisely "on the things closer to [Brazilian] culture," such as the strings and skin that Paulinho identified as the basis of his sound on *Móbile*. For the violão, with its nylon strings, for example, Celso felt that Brazilians preferred a fuller sound than Americans typically do, with more bass frequencies, and in the front of the mix. "The American always brings out the high-mid frequencies . . . to get that bright sound," but the Brazilian violão was "more intimate," "closer," as if the performer were sitting right there playing for the listener. That was "the violão that we understand," Celso said. Even when recording an acoustic guitar with steel strings, the Brazilian would try to get a sound closer to that of the violão of nylon strings, he added, with more low frequencies. (This "fuller" sound preferred for violão corresponds to Lenine's preference for more "body" on his instrument, as described in chapter 2.) But would this kind of sound not interfere with the percussion? I wondered. "No," Celso answered, because Brazilian producers and mixers "always know the place of percussion." Outside Brazil, in his experience, people sometimes hid the percussion a bit, especially if there were also electronic elements such as loops or programmed parts on sequencers. Foreign engineers and producers tended to place the acoustically performed percussion "way behind and the loop more in front." Celso preferred to have the percussion more foregrounded. The shift toward prioritizing the sounds of strings and skin for *Móbile*, as Paulinho poetically described it, thus also bore upon priorities in the mix, priorities that were, we have seen, changing during this period, in part through the efforts of Marcos Suzano.

Paulinho's contact with Suzano was a milestone in his career, like his earlier experience with Sérgio Dias. "I began to realize that he is a genius," he said of the percussionist; he was "happy to be at his side." Suzano had complained to Paulinho about ending up disappointed with so many of the recordings he worked on because the people in the control room of the studio didn't understand what kind of sound he wanted to achieve. "They just treated him like a percussionist, you know," Paulinho said with empathy. But Suzano is "an aesthete" who draws pictures and paints paintings, Paulinho thought, by "recapturing this African thing of the low frequencies" and turning it into "the contemporary." To leave his repertoire in Suzano's hands and to allow him to create a sound that *he* really loves, Paulinho concluded, was a privilege.[14] My fieldnotes record Suzano delighting in this freedom to be himself while working at AR Studios, using a version of his mini-kit:

> Suzano . . . has a drum-and-bass thing going, with [Indian] tabla [drum], a nylon percussion brush, and an inverted silver serving tray. He's sitting on a cajón [as if it were the seat of a drum kit]. . . . The sound of the tabla . . . is resonating down in the 60 to 90 Hz range, I would guess. He's just added a few [instruments] — the cajón, a small splash [cymbal], which he's not playing as a splash [would normally be played], a reco reco [scraper from samba], which he's not playing as a reco reco [would normally be used], and a pile of curved steel plates [vehicle shock absorbers]. For the second part of the song, playing with the brush in his right hand between the inverted silver [serving] tray and the splash [positioned above it], he's [also] playing a kick drum[-like] pattern [on the cajón], and sometimes hitting the tabla [with his left hand] . . . Walter just did a little pre-mix for playback and Suzano called a friend on his cellular phone to play it back for him. "*Dá um playback* [Give it a playback]," he tells Walter. "That cajón, man, sounds amazing [*é bom pá caralho*]," co-producer Celso Fonseca comments. (20 March 1999)

Here we witness the collective satisfaction that Celso and Suzano, together with the sound engineer (and well into the late hours of the night), take in hearing the instant playback of a distinctive *sound* quite outside the mainstream for Brazilian pop. (The use of the word *caralho*, in a phrase that if translated literally means "good for the penis," adds a sexual tone to the sentiment, as discussed in chapter 1.)

To mix the album, the musicians traveled to RPM Sound Studios on East 12th Street in Manhattan. For the mix engineer, Suzano chose the American Jim Ball again (with whom he had previously worked on Baez's *Play Me Backwards*, on *Olho de peixe*, and on *Sambatown*). He appreciated Ball's experience with acoustic instrumentation and sounds and knew that he would not relegate Suzano's percussion to the background. "We understood each other very well," Paulinho reflected of his musical team when we talked in New York near the end of the mixing sessions for the album. "It was very clear what we wanted." He was very excited at the time with how the project was coming together: "Today when I see everything done, I say, 'Caramba!' During mixing we listened, we talked, we went crazy, and . . . I confess to you that I am still taken by this atmosphere . . . I don't know, something inside me says that it is a *very* different album."

A Mobile in a Hurricane

Paulinho's songs probe questions of self, identity, and the search for meaning in life with lyrics that read like little poems. Love is a frequent theme, but it in fact symbolizes renewal more often than it refers to the intimate love between individuals. Key themes of existential philosophy permeate his songs, especially those on the *Móbile* album. For example, a sense of disorientation and angst with respect to the apparent lack of rational explanations for events, and a belief that subjects can create value and meaning in spite of life's absurdities; a preoccupation with intersubjectivity and with seeing other subjects in an objective relation to oneself; a sense that the past and future both also partly constitute the present, related to the existentialist concept of facticity as pertinent to the continual process of self-making; acting as one's authentic self in accordance with one's freedom (rather than following predetermined roles); and sentiments of despair in relation to external limits to the construction of one's self-identity.

For Paulinho, the opening song on the album, "Móbile no furacão (Auto-retrato nu)" (Mobile in the hurricane [Naked self-portrait]), represented his idea for the project: "simple songs, pretty, orderly melodies, within this Afro-cybernetic hurricane." A mobile in a hurricane is something that moves "even in the middle of chaos." Within "movements of extremely heavy batucada," of percussion and other sounds, "there is a violão"; there is "a song moving about inside," an artistic creation in a kinetic balance like Alexander Calder's mobiles. The track begins with a quiet B minor chord sustained on electronic keyboard with a sound somewhere in between synthesized vocal and violin timbres; layered on top of this sustained "pad" is another one with a similar timbre, but with an oscillator controlling its volume so that it pulses. Soon acoustic guitars and percussion join in to fill out the harmony and establish the rhythm, and Paulinho begins to sing lightly in the middle range of his tenor about the restlessness of existence, about always changing and "living every second." He is like a mobile loose in a hurricane, he sings, and calm only makes him feel lonely.

Meanwhile, Sacha and Suzano interfere with synthesized and acoustically performed "noises"; one such occasional iteration sounds like a depth charge in the sea. To this listener, such sounds fit well into the musical texture and hardly seem like noise at all, but they were certainly uncharacteristic for MPB at the time. Sacha also adds melodic synthesizer elaborations, some of which recall William Orbit's work. There is tremendous attention to sonic detail, to dynamic buildup and contrast between sections of the song, and to the blend of acoustic and synthesized timbres in the texture and the mix. As the song progresses, the sound grows denser and busier. The second verse is about Paulinho changing his name so that no one could find him, but being brought back to where he started, as if he'd never left—the irony of life, Paulinho concludes. Whenever his anchor grabs hold, he sings in the bridge of the song, Paulinho immediately "lights the wick" and an explosion sends him to other places and other "presents" (i.e., temporal modes). Paulinho's voice becomes more urgent as he returns to the refrain at the end of the bridge and reaches into the higher parts of his vocal range, almost shouting, "I'm a mobile alone in a hurricane!"

Guest wind instrumentalist Carlos Malta (of Pife Muderno) begins a meandering soprano saxophone solo as the song concludes, adding to the increasing impression of turbulent weather conditions swirling around the singer. After the final refrain, Carlos's solo first begins to get more intense and wild, climbing high and diving low in its range, circling through short motifs, but then calming down as all other instruments fade out completely and nothing is left but the last few embellished and sustained notes of the soprano saxophone solo, completely lacking any reverberation (i.e., room sound), as if on a wide open sea after a hurricane has passed. The saxophone sound is raw and dry as Carlos repeats a catchy melodic phrase built on a sequence of arpeggios that Sacha established earlier in the song. The "irony of life," Paulinho said in one of our interviews, extends to the way he ended up incorporating electronic sounds into the album when he had disliked synthesizer so much, and also to the fact that after four albums of pop-rock instrumentation, he was returning to where he started from—the couro and cordas so characteristic of MPB.

"It is something impressive," the author-musician Jorge Mautner wrote about Móbile in the customarily hyperbolic tradition of press releases. Paulinho "extrapolated modernism, postmodernism, tropicalism, futurism, cubism, dadaism, anthropophagy, and surrealism and reached the peak of nirvana of all the ecstasies and all the culminations of all the sensationisms, including the sensationism of [the celebrated Portuguese poet] Fernando Pessoa" (1999).[15] Mautner co-composed the lyrics to Paulinho's "Castelos de areia" (Sandcastles), a kind of funk-shuffle-baião-samba mix with Middle Eastern–sounding world music samples (e.g., a muezzin-like chant and a sampled melody with a timbre that sounds something like a zurna) provided by André Abujamra, a guest "interferer" from São Paulo.[16]

The song begins with a few seconds of Mautner playing a dissonant and strident improvisation on violin, which is suddenly interrupted by noises that sound like the static that leaps off high-power electric cables, but here emanating from Sacha's machines. Paulinho enters with a funky chord vamp on violão that is reminiscent of Lenine's guitar playing, along with a few measures of ringing sixteenth notes on the triangle, while the bassist Dunga (who also played in Lulu Santos's band) works with Suzano to hold down the groove. Paulinho also plays bell-like ostinatos on steel-stringed acoustic guitar in 6/4 meter over the 4/4 shuffle, but this instrument is electronically filtered to sound something like a sitar (the buzzy and twangy Indian chordophone). Sacha's digitized static and other sounds interfere throughout the track. The verses to "Castelos de areia" present miniature cases of dashed hopes and expectations, such as that of a pious Christian who spends a lifetime in prayer waiting to encounter Jesus, but when a burning light fills his (or her) heart, it is not Jesus but simply pain.

The last verse of the song envisions the human race achieving immortality in the year 4000. There is no longer hot or cold and no one gets ill or dies, but what still troubles people is the knowledge that despite being immortal, everyone and everything will eventually, one day, be swallowed up by a black hole. "That's right, my love," goes the refrain. "Sandcastles dissolve when the wave comes." (The line is in part an homage to Jimi Hendrix, Mautner notes, as it borrows its central metaphor from his song "Castles Made of Sand.") Interestingly, Mautner interprets the dilemmas of the lyrics as another allegory of Brazil, in reference both to Greek mythology and to Albert Camus' existentialist classic The Myth of Sisyphus (1942): "What's most important about this song is the lesson that it is precisely in defeat that strength is tested. . . . The strongest being is not the one who never falls, but rather the one who . . . upon falling profoundly . . . has the knowledge and faith to lift himself up and begin all over. It is like the myth of Sisyphus. It is like the key to the secret of the Brazilian people." Mautner also interferes in the track with "cataclysmic recitation" (as he calls it in the press release); that is, he declaims a text at the end of the track that complements the theme of the lyrics. As all the instruments drop out, Mautner's voice, distorted by a Mutator filter, is left ominously reciting, "—would inevitably, inexorably, one day or night, be swallowed by the black hole."

Carlos Malta interferes with short melodic bursts on pífano for the second track on *Móbile*, "Onde anda a onda" (Where the wave goes). This fast-paced song spins a noisy, insistent, kind of hard-bop, jungle-influenced groove unlike any other Brazilian music I know. Paulinho's wordplay lyrics speak about allowing oneself to be carried along with different kinds of waves, including sound waves, each with its own "strange spirit." Carlos also enriches the texture of Paulinho's moody, bluesy *milonga*-like "A moeda de um lado só" (One-sided coin) with bass flute.[17] "Come, let's go nowhere," Paulinho sings, reaching into his lower range. "Let's leave our clothes on the floor / Let's forget our names, our prison / Yes, I agreed to enter into your sea / without knowing where the waves would lead / to navigate only if it were for passion." Sacha's interferences on this pensive track include orchestral samples and synthesized sounds that occasionally fill out the harmonic and timbral palette.

On another track, "Tudo é possível" (Everything is possible), Sacha's samples include brief portions of what he thought might have been an Alban Berg piece (not remembering well where he had originally appropriated it)—perhaps, he said, reversed and inverted in his sequencer (a "retrograde inversion," in music theory), as well as some "spacy" sounds reminiscent of an ondes Martenot. Somewhat hidden in the percussion and rhythmic guitar playing is a 4/4 rock backbeat. The basic pulse is at first articulated by a sound that has been filtered enough to obscure its origin (Paulinho's violão?), then Dunga's electric bass repeats pulsing eighth notes of chord tones. Paulinho's violão solo on this track is also filtered into oddly plaintive, not quite "natural" but still acoustic-sounding timbres. As with the other songs, the lyrics to this one borrow themes from existential thought, in particular, a sense that time is not strictly linear. Rather, time is "a great tree of infinite branches," Paulinho sings, that bears "its most beautiful fruit in the present moment." And "tomorrow perhaps everything will be as clear to us as it was in the beginning."

Love is another theme, but not in the customary sense of a love song; rather, it refers to "a new feeling," like the intensity of emotion and newness that Paulinho experienced with the birth of his son in 1997 (Mautner 1999). It is the "same illusion of love that makes us happily leap from a new precipice," he sings in "Tudo é possível," to "feel anew the pleasure of eternity." A gem of existential pop-song poetry is "Por acaso em Osaka" (By chance in Osaka), which treats the theme of loneliness when away from home—in Paulinho's case, during performance tours. He describes wandering about alone through city streets, crying or laughing, not wanting to understand why pain sometimes "invades" him, a loneliness so raw that he has to write it down. Paulinho sings in a lilting, perambulatory melody lyrics that draw on a classic existential dilemma in which one fears falling from a height or yearns to leap or decides out of pure free will to stay put. The song's narrator, in Osaka, Japan, climbs to the top of the highest building and contemplates "the infinite landscape." He knows that "it is necessary to fly," but to leap is difficult. Then, from the heights he begins to think of life back down below ("Perhaps a visit to that exhibition"), as he experiences the existential pain that always "attacks" him when he travels, this time, by chance, in Osaka.

It is a very Zen-like sentiment, and indeed *Osaka* spelled backward is *akaso*, phonetically identical to the Portuguese *acaso*, meaning "chance." Paulinho's relaxed, offbeat groove on the guitar evokes a xote (a northeastern dance that derives from the European schottische), or even reggae a bit, and he plays an ostinato figure on the Japanese samisen. Sacha adds melodic and harmonic interferences with synthesized and sampled sounds that have wind instrument–like timbres or, in some cases, again like the ondes Martenot. Suzano's rhythmic rattlings fall on the beat, then seemingly randomly off the beat, sonically suggesting the noise of chance. This cinematic soundscape then segues into the song "A moeda de um lado só" as Carlos Malta evokes the sound of the shakuhachi on his bass flute.

"Ímã" (Magnet) is a funky shuffle blues about two individuals who cannot remember who they were before they came to know each other. It could be Paulinho and his son: "The end of your line is the beginning of mine / The place from which you will bring a new love." The "lines" are another reference to Deleuze, whose concept of the rhizome is constructed of lines of segmentarity and stratification, as well as lines of flight (see Deleuze and Guattari 1987, 21). "Sem dizer adeus" (Without saying good-bye) is another well-crafted pop tune with perhaps a more "radio-friendly" sound (a sing-along melody with fewer obvious noises or other "interferences"), and lyrics that once again treat the theme of a peregrination in search of love, in which space-time doubles back on itself. The subject of the song sings of having traveled until arriving at the last place where no one had been, only to prove "what it was to be after the end of the beyond." There is, however, another personage mentioned in the song—the intersubjective gaze—as the subject in fact only arrived where one day "you said you would depart never to return." "I was already there," he sings, "waiting for you without having said good-bye." None of the tracks, it is worth noting, sounds much like jungle, techno, or drum and bass, or like jazz for that matter. Given the transformation of these influences in Suzano's appropriations, most listeners would not make the connection. The track "Debaixo do sol, morrendo de frio" (Beneath the sun, freezing to death), however, begins in a slow dirge-like tempo with a pedal point on the bass and synthesized and percussive interferences but then suddenly switches to a jungle-like rhythm and tempo for the second verse, sounding something like William Orbit's work for Madonna on *Ray of Light*, but with a rich range of acoustic timbres.

Paulinho recorded three songs by other composers on the album, the most rousing of which is his version of Jorge Ben Jor's classic soul samba "País tropical" (Tropical country, 1969). Suzano establishes a hard-driving samba-rock rhythm on pandeiro. The thumb-stroke bass notes on his instrument are so aggressive and "tight" that they sound like hits on a kick drum. Insistent sixteenth notes from the cymbals of the pandeiro and other percussive sounds (some of which are electronically filtered) propel the song. Paulinho, similarly, plays a forcefully funky down-and-dirty acoustic guitar vamp. Dunga's bass lines hold down the bottom end and fill out the harmony. Guest musician Roberto Marques contributes a trombone solo that evokes gafieira (the brass-filled salon samba). Jorge Ben Jor's lyrics proudly tell of living in a tropical country blessed with natural beauty by God. Particularly effective are the changes in texture and groove as the musicians switch to a half-time samba-funk with a backbeat for the bridge of the song. In contrast to Paulinho's existentialist texts, "País tropical" is something of an ode to Carioca life, a celebration of carnival, soccer, the popular vw Beetle, the violão, and a lover (nega) named Tereza. (See chapter 2 for a discussion of the use of the word *nega*.) Jorge Mautner calls it "a hymn to all the music of the Brazil-Universal" (1999).

Another cover song on this album is a version of André Abujamra's "O mundo" (The world), with Lenine, Zeca Baleiro, and Chico César providing guest vocals. Paulinho chose to close the album, however, with

Benito di Paula's 1972 classic samba-canção "Retalhos de cetim" (Satin scraps), which tells of a working-class Carioca who rehearses with his samba school for an entire year and struggles to pay for his instruments and for his girlfriend's carnival costume on her promise that she would parade with him, only to have the promise broken. After the tour de force of skins and strings, of noises and interferences, of mobiles and hurricanes, Paulinho performs this song with only his violão as accompaniment, playing the chords in a xote-like offbeat rhythm, rather than as a samba. The track has an extremely "dry" sound lacking any reverb—no noises or interferences at all—with little "production" beyond recording onto tape a skillful solo performance.[18] (Interestingly, despite therefore being what Turino would call a high-fidelity recording in which liveness directly affects the recorded sound, this track sounds "less than live" because it lacks room sound, i.e., reverberation.) Paulinho thus ends the album with this unadorned voice-and-violão rendition of a classic samba about loss, heartbreak, and carnival, seeming to demand renewal or rebirth again.

Through the "False" to Freedom

In 2007 I asked Paulinho to reflect back on the recording of *Móbile* and contextualize it within his career trajectory. The album, he said, was a way for him "to get out of an abyss" (or, if we think of Deleuze, it represented a kind of "line of flight"). He wanted "to create an identity," he elaborated, and to find a "signature," a uniqueness without which he feared he would not be recognized as a musical artist in Brazil. He didn't know precisely what he was doing, but Suzano had awoken in him the desire to do something new and risky. Most importantly, Paulinho said, *Móbile* had "a sound," and "an *idea*": the flirtation with electronica, with samplers in order to incorporate them into MPB. Paulinho brought up Caetano Veloso's 1972 experimental album, *Araçá Azul* (Blue araçá), a recording that used tape loops, splicing, and even dodecaphonic techniques to create a kind of musical concrete poetry far removed from MPB. (It was in fact a failure in terms of sales.) The first time Paulinho heard the album, he related, he found it strange and difficult. But later he came to appreciate it for Caetano's audacity.[19] He came to feel that he needed to find his "signature" in Brazilian music, and that to do so he "needed to make an experience" and reflect on what kind of artist he was.

However, the experience of *Móbile* was too good, he fondly recalled: "It wasn't so good for the label," Paulinho conceded, "but it was very good for me." Three trips to Japan, and then to Europe with the live show—it was "an incredible adventure." Then EMI cut short the *Móbile* tour and requested the next album. In response, Paulinho recorded *Eu falso da minha vida o que eu quiser* in 2001, which, he noted with a laugh, was "even more radical" than *Móbile*. "The more they wanted—," I interjected as I listened to his tale. "That's right," he continued emphatically, "*the less I gave*. It was a complete rupture. . . . My last album for the label is called *I false what I want of my life!*" The album's title takes the adjective *falso* (false) and treats it like a first-person singular verb form, but it is also a reference to Deleuze, who, in *Cinema 2: The Time-Image*, elaborates on "The Powers of the False," drawing on Nietzsche's idea of the "will to power" (1989).

Discussing the film *Stavisky*, Deleuze writes that "contrary to the form of the true which is unifying and tends to the identification of a character (his discovery or simply his coherence), the power of the false cannot be separated from an irreducible multiplicity. 'I is another' ['Je est un autre'] has replaced Ego = Ego" (Deleuze 1989, 133). Paulinho was drawn to this idea of a fundamental multiplicity of the self (and its consequent potential for identifying with the Other). The following passage from Deleuze's "The Powers of the False" is revealing here: "The forger will thus be inseparable from a chain of forgers into which he metamorphoses. There is no unique forger, and, if the forger reveals something, it is the existence behind him of another forger. . . . The truthful man will form part of the chain, at one end like the artist, at the other end, the nth power of the false. And the only content of narration will be the presentation of these forgers, their sliding from one to the other, their metamorphoses into each other" (133–34). If *Móbile* was pivotal for Paulinho, *Eu falso* was more of a sonic scream that he had to let go before beginning a new phase in his career. It was a far edgier recording and it was too "noisy" for mainstream MPB audiences (that is, for radio airplay; it sold 8,000 copies). Paulinho's separation from his wife, he frankly stated in his own press release for the album, permeates the lyrics. While the album may "seem simply like a handful of romantic songs," Paulinho advised his listeners, "they are also false." A text that he declaims at the end of the last track ("Vênus"), he noted, affirms his "need for the false in questions of love," suggesting that what may seem like typically romantic lyrics are also expressions of doubt and irony, and that the musical treatment is intended to undermine their sentimentality.

Paulinho continued experimenting with Suzano, Sacha Amback, and the recording engineer Walter Costa. His encounter with these musicians, he declared, modified his "relationship with music, with sound, with life." In fact, by the middle of the *Móbile* tour, he'd begun to call his show the Móbile/Moska Quartet because, he wrote in his press release, it had become evident that the group was not merely *presenting* his music and poetry; they were researching sound. This recognition indicates a significant change in Paulinho's understanding of his creative role. Rather than having a live band or session musicians in the recording studio as a backup to the singer-songwriter whose creations they merely realize and adorn, the idea of a quartet, associated more typically with jazz and classical art music, legitimizes the sonic work of the ensemble. "It is an honor to say that we are a Quartet," Paulinho wrote. It is "a privilege to create music with them; to steal a little of their genius; to exchange, to play, to travel and be false with them." Is this not, after all, a humanist, participatory view of musical becoming, just as much as it seems eminently bourgeois?

Suzano reaffirmed "his sophistication as a producer and instrumentalist," Paulinho wrote. With his pandeiro and mini-set, Suzano emits "a truly new sound quality, with an almost magical and very unexpected polyrhythm." Samba "gushes through his blood and is imposed in between the lines of his grooves," Paulinho continued, "making the sound always Brazilian and universal." Sacha Amback, on the other hand, is a musician with such "an expansive musical culture" as to make him "someone of enviable nobility." Sacha's "atmospheres, textures, noises and interferences," Paulinho wrote, seemed "like the colors of chameleons multiplying in intense sonic paintings." And now Paulinho "adopted" the audio engineer Walter Costa "as a false musician of the Quartet," for he "manipulated, 'destroyed,' and transformed everything that was played into another sound, a false sound. Distortions, filters, effects and noises are music now. And they were 'played' by him." Walter was only a member of the quartet in the studio, Paulinho specified, while on tour, besides Suzano and Sacha, there is a bassist who is part of the quartet only in the shows. "That is, the Quartet is false." (In the studio, the bassist was Dunga, who also recorded *Móbile*.) The album, he believed, had a "pop electro-organic" character, with "the attitude of rock, MPB, samba, electronica, pop, jazz, funk, etc.," in the "alchemy of the Móbile/Moska Quartet."[20]

His press release reads like a personal letter or manifesto. It is, to be sure, a bit self-indulgent, but it is an interesting statement about how this singer-songwriter saw his personal crisis as directly relevant to his explorations of sonic difference together with his fellow "alchemists." "My name is no longer Paulinho Moska," he wrote. "Now it is just Moska. Móbile/Moska Quartet. I false what I want of my life." He elaborated on "falsehood," clearly drawing on Gilles Deleuze's writing on cinema: "False because I'm alive and life is a labyrinth of encounters in which each turn that we choose reveals the 'beginning' of a new labyrinth of possibilities. And the turns that we leave behind are transformed into 'false' realities. Encounters that we will never have. My insistence on aesthetic difference in my music is an attempt to try out some of these turns, so that they can take me down other roads, and remove me from the path of a familiar place."[21] "There is no more truth in one life than in the other," Deleuze writes. "There is only becoming, and becoming is the power of the false of life" (1989, 141). Listening to the completed album, Moska heard his "pained and vigorous" falsetto on certain songs, singing with "soul," alternately "outside of himself" and "delving into himself." He heard a "False I." The quartet's "false music," he asserted, saved him from the loneliness and pain that he experienced composing the songs.

Moska owed EMI a third album on his contract, yet *Eu falso*, the second (*Móbile* being the first), would be his last for the label. So what happened after the Móbile/Moska Quartet recorded this album that Artur Dapieve would affectionately refer to as "almost terminally depressing" (2003)? One of the artists and repertoire directors evidently started complaining that Moska was not making marketable pop music. (It was a long and complicated story, Moska said.) But Moska convinced the president of the label to end his contract and pay him a breach-of-contract fee, which he would use to record the third album: "I told the president that I would record an album of *songs*, nice songs, and this album would be mine. I would give them the licensing, but the album would be mine. And he agreed. A marvelous person. Because I play clean, you know, Fred. I tell it like it is . . . Little did I know that this would be the work that I most love in my life, this one that I did promising the president that I would make an album of songs to play on the radio, that I would not make an experimental album. And it ended up being an album that became a television show, a gallery exhibition, a DVD—the biggest project of my life. I'm doing this already for four years. I never spent so much time on one album. And I am doing *lots* of shows. I travel a lot. I don't have a reason to record another album." Moska formed his own label, Casulo Produções, to produce *Tudo novo de novo*. His glee at how he stepped into this new role is palpable in his talk:

"As soon as I freed myself of the company, to form my label—which is nothing more than a name, you know—I became the president of my company. And the first thing I did as the president of my company was to decide that I wouldn't have a deadline. I wouldn't have a deadline for composing, I wouldn't have a deadline for recording, I wouldn't have a deadline for releasing the work, I wouldn't have a deadline for rehearsing it, I wouldn't have a deadline for success, I wouldn't have a deadline for saying that the idea that I have for the project is finished." The recording companies, naturally, have production schedules: "They need to sell it quickly. So . . . they don't know how to do anything but sell records." *Tudo novo de novo*, he noted, was released in December 2003, and nearly four years later, in August 2007, he was releasing the DVD and about to begin traveling with it; he had exhibitions planned, and he had developed the television program. He was not demanding a new repertory or a new album of himself each year. "You start to work with what is flowing better, and this has been very gratifying." Surely he would not have had the luxury of this kind of time frame under his recording label contract.

A "New Kind of Artist"

As Moska recounts in his DVD *Moska: Tudo novo de novo*, he often finds himself feeling lonely when on tour and spends a lot more time walking around or sleeping or hanging out in the bathroom than he does when he is home. After he bought the digital camera during a trip to New York City, he began experimenting with the macro button. "I discovered that through a doorknob's reflection," Moska narrates on the DVD, "I could fit the whole bathroom, even myself, in the frame. From that moment on, I took pictures of every reflective object I found in the hotels I stayed in." Soon he had collected over 2,500 photographs in this manner, and he realized that he had "developed a visual language of longing and solitude." At one point in this DVD, which Moska refers to on the DVD cover as a "false documentary of a real story and of the show that resulted from this adventure," a reflection that has apparently materialized into a double of Moska sits on the sink of a cramped bathroom in a sleeveless undershirt and, scratching his head, says to his identical other, who is fiddling with a reflective surface, "Listen, don't you find this all a little narcissistic?" "I do," the other responds as he turns to look his double straight in the eye. "All you do is photograph yourself," the seated one continues. "You've got to do something with this!"

Moska thus turned his self-absorption into creative expression and entered a new phase of his career that has brought him considerable satisfaction. In one faucet Moska found an image in which it looked like his eyes were crying huge diamonds (the knobs of the faucet). He wrote a short poem about it, "Lágrimas de diamantes" (Diamond tears), and then a song with those words. Selected images inspired more songs, and eventually the album *Tudo novo de novo* came together. Although some of the themes of the poems/songs are vaguely melancholy, they are given a much livelier musical treatment than the songs on *Eu falso*, including two sambas. Moska was starting anew.

The core group of musicians remained the Móbile/Moska Quartet (but now Moska's bassist Dunga is included, while audio engineer Walter Costa, who also recorded and mixed this album, is not specifically named as part of the quartet proper). Among the notable guest musicians is Fernando Alves Pinto on the handsaw for two tracks, contributing that instrument's characteristically eerie sound (also similar to the ondes Martenot). The samba singer-songwriter Mart'nalia joins Moska for the lively pop-samba "Acordando" (Waking up). The album returns more concretely to an MPB sound within a largely pop-rock format, with drum kit (but no electric guitar), and lacking noise "interferences." The lyrics continue Moska's preoccupation with finding one's path in life. "Let us begin," are the first three words of the first song, a sort of anthem to Moska's artistic rebirth. "Let us place a final period / At least it is a signal / That everything in life has an end / Let us wake up / Today there is a different sun in the sky / Bursting with laughter in its merry-go-round / Shouting nothing is that sad / It's everything new again / Let's play where we've already been / Everything new again / Let's dive from the height we climbed." It is a beginning at the end, a serious game played where one has already been, a difference in repetition.

Moska's mastery of pop songwriting is fully evident on "Lagrimas de diamantes" and other songs such as "Cheio de vazio" (Full of emptiness) and "Pensando em você" (Thinking of you), in which clever lyrics and catchy melodies and hooks combine with familiar yet satisfyingly inventive (to this listener at least) chord progressions. "Cheio de vazio," for instance, features a restricted melody on the verses that starts on the fifth scale degree and struggles on steady eighth notes to climb stepwise just a major second, only to slink back down to where it started at the end of each line, before opening into an arching melody on the refrain with "tight," Beatles-like vocal harmonizations: "Oooo, and there on the other side of the sky / Someone pours onto a piece of paper / New poems of love."

Moska collaborated with Pedro Luís and others for the blues-shuffle "Essa é a última solidão da sua vida" (This is the last solitude of your life), and he sings a charming love song duet with the Uruguayan Jorge Drexler, "A idade do céu" (The age of the sky), at the very end of the album, in classic *nueva canción* voice-with-acoustic-guitar style. Other songs delve into the blues, funk, samba, and Cuban son. Artur Dapieve writes that "*Tudo novo de novo* could only have followed *Eu falso da minha vida o que eu quiser* and [the latter could only have followed] *Móbile* and so on (going backwards in a kind of personal 'evolutionary line'). Through them, we observe the human and artistic growth of Moska. He knows—and he teaches us—that no metamorphosis is without pain" (2003). Dapieve would seem to be in on Moska's Deleuzian reading of becoming. (Franz Kafka, author of the classic *The Metamorphosis*, served as Deleuze's principal example of a writer of minor literature, in the way that the Czech author creatively deformed the "major" language of German [Deleuze and Guattari 1983].)

As it turned out, five songs from *Tudo novo de novo* got radio airplay, more than any from Moska's previous albums, yet without any intervention from a recording label. How, I asked Moska, did he accomplish this? He approaches the stations himself, he answered, elaborating on his method:

I tell them, "Listen, I *make music. You* have a radio station. I have already been played a lot on this station because my label worked with you. Now I don't have a label, but I have music. . . . You need music, and I need you to play [mine]. So I will do the following: you play my music, and I'm your *partner*. . . . I won't give you [payola]. I'll do a show. I'll come do interviews for the station. I'll appear at events in support of the station. [switching to English and speaking deliberately] I *sit my ass in a chair in front of the directors and say*, "I'm a new kind of artist." . . . And they say, "Oh." . . . [And I say] "So, I'm the president of this side of the game, and where is the president of your [side]?" . . . I'm so polite. . . . [I say,] "I want to sit with you and talk about what we are going to do with our product." You don't have to have a manager that negotiates for you and you have to talk with him and pose like a celebrity and nobody talks with you, only with your manager. That's so crazy . . . I have been working in music for thirteen years . . . and they know me. And when they see that the artist [himself] came [to see them], it has the [effect] of "Let's be polite with him," and I sit and talk like a — like a human.

Tudo novo de novo ended up seeing modest sales (about 20,000) but, as Moska noted, by 2003 "the market was cut in half" because of the transformation in the music industry, and Moska has, in his own estimation, done well with the shows and the DVD, distributed by the Som Livre subdivision of the Globo media corporation.

Major labels and media corporations have of course not dissolved, but many musicians now enter into contracts with them only for distribution of creative products of which they retain the ownership. Musical artists, Moska felt, used to be developed following the paradigm of specialization that emerged with capitalism. It was an "extremely negative" idea, he thought, because you then have to "compete with everyone else who specializes in that same thing, and it is not possible . . . for everyone to be the best." Specialization required individuals to "go so deeply into a particular thing" that one ended up "comprehending life, the world, everything" through one lens. We have arrived in a new era of multidisciplinarity, Moska held, as individuals begin "to understand the world from various disciplines." The "new artist" is multidisciplinary, and technology and information, in his view, have allowed the contemporary artist to have "a multi-communication," and to present him- or herself in various forms, using various media — he or she had to be multiple (an idea that also draws on Deleuze; see, e.g., Badiou 2000).

Zoombido: To Make a Song

"I don't know if I invented the program just to take pictures of the artists I admire," Moska said of his cable television show during our 2007 interview, only half joking. He wasn't sure, that is, if the priority of the show Zoombido: Para se fazer uma canção (Buzz: To write a song) was talking about and playing music, or taking photographs of the musicians. Moska developed the program around a simple premise: in the first episode he creates a single verse of music and lyrics; his guests — established figures of Brazilian popular music — then add a verse on the spot, and the composition thus grows in each episode, with each new guest. This collective project, however, actually occurs at the very end of a given episode. Moska begins each episode by interviewing his guests about their lives in music, with a

focus on how they compose songs and what songwriting means to them. He then requests of his guests that they perform a couple of original songs acoustically (usually with a violão), and he advises them that he will photograph them through a glass brick. "I tell them I am going to make some images that are crazy" (see figures 18, 19, and 20).[22]

The invitee then performs while Moska takes over a hundred snapshots, of which he typically finds two or three that he likes because they have "some life" and "say something." Guest Ivan Lins, Moska reported, was shocked by the photographs of him because they were "so strange and beautiful at the same time." "He was almost scared," Moska recalled. What Moska in fact accomplishes with this photographic work is an exploration

FIGURE 18. Lenine. Photograph by Paulinho Moska.

of the meanings of portraiture. He was, on the one hand, influenced by Francis Bacon's distorted and sometimes terrifying portrait paintings (about which Gilles Deleuze has written [2005]). But we can trace also an interesting precedent in the photographic work of Brazilian modernist Mário de Andrade, who during the early 1920s "began to experiment with his 'codaquinha'" (little Kodak camera), as described by Esther Gabara (2004), and who was eminently "multidisciplinary" (a poet, novelist, musicologist, etc.). Like Moska, Mário became obsessed with the medium, assembling an archive of nearly one thousand images that became "the site for his development of a theory of a modernist sublime" (57). The author grew preoccupied with questions of truth and falsehood in portraiture,

FIGURE 19. Fernanda Abreu. Photograph by Paulinho Moska.

wherein a naturalistic representation of a "visage" may express less of an aesthetic truth than might a less "documentary" pictorial representation of a "face." Mário altered "the value of photography's indexical function," Gabara writes, such that "questions of truth and lies are no longer at the core of the ethical or aesthetic definition of photography" (54). Moska's wildly distorted digital photographs of himself in reflective surfaces, and of his friends and colleagues through glass bricks, similarly destabilize the presumed coherence of individual subjectivity in favor of reflexive and intersubjective emergence, becoming. The mirror, the glass, the lens, and the screen or the enlarged print on which the images may or may not be fixed are all forgeries, and all the more truthful for it.

FIGURE 20. Pedro Luís. Photograph by Paulinho Moska.

After Moska photographs his musical guests performing a solo song in the studio for *Zoombido*, he plays a duet with them. "The level is really high," he said, and indeed, I was captivated by the musicianship on display in the excerpts I have seen, such as one of Arnaldo Antunes singing his song "Saiba" and Moska in duet with Arnaldo on the latter's "As coisas." I savored the footage of the legendary samba musician Martinho da Vila, and of the University of São Paulo literature professor and composer José Miguel Wisnik. The program is recorded and filmed in the Palco recording studio (owned by Celso Fonseca and Gilberto Gil), in the Gávea neighborhood of the South Zone. It is fair to say that the production values for the show favor the "high-fidelity" aesthetic (Turino 2008), whereby the aesthetics of live performance influence the recorded sound. "We work in the studio with good microphones, with studio engineers," Moska emphasized. "We work with rigor [and] the sound is good." Moska's longtime associate Nilo Romero is in charge of the sound, while the cinematographer Pablo Casacuberta, from Uruguay, films each duet with six cameras trained at various angles in the recording studio, some of which capture images of the guest from various reflective surfaces placed throughout the room. You never see any of the cameras in the mirrors, Moska pointed out, and Pablo's work, he thought, was "very emotional."

Yet the audience for the program is highly restricted: it airs on a cable channel that shows only Brazilian content, mostly history programs and documentaries, and that requires an additional premium beyond basic cable (Canal Brasil). It is lamentable, Moska commented, that a Brazilian "culture channel" should have such a limited viewership, but it was precisely for this reason, he proposed, that Canal Brasil was "more free" and open to new ideas. It is a good example of Bourdieu's restricted production with a certain degree of autonomy from the mass market (Bourdieu 1984; Hesmondhalgh 2006, 214). Finally, after the interviews, performances, and photographing, Moska asks each guest composer to "make a very small work," just "one sentence" with a couple of chords, a piece of a melody, and a few lyrics—"The first idea! . . . Maybe it's not the best idea, but it's the first idea"—so that song is composed of the first musical idea of each guest added one to the other as the season progresses.

As the credits roll, the viewer hears the extended song performed by the various guests, with their distinctive voices and musicalities, a collective musicalization of becomings. One has "to find geniuses" to work with, Moska told me, and "be a very good student." Several guests, Moska claimed, told him the show was like "therapy," that it was not like a TV show at all, but rather like "life, art." Drawing on the cultural capital he has accumulated over his career (and on his connections in media circuits), Moska succeeded in establishing a space for creative expression well removed from mainstream commercial television. It was, perhaps, a space of privilege (insofar as few pop musicians are actually able to find such a creative outlet), but it was not cynical. It required what Deleuze referred to as "noble energy," as "artistic will" in "the creation of new possibilities, in the outpouring becoming" (1989, 141).

"I am doing *exactly what I want*," Moska told me, existentially affirming his lines of flight. He is a self-managed entrepreneur who seeks new forms of partnerships in order to continue creating. For example, he explained how he entered into a partnership with the Orsa Foundation, an NGO associated with a conglomerate of companies. The foundation claims to emphasize "People, Profit, and Planet" in their mission, "economically viable, socially just, and environmentally correct models for society," and social change brought about through market mechanisms (textbook neoliberal discourse).[23] In 1994 the foundation established a youth percussion group called Bate Lata (Beat Tin; recall Fernanda Abreu's song "Da lata"). As with numerous similar initiatives, the idea is social uplift through music making, typically utilizing percussion instruments (or recycled industrial materials made percussive). This kind of project accords with what George Yúdice (2003) has termed the "expediency of culture," whereby NGOs mobilize cultural practices in their efforts to reform society independently of the state. It makes for good corporate publicity, but it might be faulted for playing to stereotypes of economically disadvantaged social strata having little access to formal music education and instruments.

Moska invited Bate Lata to perform with him when he recorded the *Tudo novo de novo* DVD; he saw the children as representing "real renewal, everything new again." In exchange, the Orsa Foundation gave him half the budget he needed to film the DVD, while he negotiated with Som Livre for the other half of the production budget in exchange for the license to distribute the DVD. Meanwhile, Moska retains ownership of the master. "Tomorrow," he said in our 2007 interview, "I will have lunch with the president of Som Livre, Gustavo Ramos, about the tour for the DVD." Moska thus makes good use of his relationships with NGOs, with industry executives and radio personnel, and, finally, with his fellow musicians, in working as his own manager.

Conclusions

The first half of this chapter highlighted how Paulinho Moska's contact with Marcos Suzano facilitated a reconceptualization of his sound away from the pop-rock instrumentation he used on his albums before *Móbile*. I examined how various dimensions of sonic difference came into play in the way the musicians involved in the project went about their work. Unlike the lyrics of Lenine, Pedro Luís, and Fernanda Abreu, Moska's largely lack overt references to national identity or Carioca culture. Nevertheless, my examination of *Móbile* showed how local concerns about being "Brazilian once again" informed the production of this album, specifically in the emphasis on couro and cordas, or skin and strings, at the expense of electric guitar and drum kit. Efforts at "deterritorialization"—in purportedly universal aesthetics, song themes, or noisy interferences—are continually "reterritorialized" in cycling back through tradition, or in singing classic songs such as "País tropical" or "Retalhos de cetim," or through other references and musical practices. Deleuze argues that "movements of deterritorialization and processes of reterritalization" are always relative and connected, "caught up in one another" (Deleuze and Guattari 1987, 10), as illustrated in his example of the symbiosis between an orchid and a wasp, wherein the latter is derritorialized by "becoming a piece in the orchid's reproductive apparatus," only to reterritorialize the orchid by transporting its pollen: "Wasp and orchid, as heterogeneous elements, form a rhizome. It could be said that the orchid imitates the wasp, reproducing its image in a signifying fashion (mimesis, mimicry, lure, etc.). . . . At the same time, something else entirely is going on: not imitation at all but a capture of code, surplus value of code, an increase in valence, a veritable becoming, a becoming-wasp of the orchid and a becoming-orchid of the wasp. Each of these becomings brings about the deterritorialization of one term and the reterritorialization of the other; the two becomings interlink and form relays in a circulation of intensities pushing the deterritorialization ever further." Like the orchid and the wasp, sounds and influences from the past and "the contemporary," from local settings and international flows, from high art and pop culture, seem to have this rhizomatic relation to each other in Moska's musical trajectory.

I would like to keep questions of power, agency, and projects in this story. In his increasing self-management, Moska has surely had more room to maneuver than, for example, the youths in Bate Lata. His familiarity with the oeuvre of Deleuze speaks to a form of privilege in the Brazilian context, and some readers may find his immersion in French philosophy from a certain influential era (1960s and 1970s, especially) alienated from contemporary Brazilian realities. Indeed, intellectualism in general can enhance one's status among the more restricted cosmopolitan formation of middle-class audiences for MPB. (Chico Buarque, Caetano Veloso, and Tom Zé, for example, are public intellectuals as well as pop musicians.) I see nothing alienated, however, in the musical camaraderie found on *Zoombido*. Moska is a gifted and dedicated pop musician who can play the heck out of a classic samba—or write a lively samba of his own (or a bossa, a choro, a forró, a xote, for example). He can sculpt inventive melodies into bluesy or Beatles-esque chord changes. And there is something singular about his becoming, as a negotiation of the so-called evolutionary line of Brazilian popular song (Caetano Veloso's oft-cited term), of changing technologies and market priorities, and of his readings in philosophy.

6 ON CANNIBALS AND CHAMELEONS

The fabric of the rhizome is the conjunction, "and . . . and . . . and . . ."
—Gilles Deleuze and Félix Guattari, "What Is a Minor Literature?"

At the end of the 1990s, the musicologist Cristina Magaldi took stock of the flourish of hybrid pop music styles that had emerged in Brazil during that decade and noted that imported genres such as rock, funk, and rap were neither "enhancements" of local traditions (citing Sutton 1996, 265) nor simple "cross-fertilization[s]." Rather, they served as "positive *additions* to the choices available to Brazilians to express themselves in modern times" (Magaldi 1999, 318). Her wide-ranging analysis identified interesting trends characterizing a postdictatorship popular music scene in which Brazilians had begun to think of musical genres and styles that originated abroad "as part of their own culture" (310). Published on the eve of the new millennium, Magaldi's article was both ahead of its time and a product of it: the latter because she attributed a key role in emerging tendencies to what were then, despite widespread piracy, still comparatively confident multinational recording labels; the former because she anticipated a frictionless dynamic between "foreign" influences and "national" ones—a dynamic that was not yet, this book has shown, fully realized. "Apologies for the use of rock or any other international music" were no longer needed, Magaldi argued, and "there was no need to transform the imported sounds themselves to make them look (and sound) more 'Brazilian'" (309). Musical Brazilianness, she suggested, was no longer a fundamental preoccupation (311).

To be sure, the old paradigms (such as the national-popular model of the student left in the 1960s) had lost their relevance. The imperative to make "national" culture was gone. But the *desire* to define what it meant to be Brazilian in the contemporary world—and musically to perform Brazilianness—was as strong as ever. Foreign influences were now regarded as positive additions according to an and/and rather than either/or ideology, as Magaldi suggested (see also Sansone 1996, 207). The Tropicalists Caetano Veloso and Gilberto Gil counterposed their *som universal* (universal sound), which sought to incorporate international pop music, against the national-popular model back in 1967 at a televised song festival. Surprisingly, this dynamic once again came to be pertinent to discussions of Brazilian popular music in the 1990s. Yes, the "power to move at will between the national and the foreign" was celebrated in postdictatorship music scenes in Brazil (Magaldi 1999, 326); the "MPB: Engagement or alienation?" debate examined in the preface confirmed the importance of an ideal of absolute stylistic freedom. But while few seemed to be worried that "imported" genres would outright displace characteristically "Brazilian" ones, the balance of instrumentation, rhythms, and sounds from rock, samba, regional folkloric genres, and black diaspora influences was still actively being negotiated in Brazilian pop. In 1999 Arto Lindsay, who produced Caetano Veloso's *Estrangeiro* (among various other Brazilian recordings), told Gerald Marzorati of the *New York Times* that "in Tropicalia, you let the rough edges show, that was the point. The meaning was in the juxtaposition. The juxtaposition said something about the world" (1999). If the music examined herein really shares something with Tropicália, it is in some of the roughness of its edges (although the specific edges and roughnesses are different): it's where the *friction* is, the sticky materiality produced by desiring bodies in global encounters (Tsing 2005, 1).

As the recording industry entered into crisis and digital technologies became increasingly affordable, and as audiences for world music grew larger, many Brazilian musicians exploited the creative tensions they had always worked with to produce not only subjectivities and identities but also "products and profits" (Guilbault 2007, 265). Some have in a sense marketed discourses of inclusive mixture as the Brazilian musical brand. The popular music press has eaten it up, as demonstrated by Lenine's Paris Cité concert program, in which a journalist referred to the singer-songwriter as "le cannibale" and cited Lévi-Strauss's odyssey from civilization to barbarism and back (chapter 2). I do not write this cynically: these individuals have worked tirelessly to make a living in a difficult career path and in a setting mostly unfavorable to taking chances in creative expression or following uncertain paths. As analysts, we perhaps appreciate too little the extent to which many pop musicians must balance the need to make money from their endeavors with the desire to find meaning and intensity in them.

These are serious games, to riff on Ortner's term (1996, 12). The work that the musicians in this book accomplished (along with various peers outside the scope of my analysis) facilitated the consolidation of what some observers have begun to call the *Nova* MPB (New MPB). This New MPB still prioritizes the communicative capacity of the popular song; it remains indebted to the main singer-songwriters of the 1960s and 1970s, and in some ways to the Brazilian rock of the 1980s. However, as Fred Coelho has affirmed, it generally rejects older market formulas, and it has nurtured a generation of collaborative musician-producers who are indeed less anxious about cultural imperialism (Soares 2011). In Rio, Lenine's younger collaborator Jr Tostoi and other figures such as Alexandre Kassin have become masters of imperturbable and/and music production.

Insights from practice theory are helpful for framing the relationship between acting subjects and individual and collective projects, or for talking about class, taste, and "restricted" fields of production. But there is always *something more* happening when people sculpt their entire becoming around making music. There are those "entanglements" that are rendered audible, as Jocelyne Guilbault has put it (2005)—interconnected intensities pertaining to the construction of a democratic public sphere and the consolidation of "neoliberal" and global cultures of consumption; to Ogum and the "Afro" heritage in Brazilian culture; to Led Zeppelin, Deep Purple, and giving rock the boot while bringing percussion out from the background where it had been but a "perfume" and—*porra!*—getting a sound *do caralho* out of a goat-skin drumhead on a "detuned" tambourine; to the Nordeste, mangue beat, Pernambuco speaking to the world in côco, maracatu, forró,

CHAPTER SIX

embolada, and ciranda cyberpunk with pifes, alfaias, and violas caipiras, the Miscegenation Mass and echoes of the Portuguese "ão"; to deepening the human relationship and "pulverizing" strategies of self-promotion; to taking drum kits apart and playing batucada with rock 'n' roll pressure because no drummer has six arms — the massaroca, the suingue, carnival blocos in the South Zone, cuícas, surdos, caixas de guerra, and hubcaps, *life-groove-play-party-pleasure-joy in the here and now* (Keil 2002b, 40), the Tupy astronaut in participatory, presentational, and studio worlds of music making; to female *band leaders*, Pindorama Matriarchy, funk, lata, Funk 'n Lata, veneno da lata, good blood, the Duel between the Faithful Ones and the Lovers; to bundinha, contradiction, urban cannibals, urban violence, the divided city and the promiscuity of the South Zone; to simple songs, pretty, orderly melodies within Afro-cybernetic hurricanes, interferences, deterritorialized noises, electric guitars and Mutators; to mixing sessions with Jim Ball in New York City, mirrors, digital cameras, the false, everything new again with skin and strings — difference AND repetition!; to the Tropicália renaissance, the evolutionary line, pagode and disgusted subjects (Lawler 2005), corruption, homogenization, individuality, "artisan" production and the Real Plan; to São Sebastião and samba, samba, more samba. Becoming. Samba. Becoming-samba.

The preceding chapters trace cartographies of *milieus* — "worlds at once social, symbolic, and material, infused with the 'affects' and 'intensities' of their own subjectivities" — and of the trajectories individuals pursue as they engage their interests, their passions, their needs (Biehl and Locke 2010, 323). I am keen to embrace unfinishedness: our theorizing is inescapably incomplete and my understanding of Brazilian music making is partial. In this sense, this book is sympathetic to a recent shift in sociocultural anthropology toward drawing "mid-level" or "partial but suggestive connections" between specific aspects of large-scale problems and more localized refractions (Knauft 2006, 411). Scholars are creatively and critically mixing theoretical argumentation, ethnographic and historical narrative, subjective impressions, and sometimes "activist voicing," Bruce M. Knauft observes (411). In a somewhat similar vein, Kathleen Stewart has advocated "weak theory" for "an unfinished world" (2008).

The artists I came to know in Rio continue to develop their careers, occasionally producing new albums (including recent ones that did not make it into my analysis), and sometimes branching out into other endeavors. From Lisbon, Portugal, where I was revising this manuscript in 2010, I checked Paulinho Moska's website and found a couple of MP3s from what appeared to be a forthcoming album. A quick e-mail exchange verified that he was in fact about to release a new album (the two-CD boxed set *Muito Pouco*), and that he and his partner were expecting a new child. "Lots of work and happiness here," Moska wrote back. His television program, he noted, was already in its fifth season, and he had produced an edition of *Zoombido* for the radio. I am far from Rio de Janeiro, and much is happening there outside my purview. My knowledge of the local scene is incomplete, but interesting pieces accrue to the assemblage, often via virtual networking, but sometimes in old-fashioned ways, such as when Brazilian musicians pass through Lisbon or New York.

Pedro Luís, I learn, has published a poetic intertextual homage to Lenine and Suzano's *Olho de peixe* album: *Logo parecia que assim sempre fora: Breves inpirações livremente deliradas* (Immediately it seemed as if it had always been that way: Brief inspirations freely made delirious, 2009), sixteen years after the recording was first released. Each poem in the collection is inspired by the title of one of the songs from *Olho de peixe*. The last of them, in a chapter titled "Mais," comprises verses that begin and end with *mais além*, or "yonder," taken from the final track of *Olho de peixe*. Here is the poem in an English translation:

> Yonder, without a doubt, lies the ever after.
> I am repeating myself, most probably.
> But some poetry is bound to repeat itself,
> given that passion is often renewed.
> Some sensations, namely delights,
> will always visit upon us from time to time.
> With these visitations will come verses, seminal sighs.
> Beautiful melodies will always be welcome.
> I shall always try to be genuine.
> For you, I shall forever chase the idea that lies yonder
> —Pedro Luís, trans. Vladimir Freire

Now, what of cannibals? The theme has been present throughout this book in song lyrics and in subjects' discourse about mixture. It even made it into an album title for Lenine's *Falange canibal*. In fact, the couple of years before and after the turn of the millennium (coinciding with Fernando Henrique Cardoso's second term in office) seem to have represented some-

thing of an apex in lyrics that evoke cannibalism.[1] In this context,
sions to anthropophagy playfully postulate a kind of "cannibal mir
the national unconscious, "masticating, digesting, and rewriting th
sider" (Budasz 2005, 15). At the same time, they propose that there is an
embodied aspect to identity and becoming. What scholars often overlook
is how metaphors of ingesting the Other have become a popular talking
point in international interpretations of Brazilian music, part of the brand.
Anthropophagy does not necessarily or only indicate a radical postcolonial
method for appropriation and modernization; it has been inserted into
world music market-speak, and as a kind of explanatory shorthand, it ap-
peals to journalists.

This does not make it any less interesting to think about the cannibalist gesture. "Similar to incest, aggression, the nuclear family, and other
phenomena of universal human import," Lindenbaum writes, cannibalism "appears to be a concept on which to exercise certain theoretical programs" (2004, 480; see also Brown and Tuzin 1983, 2–3). Rather than enter
into debates over such theoretical programs, I have focused on the specific
practices that musicians describe as anthropophagic. In closing, however,
I return to a line of thought that Sara Castro-Klarén proposed in her genealogy of Oswald de Andrade's "Cannibalist Manifesto" of 1928. Whereas
Oswald conceptualized history dialectically (with a revolutionary matriarchy as the final stage in a teleological progression, in Castro-Klarén's
reading), it turns out that the anthropophagic reason of actual Tupi
peoples is non-dialectical, at least in the anthropologist Eduardo Viveiros
de Castro's elaboration of it, upon which Castro-Klarén draws.[2] Viveiros de
Castro studied ritual cannibalism among the Araweté people, who are of
the Tupi-Guaraní ethnicity. The Araweté do not "struggle to conjure away
difference" in a Euclidean dialectic (as in the Gê ethnicity famously studied
by Lévi-Strauss), or in a Lacanian model of the mirror function (Viveiros
de Castro 1992, 4).[3] They demonstrate "a passion for exteriority which . . .
inscribes Becoming" into "the very heart" of their society (1992, 3). Thus,
"the Tupí-Guaraní method of constructing the person," Viveiros de Castro
suggests, "has nothing to do with some mirror chamber of reflections and
inversion between the Self and the Other that tends towards symmetry and
stability" (4). They break the mirror, Castro claims; they destroy representation (270). They are "a society with a dynamic that dissolves those spatial
metaphors so common in sociological discourse: interior, exterior, center,
margins, boundaries, limen, etc." (270). The Tupi-Guaraní construct the

person through continual deformation. "Ego and enemy, living and dead, man and god, are interwoven, before or beyond representation, metaphorical substitution and complementary opposition" (270). Becoming is "prior to Being and unsubmissive to it" (270). Likewise, Moska's photographs are not reflections; they are de- and re-formations.

Oswald's famous redeployment of Hamlet's existential question as "Tupi, or not Tupi," Castro-Klarén concludes, was "not just a clever bilingual pun," or even "another banal instance of transculturation" (2000, 302). Rather, it posited a momentous epistemological challenge that reveals, when interpreted within a fuller genealogy, a potential alternative to the "narcissistic geometry of representation," that is, a "topological torsion of other-becoming" (Viveiros de Castro 1992, 254). "Your presence enters through the seven holes in my head," Caetano Veloso sang, and then Fernanda Abreu sang again. "It's white, green, red, blue, and yellow. It's black." What color is the chameleon on a mirror? What if the chameleon is a mirror-shattering cannibal?

APPENDIX 1

It was with the understanding of technology as an enabler of the project of mixing "Brazil" into the language of cosmopolitan pop that I viewed recording studios as important sites for conducting my field research. (In fact, a key labor performed in such studios is referred to as mixing, whereby recorded tracks are electronically modified through equalization, panning, reverberation, compression, special effects, and so on, and combined to a stereo "mix.") The larger recording facilities in Rio de Janeiro in the 1990s included Compania dos Técnicos (Company of Technicians), Estúdios Mega (Mega Studios), Nas Nuvens (In the Clouds), Estúdio AR (AR Studio), Impressão Digital (Digital Impression), and Discover. Discover, founded by Guilherme Reis, was the first all–Pro Tools (i.e., computer-based) facility in the city, and Guilherme was probably Rio's biggest enthusiast of hard disc recording before it became accepted as the norm in the first decade of the present century. While I spent considerable time in studios, however, the facilities were not in themselves my primary object of study. My concern was rather to remain attentive to the ways in which music technologies and production practices were part of these individuals' larger preoccupation with problems of modernization, national identity, and globalization.

For example, when I spoke with the sound engineer Fábio Henriques of the studio Nas Nuvens about the availability in Brazil of new and cheaper technologies brought about in part by globalization, he told me:

> The advances in technology are allowing [the construction of] more and more studios—not only in Brazil but throughout the world. The same thing is happening with music. I don't think that Brazilian music loses anything because of this very intimate contact with not just the United States but the whole world. . . . It's inevitable, and we don't have to fear it, because we have to do it, we have to "go with the flow" [in English]. What's important is not to lose the fundamental identity, that genetic thing that came from our ancestors. We carry this musical and artistic heritage from the Indians, from the African slaves, and the Europeans. It developed into something very distinct, very interesting, very rich in Brazil. This won't get lost. Actually, we'll contribute to the formation of a global artistic language. And we'll contribute a lot. Our art won't be abused in this process. We'll contribute to something bigger.

I recorded about eighty interviews on cassette tape in 1998–99, followed by several follow-up interviews in 2007 directly into MP3 format (with an Edirol R-09 digital recorder). These took place wherever I could pin busy musicians down, often in the common area of a recording facility, such as an eating space, but also occasionally in automobiles as I accompanied music makers hurrying from one location to another (including catching up with some of them in New York City when they traveled to mix in studios there), in restaurants when not so rushed, in the studio itself during breaks from recording or mixing, or in individuals' apartments. While I listened to all these, and transcribed the greater portion, I only cite from selected interviews in this book. Unless otherwise indicated, all quotations from music makers come from my interviews; I do not provide in-text citations for these; instead I make clear within the text who I am quoting, and I provide a list of cited interviews in this appendix. When the year of the interview merits mention, I do so in the text.

There are actually two processes of translation involved in extracting quotations from the interviews: from Portuguese to English, and from speech to printed text. In the latter conversion, the writer makes choices independent of the languages concerned. "Language that sparkles in conversation," Paul Berliner observed in *Thinking in Jazz*, "enhanced by inflection and by various features of nonverbal communication," may appear dull in print (1994, 9). Likewise, "the asides and redundancies of speech . . . seem disproportionately weighted in print." I have edited out most of the conversational extras that potentially impede the flow of the written quotations. Sparingly, I include my own interjections or queries in quoted conversations.

There are a few terms that I keep in Portuguese even when there exists an approximate English analogue. For example, referring to the *pandeiro* as a "tambourine"—the latter a comparatively minor instrument in the context of pop music in the United States—would not adequately convey its importance in Brazil, where it is used in numerous genres. I retain the Portuguese term for the acoustic, classical-style guitar with nylon strings, *violão*, to help distinguish it from electric guitar, referred to as *guitarra* in Brazil. Another instrument, the *surdo*, can be translated as "bass drum," but it is associated specifically with samba, while other kinds of bass drums are utilized in, for example, the *maracatu* drumming of the Northeast. A *caixa* is a kind of snare drum; I keep this in Portuguese for the sake of consistency with some of the other characteristic instruments just mentioned, and because it is usually used in Rio in reference to the *caixa de guerra* drum (lit. "war box") used in samba. (It is relatively deep, tuned quite tightly, and played with a wire snare on the top drum head, rather than on the bottom as is customary in the snare of a standard drum kit.) Another instance in which I stick with a local term is *suingue*, an interesting case since it is actually a Brazilianization of the English "swing."

Finally, a stylistic matter: It is common practice in Brazil to utilize given rather than family names to refer to many public figures, even in scholarly writing. I use that convention throughout most of this book in order to solve a minor problem of clarity: many music makers adopt an artistic name that is, for example, only a portion of their full name (e.g., Pedro Luís, instead of Pedro Luís Teixeira de Oliveira; or Tom Zé, which derives from Antônio [Tom] José [Zé] Santana Martins), or that incorporates the name of an instrument or musical genre (e.g., Paulinho da Viola, Zeca Pagodinho), or that is simply a nickname (e.g., Paulinho Moska instead of Paulo Corrêa de Araujo). With such appellations, there is no proper surname to utilize. On the other hand, it is cumbersome to use the complete artistic designation for each reference to the individual. Pedro, rather than Pedro Luís, for example, thus makes sense in such instances and avoids redundancy. To complicate matters, there are a few artists to whom Brazilian musicians typically refer by surname, including Marcos Suzano, for example, or Gilberto Gil. Meanwhile Lenine (Oswaldo Lenine Macedo Pimentel) uses only his second given name. I try to remain consistent with local preferences. When citing published literature, however, I use surnames.

Interviews Cited

Abreu, Fernanda Sampaio de Lacerda. 30 July 1999, Rio de Janeiro; and 9 August 2007, Rio de Janeiro.

Alvim, Celso. 19 May 1999, Rio de Janeiro (joint interview with C. A. Ferrari and Sidon Silva).

Amback, Sacha. 27 May 1999, Rio de Janeiro.

Campello, Rodrigo. 12 May 1999, Rio de Janeiro.

Cardoso, Fausto Borel (Fausto Fawcett), 15 July, 1999.

Corrêa de Araujo, Paulo (Paulinho Moska). 22 November 1998, Rio de Janeiro; 13 August 2007, Rio de Janeiro.

Costa, Walter. 23 March 1999, Rio de Janeiro.

Ferrari, Carlos Alexandre (C.A.). 19 May 1999, Rio de Janeiro (joint interview with Celso Alvim and Sidon Silva).

Fonseca, Celso. 11 March 1999, Rio de Janeiro.

Gonçalves, Luiz Antonio Ferreira (Tom Capone). 18 February 1999, Rio de Janeiro.

Henriques, Fábio. 11 December 1998, Rio de Janeiro.

Macedo Pimentel, Oswaldo Lenine. 1 July 1999, Rio de Janeiro.

Meirelles, Ivo. 21 July 1999, Rio de Janeiro.

Moura, Mário. 28 May 1999, Rio de Janeiro; and 3 June 1999, Rio de Janeiro (joint interview with Pedro Luís).

Neves, Chico. 7 May 1999, Rio de Janeiro.

Oliveira, Pedro Luís Teixeira de. 26 May, 1999, Rio de Janeiro; 3 June 1999, Rio de Janeiro (joint interview with Mário Moura); 9 August 2007, Rio de Janeiro.

Pacheco, Maurício. 12 July 2009, Rio de Janeiro.

Santtana, Lucas. 20 July 1999, Rio de Janeiro.

Silva, Sidon. 19 May 1999, Rio de Janeiro (joint interview with Celso Alvim and C. A. Ferrari); and 6 August 2007, Rio de Janeiro.

Suzano, Marcos. 26 April 1999, RPM Sound Studios, New York City; 22 June 1999, Rio de Janeiro; 20 July 2007, Rio de Janeiro; and 27 July 2007, Rio de Janeiro.

APPENDIX 2

I learned the basics of Suzano's method through one of his former students, Robert Saliba, a founding member of the Pandemonium ensemble of pandeiros. I also studied for a brief period with the choro pandeiro master Celsinho Silva. Samba and choro musicians generally describe the principal rhythms of these genres in 2/4 time, with each pulse divided into theoretically even sixteenth notes (although in samba, the subdivisions of the beat sometimes tend toward triplets, or the equivalent of 6/8 time, and in choro 3/4 time may also be used). On the pandeiro, the cymbals articulate these sixteenth notes (which Suzano sees as analogous to the highest atabaque drum part in the Candomblé tradition) as they shake. Normally, with the pandeiro held in front of the body, this is achieved by rhythmically rotating the instrument a short distance one way as the fingertips strike near the top of the frame, then the other way as the heel of the thumb strikes near the bottom of it, each motion lasting a sixteenth of a beat. The student must at first avoid attempting to play the characteristic swing of samba sixteenth notes, instead training the musculature to play what is called the *condução*—literally, the conduction, the drive—as evenly as possible. With this rhythmic base mastered, the percussionist can control precisely where the varied accents that distinguish specific rhythms fall in the pattern of eight steady sixteenth notes and can eventually add other strokes on top of the base. Low-range pitches (what Suzano sees as analogous to the lead atabaque in the Afro-Brazilian Candomblé drumming) are produced on the pandeiro with open strikes either with the thumb near the lower edge of the instrument or with a jab with the middle finger near the higher edge, depending on which part of the instrument is moving toward the playing hand. Slaps and other midrange pitches are produced in a variety of manners, some examples of which I describe here. In the typical choro and samba techniques for playing the pandeiro, the first sixteenth note of a given pattern is usually played with the thumb of the right hand while the fingertips of the right hand strike the second sixteenth note, and so on. Open and low sounds are then analogous to the surdo bass drum part in samba, with an accent on the second downbeat in duple meter.

Suzano's fundamental variation on this technique is to begin the patterns with the articulation at the fingertips, leaving his thumb free to accentuate the offbeats, a method that, he believes, gives him more "Afro intention." He seeks to approximate "the bass sound in Afro music," he said, in particular, in the music of the Afro-Brazilian Candomblé religious practice. In this tradition, the low rum drum "musically organizes the choreography" (Béhague 1984, 236) and functions as a kind of soloist (see also Fryer 2000, 19; and, on "Afro intention" in the Cuban context, Garcia 2006, 58–59). If, Suzano noted, he uses the thumb stoke on the downbeat of beats 1 and 2, as in the standard samba surdo part, and as the pandeiro is normally played, he loses the syncopation of the bass. Since the thumb is the strongest bass strike, he said, he keeps his thumb "always offbeat," maintaining power in syncopated low frequencies. The smaller lé and rumpi drums in Candomblé are typically responsible for steady patterns. Similarly, the cymbals on the pandeiro, in Suzano's style, generally maintain even sixteenth notes as they clang against one another, providing the fastest pulse of a given rhythm and functioning as a kind of "density referent" (Koetting 1970). The middle range on the pandeiro includes various sounds such as a muted slap on the drumhead. As Robert Saliba

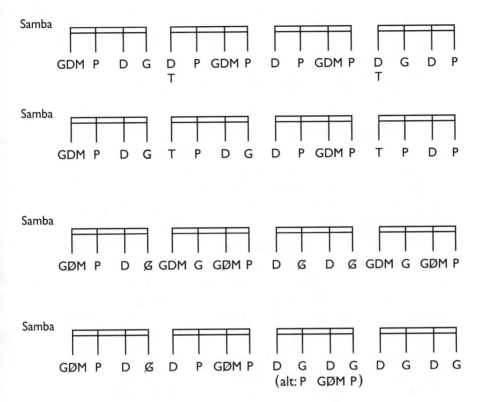

showed me, one can describe seven basic ways of striking the pandeiro with the following abbreviations for didactic purposes:

G—*Grave com o polegar.* A thumb stroke between the edge of the instrument and the middle of the drumhead producing a bass tone as the lower edge of the instrument is rotating upward toward the hand

GDM—*Grave com o dedo médio.* A bass tone made with the middle finger near the top edge of the drumhead as it is being rotated toward the fingertips (and the lower edge is moving down in the opposite motion to G [grave])

P—*Agudo com o punho.* High frequencies with the heel of the hand, a stroke that causes the cymbals to sound as part of the basic pulse (condução)

D—*Agudo com os dedos.* High frequencies with the fingertips; like P, a stroke that causes the cymbals to sound as part of the basic pulse

FIGURE 21. Variations of Marcos Suzano's samba pandeiro patterns, utilizing symbols for different hand strokes

T—*Tapa médio*. A slap in the middle of the drumhead (a mid-range sound)

Ǥ—*Médio no centro com o polegar, or grave fechado*. Mid-range or a closed low sound with the thumb striking the center of the drumhead, but dampened with the remaining fingers so that it does not resonate

G Ø M —*Médio no centro com o dedo médio or grave fechado*. Mid-range or closed low sound in the center with the middle finger; same function as G (médio), but with middle finger, and dampened

Figure 21 shows some of the exercises for pandeiro illustrating patterns of steady sixteenth notes utilizing these strokes that Robert gave me in our lessons. Note that all the samba examples begin with the bass sound produced at the first subdivision of beat 1 with the fingertips of the right hand, rather than with the thumb, allowing the low-frequency articulation on the fourth sixteenth note of beat 1, that is, a sixteenth-note anticipation of beat 2, the kind of offbeat low articulation that Suzano identifies with "Afro intention." (The last two patterns utilize more muted midrange strokes at these subdivisions.)

There is much more to his pandeiro playing than this (and indeed to pandeiro playing in general); these are but a few possible patterns. Nevertheless, this introduction gives a sense of a crucial mechanical aspect of Suzano's approach to the instrument. For more on the pandeiro, Pandemonium, and Suzano, see Crook (2009), 37–45.

NOTES

Preface

1. Quoted speech in this section is from my own transcription of the debate, which I attended. Carlos Lyra, a musician associated with the early years of bossa nova and "engaged" song, was also scheduled to participate but did not. Interestingly, thirty-two years earlier, when Marcos Valle was at the center of second-wave bossa nova, a different roundtable debate on the direction of Brazilian popular music touched on remarkably similar themes, but for different reasons. That discussion was published under the title "Que caminho seguir na música popular brasileira?" (Whither Brazilian popular music?) in the journal *Revista Civilização Brasileira*. This earlier debate is often cited as the forum in which Caetano Veloso introduced his concept of the "evolutionary line" of MPB (A. L. Barbosa et al. 1966, 384).

Introduction

1. Seu Jorge of Farofa Carioca, in fact, grew up in poverty (see, e.g., the interview with him featured in Mika Kaurismäki's film *Moro no Brasil*).

2. Rio de Janeiro is divided into North, South, and West zones, and the old downtown (the Center). The North Zone extends away from the Center and includes a mix of middle- and working-class neighborhoods. Lacking easy access to the beaches, this area is not favored by the more privileged sectors. The West Zone consists of newer middle- and upper-middle-class condominium communities, as well as working-class areas. (The Cidade de Deus neighborhood, for example, was harshly portrayed in the book and film by the same name.)

3. Musicians associated with the mangue beat music that emerged in Recife in the 1990s also tended to describe this as a scene rather than a movement, despite the media's occasional use of the latter term (see, e.g., Galinsky 2002). The ethnomusicologist Jocelyne Guilbault also uses the word *scene* in her recent study of calypso, although she links it more to a concept of genre in a flexible cosmopolitan setting with historical roots, but not necessarily fixed to a specific place (2007, 9). On the concept of a scene in popular music studies, see Bennett (2004), Cohen (1999), Hesmondhalgh (2005), Peterson and Bennett (2004), Shank (1994), and Straw (1991, 2006).

4. Homi Bhabha also famously theorized a postcolonial condition of in-betweenness (1985), but Silviano Santiago (2001) did so earlier (*The Space In-Between* is a collection of essays published earlier in Portuguese, going back to the late 1960s).

5. Rodrigo Campello, interview, 12 May 1999, Rio de Janeiro.

6. One journalist even wittily proposed the acronym MPBG for *música popular do Baixo Gávea* to refer to the work of the musicians associated with this rather specific scene (Porto 2003, 14; I thank Fred Coelho for drawing my attention to this). The area has become associated especially with the musicians of the "plus 2" collective centered on Moreno Veloso (Caetano Veloso's son), Domenico Lancelotti, and Alexandre Kassin. I conducted a number of interviews in the restaurants there. Coelho (2008) argues that journalists in Rio have attributed names to local scenes using social geographies of class rather than specifically musical criteria.

7. C. A. Ferrari, interview, 19 January 1999, Rio de Janeiro.

8. With his penchant for using sexual metaphors, Fausto Fawcett observed that Rio's tunnels function as a kind of "tight social vagina" that allow some passage, but that in fact fail fully to connect the different so-

cial worlds. He also described Rio as "the courtesan" to São Paulo, Brazil's "industrial Atlas" (Atlas in the sense of "carrying Brazil on its back" economically).

9. Brazilian books on the history of the country's popular music almost invariably begin with the notion that racial mixture is foundational to Brazilian culture (e.g., Souza, Vasconcelos, Moura, Maximo, Muggiati, Mansur, and Caurio 1988, 21).

10. I use quotation marks only in instances where I seek to draw attention to how words and phrases such as *race* and *Brazilian race* index ideologies of biological or otherwise innate difference. As a social concept, however, race—in Brazil as elsewhere—also indexes actual lived experiences of difference contoured around phenotype, so I typically use the word without quotation marks, in keeping with general practice in the social sciences. (The Portuguese word *raça* does have some culturalist overtones not necessarily connected with the word *race* in the context of the United States; moreover, there is sometimes little distinction in the Brazilian usage between the terms *raça* and *etnicidade*, ethnicity. These particularities do not, however, obviate my analyses as set forth here.) The literature on race in Brazil is extensive (and largely focused on questions of blackness and African heritage). For some relatively recent overviews in English, I point the reader to Reichmann (1999), Hanchard (1999), and Telles (2004). On blackness and the cultural sphere, see, for example, Crook and Johnson (1999) and Sansone (2003). On whiteness, see Sovik (2009).

11. Recent policies for affirmative action in government hiring and university admissions in Brazil challenge narratives of relatively harmonious race relations, as do certain hip-hop-influenced musical manifestations, such as the Afro-Reggae group and its associated NGO (Grupo Cultural Afro-Reggae), or the Central Única da Favela (CUFA) organization in Rio (see Moehn 2007; Yúdice 2003).

12. On Tom Zé, see Dunn (2001, esp. chap. 6; 2009) and Rollefson (2007). *Fabricando Tom Zé* (Manufacturing Tom Zé) is a quirky documentary on the musician, released in 2006.

13. Whether or not the Tupinambá actually practiced cannibalism (or for what reasons they might have done so) is part of a larger debate on cannibalism in anthropology. See Lindenbaum (2004) for an overview; also Conklin (2001).

14. This literature tends to focus on the modernist vanguard, national identity, and textual interpretation; the best of it offers subtle poststruc-

turalist readings of the metaphysics and power dynamics in anthropo-phagist cultural discourse (e.g., Hollanda 1998; Castro-Klarén 2000). It is in focusing on specific acting, classed subjects and their practices, how-ever, that my study differs from most of the literature on anthropophagy. (Roberto Schwarz once observed that the discourse of cultural cannibal-ism takes as its subject "the abstract Brazilian, with no class specification" [1988, 84].) Several of the chapters in Perrone and Dunn (2001) discuss cul-tural cannibalism in relation to popular music, as do Dunn (2001, 17–20), Moehn (2008), and Ulhôa Carvalho (1995). See also Budasz (2005).

15. In 1995 the group É o Tchan (formerly Gera Samba) scored a phe-nomenal success with the song "Segure o Tchan," the refrain to which went: "Segure o tchan, amarre o tchan, segure o tchan tchan tchan tchan tchan." There is no exact translation, but Mônica Leme writes that the expression *segurar o tchan* can be understood to mean, among other things, "to notice this corporeal exuberance" expressed through a prototype of beauty: "a fit body, prominent and full buttocks, grace and sensuality of movement." It is part, she observes, "of the construction of the myth of beauty of the Brazil-ian *mestiça*" (2001, 51), using another word for a woman of mixed race. The term *pagode* also refers, in an older usage, to an informal samba gathering (see Galinsky 1996).

16. Dapieve characterized "the masses" as "nourished on pork loin, blonde hair dye, and vulgarity" (1999). On the concept of "bad music," see Washburne and Derno (2004).

17. Some scholars prefer to speak of the middle *classes* in the plural. In Bra-zil, for example, the lower middle class may not enjoy many of the comforts of the middle-middle class. O'Dougherty favors the singular in order to em-phasize the "shared patterns, investments, and discourses of middle class Brazilians and about them in popular culture" (2002, 9). When I write about the middle class as an abstract social concept, I use the singular. In some in-stances, however, I may use the plural to reflect the internal differentiation of this social sector.

18. The literature generally grouped under the term *practice theory* is ex-tensive (e.g., Bourdieu 1984, 1993, 1995; Giddens 1979, 1991; Sahlins 1981, 2000; Ortner 1984, 2006). Some of the most thoughtful reflections on the topic can be found in Ortner (2006).

19. In his well-known essay "A Theory of Structure: Duality, Agency, and Transformation," William H. Sewell somewhat unhelpfully introduces an additional term when he describes a *capacity* for agency as a capacity "for de-

siring, for forming intentions, and for acting creatively" (1992, 20). Ortner seems to be seeking to clear this up with her term "agency-in-the-sense-of-power."

20. This does not mean, Gilberto Velho stresses, that the problematic of individuality is not present among the working classes, but rather that it is "a matter of dominance and context" (1992, 14).

21. Consider, for example, the following description of Bourdieu's concept of field as an arena "of production, circulation, and appropriation of goods, services, knowledge, or status, and the competitive positions held by actors in their struggle to accumulate and monopolize these different kinds of capital" (Swartz 1997, 117). Such a (Marxian) model suggests a fairly cynical view of the relationship between the individual and her social milieu. It does describe important dimensions of cultural production applicable to the present study, and I do not mean to caricaturize its terminology, but, as Nigel Rapport has argued (1997), this kind of formulation misses the more humanist side of individual becoming.

22. In a somewhat different mode, Kathleen Stewart, drawing on Eve Sedgwick's concept of "weak theory," has also sought to theorize "unfinished" worlds in ways that are less deterministic than older ways of thinking about the social (2008).

23. A more methodologically troubling reading would have been to dismiss Paulinho Moska's fascination with Deleuze as a kind of amateur philosophizing.

24. As early as 1995, Michael Kearney noted the applicability of Deleuze's concept of the rhizome and its "logic of 'both-and-and'" to the emergent anthropology of identities under globalization (in contrast to bounded "cultures"; 1995, 558–59). The rhizome contrasts with structures that are "defined by a set of points and positions, with binary relations between the points and biunivocal relationships between the positions" (Deleuze and Guattari, 1987, 21; Kearney 1995, 559). There has also been increasing interest in Deleuze and Guattari's philosophy among musicologists over the past decade or so. A recent edited volume (Hulse and Nesbitt 2010) presents some of the freshest thinking on the uses of Deleuze for theorizing contemporary art music (weighted toward European composers). This is, however, a different sort of project from thinking about how Deleuze's theories speak to the anthropology of subjectivity and becoming, and hence differs from my specific aim here (but see Kielian-Gilbert 2010, in the Hulse and Nesbitt volume). Additionally, although Deleuze wrote about modern-

ist and postmodernist art music, and about synthesizers (see Deleuze and Guatarri 1987, 108–9, 343; Scherzinger 2010, 108–9), he had little interest in popular music. Deleuze and Guattari's writing on music tends to be rather abstract, impressionistic, and inconsistent; it seems, in fact, intent on further removing musical sound "itself" from social context and actual subjects. For this reason, I engage these authors in a limited fashion in this book, and, as already noted, largely in response to Paulinho Moska's interest in Deleuze.

25. Another of Bateson's students suggested that the creature would just remain whatever color it was before approaching the mirror. In fact, chameleons are believed to change color primarily to signal specific states, not merely to camouflage in response to the color cues of its surroundings.

26. I am sympathetic to Lucas's reservations regarding hegemonic narratives about popular music, but there are contradictions to this line of reasoning that render it less useful. For example, samba has received at least as much attention from critics and scholars as MPB has, and it was historically associated with working-class populations. Moreover, Brazilian rock never really was considered MPB (nor, for that matter, was Jovem Guarda, or even Tropicália, at first). The group of musicians known as Clube da Esquina, of whom Milton Nascimento is the best known, emerged in Belo Horizonte, Minas Gerais, in the early 1970s, not in Rio or São Paulo, yet they were central to MPB. Choro, by contrast, has been a favorite of middle-class Cariocas for decades, yet it is not precisely música popular brasileira (especially because it is primarily instrumental). It is true that genres and musicians from the South and the North have had less of a presence in Rio de Janeiro. The singer-songwriter Adriana Calcanhotto, however, from Porto Alegre, in the South, moved to Rio in the late 1980s. Victor Ramil, also from Porto Alegre, has collaborated with Marcos Suzano (see chapter 1). As for middle-class Carioca critics and intellectuals, one of the more influential among them is Hermano Vianna, who published an ethnography of funk carioca (which is not considered MPB in mainstream understandings of it) as early as 1988. Also, Lucas implicates the music industries based in Rio and São Paulo in diffusing the kinds of music that middle-class critics praise. However, the music industry has arguably not prioritized the music favored by said critics, preferring instead genres that it deems easier to mass market (as the pagode phenomenon suggests). Finally, the mangue beat bands that received so much critical attention in the 1990s emerged in Recife, not Rio or São Paulo.

27. Other genres of Brazilian music accomplish some of the same identity

work for certain populations. Música sertaneja, for example, emphasizes songwriting and is influenced by North American country music (see Dent 2007, 2009; Reily 1992). Axé music, a dance-oriented genre in Bahia, hybridizes samba with Afro-pop and rock. While both clearly speak to Brazilian identities, they do not manifest a consistent preoccupation with defining the nation. They in fact retain strong regional associations for their audiences. Not all music that is "popular" and made in Brazil engages the same set of concerns. The issue with the designation música popular brasileira is only partly about what genres or places are in or out; it is also about what stories different music makers claim as theirs.

28. Modernization-minded intellectuals, by contrast, saw bossa nova as a vehicle for reversing the dynamic of imperialist cultural flows by "anthropo-phagically" digesting advanced technologies from the most industrialized countries and returning "new finished products" to them (Campos 1974, 60; Medaglia 2003, 100).

29. Perrone (1989) offers an incisive analysis focusing primarily on MPB's major stars and their song texts during the years of military rule, while Leu (2006) and Stroud (2008) probe the meanings of tradition, regionalism, style, the media, and the state in the work of major MPB artists. Dunn's *Brutality Garden* (2001) is an indispensable critical reading of the Tropicália artistic and musical movement. Vianna (1999) and Shaw (1999) go further back to the early decades of urban samba (1920s through the 1940s) to examine, among other things, how the genre came to be considered Brazil's "national" music. McCann (2004) details the role of radio in the popularization of samba, choro, baião, and other genres. By contrast, Peronne and Dunn in *Brazilian Popular Music and Globalization* (2001) include several essays on emergent sounds of postdictatorship Brazil, such as heavy metal, funk, reggae, samba-reggae, and bands associated with the mangue beat rock scene in Recife (as well as a chapter in which I offer my initial observations about the "cannibalist transnationalism" of this scene). Vargas (2007) examines hybridity in the music of mangue beat pioneers Chico Science and Nação Zumbi. Livingston-Isenhour and Garcia (2005) take a broadly historical look at the choro genre, including the flourishing of contemporary groups that emerged in the 1980s and 1990s. Individual articles of relevance include Araújo et al. (2006), Béhague (1973, 1980, 2006), Bollig (2002), Magaldi (1999), Napolitano (1998), Pardue (2004), Reily (1994), Sneed (2007), Treece (1997), Ulhôa Carvalho (1995), and Yúdice (2003). On mangue beat specifically, see, for example, Crook (2001), Galinsky (2002), Murphy (2001),

Sandroni (2009), and Vargas (2007). Herschmann (1997) is a collection of essays focused primarily on the emergence of funk and hip-hop scenes in Brazil. On hip-hop in São Paulo, see also Pardue (2008).

30. Working-class musical cultures, by contrast, have often been the focus of ethnomusicological study (e.g., Keil 1966, 1985, and Peña 1985, among various others). A notable recent contribution is Aaron Fox's *Real Country* (2004).

31. I took pandeiro lessons with Robert Saliba, a former student of Marcos Suzano and member of the Pandemonium ensemble, and with Celsinho Silva of the group Nó em Pingo d'Água. I took guitar lessons with Nelson Faria and Jorge Simas.

32. For Schwarz, who examined allegory in Tropicália, the politics of a form of capitalist development that privileged a cosmopolitan elite while perpetuating poverty remained unexamined in Brazilian popular music (1992, 139–44; see also Favaretto 1979, 65–66; Dunn 2001, 86–100).

33. Jonathan Stock gives Capwell (1991), Levin (1996), and Lortat-Jacob (1995) as other examples of ethnomusicological monographs that are sensitive to the place of the individual in a given music culture without specifically seeking to document individual music lives (2001). Monographs that have highlighted exceptional individuals include Danielson (1997), Erlmann (1991), and Stock (1996). For more on the topic, see Bohlman (1988, 69–86), Nettl (2005, 13, 172–83), and Rice (1987, 473–74). Stock (2001) offers a good overview.

34. Chapter 1 expands on my article "A Carioca Blade Runner, or How Percussionist Marcos Suzano Turned the Brazilian Tambourine into a Drum Kit, and Other Matters of (Politically) Correct Music Making," published in *Ethnomusicology* (2009), and parts of chapter 4 derive from my article "Music, Mixing, and Modernity in Rio de Janeiro," published in *Ethnomusicology Forum* (2008).

Chapter 1: Marcos Suzano

1. The term *schizophonia* is R. Murray Schafer's; it "refers to the split between an original sound and its electro-acoustic transmission or reproduction" (1977, 90). The ethnomusicologist Steven Feld later utilized Schafer's term (1994, 1996), as have I (Moehn 2005; see also Miller 2009).

2. The specific albums mentioned here are Pedro Luís e A Parede's *É tudo um real* (Everything's a dollar), Chico César's *Mapa mundi*, Zeca Baleiro's *Vô imbolá* (roughly, I'll rap it up), Lenine's *Na pressão* (Under pressure), Fernanda

Abreu's *As cidades* (Cities), Lucas Santtana's *Eletro bem dodô* (no translation), and Carlos Malta's *Pife muderno* (Modern fife).

3. With Kazufumi Miyazawa, Suzano recorded *Afrosick* (1998), and with Takashi Numazawa, *The Copacabana Sessions / Live in Naeba* (2006) and *Nenhuma canção, só música* (No songs, just music, 2007).

4. In Portugal, the name *pandeiro* is used for a similar drum in the Évora province, near Spain (Castelo-Branco and Brito 2009).

5. I compiled this list based on interviews I conducted with Suzano and other musicians who have worked with him, on my observations of the percussionist recording and performing, and on my experience studying the basics of his performance methods.

6. Some musicians felt that already in bossa nova, samba-derived Afro-Brazilian percussion was shuttered to the background of arrangements and productions. One could even go further back and say that this was the case even in the sentimental arrangements of the crooners, or "radio singers," of the late 1940s and the 1950s.

7. Carlinhos Brown from Salvador, Bahia, in the Brazilian Northeast, has followed a similar path with respect to experimenting with percussion and technology, although he also sings and composes pop songs.

8. The "conduct of conduct" phrase is attributed to Michel Foucault and pertains to the power to govern (or "conduct") people's conduct (an imperfect translation of the original "conduire des conduits"; in Foucault 1994, 237).

9. Although Mário Moura and others read the appearance of Chico Science and Nação Zumbi as an important maneuver in the project of inserting Brazil into pop, Philip Galinsky (2002) has argued that in another sense the mangue beat bands established a more direct link between the "local" and the "global," bypassing "the nation" (and the old media center of Rio de Janeiro). In my follow-up research, some of the musicians I spoke with confirmed that by the 2000s, Recife-based musicians had succeeded in establishing more direct links with the European media circuits and the touring scene. As I detail in chapter 2, Lenine played a part in strengthening this particular link.

10. In a report for the Instituto Brasileiro de Geografia e Estatística, José Eustáquio Diniz Alves discusses a variety of the male-centric expressions common in Brazil. "Do caralho," he observes, "is something very good" (2004, 27). See also DaMatta (1995).

11. Although the gonguê is often associated with Ogum because it is made

out of metal, Metz argues for a Central African rather than West African origin for the instrument (2008).

12. Lívio Sansone observed a generalized shift in "the use of 'Africa' in Brazil" in the past few decades as what was once regarded as "primitive" has "acquired status in both popular as well as high-brow culture" (1999, 39).

13. Interestingly, Ogum may also be syncretized with Saint Sebastian, the official patron saint of Rio de Janeiro, who is sometimes associated with gay subcultures in Brazil (Medeiros 2008). Suzano's apparent identification with Ogum / Saint George again seems to favor heroic tropes of masculinity over the image of the martyred Saint Sebastian and its local symbolism. Without wishing to push such associations too far, I might add that the lance can be interpreted as a phallic symbol.

14. There is in fact a literature that indexes corruption (and perceptions of corruption) to gender based on the thesis that the more "masculine" the society (emphasizing independence, achievement, power, wealth, status and "quantity of life" over quality of life [Park 2003, 36]), the higher the level of corruption. This discussion has played out primarily in the *Journal of Business Ethics* (e.g., Davis and Ruhe 2003; Husted 2002). These studies draw primarily on quantitative data and can be faulted for making generalizations based on a given, overdetermined notion of masculinity.

15. Ortner uses the phrase "agency-in-the-sense-of-(the pursuit of) projects" to identify that specific kind of agency (a form of power) that allows individuals to seek to realize projects (2006, 145). The hyphens indicate that the entire phrase represents a single concept, while the parentheses work like an embedded footnote to the concept. Although somewhat idiosyncratic, this kind of punctuation works well in the context of Ortner's elaboration of the analytical parameters of practice theory.

16. Although in rehearsal blocos may be fairly disciplined, during carnival they give the impression of being rowdy and spontaneous agglomerations of costumed musical revelers. In this way, blocos contrast with the samba schools that appear in carefully orchestrated formations in the "sambadrome" built specifically to structure the processions of the largest parades (see Moehn 2005). While most of Rio's largest samba schools are concentrated in working-class suburbs distant from the more privileged neighborhoods of Rio's South Zone, there are a number of blocos in middle- and upper-middle-class neighborhoods, among them the Monobloco group that has become tremendously popular in the South Zone (see chapter 3).

17. On choro, see, for example, Livingston-Isenhour and Garcia (2005) and McCann (2004).

18. At the time of this writing, a video of these three percussionists performing together is on YouTube: http://www.youtube.com/watch?v=WlU1 B89Q4EQ (accessed 5 December 2009).

19. The Sharp Prize was later renamed the Tim Prize (after its cellular telephone sponsor). The other core members of Aquarela Carioca for the early albums with Marcos Suzano were Lui Coimbra (cello, *charango*, violin), Paulo Muylaert (electric guitar and flute), Papito (bass), and Paulo Brandão (bass).

20. Clave is a rhythmic ostinato with roots in West African music. Sometimes it is used on pop productions to add a hint of Afro-Latin feel.

21. *Phase cancellation* refers to an adjustment made when using multiple microphones to record one sound source (e.g., a stereo pair). Typically, the signal from one of the microphones must be shifted out of phase so as not to "cancel out" (that is, essentially erase) parts of the signal from the other microphone.

22. The Curupira is a mythological forest figure believed to be of indigenous Tupinambá origin; he is a boy with red flames instead of hair, and backward feet capable of leaving misleading footprints.

23. The dark blue tones and techno aesthetic of the album cover recall the timbres of the film *Blade Runner*.

24. One of the characteristics of such narratives as told in interviews is that they may include post-facto (and possibly self-congratulatory) rationalization (see Ortner 2006, 135). Was Suzano really so clear about his motivations, so certain of the meanings of his actions at the time he first attempted them? Based on the way others in this setting talked to me about him as early as the mid-1990s, I am inclined to think that for the most part, he was. That said, Ortner's "serious games" framework allows that intentions do not always generate predictable results. (Other scholars have pointed this out too, e.g., Comaroff and Comaroff 1992.) Moreover, his very shaping of his personal narrative speaks to his intentions *at the time of the interview*, to his desire to assert his narrative version of events over other potential ones.

25. Filters such as Suzano's Belgian-made Sherman unit remove a specified band of frequencies from the sound that enters the device and send back out what remains. There are a variety of uses for such frequency filtering devices; for example, a "low pass" filter eliminates all frequencies above a specific cutoff point and may be used to eliminate hiss-like sounds. The kinds of devices used in electronic dance musics generally feature oscillators that mechanically control which frequencies are filtered. In this manner, a "band" of frequencies is attenuated from the sound source, but the center point of that band sweeps through a range at a specified tempo (that is, this

oscillation has its own frequency). In dance music the oscillation is set to a tempo that is metrically appropriate for the song.

26. Quote from www.sherman.be (accessed 18 January 2011).

27. "Voodoo" is Anglicized orthography for Vodoun (or Vodou). In popular usage, however, this spelling of the term has come to be a gloss for "black magic" or superstitious, irrational beliefs. In the United States, Voodoo can refer to "witchcraft," as thought to be practiced in and around New Orleans. For those who adhere to Vodoun as a deep-rooted African diaspora religion, such associations can be offensive. Hence "Voodoo" is not the preferred spelling.

28. *Satolep* is *Pelotas*—Ramil's hometown—spelled backward, whereas Sambatown is, of course, Suzano's city.

29. Lucas Santtana's *Three Sessions in a Greenhouse*, for example, was funded by a grant from the cultural foundation of the national oil company, Petrobras.

30. On different registers of musical masculinity, see especially Meintjes (2004) and Solis (2007).

Chapter 2: Lenine

1. In an interview for MTV Brasil in 1999, Caetano Veloso called Lenine's debut solo album (*O dia em que faremos contato*) a "masterpiece" (cited in a press release from the Swiss booking agency Latitude Music, http://www.latitudemusic.com/lenine [accessed 17 August 2008]). The remaining musicians Veloso invited to the Cité concert were the cellist and arranger Jacques Morelenbaum, the drummer Ronaldinho Silva, the guitarist Luiz Brasil, and the bassist Alberto Continentino, while Lenine brought the wind instrumentalist Carlos Malta and the percussionist Marco Lobo. The shows took place on 14–16 May 1999.

2. Quoted from the *In Cité* concert program notes (my translation).

3. The North American singer Dionne Warwick recorded a version of his samba "Virou areia" with English lyrics in 1995. (*Virou areia* means "it turned to sand," but Warwick's version keeps this in Portuguese.) With Bráulio Tavares, Lenine wrote the sambas de enredo "Bundalelê" (no exact translation; it means, among other things, "a party") for the Suvaco do Cristo carnival bloco. Lenine's song "Do It" (co-composed with Ivan Santos) was included in the soundtrack for the telenovela *Belíssima*, while his song "Mero detalhe" was featured on *As filhas da mãe*, and "O silêncio das estrelas" (composed with Dudu Falcão) on the telenovela *O Clone*.

4. In Europe, the wood was used to produce a red dye, while a variety of brazilwood from Pernambuco was also among the preferred materials for making bows for the viol and the violin in Europe. See Woodfield and Robinson n.d.

5. The battle against Canudos was famously documented by the journalist and civil engineer Euclides da Cunha in his book, *Os sertões* (*Rebellion in the Backlands*, 1902).

6. Northeastern musical traditions were an important element in the writings of the modernist thinker Mário de Andrade, who proposed carefully fusing local folklore with European forms to advance Brazilian art music. In 1938 Mário oversaw the Missão de Pesquisas Folclóricas (Folkloric Research Mission), an ethnographic project that documented musical traditions of the North and Northeast. The continued importance of the region's music to the national cultural patrimony is indicated by the relatively recent release of a handsomely illustrated six-CD boxed set of a selection of these recordings, with accompanying essays in both Portuguese and English translation.

7. During our interview Lenine illustrated the *peleja* tradition by singing for me the memorable refrain to a duel between the northeasterners Cego Aderaldo and Zé Pretinho, in which the former incorporated a set of variations on an alliterative phrase into his response to his verbal adversary: "Quem a paca cara compra, paca cara pagará," Lenine recited, followed by his own variation of the refrain "Quem a paca cara compra, paca cara pagará pá caralho!" (loosely translated, "Whosoever buys the expensive *paca* [a rodent] will pay through the nose for it"). Cego Aderaldo was born in 1878; I found the complete text of this lengthy peleja at http://www.releituras.com/cegoaderaldo_paca.asp (accessed 14 August 2008).

8. Crook refers to this loose collection of related styles as the "forró complex" (2005, 89). The term *forró* probably derives from *forrobodó*, meaning something like "commotion," or "party."

9. The baião rhythm is related to similar patterns in numerous Afro-Brazilian musical forms of the Northeast, such as the *baiano* (meaning "from Bahia").

10. In 2007 the municipality of Recife promoted a celebration called 100 Years of Frevo (based on the first printed use of the term in a Recife newspaper in 1907), and in Rio de Janeiro the oldest samba school of the city, Mangueira, chose "100 Years of Frevo" for its 2008 carnival theme.

11. Lenine released "Prova de fogo" later in 1981 as a single, and it was included on the album Lenine recorded with Lula Queiroga, *Baque solto* (1983).

12. The quotation about Lenine's "anachronistic" relationship with BMG is from an interview with the *Correio Braziliense* (Cavalcanti 2002).

13. Other instruments are utilized sparingly on the album, such as soprano saxophone (on the title song) and electric guitar on "Lá e lô" (roughly, Front and back), in addition to the already mentioned limited use of synthesizers (most prominent on the song "Escrúpulo" [Scruple]).

14. Vianna is an astute critic of Brazilian music and society and my aim is not to disqualify his interpretation but rather to highlight how *O dia em que faremos contato* was interpreted locally. We may bear in mind also that it is customary practice to indulge in hyperbole in album release texts.

15. Bourdieu has used the phrase "production for producers" for art that reaches only a highly "restricted" public, and as Hesmondhalgh observes, the subfield of small-scale (or restricted) production "involves *very* low levels of economic capital, and *very* high levels of field-specific symbolic capital" (2006, 214). This does not really occur in pop music as such, so what we have in the present setting is closer to Bourdieu's subfield of mass production for the bourgeoisie, as compared with "popular" mass production (215).

16. Interestingly, Chico cited a major industry insider, André Midani, as the individual who counseled him years before that if he wanted to make music, he would have to stay out of the music *business*. Midani, under whom I worked for a summer at Warner Music Latin America in New York City, is a legend in the Brazilian popular music business. He contracted many of the main singer-songwriters of MPB and become a leading international music industry executive. *Billboard* magazine selected him as one of the ninety most important people in the history of the global music industry.

17. After Lenine's first solo album, Chico returned to Real World in the following two years to mix Os Paralamas do Sucesso's *Hey na na* (1998), Arnaldo Antunes's *O som* (1998), Lucas Santtana's *Eletrobemdodô* (1999), and O Rappa's *Lado B lado A* (1999).

18. Caju and Castanha performed at the release party for *O dia em que faremos contato* in Rio. Caju passed away in 2001, and his nephew Ricardo Alves da Silva took his place in the duo.

19. Claude Sicre, the founder of Les Fabulous Trobadors, traveled to Brazil in the early 1980s and discovered the embolada singers of the Northeast (see Haines 2004, 145).

20. The underlying idea with the term *nega*, Carvalho elaborates, "is that real sexual pleasure is normally achieved outside marriage, mostly with a black woman, who comes to represent total openness, as opposed to the wife, who represents controlled and conventional desire" (1994, 23).

21. Other Brazilian racial typologies that Lenine pokes fun at in this song include *um mulato muito louco* (a very crazy mulato) which, like *um mameluco maluco*, recalls positivist discourses about race mixture leading to insanity. Lenine also describes a *moreno* (light-skinned mulato) who is together with a *cafuzo* (African and Amerindian), and a *sarará* (a light-skinned person who has "kinky" hair [Sanjek 1971, 1132]) with a *coboclo* (Amerindian and Portuguese). While the lyrics ridicule such terms, they simultaneously celebrate miscegenation.

22. I transcribed these quotations from my field recording of their conversation on 16 March 1999.

23. Lenine recorded another version of "Jack soul brasileiro" for the collection *Jackson do Pandeiro revisito e sampleado* and also performed it on the two live recordings, *Acústico* MTV and *In Cité*. Fernanda Abreu recorded a version of the song with Lenine on her 1997 album, *Raio X* (see chapter 4).

24. In Swahili and other African languages the word *mganga* refers to a medicine man, a doctor (see Madan 1902, 403). Luís da Câmera Cascudo (1999, 404) writes that in Brazil *muganga* (with the "u" possibly added to mganga to Latinize it) came to refer to "exuberant gesticulations" and "harsh movements." Castro (2001) lists *dengo* (affection, tenderness) as coming from Bantu. Nei Lopes (1995, 158) suggests a possible etymology for *mamulengo* from the Kikongo *mi-lengo*, meaning "miracle."

25. *Banguela* may derive from the slave port São Filipe de Benguela in Angola. Many of the Africans exported to Brazil from this port, it is said, had the custom of filing down their incisor teeth (see N. Lopes 1995, 42).

26. The orthographic neighbor is a linguistic concept that pertains to facility for naming words. Neighbors differ in one letter only; utilizing the principle loosely in "Meu Amanhã (Intuindootil)," Lenine extends the idea to two letters in a few instances. He also utilizes what some linguists have called "phonographic neighbors" (words differing in one letter and one phoneme, e.g., *stove* and *stone*; see Adelman and Brown 2007).

27. Universidade Federal de Londrina, Concurso Vestubular 2005 (sample exam), at http://www.cops.uel.br/vestibular/2005/provas/03_Bio_Fis.pdf (accessed 20 August 2008); Prova de Conhecimentos Específicos, PROAC/ COSEAC—Curso de Serviço Social (pp. 5–6), PDF at www.coseac.uff.br/ . . . / Transferencia_UFF_2007_Ssocial_Campos.PDF (accessed 3 September 2011).

28. The metaphoric image of the stop light is potent in Rio de Janeiro, where the distinction between those who have cars and those who do not is a particularly noticeable marker of class divisions. While the middle and

upper classes may encounter children selling or begging at a red light, they may also encounter armed thieves who seek to steal their vehicle. Meetings of the social classes at intersections are thus charged with guilt, fear, perhaps anger, or even expectation (from the perspective of someone trying to sell candy, for example).

29. In 1526 Paraguaçu traveled with Carumuru to France, where Queen Catherine de Medici baptized her and gave her the name Catarina.

30. Although the country was shocked by the crime, it took years to prosecute the youths.

31. From Lenine's commentary in the CD listening notes.

32. Lenine subsequently chose this song as his contribution to the Drop the Debt project, which emerged out of the Jubilee 2000 international movement to cancel third world debt by the year 2000. The Drop the Debt NGO produced an eponymous album in 2003 with artists from developing countries (including Fernanda Abreu) and directed the profits toward debt negotiations.

33. Lenine's album *Labiata* (2008), produced by Jr Tostoi, is again more rock-oriented, moving away from the jazzy pop world music kind of sound. Given my focus on Lenine's earlier work, and for concerns of length, I chose not to discuss this album here.

Chapter 3: Pedro Luís and The Wall

1. Harris M. Berger and Cornelia Fales (2005) have analyzed timbre in rock, particularly in the distorted guitar sounds, focusing on how to quantify relative sensations of heaviness. See also Berger (1999), Fast (2000), Frith and McRobbie (1978), Holm-Hudson (2002), and Walser (1993). This literature, focused on the United States and the United Kingdom, cannot address how Brazilian musicians' appreciation of heavy rock sounds from abroad served to indicate their country's "underdevelopment" in music production (whether this perception was justified is a separate question), and how it would eventually inspire them to create a completely different hybrid aesthetic of musical "heaviness" that drew on both rock and samba.

2. Around this time Pedro also co-produced, with Arícia Mess, Mathilda Kóvak, and Suely Mesquita, a CD titled *O Ovo*, which highlighted a variety of new songwriters in the local scene, including Rodrigo Campello, later co-owner of the MiniStereo studio.

3. PLAP credit the composer Antônio Saraiva as one of their initial inspirations for their approach to batucada.

4. The event was "CEP 20.000," which took place in March 1996 at the Sergio Porto Cultural Space and was organized by the poets Chacal and Michel Melamed.

5. In citing Keil here, I leave aside the theoretical problems that arise when we ask what "socially valuable" means (and who determines this), or why participatory music making is out of tune, or of time, rather than alternatively tuned and timed.

6. One of Gerischer's interviewees used similar language to describe suingue baiano: "If you use a drum machine it would be hard. The suingue is exactly that oscillation, which is neither wrong nor exactly correct" (Tustão, cited in Gerischer 2006, 103).

7. Washburne (1998) looks at swing in salsa.

8. Reebee Garofalo (1993) similarly noted that the flow of popular musics from the United States to what tended to be called "the periphery" in the 1990s was not necessarily negative.

9. As noted in chapter 1, for Mário Moura, CSNZ in particular offered "strong, vigorous sounds" that sparked national pride among middle-class youths. This sonic vigor appears to evoke the kind of "masculine energy" that Pedro conceded attracted male youths to rock 'n' roll.

10. Thomas Porcello (2002) has shown that despite Charles Keil's personal animus toward technology, PDs may very well be prioritized in the recording studio (as in the "Austin sound"), and we see this kind of move here framed in relation to instrumentation and terminology taken from distinctly Brazilian sound worlds.

11. Perhaps it is worth noting here how the metaphor of "dropping a grenade" recalls the bellicose aspect of maracatu drumming and of the figure of Ogum as mentioned in my analysis of Suzano's musical invention.

12. Weid (2007) offers an interesting ethnographic study of an underground swinging scene in Rio's South Zone.

13. There were, of course, contemporary voices of social critique emerging from the favelas too, generally less celebratory of the life (most notably, Afro-Reggae; see, e.g., Moehn 2007; Yúdice 2003).

14. The name also recalled a bus line that went from Tijuca to Copacabana and that utilized a Mercedes-Benz vehicle known as a "Monobloco Mercedes." (Its frame was made out of a single block of metal.)

15. New York is a good example. In the 1990s I performed regularly with Brazilian expat Ivo Araújo's Manhattan Samba group. In recent years the ethnomusicologist Philip Galinsky has built up his Samba New York! or-

ganization, which, like Monobloco, conducts workshops, performs shows, and participates in street parades (such as the Halloween Day Parade). Maracatu New York, directed by Scott Kettner, is similar, but with a greater focus on Northeastern drumming. There are numerous other examples in cities worldwide.

16. The reader may have noted that Sidon uses "Carioca" in these quoted passages to refer specifically to middle-class residents of the South Zone. While this suggests that the normative usage of this term has a class bias, this is not precisely the case. There is a sense in which the popular image of the Carioca tends to suggest a South Zone beach-goer, but "samba carioca," and "funk carioca," for example, refer to working-class manifestations (hence my follow-up question to Sidon).

17. Monobloco in fact confronts some of the same technical challenges that the major samba schools must work around with respect to amplification when performing on the street. For example, it is difficult to synchronize the musicians who remain atop a flatbed truck as the bloco moves through the streets (e.g., the singer, guitar, keyboards, and *cavaquinho*) with the drum corps following on foot at some distance on the street below. In order to do so, technicians must aim a microphone at key drums and send the sound to monitors on the truck. (In the sambadrome, however, the problem of acoustic delay is considerably more complicated, as I detailed in "The Disc Is Not the Avenue" [2005].) In recent years the group began to parade on the avenue in front of the beach of Copacabana (from Posto 6 to Figueiredo Magalhães Street).

18. Fundo de Quintal play what is understood by many local musicians as "authentic" pagode, distinct from the more commercialized genre of the same name that exploded in the 1990s (see Galinsky 1996).

19. The album also features several songs not penned by Pedro, including "Morbidance" (as in "morbid dance," by Lula Queiroga, Felipe Falcão, and Lucky Luciano), "Saudação a Toco Preto" (by the legendary Mangueira sambista Candeia), "Do Leme ao Leblon" (by Carlos Negreiros, Marcos Suzano's partner in the Batucum group), and "Nega de Obaluaê" (an old and rarely heard samba by the romantic singer Wanderley Alves dos Reis, known as Wando).

20. Tom's wife continues to run the Toca do Bandido studio since his passing. The members of PLAP did release some other recordings in the years immediately after Tom's passing: a collaboration with the singer Ney Matogrosso (*Vagabundo* [Lazy bum] and the corresponding live CD of the

show), the second Monobloco album and live DVD, and a greatest-hits collection.

21. For more on the folia de reis, see Reily (2002) and Tremura (2004).

22. "MiniStereo" refers both to Rodrigo Campello and Jr Tostoi as a performing-arranging-producing duo and to their recording facility.

23. For more on Turino's book, Keil's harrumph of a review of it is also worth reading (2009).

Chapter 4: Fernanda Abreu

1. Elijah Wald has suggested that female fans of both jazz and rock 'n' roll have historically been more interested in dance than male fans (Wald 2009). As Burkett points out, however, lacking "detailed accounts of women listening attentively to live performances, collecting recordings, or working as professional musicians themselves" (2010, 424), Wald's argument remains too much of a generalization. While jazz criticism and historiography have tended to emphasize male figures, the essays in Rustin and Tucker (2008) provide detailed critical accounts of women's participation in jazz as performers, arrangers, composers, and listeners.

2. "Who qualifies as a rockera?" the journalist Tim Padgett asked in the article. "Most Latin Music critics," he answers, "say that the term can mean almost any singer who departs from mainstream Latin American pop. Even pop-rock can qualify, so long as it's written and performed artfully, intelligently and with a hint of nonconformity. The same goes for folk rock, glam rock, even Brazilian samba-funk-rock" (1998, 38).

3. I have taken parts of this description of Fernanda's childhood from the autobiographical text she published on her website: http://fernandaabreu .uol.com.br/home.htm (accessed 2 June 2008). Regarding the Post 9 beach hangout, James Freeman has observed that it is "more a lifestyle than an actual lifeguard station" (2002, 14). Rio's beaches are often touted as profoundly democratic public spaces with respect to race and class, but a visit to Post 9, peopled mostly by light-skinned middle- and upper-middle-class youths, reveals this claim to be only partially valid (see Rohter 2007).

4. Bi Ribeiro's father was a diplomat, for example, while Herbert Vianna's father was in the military.

5. DJ Marlboro's 1989 mix album Funk Brasil was a tremendous success, even lacking promotional support from PolyGram, the label that released it (Cumming 2003). For more on the 1970s soul movement in Rio de Janeiro, see Alberto (2009) and McCann (2002).

6. The Rio-based journalist Danuza Leão turned this rather South Zone habit of exaggeratedly accenting each syllable of certain words into a characteristic of her society column in the 1990s.

7. Marcos Suzano suggested, plausibly, that funk carioca emerged from a fusion of the basic Miami bass rhythm with the Afro-Brazilian *curimba*, which has some similar key syncopations. He thought, further, that it took hold so forcefully in Brazil precisely as a kind of electrification and amplification of this rhythm already known in the Umbanda religious practice.

8. There are occasional references to *branco* in Brazilian song lyrics—for example, in Caetano Veloso's "A tua presença," discussed in the following pages, or in his and Gilberto Gil's "Haiti" (see Sovik 2002). An alternative interpretation of the numerous terms for blackness might read these terms as indicating not so much a "multiplicity" of black identities, to use Carvalho's term, but rather the dynamics of power behind the ability to attribute names: *neguinho*, for example, which literally means "little black man," undoubtedly indexes the right that whites historically have felt to proclaim intimacy with Afro-Brazilians within relations of racial patriarchy. Carvalho describes the figure of the neguinho as "the happy black *malandro* (hustler) who lives in the favelas and is a samba composer." He "provides fun and doesn't threaten the whites, for he only operates inside the established hierarchy" (1994, 20).

9. See also the 2005 documentary film, *Sou feia mas tô na moda*, directed by Denise Garcia, which focused especially on women in funk carioca.

10. Deleuze specifically theorizes becoming-woman as a "fundamental step in the process of becoming, for both sexes" (Braidotti 2003, 49). Becoming-woman is part of his theory of the subject as multiple and emergent. Braidotti observes that "the reference to 'woman' in the process of 'becoming-woman,' however, does not refer to empirical females, but rather to socio-symbolic constructions, topological positions, degrees and levels of intensity, affective states."

11. Fernanda's recording of "É hoje" was also utilized for a 1996 Rider Sandal television commercial that featured images of Copacabana and Ipanema beaches.

12. In her video of this song, Fernanda appears as a platinum blonde with long, straight hair, in a white dress, with white lipstick, white earrings, large white-rimmed sport glasses, and white boots, driving a white Mustang convertible, hair blowing, waving a pistol in her hand, and three gangsters armed with machine guns riding in the back seat, one of whom is her *figu-*

rão, that is, the trafficker. Fernanda's exaggerated blondness, her platinum wig, and her tight white dress also play on the role of the *travesti* in Brazilian culture, which is not precisely the same as that of the transvestite. Travestis cross-dress and may take female hormone treatments or silicone injections in order to appear more attractive to males, Don Kulick writes, but they do not usually self-identify as women or undergo sex-change operations, even while they use female-gendered names (1998, 5–6).

13. Fernanda related that she did not want to "dress up all in white in a Gandhi-like stance" for the album cover, because she feared the album would attract people who already identify with that kind of image, while others might look at it and think, "That's not my tribe."

14. David McDonald has argued for the context of the Israel-Palestinian conflict that "in studying performative media we come to understand how experiences of violence influence aesthetics, and conversely how the aesthetics of performance contour modes of enacting and/or negotiating everyday violence" (2009, 82). Individuals navigating "formations of violence," he proposes, "create their own understandings of conflict, and shape their perceptions of self and other." It is tempting to try to engage his arguments here, but I am wary of generalizing "violence" as a theoretical trope that can be transposed from one context to another; a context in which suicide bombing carries heroic connotations is different from one in which violence is associated with trafficking, poverty, and policing, and in which it is attributed primarily to one sector of the population. For the Rio context, Araújo et al. (2006) and Araújo with Grupo Musicultura (2010) offer thoughtful analyses and methodologies.

15. The nightclub, although short-lived, was wildly successful, generating a Globo Network telenovela in 1978, and the club's reopening on the Sugarloaf of Urca.

Chapter 5: Paulinho Moska

1. A small sampling of the vast literature that specifically theorizes difference in music might include a number of books on gender (e.g., Solie 1993; Magrini 2003; Moisala and Diamond 2000) and publications on world music (e.g., Erlmann 1993, 1996; Feld 1994, 1996, 2000; Taylor 1997) and on Orientalism and exoticism in Western music (e.g., Born and Hesmondhalgh 2000; Taylor 2007), or on race (e.g., Radano and Bohlman 2000). Meintjes (2003) is of special interest for showing how difference is produced through mediation, specifically in the recording process.

2. The title of this chapter is a reference to Deleuze's *Difference and Repetition*, first published in 1968. It is a complex work in which the thinker develops a theory of difference in relation to central problems of philosophy; I do not claim to have studied it. However, what Paulinho Moska understood of this work clearly influenced his thinking, and I have looked at some of the secondary literature (see, e.g., Ansell-Pearson 1999; Colebrook 2000, 2006; McMahon 2005; Williams 2003).

3. This was the popular nightclub first opened as a disco by Nelson Motta in a shopping center in the South Zone (see Motta 2000, 304–10).

4. Inimigos do Rei can be seen performing "Adeleide" on the *Xou da Xuxa* (Xuxa show) on YouTube at http://www.youtube.com/watch?v=UgttrS_DF TE&feature=related (accessed 29 June 2009).

5. From Sérgio Dias's publicity release for *Vontade*, written in 1993 and subsequently published on Paulinho Moska's website: http://paulinhomoska .com.br (accessed 23 September 2009).

6. Reporting on these gatherings where architects, psychoanalysts, professors, and artists debated "concepts of time, body, reason, and thinking until dawn," one journalist noted how, for Paulinho's generation, such discussions could also be associated with a kind of liberation from the intellectual strictures of the military regime (Pessoa 1987).

7. From Gilberto Gil's album release for *Pensar é fazer música*, written in 1995 and subsequently published on Paulinho Moska's website: http:// paulinhomoska.com.br (accessed 23 September 2009).

8. SESC refers to Serviço Social do Comércio (Social Service of Business), a system by which commercial interests essentially pay a direct tax to support cultural productions at various state-owned theaters. Not surprisingly, the system has been especially successful in São Paulo, the center of industry in the country.

9. Tom Zé developed an interesting theory of androids as inexpensive third world laboring subjects that nevertheless have "defects" to the extent that they think, dance, and dream (see Dunn 2001, 201). Paulinho does not seem to be referencing Tom Zé's concept here.

10. Before embarking on a career as a solo artist, Celso Fonseca played guitar in Gilberto Gil's band, yet another connection with a protagonist of Tropicália. Celso produced Gilberto Gil's album *Eterno Deus mu dança* (1989), and he is a partner with Gil in the Geléia Geral label and their recording studio Palco.

11. The morro here symbolizes a broader context in which popular music

that is considered national typically has roots in working-class cultural practices (although youths in the morros had meanwhile grown increasingly interested in commercial pagode, rap, hip-hop, and funk).

12. For Deleuze and Guattari, the synthesizer is the "assemblage" of the "sound machine" (referring to Edgard Varèse's music): it "makes audible the sound process itself, the production of that process, and puts us in contact with still other elements beyond sound matter. It unites disparate elements in the material, and transposes the parameters from one formula to another" (1987, 343).

13. Walter Costa had the impression that it would be easier to mix a Brazilian album in Nashville than in Los Angeles or New York. Country music, he thought, was perhaps closer to Brazilian music in terms of the production sound. Thomas Porcello (2002) has observed how the "clean," "crisp," and "neotraditional" sound of Nashville productions contrasts with "the Austin sound." Although such values are contested, fluid, and highly context dependent, Walter may have a point, at least when it comes to MPB, in which a "clean," neotraditional acoustic aesthetic has been predominant. We may recall too that it was in fact in Nashville, with Joan Baez, where Marcos Suzano met the recording engineer Jim Ball, who had worked for several years in that city, and who influenced the development of Suzano's recorded pandeiro sound with the clarity of his stereo image.

14. The idea of Suzano as an aesthete seems to contrast somewhat with the Blade Runner image also proposed by Paulinho Moska. I think this speaks to two different spheres of practice: Suzano had to be a more aggressive figure in his early recording career to get his point of view across; in the Móbile project, however, he was given free rein to work out his aesthetic preferences. These varied readings of Suzano's presence also highlight the multidimensionality of individual becoming.

15. Sensationism is especially associated with the French philosopher Étienne Bonnot de Condillac, who proposed in his Traité des sensations (1754) that all mental faculties and ideas derive from sensations. Jorge Mautner collaborated with the Tropicalist leaders Gilberto Gil and Caetano Veloso in the early 1970s, although he began his career as an author well before Tropicália. His best-known song is "Maracatu atômico" of 1972, for which he wrote the lyrics. Gilberto Gil made a hit of it in 1974, and Chico Science and Nação Zumbi revived it in the mid-1990s (see Perrone 2000). In the 1960s Mautner, a kind of radical humanist, developed what he called the "Mythology of Kaos," a rather loose assemblage of images, references, and

discourses that "assimilates elements of paganism, Greek thought (Dionysian strains), Christianity, Nietzsche and other German philosophers, and existentialism" (Perrone 2000, 162; see also Mautner 1980, 2002). With *Móbile*, Mautner wrote in the press release, Paulinho Moska "reached the core of Kaos."

16. For more on André Abujamra and his group Karnak, see Murphy (2002).

17. Milonga is associated with Uruguay, Argentina, and with Brazilian gaúcho culture. It is similar to the tango and features a 3 + 3 + 2 rhythmic pattern.

18. The dry, no-reverb sound is also a response to the broader trends in music production: various music makers complained of a tendency in Brazilian productions (especially in the 1980s) to overuse reverberation and echo, whereas in pop productions from the United States and the United Kingdom, such an aesthetic had gone out of fashion.

19. According to Dunn, for *Araçá Azul*, "Polygram gave Veloso free reign to 'play' in the studio and create a highly personal and cryptic album" (2001, 168), or what Turino refers to as "studio audio art" (2008). It is interesting that this freedom came from the label in 1972, while none of the musicians I researched in 1998–99 felt that they were granted this kind of freedom by their recording companies.

20. Additional studio musicians for this album included Nilo Romero (the producer of Paulinho's first four albums) and the Japanese drummer Takashi Numazawa, who traveled to Brazil to record the album. Thus while Suzano's percussion and sonic experimentation remained fundamental to Paulinho's sound, the drum kit returned for *Eu falso*.

21. In *Cinema 2: The Time-Image*, Deleuze writes of "Borges's reply to Leibniz: the straight line as force of time, as labyrinth of time, is also the line which forks and keeps on forking, passing through *incompossible presents*, returning to *not-necessarily true pasts*" (1989, 131). Deleuze also delineates "organic" versus "crystalline" regimes of the image here, which seems to have influenced Paulinho's photography as well.

22. Paulinho Moska has a website where he posts his photographs for the public, and where he often receives comments on his visual work. The title of his site is Moska aksoM — Reflexos e Reflexões (Mirror reflections and thought reflections). Its address is http://paulinhomoska.multiply.com (accessed 7 December 2009).

23. From the Orsa Foundation website: http://www.fundacaoorsa.org.br/web/pt/institucional/filosofia.htm (accessed 7 December 2009).

Chapter 6: On Cannibals and Chameleons

1. Even in July 2007, however, I encountered graffiti on a wall in Rio de Janeiro with the caption "Canibalismo é um ato de amorrrr" ("Cannibalism is an act of luuuv"; see Moehn [2008, 195] for a photo of the wall).

2. Castro-Klarén's assertion that Oswald de Andrade was "not prepared to understand or develop the full implications of Tupi meta\physics," in which "everything is in flux" (2000, 311), is a little unfair since Oswald was writing in the 1920s, about sixty years before Viveiros de Castro published the monograph upon which Castro-Klarén draws for her understanding of the Tupi anthropophagic reason.

3. The Gê, Viveiros de Castro writes, "appear to be one of the strongest cases supporting structural anthropology," quite in contrast to the Araweté (1992, 5).

REFERENCES

Adelman, James S., and Gordon D. A. Brown. 2007. "Phonographic Neighbors, Not Orthographic Neighbors, Determine Word Naming Latencies." *Psychonomic Bulletin and Review* 14 (3): 455–59.

Alberto, Paulina L. 2009. "When Rio Was Black: Soul Music, National Culture, and the Politics of Racial Comparison in 1970s Brazil." *Hispanic American Historical Review* 89 (1): 3–39.

Albuquerque, Durval Muniz de, Jr. 2004. "Weaving Tradition: The Invention of the Brazilian Northeast." Trans. Laurence Hallewell. *Latin American Perspectives* 31 (2): 42–61.

Alves, José Eustáquio Diniz. 2004. *A linguagem e as representações da masculinidade*. Rio de Janeiro: Escola Nacional de Ciências Estatísticas / Instituto Brasileiro de Geografia e Estatística. Textos para Discussão 11.

Andrade, Mário de. 1987. *Poesias completas*. Ed. Diléa Zanotto Manfio. Belo Horizonte, Brazil: Itatiaia.

————. 1999. *Dicionário musical brasileiro*. Belo Horizonte, Brazil: Itatiaia.

Andrade, Oswald de. 1995 [1928]. "Manifesto antropófago." *Vanguardas latino-americanas: Polêmicas, manifestos, e textos críticos*, ed. Jorge Schwartz, 142–47. São Paulo: Iluminuras.

————. 1999 [1928]. "The Cannibalist Manifesto." *Third Text* 46:92–96.

Ansell-Pearson, Keith. 1999. *Germinal Life: The Difference and Repetition of Deleuze*. London: Routledge.

Araújo, Samuel, et al. 2006. "Conflict and Violence as Theoretical Tools in Present-Day Ethnomusicology: Notes on a Dialogic Ethnography of Sound Practices in Rio de Janeiro." *Ethnomusicology* 50 (2): 287–313.

Araújo, Samuel, with Grupo Musicultura. 2010. "Sound Praxis: Music, Politics, and Violence in Brazil." *Music and Conflict*, ed. John Morgan O'Connell and Salwa El-Shawan Castelo-Branco, 217–31. Urbana: University of Illinois Press.

Attali, Jacques. 1985 [1977]. *Noise: The Political Economy of Music*. Trans. Brian Massumi. Minneapolis: University of Minnesota Press.

Averill, Gage, and Yuen-Ming David Yih. 2000. "Militarism in Haitian Music." *The African Diaspora: A Musical Perspective*, ed. Ingrid Monson, 267–94. New York: Garland.

Badiou, Alain. 2000. "Un, multiple, multiplicité(s)." *Multitudes* 1 (1): 195–211.

Barbosa, Airton Lima, et al. 1966. "Que caminho seguir na música popular brasileira?" *Revista Civilização Brasileira* 1 (7): 375–85.

Barbosa, Marco Antonio. 2001. "Pedro Luís & A Parede: Tirando a ordem da casa." http://www.allbrazilianmusic.com/br/Acontecendo/Acontecendo.asp?Nu_materia=3190 (accessed 31 May 2009).

Barcellos, Mário Cesar. 1997. *Os orixás e a personalidade humana*. Rio de Janeiro: Pallas.

Barnes, Sandra T. 1997. *Africa's Ogun: Old World and New*. 2nd ed. Bloomington: Indiana University Press.

Becker, Howard. 1982. *Art Worlds*. Berkeley: University of California Press.

Béhague, Gerard. 1973. "Bossa and Bossas: Recent Changes in Brazilian Urban Popular Music." *Ethnomusicology* 17 (2): 209–34.

————. 1980. "Brazilian Musical Values of the 1960s and 1970s: Popular Urban Music from Bossa Nova to Tropicália." *Journal of Popular Culture* 14 (3): 437–52.

————. 1984. "Patterns of Candomblé Music Performance: An Afro-Brazilian Religious Setting." *Performance Practice: Ethnomusicological Perspectives*, ed. Gerard Béhague, 222–54. Westport, Conn.: Greenwood.

————. 2006. "Rap, Reggae, Rock, or Samba: The Local and the Global in

Brazilian Popular Music (1985–95)." *Latin American Music Review* 27 (1): 79–90.

Bennett, Andy. 2004. "Consolidating the Music Scenes Perspective." *Poetics* 32: 223–34.

Berg, Stephen. 1999. "An Introduction to Oswald de Andrade's *Cannibalist Manifesto*." *Third Text* 46: 89–91.

Berger, Harris. 1999. *Metal, Rock, and Jazz: Perception and the Phenomenology of Musical Experience*. Middletown, Conn.: Wesleyan University Press.

Berger, Harris M., and Cornelia Fales. 2005. "'Heaviness' in the Perception of Heavy Metal Guitar Timbres: The Match of Perceptual and Acoustic Features over Time." *Wired for Sound: Engineering and Technologies in Sonic Cultures*, ed. Paul D. Greene and Thomas Porcello, 181–97. Middletown, Conn.: Wesleyan University Press.

Berliner, Paul. 1994. *Thinking in Jazz: The Infinite Art of Improvisation*. Chicago: University of Chicago Press.

Berozu, Tetsuo. 1998. "Dirty Trick: How to Cuss in 'Brazilian.'" *Brazzil*, May. http://www.brazzil.com/blamay98.htm (accessed 16 June 2009).

Beserra, Bernadete. 2004. Introduction to "Brazilian Northeast: Globalization, Labor, and Poverty." Trans. Laurence Hallewell. Special issue, *Latin American Perspectives* 31 (2): 3–15.

Bhabha, Homi. 1985. "Signs Taken for Wonders: Questions of Ambivalence and Authority under a Tree outside Delhi, May 1817." *Critical Inquiry* 12 (1): 144–65.

Biehl, João, Byron Good, and Arthur Kleinman, eds. 2007. *Subjectivity: Ethnographic Investigations*. Berkeley: University of California Press.

Biehl, João, and Peter Locke. 2010. "Deleuze and the Anthropology of Becoming." *Current Anthropology* 51 (3): 317–51.

Bohlman, Philip V. 1988. *The Study of Folk Music in the Modern World*. Bloomington: Indiana University Press.

Bollig, Ben. 2002. "White Rapper / Black Beats: Discovering a Race Problem in the Music of Gabriel o Pensador." *Latin American Music Review / Revista de Música Latinoamericana* 23 (2): 159–78.

Bonnett, Alastair. 2002. "A White World? Whiteness and the Meaning of Modernity in Latin America and Japan." *Working through Whiteness: International Perspectives*, ed. C. Levine-Rasky, 69–106. Albany: State University of New York Press.

Born, Georgina, and David Hesmondhalgh. 2000. "Introduction: On Difference, Representation, and Appropriation in Music." *Western Music and Its Others: Difference, Representation, and Appropriation in Music*, ed. Georgina

Born and David Hesmondhalgh, 1–58. Berkeley: University of California Press.

Bourdieu, Pierre. 1984. *Distinction: A Social Critique of the Judgment of Taste.* Trans. Richard Nice. Cambridge: Harvard University Press.

———. 1993. *The Field of Cultural Production: Essays on Art and Literature.* New York: Columbia University Press.

———. 1995 [1977]. *Outline of a Theory of Practice.* New York: Cambridge University Press.

Braidotti, Rosi. 2003. "Becoming Woman; or, Sexual Difference Revisited." *Theory, Culture and Society* 20 (3): 43–64.

Brand, Stewart. 1974. *Whole Earth Catalog.* Baltimore: Penguin.

Brenner, Neil, and Nik Theodore. 2002. "Cities and the Geographies of 'Actually Existing Neoliberalism.'" *Antipode* 34 (3): 349–79.

Brown, Paula, and Donald F. Tuzin, eds. 1983. *The Ethnography of Cannibalism.* Washington: Society for Psychological Anthropolology.

Brown, Steven D. 2002. "Michel Serres: Science, Translation and the Logic of the Parasite." *Theory, Culture and Society* 19 (3): 1–27.

Budasz, Rogério. 2005. "Of Cannibals and the Recycling of Otherness." *Music and Letters* 87 (1): 1–15.

Burkett, Lyn Ellen. 2010. Review of *How the Beatles Destroyed Rock 'n' Roll: An Alternative History of American Popular Music,* by Elijah Wald. *Popular Music and Society* 33 (3): 423–25.

Caminha, Pero Vaz de. 1999 [1500]. "Carta de Pero Vaz de Caminha." *Os três únicos testemunhos do descobrimento do Brasil,* ed. Paulo Roberto Pereira, 31–59. Rio de Janeiro: Lacerda.

Campanér, Laura. 1999. "Pedro Luís vai cantar para toda nação." *Revista Interativa Borage* 1 (13): 4–20. http://www2.uol.com.br/borage/rbi13/brgr13_lancamentos.htm (accessed 31 May 2009).

Campos, Augusto de. 1974 [1968]. "Boa palavra sobre a música popular." *Balanço da bossa e outras bossas,* ed. Augusto de Campos, 59–66. São Paulo: Perspectiva.

Capwell, Charles. 1991. "Marginality and Musicology in Nineteenth Century Calcutta: The Case of Sourindro Mohun Tagore." *Comparative Musicology and the Anthropology of Music: Essays on the History of Ethmomusicology,* ed. Bruno Nettl and Philip V. Bohlman, 228–43. Chicago: University of Chicago Press.

Carpegianni, Schneider. 2000. "A música brasileira é predatória há 500 anos." *Jornal do Commercio,* 21 January.

Carvalho, José Jorge de. 1994. "The Multiplicity of Black Identities in Brazilian Popular Music." *Série Antropologia* 163: 1–40.

Cascudo, Luís da Câmera. 1999. *Dicionário do folclore brasileiro*. São Paulo: Global.

Castelo-Branco, Salwa El-Shawan, and Manuel Carlos de Brito. N.d. "Portugal." *Grove Dictionary of Music*. Oxford Music Online. http://www.oxfordmusiconline.com/subscriber/article/grove/music/22157 (accessed 7 November 2009).

Castro, Yeda Pessoa de. 2001. *Falares africanos na Bahia: Um vocabulário afro-brasileiro*. Rio de Janeiro: Topbooks.

Castro-Klarén, Sara. 2000. "A Genealogy for the 'Manifesto Antropófago,' or 'The Struggle between Socrates and the Caraïbe.'" *Nepantla: Views from the South* 1 (2): 295–322.

Cavalcanti, Leonardo. 2002. "Lenine, o universal." *Correio Braziliense*, 16 March. Online source, printed copy on file with author.

Clark, Nigel. 2000. "'Botanizing on the Asphalt'? The Complex Life of Cosmopolitan Bodies." *Body and Society* 6 (3–4): 12–33.

Coelho, Frederico. 2008. "Suingue e agitação: Apontamentos sobre a música carioca contemporânea." *Leituras sobre música popular: Reflexões sobre sonoridades e cultura*, ed. Emerson Giumbelli, Júlio Cesar Valadão Diniz, and Santuza Cambraia Naves, 98–113. Rio de Janeiro: 7 Letras.

Cohen, Sara. 1999. "Scenes." *Key Terms in Popular Music and Culture*, ed. Bruce Horner and Thomas Swiss, 239–50. Malden, Mass.: Blackwell.

Colebrook, Claire. 2002. *Gilles Deleuze*. New York: Routledge.

———. 2006. *Deleuze: A Guide for the Perplexed*. London: Continuum.

Collier, Stephen J., and Aihwa Ong. 2005. "Global Assemblages, Anthropological Problems." *Global Assemblages: Technology, Politics, and Ethics as Anthropological Problems*, ed. Aihwa Ong and Stephen J. Collier, 3–21. Malden, Mass.: Blackwell.

Comaroff, Jean, and John L. Comaroff. 1992. *Ethnography and the Historical Imagination*. Boulder: Westview.

Conklin, Beth A. 2001. *Consuming Grief: Compassionate Cannibalism in an Amazonian Society*. Austin: University of Texas Press.

Cooley, Timothy J., Katherine Meizel, and Nasir Syed. 2008. "Virtual Fieldwork: Three Case Studies." *Shadows in the Field: New Perspectives for Fieldwork in Ethnomusicology*. 2nd ed., ed. Gregory Barz and Timothy J. Cooley, 90–107. New York: Oxford University Press.

Crook, Larry. 1993. "Black Consciousness, Samba Reggae, and the Re-

Africanization of Bahian Carnival Music in Brazil." *World of Music* 35 (2): 90–108.

———. 2001. "Turned-Around Beat: *Maracatu de Baque Virado* and Chico Science." *Brazilian Popular Music and Globalization*, ed. Charles Perrone and Christopher Dunn, 233–44. Gainesville: University Press of Florida.

———. 2005. *Brazilian Music: Northeastern Traditions and the Heartbeat of a Modern Nation*. Santa Barbara: ABC-CLIO.

———. 2009. *Focus: Music of Northeast Brazil*. 2nd ed. New York: Routledge.

Crook, Larry, and Randal Johnson. 1999. *Black Brazil: Culture, Identity, and Social Mobilization*. Los Angeles: UCLA Latin American Center Publications.

Cumming, Andy. 2003. "An Interview with DJ Marlboro June 2003." *Hyperdub*. http://web.archive.org/web/20040422141408/http://www.hyperdub.com/softwar/marlboro.cfm (accessed 1 June 2009).

DaMatta, Roberto A. 1995 [1978]. "For an Anthropology of the Brazilian Tradition; or, A Virtude Está No Meio." *The Brazilian Puzzle: Culture on the Borderlands of the Western World*, ed. D. J. Hess and R. A. DaMatta, 270–91. New York: Columbia University Press.

Danielsen, Anne. 2006. *Presence and Pleasure: The Funk Grooves of James Brown and Parliament*. Middletown, Conn.: Wesleyan University Press.

Danielson, Virginia. 1997. *The Voice of Egypt: Umm Kulthum, Arabic Song, and Egyptian Society in the Twentieth Century*. Chicago: University of Chicago Press.

Dapieve, Artur. 1995. *Brock: O rock brasileiro dos anos 80*. São Paulo: Editora 34.

———. 1999. "MTV—bunda, ainda." *O Globo*, 6 March.

———. 2003. "Dores de crescimento." Press release for Paulinho Moska's album *Tudo novo de novo*. http://paulinhomoska.com.br/html/obra/discos/tudonovo/release.htm (accessed 4 December 2009).

Davis, James H., and John A. Ruhe. 2003. "Perceptions of Country Corruption: Antecedents and Outcomes." *Journal of Business Ethics* 43 (4): 275–88.

Deleuze, Gilles. 1989. *Cinema 2: The Time-Image*. Trans. Hugh Tomlinson and Robert Galeta. Minneapolis: University of Minnesota Press.

———. 1995. *Negotiations, 1972–1990*. Trans. Martin Joughin. New York: Columbia University Press.

———. 2005 [1981]. *Francis Bacon: The Logic of Sensation*. Trans. Daniel W. Smith. New York: Continuum.

———. 2006. *Two Regimes of Madness: Texts and Interviews, 1975–1995*. Ed. David Lapoujade, trans. Ames Hodges and Mike Taormina. Los Angeles: Semiotext(e).

Deleuze, Gilles, and Félix Guattari. 1983. "What Is a Minor Literature?" Trans. Robert Brinkley. *Mississippi Review* 11 (3): 13–33.

———. 1987. *A Thousand Plateaus: Capitalism and Schizophrenia.* Trans. Brian Massumi. Minneapolis: University of Minnesota Press.

Dent, Alexander Sebastian. 2007. "Country Brothers: Kinship and Chronotope in Brazilian Rural Public Culture." *Anthropological Quarterly* 80 (2): 455–95.

———. 2009. *River of Tears: Country Music, Memory, and Modernity in Brazil.* Durham: Duke University Press.

Diouf, Sylviane Anna. 2003. "Devils or Sorcerers, Muslims or Studs: Manding in the Americas." *Trans-Atlantic Dimensions of Ethnicity in the Americas*, ed. Paul E. Lovejoy and David V. Trotman, 139–57. New York: Continuum.

Dordor, Francis. 2004. "Le cannibale." Cité de la Musique, Paris, 29–30 April. http://www.arkoiris.fr/lenine/IMG/pdf/040429_nuit_bresil-2.pdf (accessed 18 November 2009).

Dunn, Christopher. 2001. *Brutality Garden: Tropicália and the Emergence of a Brazilian Counterculture.* Chapel Hill: University of North Carolina Press.

———. 2007. "Black Rome and the Chocolate City: The Race of Place." *Callaloo* 30 (3): 847–61.

———. 2009. "Tom Zé and the Performance of Citizenship in Brazil." *Popular Music* 28 (2): 217–37.

Erlmann, Veit. 1991. *African Stars: Studies in Black South African Performance.* Chicago: University of Chicago Press.

———. 1993. "The Politics and Aesthetics of Transnational Musics." *World of Music* 35 (2): 3–15.

———. 1996. "The Aesthetics of the Global Imagination: Reflections on World Music in the 1990s." *Public Culture* 8: 467–87.

Fales, Cornelia. 2005. "Short-Circuiting Perceptual Systems: Timbre in Ambient and Techno Music." *Wired for Sound: Engineering and Technologies in Sonic Cultures*, ed. Paul D. Greene and Thomas Porcello, 156–80. Middletown, Conn.: Wesleyan University Press.

Fast, Susan. 2000. "Rethinking Issues of Gender and Sexuality in Led Zeppelin: A Woman's View of Pleasure and Power in Hard Rock." *American Music* 17 (3): 245–99.

Favaretto, Celso. 1979. *Tropicália: Alegoria, alegria.* São Paulo: Ateliê.

Fawcett, Fausto. 1995. "A lata nua!" Press release for Fernanda Abreu's album *Da lata.* http://fernandaabreu.uol.com.br/home.htm (accessed 13 October 2009).

———. 2004. "A novidade da Fernanda." Press release for Fernanda Abreu's album *Na paz.* http://fernandaabreu.uol.com.br/home.htm (accessed 13 October 2009).

Feld, Steven. 1994. "From Schizophonia to Schismogenesis: On the Discourses and Commodification Practices of 'World Music' and 'World Beat.'" *Music Grooves: Essays and Dialogues,* by Charles Keil and Steven Feld, 257–89. Chicago: University of Chicago Press.

———. 1996. "Pygmy POP: A Genealogy of Schizophonic Mimesis." *Yearbook for Traditional Music* 28: 1–35.

———. 2000. "A Sweet Lullaby for World Music." *Public Culture* 12 (1): 145–71.

Foucault, Michel. 1972. *The Archeology of Knowledge.* Trans. A. M. Sheridan Smith. New York: Pantheon.

———. 1994. *Dits et écrits IV.* Paris: Gallimard.

Fox, Aaron. 2004. *Real Country: Music and Language in Working-Class Culture.* Durham: Duke University Press.

Frankenberg, Ruth. 1997. "Introduction: Local Whiteness, Localizing Whiteness." *Displacing Whiteness: Essays in Social and Cultural Criticism,* ed. Ruth Frankenberg, 1–34. Durham: Duke University Press.

———. 2001. *The Making and Unmaking of Whiteness.* Durham: Duke University Press.

Freeman, James. 2002. "Democracy and Danger on the Beach: Class Relations in the Public Space of Rio de Janeiro." *Space and Culture* 5 (1): 9–28.

Frith, Simon, and Angela McRobbie. 1978. "Rock and Sexuality." *Screen Education* 29: 3–19.

Fryer, Peter. 2000. *Rhythms of Resistance: African Musical Heritage in Brazil.* Hanover, N.H.: University Press of New England.

Gabara, Esther. 2004. "Facing Brazil: The Problem of Portraiture and the Modernist Sublime." *CR: The New Centennial Review* 4 (2): 33–76.

Galinsky, Philip. 1996. "Co-option, Cultural Resistance, and Afro-Brazilian Identity: A History of the 'Pagode' Samba Movement in Rio de Janeiro." *Latin American Music Review / Revista de Música Latinoamericana* 17 (2): 120–49.

———. 2002. *"Maracatu Atômico": Tradition, Modernity, and Postmodernity in the Mangue Movement and "New Music Scene" of Recife, Pernambuco, Brazil.* New York: Routledge.

Galm, Eric A. 2010. *The Berimbau: Soul of Brazilian Music.* Jackson: University Press of Mississippi.

Galvão, Walnice Nogueira. 1976. "MMPB: Uma análise ideológica." *Saco de Gatos,* 93–119. São Paulo: Duas Cidades.

Garcia, David F. 2006. *Arsenio Rodríguez and the Transnational Flows of Latin Popular Music.* Philadelphia: Temple University Press.

Garofalo, Reebee. 1993. "Whose World, What Beat: The Transnational Music Industry, Identity, and Cultural Imperialism." *World of Music* 35 (2): 16–31.

Gaunt, Kyra. 2002. "Got Rhythm? Difficult Encounters in Theory and Practice and Other Participatory Discrepancies in Music." *City and Society* 14 (1): 119–40.

Gerischer, Christiane. 2006. "O Suingue Baiano: Rhythmic Feeling and Microrhythmic Phenomena in Brazilian Percussion." *Ethnomusicology* 50 (1): 99–119.

Giddens, Anthony. 1979. *Central Problems in Social Theory: Action, Structure, and Contradiction in Social Analysis.* Berkeley: University of California Press.

———. 1991. *Modernity and Self-Identity: Self and Society in the Late Modern Age.* Stanford: Stanford University Press.

Gilman, Bruce. 2006. "Brazil's Planetary Troubadour." *Brazzil,* 14 August. http://www.brazzil.com/component/content/article/170-august-2006/9670.html (accessed 4 May 2009).

Gledhill, John. 2004. "Neoliberalism." *A Companion to the Anthropology of Politics,* ed. David Nugent and Joan Vincent, 332–48. Malden, Mass.: Blackwell.

Goldenberg, Mirian, ed. 2002. *Nu e vestido: Dez antropólogos revelam a cultura do corpo carioca.* Rio de Janeiro: Record.

Gontijo, Fabiano. 2002. "Carioquice ou carioquidade? Ensaio etnográfico das imagens identitárias cariocas." *Nu e vestido: Dez antropólogos revelam a cultura do corpo carioca,* ed. Mirian Goldenberg, 41–77. Rio de Janeiro: Record.

Greene, Paul, and Thomas Porcello, eds. 2005. *Wired for Sound: Engineering and Technologies in Sonic Cultures.* Middletown, Conn.: Wesleyan University Press.

Grosz, Elizabeth. 1998. "Bodies-Cities." *Places through the Body,* ed. Heidi J. Nast and Steve Pile, 42–51. New York: Routledge.

Guilbault, Jocelyne. 2005. "Audible Entanglements: Nation and Diasporas in Trinidad's Calypso Music Scene." *Small Axe* 17: 40–63.

———. 2007. *Governing Sound: The Cultural Politics of Trinidad's Carnival Musics.* Chicago: University of Chicago Press.

Haines, John. 2004. "Living Troubadours and Other Recent Uses for Medieval Music." *Popular Music* 23 (2): 133–53.

Hanchard, Michael, ed. 1999. *Racial Politics in Contemporary Brazil*. Durham: Duke University Press.

Haraway, Donna. 1991. *Simians, Cyborgs and Women: The Reinvention of Nature*. New York: Routledge.

Herschmann, Micael. 1997. *Abalando os anos 90 funk e hip-hop: Globalização, violência e estilo cultural*. Rio de Janeiro: Rocco.

———. 2007. "O circuito cultural do samba e do choro da Lapa." *Lapa, cidade da música: Desafios e perspectivas para o crescimento do Rio de Janeiro e da indústria da música independente nacional*, 33–70. Rio de Janeiro: Mauad.

Hesmondhalgh, David. 2005. "Subcultures, Scenes or Tribes? None of the Above." *Journal of Youth Studies* 8 (1): 21–40.

———. 2006. "Bourdieu, the Media, and Cultural Production." *Media, Culture and Society* 28 (2): 211–31.

Hollanda, Heloisa Buarque de. 1998. "The Law of the Cannibal, or How to Deal with the Idea of 'Difference' in Brazil." http://www.pacc.ufrj.br/heloisa/paper1.html (accessed 12 August 2009).

———. 2002. "Gender Studies: Rough Notes from a Very Local Perspective." *Journal of Latin American Cultural Studies* 11 (3): 321–31.

Holm-Hudson, Kevin. 2002. *Progressive Rock Reconsidered*. New York: Routledge.

Hulse, Brian, and Nick Nesbitt. 2010. *Sounding the Virtual: Gilles Deleuze and the Theory and Philosophy of Music*. Burlington, Vt.: Ashgate.

Husted, Bryan W. 2002. "Culture and International Anti-corruption Agreements in Latin America." *Journal of Business Ethics* 37 (4): 413–22.

Isfahani-Hammond, Alexandra. 2008. *White Negritude: Race, Writing, and Brazilian Cultural Identity*. New York: Palgrave.

Jabor, Arnaldo. 1998. "Fim de papo, malandragem: Quebra das bolsas une pobres e ricos na crise neoliberal." *Jornal do Brasil*, 22 September.

Jaguaribe, Beatriz. 2007. "Cities without Maps: Favelas and the Aesthetics of Realism." *Locating the Modern City*, ed. Alev Çinar and Thomas Bender, 100–120. Minneapolis: University of Minnesota Press.

Jairazbhoy, Nazir A. 1983. "Nominal Units of Time: A Counterpart for Ellis' System of Cents." *Selected Reports in Ethnomusicology* 4: 113–21.

Kearney, Michael. 1995. "The Local and the Global: The Anthropology of Globalization and Transnationalism." *Annual Review of Anthropology* 24: 547–65.

Keil, Charles. 1966. *Urban Blues*. Chicago: University of Chicago Press.

———. "People's Music Comparatively: Style and Stereotype, Class and Hegemony." *Dialectical Anthropology* 10 (1–2): 119–30.

———. 1987. "Participatory Discrepancies and the Power of Music." *Cultural Anthropology* 2 (3): 275–83.

———. 1995. "The Theory of Participatory Discrepancies: A Progress Report." *Ethnomusicology* 39 (1): 1–19.

———. 2002a. "Response to Papers." *City and Society* 14 (1): 141–46.

———. 2002b. "They Want the Music but They Don't Want the People." *City and Society* 14 (1): 37–57.

———. 2009. Review of *Music as Social Life: The Politics of Participation*, by Thomas Turino. *Yearbook for Traditional Music* 41: 221–23.

Kielian-Gilbert, Marianne. 2010. "Music and the Difference in Becoming." *Sounding the Virtual: Gilles Deleuze and the Theory and Philosophy of Music*, ed. Brian Hulse and Nick Nesbitt, 199–225. Burlington, Vt.: Ashgate.

Kingfisher, Catherine, and Jeff Maskovsky. 2008. "Introduction: The Limits of Neoliberalism." *Critique of Anthropology* 28 (2): 115–26.

Knauft, Bruce M. 2006. "Anthropology in the Middle." *Anthropological Theory* 6 (4): 407–30.

Koetting, James. 1970. "Analysis Annotation of West African Drum Ensemble Music." *Selected Reports in Ethnomusicology* 1 (3): 116–46.

Kulick, Don. 1998. *Travesti: Sex, Gender, and Culture among Brazilian Transgendered Prostitutes*. Chicago: University of Chicago Press.

Kun, Josh. 2005. *Audiotopia: Music, Race, and America*. Berkeley: University of California Press.

Larner, Wendy. 2003. "Neoliberalism?" *Environment and Planning D: Society and Space* 21: 509–12.

Lawler, Stephanie. 2005. "Disgusted Subjects: The Making of Middle-Class Identities." *Sociological Review* 53 (3): 429–46.

Leme, Mônica. 2001. "'Segure o tchan!' Identidade na 'axé-music' dos anos 80 e 90." *Cadernos do Colóquio* (Annual publication of the Graduate Program in Music at the State University of Rio de Janeiro), 45–52.

Lemos, Nina. 2005. "Vida de cachorra." *Folha de São Paulo*, 6 March.

Lessa, Patricia. 2005. *Mulheres à venda: Uma leitura do discurso publicitário nos outdoors*. Londrina: Eduel.

Leu, Lorraine. 2006. *Brazilian Popular Music: Caetano Veloso and the Regeneration of Tradition*. Burlington, Vt.: Ashgate.

Levin, Theodore. 1996. *The Hundred Thousand Fools of God: Musical Travels in Central Asia (and Queens, New York)*. Bloomington: Indiana University Press.

Liechty, Mark. 2003. *Suitably Modern: Making Middle-Class Culture in a New Consumer Society*. Princeton: Princeton University Press.

Lindenbaum, Shirley. 2004. "Thinking about Cannibalism." *Annual Review of Anthropology* 33 (1): 475–98.

Livingston, Tamara E. 1999. "Music Revivals: Towards a General Theory." *Ethnomusicology* 43(1): 66–85.

Livingston-Isenhour, Tamara E., and Thomas G. C. Garcia. 2005. *Choro: A Social History of a Brazilian Popular Music*. Bloomington: Indiana University Press.

Lopes, Denise. 1999. "Carta blanca para Caetano na França." *Jornal do Brasil*, 5 May.

Lopes, Nei. 1995. *Dicionário banto do Brasil*. Rio de Janeiro: Centro Cultural José Bonifácio.

Lortat-Jacob, Bernard. 1995. *Sardinian Chronicles*. Trans. Teresa Lavender Fagan. Chicago: University of Chicago Press.

Lucas, Maria Elizabeth. 2000. "Gaucho Musical Regionalism." *Ethnomusicology Forum* 9 (1): 41–60.

Luís, Pedro. 2009. *Logo parecia que assim sempre fora: Breves inspirações*. Rio de Janeiro: Língual Geral.

Lysloff, René T. A., and Leslie C. Gay Jr. 2003. *Music and Technoculture*. Middletown, Conn.: Wesleyan University Press.

MacIntyre, Alasdair. 1984. *After Virtue: A Study in Moral Theory*. Notre Dame, Ind.: University of Notre Dame Press.

Madan, Arthur Cornwallis. 1902. *English-Swahili Dictionary*. 2nd ed. Oxford: Clarendon.

Madeira, Angelica. 1991. "Rhythm and Irreverence: Notes about the Rock Music Movement in Brasilia." *Popular Music and Society* 15 (4): 58–70.

Magaldi, Cristina. 1999. "Adopting Imports: New Images and Alliances in Brazilian Popular Music of the 1990s." *Popular Music* 18 (3): 309–29.

Magrini, Tullia, ed. 2003. *Music and Gender: Perspectives from the Mediterranean*. Chicago: University of Chicago Press.

Marcus, George E., and Erkan Saka. 2006. "Assemblage." *Theory, Culture and Society* 23 (2–3): 101–6.

Marques, Mário. 1998. "Novos acordes do Rio: Inspirada pela bossa nova, a música popular carioca firma-se como movimento na cidade." *O Globo*, 12 January.

Marsh, Charity, and Melissa West. 2003. "The Nature/Technology Binary Opposition Dismantled in the Music of Madonna and Björk." *Music and Technoculture*, ed. René T. A. Lysloff and Leslie C. Gay Jr., 182–203. Middletown, Conn.: Wesleyan University Press.

Marzorati, Gerald. 1999. "Tropicalia, Agora!" *New York Times Magazine*, 25 April.

Matory, James L. 2005. *Black Atlantic Religion: Tradition, Transnationalism, and Matriarchy in the Afro-Brazilian Candomblé*. Princeton: Princeton University Press.

Mautner, Jorge. 1980. *Panfletos da nova era*. São Paulo: Global.

———. 1999. Press release for Paulinho Moska's album *Móbile*. http://paulinhomoska.com.br/html/obra/discos/mobile/release.htm (accessed 3 December 2009).

———. 2002. "O mestre do Kaos." *JB Online*, 21 June.

McCann, Bryan. 2002. "Black Pau: Uncovering the History of Brazilian Soul." *Journal of Popular Music Studies* 13 (1): 33–62.

———. 2004. *Hello, Hello Brazil: Popular Music in the Making of Modern Brazil*. Durham: Duke University Press.

McDonald. David A. 2009. "Poetics and the Performance of Violence in Israel/Palestine." *Ethnomusicology* 53 (1): 58–85.

McMahon, Melissa. 2005. "Difference, Repetition." *Gilles Deleuze: Key Concepts*, ed. Charles J. Stivale, 42–52. Montreal: McGill-Queen's University Press.

Medaglia, Júlio. 2003 [1966]. "Balanço da bossa nova." *Balanço da bossa e outras bossas*, ed. Augusto de Campos, 67–123. São Paulo: Perspectiva.

Medeiros, Bartolomeu Tito Figueirôa de. 2008. "Deslocamentos em dois cortejos processionais católicos." *Religião e Sociedade* 28 (1): 125–45.

Meintjes, Louise. 2003. *Sound of Africa! Making Music Zulu in a South African Studio*. Durham: Duke University Press.

———. 2004. "Shoot the Sergeant, Shatter the Mountain: The Production of Masculinity in Zulu Ngoma Song and Dance in Post-Apartheid South Africa." *Ethnomusicology Forum* 13 (2): 173–201.

Metz, Jerry D. 2008. "Cultural Geographies of Afro-Brazilian Symbolic Practice: Tradition and Change in *Maracatu de Nação* (Recife, Pernambuco, Brazil)." *Latin American Music Review / Revista de Música Latinoamericana* 29 (1): 64–95.

Miller, Kiri. 2009. "Schizophonic Performance: *Guitar Hero*, *Rock Band*, and Virtual Virtuosity." *Journal of the Society for American Music* 3 (4): 395–429.

Moehn, Frederick. 2005. "The Disc Is Not the Avenue: Schismogenetic Mimesis in Samba Recording." *Wired for Sound: Engineering and Technologies in Sonic Cultures*, ed. Paul Greene and Thomas Porcello, 47–83. Middletown, Conn.: Wesleyan University Press.

————. 2007. "Music, Citizenship, and Violence in Postdictatorship Brazil." *Latin American Music Review / Revista de Música Latinoamericana* 28 (2): 180–219.

————. 2008. "Music, Mixing, and Modernity in Rio de Janeiro." *Ethnomusicology Forum* 17 (2): 165–202.

————. 2009. "A Carioca Blade Runner, or How Percussionist Marcos Suzano Turned the Brazilian Tambourine into a Drum Kit, and Other Matters of (Politically) Correct Music Making." *Ethnomusicology* 53 (2): 276–307.

Moisala, Pirkko, and Beverley Diamond, eds. 2000. *Music and Gender.* Urbana: University of Illinois Press.

Monteiro, Pedro Meira. 2009. "As raízes do Brasil no espelho de próspero." *Novos Estudos* 83: 159–82.

Morse, Richard M. 1988. *Espelho de próspero: Cultura e ideias nas Américas.* São Paulo: Companhia das Letras.

Moska, Paulinho. 2004. *Graphia:* Bio. http://www.paulinhomoska.com.br (accessed 8 August 2009).

Motta, Nelson. 2000. *Noites tropicais: Solos, improvisos e memórias musicais.* Rio de Janeiro: Objetiva.

Murphy, John. 2001. "Self-discovery in Brazilian Popular Music: Mestre Ambrósio." *Brazilian Popular Music and Globalization,* ed. Charles Perrone and Christopher Dunn, 245–47. Gainesville: University Press of Florida.

————. 2002. "Viral Creativity: A Memetic Approach to the Music of André Abujamra and Karnak." *From Tejano to Tango: Latin American Popular Music,* ed. Walter Aaron Clark, 240–51. New York: Routledge.

Napolitano, Marcos. 1998. "A invenção da música popular brasileira: Um campo de reflexão para a história social." *Latin American Music Review / Revista de Música Latinoamericana* 19 (1): 92–105.

Naves, Santuza Cambraia. 2000. "Da bossa nova à Tropicália: Contenção e excesso na música popular." *Revista Brasileira de Ciências Sociais* 15 (43): 35–44.

Nayak, Anoop. 2007. "Critical Whiteness Studies." *Sociology Compass* 1–2: 737–55.

Nettl, Bruno. 2005. *The Study of Ethnomusicology: Thirty-one Issues and Concepts.* Urbana: University of Illinois Press.

Nunes, Benedito. 1990. "Antropofagia ao alcance de todos." *A utopia antropofágica,* by Oswald de Andrade, 5–39. São Paulo: Globo.

Nunes, Zita. 1994. "Anthropology and Race in Brazilian Modernism." *Colo-*

nial Discourse, Postcolonial Theory, ed. Francis Barker, Peter Hulme, and Margaret Iversen, 115–25. Manchester: Manchester University Press.

O'Dougherty, Maureen. 2002. Consumption Intensified: The Politics of Middle-Class Daily Life in Brazil. Durham: Duke University Press.

Ong, Aihwa, and Stephen J. Collier, eds. 2005. Global Assemblages: Technology, Politics, and Ethics as Anthropological Problems. Malden, Mass.: Blackwell.

Ortner, Sherry B. 1984. "Theory in Anthropology since the Sixties." Comparative Studies in Society and History 26 (1): 126–66.

———. 1996. Making Gender: The Politics and Erotics of Culture. Boston: Beacon.

———. 2006. Anthropology and Social Theory: Culture, Power, and the Acting Subject. Durham: Duke University Press.

Owensby, Brian. 1994. "Stuck in the Middle": Middle Class and Class Society in Modern Brazil, 1850 to 1950. PhD diss., Princeton University.

———. 1999. Intimate Ironies: Modernity and the Making of Middle-Class Lives in Brazil. Stanford: Stanford University Press.

Padgett, Tim. 1998. "Rising Stars." Time, Latin American edition, 3 August.

Pardue, Derek. 2004. "Putting Mano to Music: The Mediation of Race in Brazilian Rap." Ethnomusicology Forum 13 (2): 253–86.

———. 2008. Ideologies of Marginality in Brazilian Hip Hop. New York: Palgrave Macmillan.

Pareles, Jon. 1997. "A Brazilian Feast Welcomes Summer." New York Times, 21 June.

———. 2007. "At Home Again in the Unknown." New York Times, 29 April.

Park, Hoon. 2003. "Determinants of Corruption: A Cross-National Analysis." Multinational Business Review 11 (2): 29–48.

Parker, Richard G. 2009 [1991]. Bodies, Pleasures, and Passions: Sexual Culture in Contemporary Brazil. Nashville: Vanderbilt University Press.

Peña, Manuel H. 1985. The Texas-Mexican Conjunto: History of a Working-Class Music. Austin: University of Texas Press.

Perrone, Charles A. 1989. Masters of Contemporary Brazilian Song: MPB, 1965–1985. Austin: University of Texas Press.

———. 1990. "Changing of the Guard: Questions and Contrasts of Brazilian Rock Phenomena." Studies in Latin American Popular Culture 9 (1990): 65–83.

———. 2000. "Do bebop e o Kaos ao chaos e o triphop: Dois fios ecumenicos no escopo semimilenar do Tropicalismo." Linha de Pesquisa 1 (1): 155–70.

Perrone, Charles A., and Christopher Dunn, eds. 2001. Brazilian Popular Music and Globalization. Gainesville: University Press of Florida.

Pessoa, Isa. 1987. "Filosofia está na moda." *O Globo*, 15 October.

Peterson, Richard A., and Andy Bennett. 2004. "Introducing Music Scenes." *Music Scenes: Local, Translocal, and Virtual*, ed. Andy Bennett and Richard A. Peterson, 1–16. Nashville: Vanderbilt University Press.

Porcello, Tom. 2002. "Music Mediated as Live in Austin: Sound, Technology, and Recording Practice." *City and Society* 14 (1): 69–86.

Porto, Bruno. 2003. "Som do BG." *O Globo Magazine*, 17 June.

Prögler, J. A. 1995. "Searching for Swing: Participatory Discrepancies in the Jazz Rhythm Section." *Ethnomusicology* 39 (1): 21–54.

Radano, Ronald, and Philip V. Bohlman. 2000. *Music and the Racial Imagination*. Chicago: University of Chicago Press.

Rapport, Nigel. 1997. *Transcendent Individual: Towards a Literary and Liberal Anthropology*. New York: Routledge.

Reichmann, Rebecca, ed. 1999. *Race in Contemporary Brazil: From Indifference to Inequality*. University Park: Pennsylvania State University Press.

Reily, Suzel Ana. 1992. "Música Sertaneja and Migrant Identity: The Stylistic Development of a Brazilian Genre." *Popular Music* 11 (3): 337–58.

———. 1994. "Macunaíma's Music: National Identity and Ethnomusicological Research in Brazil." *Ethnicity, Identity and Music: The Musical Construction of Place*, ed. Martin Stokes, 67–81. Oxford: Berg.

———. 2000. "Introduction: Brazilian Musics, Brazilian Identities." *Ethnomusicology Forum* 9 (1): 1–10.

———. 2002. *Voices of the Magi: Enchanted Journeys in Southeast Brazil*. Chicago: University of Chicago Press.

Reis, Sérgio Rodrigo. 2008. "Pedro Luís e a Parede lançam álbum com marca autoral." *Diverta-se* (17 September). http://www.new.divirtase.uai .com.br/html/sessao_19/2008/09/17/ficha_musica/id_sessao=19&id_ noticia=2927/ficha_musica.shtml (accessed 26 May 2009).

Renegar, Valerie R., and Stacey K. Sowards. 2009. "Contradiction as Agency: Self-Determination, Transcendence, and Counter-imagination in Third Wave Feminism." *Hypatia* 24 (2): 1–20.

Rice, Timothy. 1987. "Toward the Remodeling of Ethnomusicology." *Ethnomusicology* 31 (3): 469–88.

Ridenti, Marcelo. 2000. *Em busca do povo brasileiro: Artistas da revolução, do CPC à era da TV*. Rio de Janeiro: Record.

Rocha, João Cezar de Castro, and Jorge Ruffinelli, eds. 1999. "Anthropophagy Today?" Special issue, *Nuevo Texto Crítico* 23–24.

Rohter, Larry. 2007. "Rio de Janeiro Journal: Drawing Lines across the Sand." *New York Times*, 6 February.

Rollefson, J. Griffith. 2007. "Tom Zé's *Fabrication Defect* and the 'Esthetics of Plagiarism': A Postmodern/Postcolonial 'Cannibalist Manifesto.'" *Popular Music and Society* 30 (3): 305–27.

Rustin, Nicole T., and Sherrie Tucker. 2008. *Big Ears: Listening for Gender in Jazz Studies.* Durham: Duke University Press.

Sahlins, Marshall. 1981. *Historical Metaphors and Mythical Realities: Structure in the Early History of the Sandwich Islands Kingdom.* Ann Arbor: University of Michigan Press.

———. 2000. *Culture in Practice: Selected Essays.* New York: Zone.

Sandroni, Carlos. 2009. "O mangue e o mundo: Notas sobre a globalização musical em Pernambuco." *Claves* 7: 63–70. http://www.cchla.ufpb.br/claves/index (accessed 16 June 2010).

Sanjek, Roger. 1971. "Brazilian Racial Terms: Some Aspects of Meaning and Learning." *American Anthropologist* 73 (5): 1126–43.

Sansone, Lívio. 1996. "The Local and the Global in Today's Afro-Bahia." *The Legacy of the Disinherited: Popular Culture in Latin America: Modernity, Globalization, Hybridity and Authenticity,* ed. Ton Salman and Anke van Dam, 196–219. Amsterdam: CEDLA.

———. 1999. *From Africa to Afro: Use and Abuse of Africa in Brazil.* Amsterdam: SEPHIS. Available at http://sephis.org (accessed 27 June 2010).

———. 2003. *Blackness without Ethnicity: Constructing Race in Brazil.* New York: Palgrave Macmillan.

Santiago, Silviano. 2001 [1973]. *The Space In-Between: Essays on Latin American Culture.* Ed. A. L. Gazzola. Durham: Duke University Press.

Schafer, R. Murray. 1977. *The Tuning of the World.* New York: Alfred A. Knopf.

Scherzinger, Martin. 2010. "Enforced Deterritorialization, or the Trouble with Musical Politics. Music and the Difference in Becoming." *Sounding the Virtual: Gilles Deleuze and the Theory and Philosophy of Music,* ed. Brian Hulse and Nick Nesbitt, 103–28. Burlington, Vt.: Ashgate.

Schwarz, Roberto. 1988. "Brazilian Culture: Nationalism by Elimination." *New Left Review* 167: 77–90.

———. 1992. *Misplaced Ideas: Essays on Brazilian Culture.* New York: Verso.

Sewell, William H. Jr. 1992. "A Theory of Structure: Duality, Agency, and Transformation." *American Journal of Sociology* 98 (1): 1–29.

Shank, Barry. 1994. *Dissonant Identities: The Rock 'n' Roll Scene in Austin, Texas.* Hanover, N.H.: University Press of New England.

Shaw, Lisa. 1999. *The Social History of the Brazilian Samba.* Burlington, Vt.: Ashgate.

Shohat, Ella, and Robert Stam. 1994. *Unthinking Eurocentrism: Multiculturalism and the Media*. New York: Routledge.

Skidmore, Thomas. 1993 [1974]. *Black into White: Race and Nationality in Brazilian Thought*. Durham: Duke University Press.

Sneed, Paul. 2007. "Bandidos de Cristo: Representations of the Power of Criminal Factions in Rio's Proibidão Funk." *Latin American Music Review / Revista de Música Latinoamericana* 28 (2): 220–41.

Soares, Ana Cecília. 2011. "Ruptura e renovação: Entrevista com Frederico Coelho." *Diário do Nordeste*, Caderno 3, 4 September.

Soares, José Celso de Macedo. 1999. "Globalization." *Jornal do Brasil*, 12 July.

Solie, Ruth. 1993. *Musicology and Difference: Gender and Sexuality in Music Scholarship*. Berkeley: University of California Press.

Solis, Gabriel. 2007. " 'Workin' Hard, Hardly Workin' / Hey Man, You Know Me': Tom Waits, Sound, and the Theatrics of Masculinity." *Journal of Popular Music Studies* 19 (1): 26–58.

Souza, Tarik de, Ary Vasconcelos, Roberto M. Moura, Joao Maximo, Roberto Muggiati, Luiz Carlos Mansur, and Rita Caurio. 1988. *Brasil musical Brazil: Viagem pelos sons e ritmos populares / A Journey through Popular Sounds and Rhythms*. Rio de Janeiro: Art Bureau.

Sovik, Liv. 2002. " 'O Haiti é aqui / O Haiti não é aquí': Música popular, dependência cultural e identidade brasileira na polêmica Schwarz-Silviano Santiago." *Estudios y otras prácticas intelectuales latinoamericanas en Cultura y Poder*, ed. Daniel Mato, 277–86. Caracas: CLASCO and CEAP, FACES, Universidad Central de Venezuela.

———. 2004. "O travesti, o híbrido e o integrado: Identidades brancas na música popular brasileira." *Comunicação, representação e práticas sociais*, ed. Miguel Pereira, Renato Cordeiro Gomes, and Vera Lúcia Follain de Figueiredo, 231–41. Rio de Janeiro: PUC-Rio.

———. 2009. *Aqui ninguém é branco*. Rio de Janeiro: Aeroplano.

Stewart, Kathleen. 2008. "Weak Theory in an Unfinished World." *Journal of Folklore Research* 45 (1): 71–82.

Still, Judith. 1999. "Introduction: Identity and Difference." *Brazilian Feminisms*, ed. S. R. de Oliveira and J. Still, 1–14. Nottingham: University of Nottingham Monographs in the Humanities.

Stock, Jonathan. 1996. *Musical Creativity in Twentieth-Century China: Abing, His Music and Its Changing Meanings*. Rochester: University of Rochester Press.

———. 2001. "Toward an Ethnomusicology of the Individual, or Biographical Writing in Ethnomusicology." *World of Music* 43 (1): 5–19.

Straw, Will. 1991. "Systems of Articulation, Logics of Change: Communities and Scenes in Popular Music." *Cultural Studies* 5 (3): 368–88.

———. 2006. "Scenes and Sensibilities." *E-Compós: Revista da Associação Nacional dos Programas de Pós-Graduação em Comunicação* 6: 1–16. http://www.e-compos.org.br (accessed 10 March 2010).

Stroud, Sean. 2008. *The Defense of Tradition in Brazilian Popular Music: Politics, Culture, and the Creation of Música Popular Brasileira*. Burlington, Vt.: Ashgate.

Sugarman, Jane. 1997. *Engendering Song: Singing and Subjectivity at Prespa Albanian Weddings*. Chicago: University of Chicago Press.

Sutton, R. Anderson. 1996. "Interpreting Electronic Sound Technology in the Contemporary Javanese Soundscape." *Ethnomusicology* 40 (2): 249–68.

Swartz, David. 1997. *Culture and Power: The Sociology of Pierre Bourdieu*. Chicago: University of Chicago Press.

Tas, Marcelo. 1995. "Fernanda da lata." Press release for Fernanda Abreu's *Da lata* album. http://fernandaabreu.uol.com.br/home.htm (accessed 13 October 2009).

Taylor, Timothy. 1997. *Global Pop: World Music, World Markets*. New York: Routledge.

———. 2001. *Strange Sounds: Music, Technology, and Culture*. New York: Routledge.

———. 2007. *Beyond Exoticism: Western Music and the World*. Durham: Duke University Press.

Telles, Edward Eric. 2004. *Race in Another America: The Significance of Skin Color in Brazil*. Princeton: Princeton University Press.

Théberge, Paul. 1997. *Any Sound You Can Imagine: Making Music / Consuming Technology*. Middletown, Conn.: Wesleyan University Press.

Tinhorão, José Ramos. 1997. *Música popular: Um tema em debate*. 3rd ed. São Paulo: Editora 34.

Tinoco, Pedro. 1999. "Vozes da rua: A cidade pulsa na música de Marcelo Yuka e Pedro Luís." *Veja Rio*, 8 September.

Tinoco, Pedro, and Monica Weinberg. 1998. "O som da cidade partida: As bandas cariocas que mostram o Rio sem retoques." *Veja Rio*, 16 September.

Treece, David. 1997. "Guns and Roses: Bossa Nova and Brazil's Music of Popular Protest, 1958–68." *Popular Music* 16 (1): 1–29.

Tremura, Welson Alves. 2004. "With an Open Heart: *Folia de Reis*, a Brazilian Spiritual Journey through Song." PhD diss., Florida State University.

Tsing, Anna Lowenhaupt. 2005. *Friction: An Ethnography of Global Connection*. Princeton: Princeton University Press.

Turino, Thomas. 2000. *Nationalists, Cosmopolitans, and Popular Music in Zimbabwe*. Chicago: University of Chicago Press.

———. 2008. *Music as Social Life: The Politics of Participation*. Chicago: University of Chicago Press.

Twine, France Winddance, and Charles Gallagher. 2008. "The Future of Whiteness: A Map of the 'Third Wave.'" *Ethnic and Racial Studies* 31 (1): 4–24.

Ulhôa Carvalho, Martha de. 1995. "Tupi or Not Tupi MPB: Popular Music and Identity in Brazil." *The Brazilian Puzzle: Culture on the Borderlands of the Western World*, ed. David J. Hess and Robert DaMatta, 159–79. New York: Columbia University Press.

Vargas, Herom. 2007. *Hibridismos musicais de Chico Science e Nação Zumbi*. Cotia, São Paulo: Ateliê.

Veal, Michael. 2007. *Dub: Soundscapes and Shattered Songs in Jamaican Reggae*. Middletown, Conn.: Wesleyan University Press.

Velho, Gilberto. 1992 [1981]. "Project, Emotion, and Orientation in Complex Societies." Trans. Howard S. Becker. *Sociological Theory* 10 (1): 6–20.

Veloso, Caetano. 1977. *Alegria, alegria*. Ed. Wally Salomão. Rio de Janeiro: Pedra Q Ronca.

Ventura, Zuenir. 1994. *Cidade partida*. São Paulo: Companhia das Letras.

Vianna, Hermano. 1990. *O mundo funk carioca*. Rio de Janeiro: Jorge Zahar.

———. 1992. "Release do disco SLA2—*Be Sample*, de Fernanda Abreu—1992." http://www.overmundo.com.br/banco/release-para-o-disco-sla-2-be-sample-de-fernanda-abreu (accessed 4 December 2009).

———. 1995. "Release para o disco *Da Lata*, de Fernanda Abreu—1995." http://www.overmundo.com.br/banco/release-para-o-disco-da-lata-de-fernanda-abreu (accessed 4 December 2009).

———. 1999 [1995]. *The Mystery of Samba: Popular Music and National Identity in Brazil*. Ed. and trans. John Charles Chasteen. Chapel Hill: University of North Carolina Press.

———. 2000. "About *O dia em que faremos contato*." Press release for the Swiss booking agency Latitude Music, http://www.latitudemusic.com/lenine (accessed 17 August 2008).

———. 2004. "Cotas da discordia: Risco da reserva de vagas nas universidades do Brasil." *Folha de Sao Paulo*, 27 June.

Viveiros de Castro, Eduardo. 1992. *From the Enemy's Point of View: Humanity* and *Divinity in an Amazonian Society*. Trans. Catherine V. Howard. Chicago: University of Chicago Press.

Wade, Peter. 2004. "Images of Latin American Mestizaje and the Politics of Comparison." *Bulletin of Latin American Research* 23 (3): 355–66.

Wald, Elijah. 2009. *How the Beatles Destroyed Rock 'n' Roll: An Alternative History of American Popular Music*. New York: Oxford University Press.

Walden, Stephen Thomas. 1996. "Brazilidade: Brazilian *Rock Nacional* in the Context of National Cultural Identity." PhD diss., University of Georgia.

Walser, Robert. 1993. *Running with the Devil: Power, Gender, and Madness in Heavy Metal Music*. Middletown, Conn.: Wesleyan University Press.

Washburne, Christopher. 1998. "Play It 'Con Filin!' The Swing and Expression of Salsa." *Latin American Music Review* 19 (2): 160–85.

Washburne, Christopher J., and Maiken Derno, eds. 2004. *Bad Music: The Music We Love to Hate*. New York: Routledge.

Waterman, Christopher. 1993. "Jùjú History: Toward a Theory of Socio-musical Practice." *Ethnomusicology and Modern Music History*, ed. Stephen Blum, Philip V. Bohlman, and Daniel M. Neuman, 49–67. Urbana: University of Illinois Press.

Weid, Olivia von der. 2007. "Troca de casais: Gênero e sexualidade nos novos arranjos conjugais." *O corpo como capital: Estudos sobre gênero, sexualidade e moda na cultura brasileira*, ed. Mirian Goldenberg, 72–97. Burueri, Brazil: Estação das Letras.

Weinschelbaum, Violeta. 2006. *Estação Brasil: Conversas com músicos brasileiros*. São Paulo: Editora 34.

Williams, James. 2003. *Gilles Deleuze's "Difference and Repetition": A Critical Introduction and Guide*. Edinburgh: Edinburgh University Press.

Woodfield, Ian, and Lucy Robinson. N.d. "Viol." *Grove Dictionary of Music*. Oxford Music Online, http://www.oxfordmusiconline.com/subscriber/article/grove/music/29435 (accessed 8 July 2008).

Yúdice, George. 2003. "Parlaying Culture into Social Justice." *The Expediency of Culture*, 133–59. Durham: Duke University Press.

DISCOGRAPHY

Abreu, Fernanda. 1990. *Sla radical dance disco club*. Compact disc. EMI-Odeon 066 794631-1.

———. 1992. *SLA2—Be Sample*. Compact disc. EMI-Odeon 364 780404-2.

———. 1995. *Da lata*. Compact disc. EMI 837397-2.

———. 1997. *Raio X*. Compact disc. EMI 859283-2.

———. 2000. *Entidade urbana*. Compact disc. EMI 528232-2.

———. 2004. *Na paz*. Garota Sangue Bom / EMI 07243 5772662-2.

Baez, Joan. 1992. *Play Me Backwards*. Compact disc. Virgin Records 86458-2.

Gabriel O Pensador. 1993. *Gabriel O Pensador*. Chaos / Sony Music 2-464423.

———. 2002. *Nádegas a declarar*. Compact disc. Sony Brazil 75371.

Kaurismäki, Mika. 2007. *The Sound of Rio: Brasileirinho*. Milan Entertainment DVD M2-36182.

Lenine. 1997. *O dia em que faremos contato*. Compact disc. BMG Brazil 74321-50211-2.

———. 1999. *Na pressão*. Compact disc. BMG Brazil 74321-71076-2.

———. 2002. *Falange canibal*. Compact disc. BMG Brazil 74321-89351-2.

———. 2006. *In Cité: Ao vivo*. Compact disc. Mr. Bongo 861654.

———. 2008. *Labiata*. Compact disc. BMG/Universal 78932-5100007-2.

Lenine and Lula Queiroga. 1983. *Baque solto*. Compact disc. MP, B Discos 398424121-2.

Lenine and [Marcos] Suzano. 1993. *Olho de peixe*. Velas CD 11-V018.

Monobloco. 2002. *Monobloco 2002*. Compact disc. MP, B/Universal 325912004992.

———. 2006. *Ao vivo*. Compact disc. Msi Music Corp. 07891430021023.

Moska, Paulinho. 1997. *Através do espelho*. Compact disc. EMI 823852-2.

———. 1997. *Contrasenso*. Compact disc. EMI 856849-0.

———. 1999. *Móbile*. Compact disc. EMI 521733-2.

———. 2001. *Eu falso da minha vida o que eu quiser*. Compact disc. EMI 5339312.

———. 2003. *Tudo novo de novo*. Compact disc. Casulo Produções / EMI 594905-2.

———.2007. *Moska + novo de novo*. DVD. Som Livre 0203-9.

———. 2010. *Muito Pouco*. Two-CD boxed set. Biscoito Fino BF 333.

Nó em Pingo D'água. 1987. *Salvador*. Visom LP VO-017.

———. 1991. *Receita de Samba*. Visom CD 00064.

Pedro Luís e A Parede. 1997. *Astronauta Tupy*. Compact disc. Dubas Música / Warner Brothers 063109483-2.

———. 1999. *É tudo um real*. Compact disc. MP, B/Universal 32591200655-2.

———. 2001. *Zona e progresso*. Compact disc. MP, B/Universal 32591 2003552-3.

———. 2008. *Ponto enredo*. Compact disc. EMI 242074-2.

Possi, Zizi. 1991. *Sobre todas as coisas*. Eldorado CD 946007.

Ramil,Vitor, and Marcos Suzano. 2007. *Satolep Sambatown*. MP, B/Universal 1422263.

Suzano, Marcos. 1996. *Sambatown*. Compact disc. MP, B/Warner 063016719-2.

———. 2000. *Flash*. Compact disc. Trama T500 065-2.

INDEX

Page numbers in italics indicate figures and illustrations.

alfaia, 25–26, 62, 81

alienation and engagement debates, xi–xvi, xii, xviii, 166, 170, 205, 219n1

Alvim, Celso, 85, 98–100, 102, 105–6, 115

Amback, Sacha, 176–79, 184, 186–89, 190–91, 194, 202

Americanization/Americanoid, xxi, 105, 128, 168, 175, 235n8. *See also* United States

Andrade, Mário de, 10, 60, 85, 107, 153, 167, 198–99, 209, 231n6

Andrade, Oswald de, 10, 85, 107, 165, 209, 210, 243n3

androids, use of term, 174, 240n9. *See also* technologies and sonic practices

anthropophagy metaphor (cannibalism metaphor). *See* cannibalism metaphor (anthropophagy metaphor)

Antunes, Arnaldo, 81, 169, 200, 232n17

AR Studios (Estúdio AR), 108, 122, 168, 182

Araújo, Paulo Roberto Pereira de (Paulão 7 Cordas), 123

Arawaté people, 209, 243n3. *See also* Tupinambá (Tupi or Tupy)

art music theory, 223n24

artisanal style, 65, 67, 169, 179

Asdrúbal Trouxe o Trombone, 97–98, 133

asphalt (asfalto or condominium neighborhoods), 7, 121, 151, 154, 156, 160–61

assemblage concept, 129, 132, 146–47, 162, 208

Attali, Jacques, 167

authenticity concept, 106–7, 128–29

axé, xiv, xix, xx, 112, 225n27

Baez, Joan, 40, 182, 241n13

Bahia: axé and, xiv, xix, xx, 225n27; Candomblé and, 102; consumerism and, xiii; music scene in, xix; pagode and, 11; race and ethnicity centrality in, 33; Salvador, xix, 11, 41, 58–59, 86, 109, 112, 227n7; suingue baiano and, 102, 109–10, 235n6. *See also* Northeast of Brazil

baião, 62, 64, 106, 122, 231n9

bailes, 119–20, 136, 138, 146, 149, 155

Ball, Jim, 40, 42–43, 67, 73, 182–83, 207, 229n21, 241n13

bandas de pífano (fife-and-drum ensembles), 44, 61–62, 98

Bandeira, Luiz, 76

Barnes, Sandra T., 32–33

bass, Miami, 136–37, 238n7

Bate Lata, 201, 202

baterias, 102, 117, 119, 158

Bateson, Gregory, 17

batucada: overview of, 96; Abreu and, 148, 150, 151, 158; as masculine gendered, 102; Paulinho and, 183; Pedro Luís and, 98; percussion in hierarchy of music production and, 41; PLAP and, 96, 98, 100–101, 103, 109, 115, 122, 126, 234n3; technologies and sonic practices and, 148

beatboxes, 50, 164

the Beatles, 172, 194–95

becoming: becoming middle class and, 13–17, 222n19, 223nn20–24, 224n25; becoming race and, 9; becoming-woman and, 147, 238n10; cannibalism metaphor and, 209–10, 243nn2–3; men and, 147, 238n10; music making and, 181–82, 195, 200–201, 241n14; national identity and, 9; project as musical becoming and, 170. *See also* agency

being middle class, 13–17, 222n19, 223nn20–24, 224n25

being musical, 15–16

Belo Horizonte, 6, 19, 224n26

Benito di Paula, 188–89

Berliner, Paul, 213

Beto Cazes, 40

betweenness, 5, 13–14, 16, 102, 220n4

Biehl, João, 16, 147, 207

Björk, 49–50, 230n27

black dance music (African American dance music), 137, 149, 150–51, 153, 164

black diasporic traditions (Afro-diasporic traditions): black dance music and, 137, 149, 150–51, 153, 164; CSNZ and, 41; influences of, 4, 205; mixtures and, 31; Suzano and, 44–46, 229n24; from United States and, 23, 137, 139, 149, 150–51, 153, 164

black identity, 4, 33, 77–78, 124, 139–40, 151–53, 232n20, 238n8

Blade Runner (film), 30, 229n23. *See also* "Carioca Blade Runner"

Blitz, xi, xv, 23, 132–35, 164

blocos, 23, 37, 57, 80, 114–15, 117, 228n16. *See also* carnival; Monobloco project

blogs, 126–28

Renato, Zé, 126
Renegar, Valerie R., 145–46
Renno, Carlos, 125–26
repentistas, 60–61, 70
repetition, 170, 194
research methods, xix–xxi, 22, 211–14, 226n31. *See also* ethnomusicology
restricted production, 200
rhizome concept, 96–97, 187, 202, 204, 223n24
rhythm and blues (R&B): overview of, 136; Abreu and, 139, 156, 159; Lenine and, 77; Paulinho and, 173; PLAP and, 110, 112–13; Suzano and, 44. *See also* blues/bluesy
Ribeiro, Felipe "Bi," 134–35, 237n4
Ridenti, Marcelo, 56–57
Rio de Janeiro: overview and history of, 6, 18, 220n2; carnival revival in, 116; choro in, 18, 23, 96, 115, 224n26; divided-city metaphor and, 2, 7, 207; garota carioca and, 140–41; hegemonic narratives about middle-class audiences and, 224n26; mixtures and, 39; music industry and, 19; music scene in, xix, 18–19; race and ethnicity and, 18; recording studios in, xx; samba and, 115; social relations and, 7, 220n8; West Zone of, 80, 220n2. *See also* morro; North Zone of Rio; South Zone of Rio; violence in Rio
Rio funk (funk carioca). *See* funk carioca (Rio funk)
Rio musicians. *See specific artists*
Rita Lee, 20, 133, 164
Rocha, Zé, 64, 113–14, 231n11
rock: overview and use of term, 237n2; Abreu and, 132, 237n2; "Brazilian" music and, 4, 97, 135, 234n1; Brock compared with, xx–xxi, 135; heaviness and, 23, 96–97, 234n1; hegemonic narratives about middle-class audiences and, 19–20, 224n26; Lenine's mix of traditions with, 61, 63–64, 66, 74–75, 77, 81–82, 85, 87–89; as masculine gendered, 102, 132, 235n9; mixtures and, xxi, 1–2, 61, 81–82, 204; Paulinho and, 97, 168, 171, 173–75; PLAP and, 96, 98, 106, 110, 112, 122, 125–26; rock-funk and, 110; samba-funk-rock and, 132, 237n2; ska-rock and, 113, 134; in United Kingdom, 234n1; United States and, 234n1. *See also* Brock

roda (circle) concept, 159–60
Roland TR-808 (808), 136, 150–51, 179
rural maracatu (maracatu rural), 62–63, 64, 81

saints in Christianity, 33, 228n13
Saliba, Robert, 215, 216–17, 226n31
Salvador de Bahia, xix, 11, 41, 58–59, 86, 109, 112, 227n7. *See also* Bahia
samba: overview of, xxi, 18–19; Abreu and, 149–50, 151, 154, 156–58, 159, 163; Bahia and, 102; "Brazilian" music and, 234n1; côco and, 18; hegemonic narratives about MPB's audiences and, 224n26; intensity in, 46–48, 48; jazz repertory and, xviii; mixtures and, xxi; Monobloco project and, 115; national identity and, 23; North of Brazil and, 18; Paulinho and, 194, 195; PLAP and, 96, 98, 100, 106, 122–23, 125–26; Rio and, 115; simplification of, 81–82; sociopolitical issues and, 134; stereotypes and, 4; suingue and, 102; Suzano on intensity of, 46–48, 48; violão and, xv, 61. *See also* samba schools
samba-canção, 19, 53, 122, 189
samba de enredo, 80, 230n3
samba-funk, 142, 148–51, 154–55, 162, 188
samba-funk-rock, 132, 237n2
samba-reggae, 109–10
samba-rock, 188
samba schools: baterias and, 102, 117, 119, 158; Mangueira and, xix, 87, 88, 118, 151, 154, 157–58; Monobloco project and, 117–20, 236n17; sambadromes and, 37, 228n16; sociopolitical issues and, 118–19; technologies and sonic practices and, 236n17; working-class suburbs and, 228n16. *See also* samba
samplers and samples: Abreu and, 132, 147–49, 151, 158; Lenine and, 81; local and global debates, 147; Neves and, 72, 74; Paulinho and, 173, 177, 185, 186, 189; world music and, 185
Sansone, Lívio, 228n12
Santana Martins, Antônio (Tom) José (Zé) [Tom Zé], 10, 19–20, 113, 221n12, 240n9
Santtana, Lucas, 26, 45, 227n3, 230n29, 232n17
São Paulo: map of, 6; middle classes and, 13, 224n26; pagode and, 11; production

São Paulo (*continued*)
   in, 5; rap and, 118; SESC Vila Mariana
   and, 114, 127, 173, 240n8; social relations between Rio and, 220n8
scene(s), 3–4, 5, 7, 220n3, 220n6,
   224nn26–27. *See also specific music scenes*
Schafer, R. Murray, 226n1
schizophonia, 26, 226n1
schottische, 37, 187
Schwartz, Roberto, 22, 222n14, 226n32
Science, Chico, xv, xix, 39, 41. *See also* Chico
   Science e Nação Zumbi (CSNZ); Recife
Sebastian (saint), 228n13
self-management. *See* musical entrepreneurship
sensationism, 184–85, 241n15
sequencers, 132, 164, 169, 181
"serious games," 33–36, 50, 194, 206,
   229n24
SESC Vila Mariana, 114, 127, 173, 240n8
Seu Jorge (Farofa Carioca), 1, 2, 220n1
Sewell, William H., 15, 222n19
sexuality, as inseparable from music
   making, 31, 33–35, 182, 227n10
Sharp Prize (Tim Prize), 38, 39, 43, 75, 89,
   229n19
Sicre, Claude, 87, 232n19
Silva, Aloíso, 163
Silva, Celsinho, 38, 215, 226n31
Silva, Gerson, 47
Silva, Sidon, 3, 85, 93, 98, 104, 116–17,
   236n16
Silva Filho, Jessé Gomes da (Zeca Pa-
   godinho), xvii, 123
ska-rock, 113, 134
Skidmore, Thomas, 153
Sneed, Paul, 136, 137
Soares, José Celso de Macedo, xi
social relations: Fausto on, 8, 220n8;
   Lenine on, 55, 90–91; music making
   and, 111, 128; people-in-(power)-
   relationships-in-projects, 35, 129; PLAP
   and, 111, 128; power in, 35, 109, 129,
   141–42, 145–46; in Rio, 7–8, 220n8; in
   São Paulo, 220n8
sociopolitical issues: overview of, xviii, 23,
   33; affirmative action and, 152, 221n11;
   "Brazilian" music and, 4; dictatorship
   and, xii–xiv, xvi, 4, 9, 13, 20, 36, 54, 134;
   ethics and, xiv, 11, 72, 132, 169, 199;
   MPB and, xi; music making and, xii–

xiii, 9, 13; national identity and, 58–60;
   peace messages and, 161–62, 163,
   239n13; "planetary vision" and, 56, 67,
   89; PLAP and, 109–10, 113–14; poverty
   and suingue coexistence and, 110–11,
   235n13; prison system and, 125–26;
   privilege and, 100, 140, 146, 166, 201–2,
   226n32; samba and samba schools and,
   118–19, 134; social inequalities and,
   9, 109–10, 131, 133, 141–42, 146, 166,
   221n11; social justice and, 201; Suzano
   and, 36, 39–40, 43; United States and,
   xiv, xvii. *See also* consumerism; economics; race and ethnicity
som universal, 205
sonic practices and technologies. *See* technologies and sonic practices
Soul II Soul, 149–50
South and Southeast of Brazil, 59, 89–90,
   224n26. *See also specific cities*
South Zone of Rio: overview of, xv–xvi, 5,
   6, 220n2; blocos and, 57, 80, 228n16;
   bossa nova and, 5; Brock and, 133–34;
   Dancing Days nightclub in, 164, 239n15;
   gafieira and, 115; Monobloco project
   and, 115, 116, 116–17, 228n16, 236n16;
   MPC and, 1–3; race and ethnicity and,
   xix, 5; recording studios in, 7; social
   relations in, 7–8, 220n8; upper-class
   and, xix, 5; violence in, 7. *See also* Rio de
   Janeiro
Sovik, Liv, 138–39, 166
Sowards, Stacey K., 145–46
stereotypes and typologies, 4, 78, 233n21
Stewart, Kathleen, 207, 223n22
Stock, Jonathan, 22, 226n33
Studio 304 (Estúdio 304), 70, 72, 159
studios. *See* recording studios; *specific studios*
stuttering guitar, xviii. *See also* guitars
subjectivity and subject formation: overview of, 205–6, 207; cannibalism metaphor and, 90–91; mirror trope and, 5,
   17, 79, 121, 167, 199, 209–10
Sugarman, Jane, 14
suingue ("swing"): overview of, 101–2, 213;
   Abreu and, 141–42, 154–56; as feminine gendered, 102; Lenine and, 82, 84,
   85; PLAP and, 102–4, 109–11, 235n6,
   235n13; poverty's coexistence with,
   110–11, 235n13; samba and, 102; suingue
   baiano and, 102, 109–10, 235n6

Paulinho and, 174–76, 181, 183, 185–86, 188–89, 197; PLAP and, 101; samba and, xv, 61; Suzano and, 40. *See also* guitars

violence in Rio: overview of, 7; Abreu on, 148–49, 158, 161–62, 239nn13–14; carnival, 113; funk and, 111, 136; funk carioca and, 136–37; hip-hop and, 163; Lenine on, 86–87. *See also* Rio de Janeiro

virtual and real as co-constitutive, 127–28

Viveiros de Castro, Eduardo, 209–10, 243nn2–3

Vulgue Tostoi, 87–88, 92

Wade, Peter, 9, 104

Wald, Elijah, 237n1

"weak theory," 207, 223n22

West, Melissa, 49

West Zone of Rio, 80, 220n2. *See also* Rio de Janeiro

whiteness, 138–40, 146, 151–53, 166, 238n8

women and feminine gendered: becoming-woman and, 147, 238n10; bunda as term for, 11–12, 133, 155, 164–65; garota carioca and, 141, 142–44, 156, 164–65; inequalities and, 131, 133, 141–42, 166; jazz fans as, 131, 237n1; male gaze on, 156, 158, 164–65; motherhood and, 142–45, 165–66; nega and, 77–78, 139–40, 232n20; neoliberal globalization affects

as, 35; Pindorama matriarchy and, 165, 207; power of, 141–42, 145–46; suingue as, 102. *See also* men and masculine gendered

wordplay, 82–84, 88–89, 113, 154, 186, 187, 233nn24–26

working class: overview of, 220n2; baile and, 136; blocos and, 117, 228n16; middle classes' relations with, 154; MPB and, 136, 224n26, 240n11; music and music making and, 19, 95, 111, 226n30, 236n16. *See also* class

world music: Brazilian perspective on, xxi; difference and, 170; growth of audience for, 10, 66, 205; literature on, 239n1; marketing language of, 209, 234n33; Real World Studios and, 73, 90; samples of used in recording, 185. *See also* music and music making

xote, 62, 113, 115, 187, 189

Yoruba, 75, 124–26. *See also* Ogum

zabumba, 25, 61–62, 77, 82, 98–99

Zeca Pagodinho (Jessé Gomes da Silva Filho), xvii, 123

Zumbi (of Palmares), 59, 80. *See also* Chico Science e Nação Zumbi (CSNZ)

FREDERICK MOEHN is a research associate at the Institute for
Ethnomusicology–Center for Music and Dance of the Universidade
Nova de Lisboa in Portugal.

Library of Congress Cataloging-in-Publication Data
Moehn, Frederick
Contemporary Carioca : technologies of mixing in a
Brazilian music scene / Frederick Moehn.
p. cm.
Includes bibliographical references and index.
ISBN 978-0-8223-5141-2 (cloth : alk. paper)
ISBN 978-0-8223-5155-9 (pbk. : alk. paper)
1. Popular music—Brazil—History and criticism.
2. Sound—Recording and reproducing—Digital techniques.
3. Suzano, Marcos. I. Title.
ML3487.B7M59 2012
781.640981′09049—dc23
2011041908